D0420366

09

/cam

P.P

F
i
h

D
B

Dat

29, M
5 FEB

1 3 MAY

3 0 J

1 2 SEP

CAMUS at *Combat*

CAMUS at *Combat*

Writing 1944–1947

**EDITED AND ANNOTATED BY
JACQUELINE LÉVI-VALENSI**

FOREWORD BY DAVID CARROLL

TRANSLATED BY ARTHUR GOLDHAMMER

PRINCETON UNIVERSITY PRESS

PRINCETON AND OXFORD

Copyright © 2006 by Princeton University Press
French edition © Editions Gallimard, Paris, 2002
Camus *à Combat*: Éditoriaux et articles (1944–1947)
Édition de Jacqueline Lévi-Valensi
Published by Princeton University Press, 41 William Street, Princeton, New Jersey 08540
In the United Kingdom: Princeton University Press, 3 Market Place, Woodstock,
Oxfordshire OX20 1SY
All Rights Reserved

Second printing, and first paperback printing, 2007
Paperback ISBN: 978-0-691-13376-8

The Library of Congress has cataloged the cloth edition of this book as follows

Camus, Albert, 1913–1960.
[Camus à Combat. English]
Camus at Combat : writing 1944–1947 / edited and annotated by Jacqueline Lévi-Valensi;
foreword by David Carroll ; translated by Arthur Goldhammer.
p.   cm.
Includes bibliographical references and index.
ISBN-13: 978-0-691-12004-1
ISBN-10: 0-691-12004-8
1. World War, 1939–1945—Underground literature—France.   2. World War, 1939–1945—
Underground movements—France.   3. Politics and literature—France—History—20th
century.   4. Combat (Paris, France : 1940)   5. Camus, Albert, 1913–1960.   6. France—
History—German occupation, 1940–1945.   I. Lévi-Valensi, Jacqueline.   II. Goldhammer,
Arthur.   III. Title.
D802.F8C34413 2006
844'.914—dc22   2005040564

This work is published with the support of the French Ministry of Culture—
Centre Nationale du Livre

Ouvrage publié avec le concours du Ministére français chargé de la culture—
Centre nationale du livre

British Library Cataloging-in-Publication Data is available

This book has been composed in Adobe Garamond and Helvetica Neue

Printed on acid-free paper. ∞

press.princeton.edu

Printed in the United States of America

10 9 8 7 6 5 4 3 2

CONTENTS

Foreword by David Carroll   vii

Preface   xxvii

Acknowledgments   xxix

Introduction by Jacqueline Lévi-Valensi   xxxi

Thematic Classification   xxxiii

CHAPTER 1   *Combat* Underground: March–July 1944   1

CHAPTER 2   August 21, 1944–November 15, 1945   11

CHAPTER 3   November 19–30, 1946   255

CHAPTER 4   March 17–June 3, 1947   277

CHAPTER 5   1948–1949   295

Chronology of Principal Events, 1944–1948   311

Partial Bibliography   333

Albert Camus—Political Journalist: Democracy in an Age of Terror

> Our twentieth century is the century of fear. . . . We live in terror.

> —ALBERT CAMUS,
>
> "The Century of Fear" (*Combat*, November 19, 1946)

> I have always believed that if people who placed their hopes in the human condition were mad, those who despaired of events were cowards. Henceforth there will be only one honorable choice: to wager everything on the belief that in the end words will prove stronger than bullets.

> —ALBERT CAMUS,
>
> "Toward Dialogue" (*Combat*, November 30, 1946)

In the fall of 1943, at the age of thirty and having recently recovered from a recurrence of tuberculosis, Albert Camus joined the Resistance and began writing articles for the clandestine Resistance newspaper *Combat*. Generally unknown outside of Algeria before he published *The Stranger* and *The Myth of Sisyphus* in occupied Paris in 1942, Camus began work as a reader for the Editions Gallimard in November 1943 and at approximately the same time became editor in chief of *Combat*, a newspaper that represented various Resistance groups and that had been published irregularly since December 1941. The texts included in the present collection and admirably translated by Arthur Goldhammer comprise the editorials and articles written by Camus for *Combat* from 1944 to 1947, along with four short articles he published in 1948 and 1949.

Jacqueline Lévi-Valensi, the noted Camus scholar who has both edited and provided indispensable historical notes for this collection, has indicated that Camus published a total of 165 entries in *Combat* between August 21, 1944, and June 3, 1947: 138 editorials and 27 articles, with his most productive period between August 21 and November 30, 1944, when he contributed 70 editorials and 7 articles.[1] The present volume includes the articles signed by Camus, a

---

[1] These figures are given by Jacqueline Lévi-Valensi in one of the two introductions she wrote for the original French edition of this collection. She acknowledges that of the seventy editorials attributed to

number of others he did not sign but for which there is strong supporting evidence that he was the author, and those whose style and mode of argumentation suggest that they were also written by him.[2]

What is the relevance of this collection of editorials and articles today? First of all, it is of obvious historical interest, since Camus' editorials vividly describe the most important events of the immediate postwar period and analyze the major political issues faced by France from the liberation of Paris through the early years of the Cold War. It would be difficult to imagine a livelier "historian of the moment" (which is Camus' expression for journalists), and at the same time a more reflective, critical guide to these chaotic times than Albert Camus. It certainly does not detract from the interest of these essays that their author was a recognized novelist, playwright, and essayist who would win the Nobel Prize in 1957 and who for the time he was editor in chief of *Combat* was also writing *The Plague* (1947), and allegorical account of the Resistance that presents in a fictional context the most important moral and political issues originally addressed in his editorials.

But if Camus' editorials for *Combat* have both an obvious historical and literary interest, their primary interest is above all political. For along with his Resistance comrades at *Combat*, Camus was fully engaged not only as a journalist in reporting the news but also in the daily political struggles for freedom, first in occupied and later in liberated France. In addition, in his most important editorials, he contributed to the debates concerning the restoration of democracy in France and analyzed the larger political issues that would shape the postwar period and in fact the rest of the twentieth century—issues that continue to concern us today.

From Enthusiasm to Terror

Along with his comrades at *Combat*, Camus enthusiastically supported the idea of a "liberal revolution" that would result in the formation of a social democracy in France. His support of "revolution" might surprise some readers, given that Camus would publish an extremely harsh critique of revolution in *L'Homme*

Camus during this period, nine would have to be considered only "probable" in terms of Camus's authorship ("Un écrivain face à l'histoire," *Camus à* Combat, Jacqueline Lévi-Valensi, ed. [Paris: Gallimard, 2002], 70). From the time Camus joined the editorial staff of *Combat* in September 1944 until the end of 1945, Lévi-Valensi calculates that he wrote "133 editorials—of which 92 were signed or authenticated—and 16 articles, one of which is only probable" (72). After September 1945, Camus no longer regularly contributed editorials to the journal.

[2] During its clandestine period, the editors of *Combat* naturally could not publish their names in the paper. After the liberation of Paris, on August 27 and 28, 1944, the editors are for the first time listed in the following way: "Albert Camus, Henri Frédéric, Marcel Gimont, Albert Olivier and Pascal Pia currently edit Combat after having edited it underground." On November 3, 1944, another formula is used and will continued to be used until October 1945: "Editorial Committee: Pascal Pia, Director; Albert Camus, editor in chief; Marcel Gimont and Albert Ollivier" (Jacqueline Lévi-Valensi, "Un journal dans l'histoire," in *Camus à* Combat, 46).

révolté (*The Rebel*) in 1951.[3] But after the rout of the French army at the beginning of the war, the destruction of the Third Republic by the parliamentary vote
that granted Maréchal Pétain "full powers" and thus absolute authority, followed
by four years of German Occupation and Vichy rule, it is not difficult to imagine the reasons for such enthusiasm for both democracy and social justice on the
part of a writer such as Camus, whose political commitments and journalistic
experience before the war had been on the political left.

It was precisely because their political commitments were on the left that
Camus and his fellow editorialists at *Combat* refused to accept a return to the
compromised values and practices of the French Third Republic or the formation of a new Republic that would be democratic in name only. But because of
the passion of his political commitments and the clarity, sincerity, and force of
his writing, Camus quickly became one of the most influential voices on the
non-Communist left demanding that an important role be given to the Resistance in postwar French governments—for all factions within the Resistance,
including Communists.

Camus' earliest postwar articles argue for the creation of a social-democratic
state out of the ruins of Vichy France. They express confidence that because of
the horrible experience of the war and the sacrifices made by those who actively
opposed Nazi tyranny the French people as a whole would be willing and able to
overcome their political differences and work together to form a truly democratic
state in the same way factions of the Resistance had been able to work together
to defeat a common enemy. The writer of these articles clearly believed that after
the war the French had both a unique opportunity and an obligation to get
democracy right. Camus' editorials remind us once again that what is most often
accepted as democracy is not all that democracy necessarily could or should be.

Camus argues in numerous editorials that protection of individual freedoms
without the guarantee of social justice would not only perpetuate or exacerbate
existing social and economic inequities but also lead to the further limitation or
even destruction of the freedom of the poor and the oppressed. On the other
hand, to sacrifice freedom in order to pursue the goal of social justice would
inevitably result in the formation of an oppressive, centralized, bureaucratic state
in which equality was abstract rather than real. If Communists and Catholics,
socialists and Gaullists, conservative nationalists and revolutionary internationalists could work together in the Resistance in a common struggle for freedom
and justice, Camus saw no reason why French society as a whole, and ultimately

---

[3] In his preface to the publication of a selection of his essays from *Combat* in *Actuelles I: Chroniques
1944–1948* (Paris: Gallimard, 1950), Camus describes his journalistic experience in the following way:
"This volume represents the experience of a writer involved for four years in the public life of his country. . . . This experience ends, as is only natural, with the loss of several illusions and the reinforcement of
a more profound conviction. . . . To tell the truth, I cannot read one or two [of the editorials] today without distress and sadness, and I had to make a real effort in order to republish them" (Albert Camus,
"Avant-Propos," *Essais* [Paris: Gallimard, 1965], 251; all translations from the *Essais* are my own).

the entire world community, could not work together in the same way. But this could happen only if what he called ideological "abstractions" did not determine the politics of each group, only if politics could be made more "moral" and less ideological.[4]

"The introduction of the language of morality into politics" is in fact one of the constant themes of the editorials Camus wrote for *Combat*, but the meaning of this phrase is not what might at first be assumed. It certainly does not mean that Camus believed that politics should conform to a particular moral or religious system, since he distrusted all systems, whether religious, moral, or political. It was also not meant to encourage a withdrawal from politics, but on the contrary a more critical, self-reflexive, and "moral" form of political commitment, which, for example, might appear to "give with one hand what we seem to take away with the other. . . . What this comes down to is saying yes and no at the same time, and saying both with the same seriousness and the same objectivity" (October 7, 1944). Camus is of course not advocating here either crass opportunism or the superficial support of one political position and then another. Rather, he is highlighting what he feels is or should be the contradictory nature of all political commitment and demanding that no commitment be blind or total, no matter what cause is being defended or what end is being pursued.

If there should be a "no" at the core of every "yes," it is in order to create a space for questioning, doubt, and critical judgment. It is also to impose limits on all political action and thus to ensure that not everything will be permitted in the pursuit of any cause, no matter how noble. The ultimate limit that Camus will impose on political involvement, the "no" that always be uttered, is the refusal to accept the murder of innocent civilians as a legitimate means to any end. This principle applies both to civilians targeted by the military during war and those who would be the victims of terrorist acts outside of war. It would apply as much to the French Resistance during World War II as to FLN terrorism and French counterterrorist activities during the Algerian War. There was in fact no cause to which Camus would ever have said simply "yes"—especially if "yes" meant that murder would have to be excused and defended.

As the experience of the Resistance faded into the past and the euphoria of the Liberation lessened with time, Camus' articles for *Combat* gradually took on a less enthusiastic, more critical tone. I would suggest that this was due in large part to what his essays present as three major failures of French democracy in the immediate postwar period. The first failure, which occurred immediately after the

---

[4] In arguing that the Resistance should have a major role in postwar governments, Camus characterizes the revolution he advocates as one in which politics would be replaced with morality: "The affairs of this country should be managed by those who paid and answered for it. In other words, we are determined to replace politics with morality. That is what we call a revolution" (September 4, 1944). In another editorial Camus acknowledges how easy it is for "morality" to degenerate into "moralism": "If we point out the limitations of certain ideas or political actions, we are naturally aware of our own limitations as well, and we try to make up for them by adhering to two or three basic principles. But reporting the news is a demanding business, and the boundary between morality and moralism is never clear. Sometimes one crosses it owing to fatigue or negligence" (November 22, 1944).

Liberation, resulted from the inability of the French to deal effectively and, more important, justly with the traitors and criminals of the war period in the purge trials (*l'épuration*). The second was the failure of France to recognize the injustices of colonialism and to uphold the same democratic principles in its colonies for which the Resistance had fought and which the French people demanded for themselves. The third major failure of democracy was related to the inadequacy of the free press in general, but particularly to *Combat's* own inability to remain independent and thus in Camus' terms faithful to its democratic mission. Taken together these particular failures represented a general failure in or of democracy itself.

This explains why at the end of Camus' service as editor in chief of *Combat*, there is little evidence in his editorials of the enthusiasm characteristic of his earliest articles. The main problem he confronts in his later articles, and especially the last major series of articles he published in *Combat* under the title "Neither Victims nor Executioners" (November 19–30, 1946), is no longer how to move from the Resistance (revolt) to revolution (social democracy), but rather how to work effectively for freedom and justice in an increasingly oppressive climate of terror. It is not just how to defend democracy from its totalitarian enemies but also how to defend democracy from itself. I shall focus primarily on the editorials that analyze the failures of democracy in postwar France, for in them we get the best picture of what Camus meant by and expected of democracy—and of what still could be expected of democracy today.

The Failure of Justice: The Purge Trials

No issue was more difficult for Camus to deal with, no issue in its harsh reality clashed more directly with his dreams of creating a social democracy in France in which justice would prevail, than the one the French confronted immediately at the time of the Liberation: how to deal with French collaborators, especially those who had committed atrocious crimes, ordered or encouraged others to commit them, or supported policies that resulted either directly or indirectly in the imprisonment, torture, deportation, or death of others. This included both important and insignificant officials of the Vichy regime, members of the French Milice,[5] and opportunistic or ideologically committed collaborationist journalists and intellectuals.

It is clear from reading his earliest articles on the purge that Camus felt very strongly that too many members of the Resistance and too many innocent civilians had been tortured, too many had been deported, too many had died, to pardon those responsible for the crimes committed against them. For to pardon them would be to forget or ignore the sacrifices made by the victims. No legitimate republic could be formed until the matter of how to deal with the wide range of collaborators was resolved, for to act as if the sacrifices of so many

---

[5] The Milice was a paramilitary organization created in 1943 by Joseph Darnand, Vichy secretary of state, to support German actions taken against the Resistance and to aid in the arrest and deportation of Jews.

victims of Nazi and Vichy oppression did not really matter would be to found a republic on the basis of the denial of those who had given their lives to make the Republic possible. Justice demanded that the victims of Nazi and Vichy crimes not be forgotten and that the criminals responsible for the worst crimes be punished severely—which meant that those guilty of the worst crimes should themselves be executed.

As was the case with all the most controversial issues of the post-Liberation period, Camus was at the center of debates over how extensively and severely to punish collaborators and which crimes actually merited the death penalty. Camus, like most of those involved in the Resistance, initially supported the harshest punishment for those responsible for the most heinous crimes, and even before the Liberation, *Combat*, like other Resistance journals, denounced the crimes of collaborators both to encourage more of the French to join the Resistance and to threaten those who continued to collaborate with the consequences of their acts. For example, an article attributed to Camus and appearing in *Combat* during the period when it was still being published clandestinely refers to the members of the French Milice as "rotten branches that cannot be left attached to the tree" but should be "lopped off, reduced to sawdust, and scattered on the ground. . . . Courts-martial would be pointless, moreover. The Milice is its own tribunal. It has judged itself and sentenced itself to death. Those sentences will be carried out" ("Outlaws," *Combat*, underground no. 56, April 1944). Justice is unproblematic and absolute in such extreme cases and does not need laws, courts, judges, or juries to be implemented: "The Milice has placed itself outside the law. It must be made quite clear that each militiaman, in signing his enlistment papers, is ratifying his own death sentence." Justice for those so egregiously outside the law—not the actual law of Vichy but a higher law, the law of justice—is obvious and transcends any legal code. The perpetrators of the crimes know that their own acts judge them, that by their crimes they have in fact sentenced themselves to death.

In another article attributed to him, Camus describes in vivid detail the massacre of a French village by German soldiers and demands that those responsible for such atrocious acts pay for them: "For the question is not whether these crimes will be forgiven; it is whether anyone will pay for them. And if we were inclined to doubt it, the image of this village soaked in blood and from this day forth populated solely by widows and orphans should suffice to assure us that someone will pay for this crime, because the decision is now in the hands of all the French, and in the face of this new massacre we are discovering the solidarity of martyrdom and the power that grows out of vengeance" ("For Three Hours They Shot Frenchmen," *Combat*, underground no. 57, May 1944).[6] Vengeance in such cases would be equivalent to justice, for it would be taken not

---

[6] This article of course was not signed by Camus because *Combat* at the time was still an underground newspaper, but Lévi-Valensi argues that there exists unanimous agreement that he wrote it because, as she puts it in a note, "the vigor of the style, the visionary realism, and, once again, the central idea of solidarity leave little room for doubt."

out of self-interest or for political ends but rather in the name and memory of those who were massacred and by a newly reunified people who recognize their sacrifice. The solidarity of martyrdom, however, is an unstable and dangerous foundation on which to build a democracy, for the power of vengeance is difficult, if not impossible, to limit and control once it is set loose, as the purge itself would clearly demonstrate.

Camus justifies his support of immediate justice and capital punishment for French collaborators guilty of crimes of torture or murder not by legal or political arguments but by simply describing the horrendous nature of the crimes themselves, as if the description of the crime in itself dictated the appropriate punishment. In one of the earliest editorials he published in *Combat* after the liberation of Paris, Camus describes the discovery at Vincennes, on the outskirts of Paris, of the bodies of thirty-four Frenchmen who had been tortured before being executed and mutilated: "We learn of comrades who had their guts ripped out, their limbs torn off, and their faces kicked in. And the men who did these things were men polite enough to give up their seats on the subway.... Who in such circumstances would dare to speak of fogiveness? ... It is not hatred that will speak out tomorrow but justice itself, justice based on memory" ("The Age of Contempt," *Combat*, August 30, 1944). Camus characterizes a justice based on the memory of such suffering and horror as "absolute" because the victims had already paid an absolute price for resisting tyranny. Atrocities of the kind described by Camus allow for no possibility of restraint, mitigation, or of course pardon. For Camus, granting pardons to such criminals would not reunite the French, as some argued, but further divide them; it would not put an end to the Franco-French war of the last years of the Occupation but perpetuate it.

Camus, of course, would eventually modify his position on absolute justice, but only after he had supported the necessity of such trials and engaged in an extended polemic with François Mauriac over whether charity or justice should prevail in deciding such cases.[7] Camus, of course, defended justice, which for him meant the most severe punishment for the worst crimes. In an article he wrote on Pierre Laval and Maréchal Pétain, whom he labels "the President of Compromise and the Marshal of Confusion," Camus unequivocally states that they should be treated as murderers: "These men, who rationed everything except shame, who dispensed blessings with one hand while they killed with the

---

[7] Mauriac was a well-known, respected conservative Catholic novelist and fellow *résistant* and wrote for *Le Figaro*. Camus summarizes his differences with Mauriac in the following way: "Whenever I used the word *justice* in connection with the purge, M. Mauriac spoke of *charity*. So singular is the virtue of charity, moreover, that in calling for justice I seemed to be pleading on behalf of hatred. To hear M. Mauriac tell it, it truly seems that in dealing with these mundane matters we must make an absolute choice between the love of Christ and the hatred of men. Surely not! Some of us reject both the cries of enmity that reach our ears from one side and the tender solicitations that come to us from the other. Between these two extremes, we are searching for the just voice that will give us truth without shame.... This is what allows me to say that charity has no business here" ("Justice and Charity," January 11, 1945). But in a talk given to a Dominican community in 1948, Camus acknowledged that "concerning the substance and on the precise point of our controversy, Mr. François Mauriac was right" (*Essais*, 372).

other, who combined hypocrisy with terror, and who for four years treated us to an appalling mixture of sermons and executions, homilies and torture—these men could expect neither forgiveness nor indulgence from France. . . . We are not men of hate. But we must be men of justice. And justice dictates that those who killed and those who permitted murder are equally responsible before their victims" ("Time for Justice," August 22, 1944). The only conclusion that could be drawn from such arguments is that both Laval and Pétain deserved to die.[8]

In an article written on the proposal to establish a High Court of Justice to judge the prominent members of the Vichy government, Camus once again expresses his support for the strongest punishments: "If there are some cases in which our duty is not clear or justice is difficult to define, in this case we take our stand without hesitation. The voices of the tortured and humiliated join with ours in calling for justice of the most pitiless and decisive kind" (November 2, 1944). Pitiless, decisive justice is the only form of justice for Camus that would not have the effect of silencing the voices of the victims and their survivors, who alone have absolute authority.[9] Camus thus makes the choice between execution and pardon a choice between innocent victims, on the one side, and perverse torturers and executioners, on the other. And when a choice is presented in this way, justice is obviously on the side of the victims and legitimately "pitiless."

But even during this period when Camus argued that "the purge is necessary" and most enthusiastically supported capital punishment for the traitors responsible for the crimes of torture, deportation, and murder, he still argued that the principle of proportion had to be respected: "The point is not to purge a lot but to purge well. But what does it mean to purge well? It means to respect the general principle of justice without failing to make allowances in individual cases" (October 18, 1944). For without proportion there could be no possibility of justice. Even or especially in the most extreme cases Camus argues that there needs to be a balance between two radically opposed feelings: between the repugnance that would be felt by honorable people if the death sentences of those responsible for torture, deportation, and murder were actually carried out and the repulsion, anger, or horror experienced when the suffering of the victims is remembered and which would increase if the guilty were pardoned. It is precisely because balance or proportion is so difficult to determine and achieve in such instances that it is necessary.

Camus was nevertheless for a brief time a conflicted but nonetheless resolute supporter of the death penalty for particularly atrocious war crimes, but only if

---

[8] Both, of course, were sentenced to death, but only Laval would actually be executed. Pétain died in prison after de Gaulle had commuted his death sentence to one of life imprisonment.
[9] Camus insists that only the families of the victims have the right to speak of pardon: "I see for our country two ways unto death (and there are ways of surviving that are no better than death): the way of hatred and the way of pardon. One seems to me as disastrous as the other. . . . I shall join M. Mauriac in granting open pardons when Vélin's parents and Leynaud's wife tell me that I can. But not before. Never before" ("Justice and Charity"). Vélin, or André Bollier, was *Combat*'s printer, who committed suicide rather than be captured by the Gestapo. René Leynaud was a poet and early contributor to *Combat*; he was captured by the French Milice and executed by the Germans just before the Liberation in June 1944. Camus published a moving tribute to him in *Combat* (October 27, 1944).

justice was "prompt" rather than "precipitous": "We have never called for blind or precipitous justice. We detest arbitrary judgment and criminal stupidity, and we would prefer that France keep her hands clean. But to that end we want justice to be prompt, and we want all prosecution for crimes of collaboration to end at some fixed date. We want the most obvious crimes to be punished immediately, and then, since nothing can be done without mediocrity, we want the errors that so many Frenchmen have indeed committed consigned to carefully considered oblivion" (October 25, 1944). It soon became clear to Camus and almost everyone else that the opposite was occurring: justice was in almost all instances rapid and severe for lesser crimes and painfully slow and indulgent for the greater crimes committed by Vichy officials and important industrialists. In Camus' own terms, the justice that was being meted out was anything but proportional, which means it was anything but just in either a legal or a moral sense.

It is clear that by the summer of 1945 Camus had changed his position on the necessity for the purge after he had been confronted with its grotesque reality: "The word 'purge' itself was already rather distressing. The actual thing became odious. . . . The failure is complete" (August 30, 1945). In an earlier editorial, however, Camus already criticizes the purge trials, given that they had repeatedly produced further injustices, especially when indefensible crimes were being judged. Camus attacks the trials for producing only "absurd sentences and preposterous instances of leniency. In between, prisoners are snatched from their prisons and shot because they were pardoned. We want to say simply that all of this was to be expected and that it is probably too late now for justice to be done" (January 5, 1945). He deplores the fact that "they will go on handing out death sentences to journalists who don't deserve as much. They will go on half-acquitting recruiters with silver tongues. And the people, tired of their sick justice, will continue to intervene from time to time in cases that should no longer be their concern" (January 5, 1945). The moment for a higher, moral form of justice rooted in the need to respect the memory of the victims of Nazism and the Vichy state, a justice demanded by their silenced voices and carried out in their name, the moment for what Camus also called pure or absolute justice, had thus passed very quickly, as if it had never really been possible to achieve. But the obligation to honor the memory of the victims remained, even if in reality it proved to be difficult, if not impossible, to fulfill.

The failure of justice in the purge trials increased Camus' doubts about the legitimacy of capital punishment in general and led him to become a resolute opponent of the death penalty. It was with reference to his general opposition to the death penalty that he justified signing petitions to save the lives of two infamous literary collaborators, Robert Brasillach, who, despite the petition, was nonetheless executed immediately after his trial in February 1945, and Lucien Rebatet, whose death sentence was commuted and who was ultimately released from prison in the amnesty of 1950. Camus' reason for signing both petitions was the same: even though he admits he felt nothing but disdain for both Brasillach and Rebatet and considers their writings and actions to be criminal, he claims he holds the death penalty in greater horror than he does these two militant anti-Semites, collaborators, and Nazi propagandists.[10]

It would thus seem that it was his perception of the injustices of the purge trials themselves that convinced Camus that the only coherent and, more important, the only just position was to oppose capital punishment in all situations, even for those criminals he most abhorred. He realized that his obligation to the victims of criminal injustice was not to avenge them but rather to honor their memory in a completely different way: by a steadfast opposition to capital punishment, which for him amounted to "murder" being committed in their name or in the name of the state or the people. Camus thus decided to choose life before justice, even the life of criminal enemies of justice for whom he had the greatest contempt. Ten years later, during the Algerian War, he would be much criticized and grossly misunderstood for taking a similar position and announcing that if he were forced to choose between defending justice and defending the life of his mother, he would choose first to defend his mother.[11] This did not in fact, as has often been argued, reveal that he was a supporter of colonialism in Algeria and an opponent of freedom and justice for all Algerians. It rather constituted a statement of principle: that priority should always be given to human life, which had to be defended before ideals, no matter the legitimacy of the ideals and the cause being pursued.

For Camus the failure of justice in the purge trials was both a sign and a cause of the impending failure of France to "remake itself" and become a true democracy. As he put it, "a country that fails to purge itself is preparing to fail to remake itself. The face that a nation wears is that of its system of justice" (January 5, 1945). And the face of "sick justice" the French nation wore immediately after the Liberation was certainly far from the ideal of justice Camus proposed in his earliest articles. In this instance and in general, a democracy whose system of justice is sick cannot really be considered a democracy at all.

[10] In a letter Camus sent on January 27, 1945, to the novelist Marcel Aymé, who had written Camus to ask him to sign a petition to de Gaulle asking that Brasillach's life be spared, Camus reluctantly agreed to sign the petition and explained why: "I have always been horrified by the death penalty, and I have judged that as an individual the least I could do is not participate in it, even by abstention. . . . This is a scruple that I suppose would make the friends of Brasillach laugh. And as for him, if his life is spared and if an amnesty frees him as it probably will in one or two years, I would like him to be told the following as concerns my letter: it is not for him that I join my signature with yours, it is not for the writer, whom I consider to be worth nothing, nor for the individual, for whom I have the strongest contempt" (cited in Olivier Todd, *Albert Camus: Une vie* [Paris: Gallimard, 1996], 374).
[11] After receiving the Nobel Prize in 1957 and during a discussion with a group of students in Sweden, one of whom was Algerian and who repeatedly interrupted Camus with questions about democracy and justice in Algeria, Camus made the following remark: "I have always supported a just Algeria, where the two populations must live in peace and equality. I have said and repeated that we have to bring justice to the Algerian people and grant them a fully democratic regime. . . . I have always condemned terror. I must also condemn a terrorism that is practiced blindly, in the streets of Algiers, for example, and which one day could strike my mother or my family. I believe in justice, but I will defend my mother before justice" (*Le Monde*, December 14, 1957, in *Essais*, 1881–82).

The Failure of Politics: Colonialism

It may surprise some critics of Camus' position on the Algerian War to discover in this collection of editorials and articles from *Combat* that as early 1945 he wrote insistently about the necessity to resolve the injustices caused by colonialism, even or especially at a time when the seemingly more urgent problem facing France was the monumental task of rebuilding itself after four years of deprivation, physical devastation, occupation, and in the end what amounted to a civil war. The colonial question and more generally European imperialism were not, however, peripheral issues for Camus, either during or immediately after the war. On the contrary, he felt that the injustices of French colonialism constituted a serious threat to democracy in France, and that European, American, and Soviet imperialisms were obstacles to the creation of a truly democratic world order. It seemed to Camus not only illogical and incoherent but, more important, unjust for the French, who had regained their own freedom at the end of the war, to continue to deny that same freedom to those living in the different French colonies, some of whom had in fact fought alongside the French in the war against Germany. It was for him not just hypocritical but strictly speaking impossible to attempt to create an authentic democracy within France if France continued to deny social justice and democratic rights to its colonies.

For Camus, the basic issue was simple and clear: freedom and justice cannot be for some but not for others. Camus not only argues that France could not continue to have two different and even opposed policies concerning democracy, "one granting justice to the people of France and the other confirming injustice toward the Empire" (October 13, 1944). But in an article on France's Indochina policy, he also calls overtly for "a policy of emancipation": "Indochina will be with us if France leads the way by introducing both democracy and freedom there. But if we hesitate at all, Indochina will join forces with anyone at all, provided they are against us" (March 29, 1945). France, of course, never implemented such a policy, and thus independence in Vietnam, as well as Algeria, was achieved by other, more violent means and at a horrible cost in human lives.

Camus' most extended analysis in *Combat* of the injustices of colonialism is contained in the series of articles he published on Algeria in May and June 1945, immediately after the riots and massacres at Sétif and Guelema. More than a hundred French citizens were killed when demonstrations in various cities turned into riots, with women and children savagely mutilated. In retaliation, thousands of innocent Algerian men, women, and children were massacred by French civilians and police.[12] The massacre of Arab Algerians by French authorities and civilians nine years before the organization of an armed insurrection is now seen by most historians as the unofficial beginning of the Algerian War.

---

[12] Historians agree that the figure of 1,500 Algerian deaths given by the French administration is incredibly low, while the figure of 40,000 deaths given by the FLN is grossly inflated. Most place the number of deaths resulting from the French retaliation to be between 6,000 and 10,000, but some still argue the figure might be even higher.

Camus was one of the very few journalists at this time who attempted to understand the cause of the riots and who defended the rights of Arab Algerians in an
atmosphere of hatred and revenge.

In his articles Camus demands not only that Algeria not be forgotten in the
euphoria of the Liberation of metropolitan France but also that "the Arab people" of Algeria should finally be recognized as a people: "I want to point out that
the Arab people also exist. By that I mean that they aren't the wretched, faceless
mob in which Westerners see nothing worth respecting or defending. On the
contrary, they are a people of impressive traditions, whose virtues are eminently
clear to anyone willing to approach them without prejudice. These people are
not inferior except in regard to the conditions in which they must live, and we
have as much to learn from them as they from us" ("Crisis in Algeria," May
13–14, 1945). Recognition of the existence of "the Arab people" for Camus
means recognizing Arab Algerians as a people different from but equal to the
French. Refusing to accept the indifference, if not racist hostility, of both metropolitan French and French Algerians toward "the Arab people," Camus warns of
increased difficulties and violence if immediate steps are not taken to vastly
improve economic and political conditions in Algeria. It was a message virtually
no one in France in 1945 wanted to hear. Camus was thus at this pivotal
moment one of the very few French intellectuals or journalists who defended the
rights of Arab and Berber Algerians and their demands for freedom and justice,
and he would remain faithful to this position throughout the Algerian War itself,
even as he opposed the politics and actions of the FLN.

Camus argues that the French should be especially sensitive to the injustices
suffered by Algerians for a very particular reason: "We cannot remain indifferent
to their suffering, because we have experienced it ourselves. Rather than respond
with condemnations, let us try to understand the reasons for their demands and
invoke on their behalf the same democratic principles that we claim for ourselves" ("Crisis in Algeria"). His position on Algeria is thus the same as the one
he took on Indochina: everyone has the right to the same freedom and the same
justice. Even though Camus is not advocating a totally independent Algeria in
these articles and never supported such a proposal, it is still difficult to see how
Algeria could become the kind of democratic society Camus envisioned, with
all its inhabitants granted the rights of full citizens, without colonialism itself
coming to an end. A democratic Algeria with an Arab majority could not have
remained "French," except by means of a system of federation that moderate
Arab-Algerian nationalists had in fact proposed before the outbreak of World
War II and that Camus would continue to support during the Algerian War,
even when the intransigence of the overwhelming majority of French Algerians
had convinced moderate nationalists that such a system could no longer be
created.

Given the general hostility among French colonialists to democratic reforms
in Algeria, in these articles Camus presents the French with a simple choice: (1)
either acknowledge openly that indigenous Algerians will always be treated as a
conquered, inferior, colonized people, with limited rights and totally dependent

on and subservient to the French; (2) or acknowledge that democratic principles are universal and have to be applied to all situations given the fundamental right of all peoples to be free. In fact, the French, in principle although not in fact, had already chosen the latter alternative long before, Camus argues, and therefore it had always been and still was the responsibility of France to apply democratic principles in Algeria. What he provocatively calls the "reconquest" of Algeria would thus constitute the conquest of freedom in Algeria for all Algerians. That this would mean the end of colonialism had not escaped Camus, since he proclaims in another article in the series that "the era of Western imperialism is over" ("It Is Justice That Will Save Algeria from Hatred," May 23, 1945), even if it would in fact not be until 1962 and after eight years of horrible war that French colonialism would finally come to an end in Algeria.

The fundamental problem in Algeria, Camus argues, is not just that its Arab and Berber populations no longer believed in the possibility of their assimilation into French culture and economic-political life. More serious is that they also no longer believed in democracy, especially given the grotesque form in which it had been presented to them: "But the Arabs seem to have lost their faith in democracy, of which they were offered only a caricature. They hope to achieve by other means a goal that has never changed: an improvement in their condition" (May 18, 1945). The issue for Camus in 1945 was not *whether* to work for democracy in Algeria and thus improve the horrible living conditions of Berber and Arab Algerians but rather *how* best to do it. He was convinced that if nothing was done and conditions continued to worsen, violence would also increase—which is exactly what occurred. In Camus' view, though, neither France nor any other nation could claim to be a true democracy if it remained a colonial or imperialist power and subjugated and oppressed other peoples, if it denied others the very freedoms it claimed for itself. The failure to peacefully put an end to colonialism in the aftermath of World War II thus also constituted for Camus a serious, if not the most serious, failure of French democracy itself.

The Failure of the Free Press: Terror and Silence

"We live in terror," writes Camus in the first article of the series he published in *Combat* under the general title "Neither Victims nor Executioners," and then adds that the entire twentieth century could be characterized as "the century of fear." Camus did not, however, write this series of articles during the worst moments of World War II. Nor does the phrase "we live in terror" refer exclusively to the past atrocities of the Nazi Occupation or the crimes of the Vichy state, some of which he had dramatically described in articles published in the days immediately preceding and following the liberation of Paris. The series, "Neither Victims nor Executioners," was in fact published in November 1946, well after France had been liberated and Nazi Germany defeated.

Europe was finally at peace. Soldiers were no longer dying in battles in Europe and the East, and civilians were no longer living in immediate terror for their lives in the cities that both Nazi and Allied forces had targeted at different moments of the war. Camus' Resistance comrades and other political opponents of Nazi Germany and Vichy France were no longer being tortured, summarily executed, or deported to concentration camps to live and die under atrocious conditions. Jews were no longer being deported to death camps and systematically exterminated by the millions. Nazi oppression, torture, deportation, and mass murder were thus horrible memories of the recent past but no longer part of everyday reality. But despite all these facts, Camus argues that the reign of terror was continuing and for a very specific reason: it served a political purpose. For "even if fear can't be considered a science in itself," Camus argues, "there is no question that it is a method" ("The Century of Fear," November 19, 1946). And as a method, terror was in fact working all too well to silence opposition, prevent dialogue, and force people to choose one side or the other in a battle that each side presented as one between freedom and enslavement, justice and injustice, and ultimately between "Good" and "Evil." The effect of terror was to ensure that no other choices were available, that one had to choose one side over the other. This was the method in its madness.

Camus presents terror as being even more insidious in the postwar period than during the war, since it had spread across the political spectrum. Its primary source was no longer Nazi Germany but other "deadly ideologies" that were continuing to struggle for hegemony in Europe and the rest of the world: "Today, no one is talking (apart from those who repeat themselves), because the world seems to us to be led by forces blind and deaf to warnings, advice, and supplications. . . . There is no way of persuading an abstraction, or, to put it another way, the representative of an ideology. The long dialogue among human beings has now come to an end" ("The Century of Fear"). The silence produced by such ideological terror represents for Camus a deadly threat not only to freedom but also "for all who cannot live without dialogue and the friendship of other human beings, . . . the end of the world." Camus thus fears that the world is on the verge of ending not with a bang or even a whimper but with total silence, a silence created by the messianic abstractions (ideologies) that dominate the public sphere, with people both afraid and reluctant to speak because their only choice is between equally unacceptable abstractions.

Terror thrives in "a world of abstraction, a world of bureaucracy and machinery, of absolute ideas and of messianism without subtlety, . . . among people who believe they are absolutely right, whether it be in their machines or their ideas." In this way history becomes a process of death, not of life, the product of mechanical abstractions rather than living human beings. Camus in fact considers all the ideologies struggling for dominance in the postwar period to be potentially deadly, with each of them in its own way contributing to the creation of a state of terror and the depreciation of life: "Because persuasion is no longer possible, because man has been delivered entirely into the hands of history and can no longer turn toward that part of himself which is as true as the historic part, and which he discovers when he confronts the beauty of the world and of people's faces" ("The Century of Fear"). And human beings who have been delivered to history and accept being determined by history become one-dimensional, muted creatures who have an ever-diminishing moral and aesthetic sense and thus a diminished sense of the possibilities of history itself. Above all, they lose their sense of both natural beauty and the beauty of other human faces, and with this loss of aesthetic judgment and a lack of recognition of the worth of others they lose the capacity for moral judgment as well. Above all, they lose all sense of justice.

Camus writes in this series as if the end had already occurred, as if terror had won, as if silence was already the norm: "A man who cannot be persuaded is a man who makes others afraid. So that alongside people who stopped speaking because they deemed it pointless to try, a vast conspiracy of silence has arisen and continues to spread, a conspiracy accepted by those who quake in fear" ("The Century of Fear"). Against terror, Camus continued to defend the power of words and thus of responsible political journalism, which he felt had as crucial a role to play in the resistance to the conspiracy of silence as it had in the French Resistance to Nazism.

Arguments "against ideology" are by now very familiar. But many, if not most of these arguments are in fact ideologically motivated defenses of capitalism and a particular form of liberal democracy. In other words, "the end of ideology" has come to signify the end of "their" ideology—the end of Communism, for example—and the triumph of democracy. This was not, however, Camus' position, for if he was a staunch defender of democracy and an increasingly outspoken critic of Marxism,[13] it is not because he felt democracy was the ideal form of government. Rather, as he states in an article written after "Neither Victims nor Executioners," it is because democracy is "the least bad" political alternative. He argues that in its best sense, democracy is "an exercise in modesty" ("Democracy and Modesty," April 30, 1947), an open, unfinished project, always "to be made," never already achieved once and for all time.[14]

Modesty means that democracies have to acknowledge that all progress toward greater freedom and justice is relative and can be destroyed or reversed at any time, that freedoms already formally guaranteed and in principle protected can be destroyed or in fact do not even actually exist, that injustices and inequalities that have in principle been eliminated can in fact continue to exist, and perhaps even increase. Modesty also means that democracies should never silence those who call attention to such reversals, contradictions, and inadequacies, those who demand that more still needs to be done, that democracies have to become increasingly more democratic and thus more just. It is certainly true that Camus' increasingly "anti-Communist" political position, which is expressed in a more

[13] In a letter to Roger Quillot (June 30, 1948), he asserts that "the Marxist conception of the world is not only false but it is also becoming lethal" (*Essais*, 1579).

[14] The title of one of Camus' early editorials, "La Démocratie à faire" ("The Democracy to Come," September 2, 1944) could in fact characterize all his remarks on democracy: that it is always "to come," always "to be made," never already made.

developed form in *The Rebel*, is evident in his editorials from 1946 and 1947. But what is more interesting and relevant to us and certainly more vital for our own world, in which a different climate of terror reigns, is the way Camus defends democracy: by offering a severe critique of the immodesty, short-comings, and failures of actual democracies and thus of their failure to live up to what he argues democracy could and should be. It is a critique perhaps more nec-essary today than ever before.

If modesty is democracy's strength, it follows that to triumph over political adversaries by force can never be considered proof of democracy's superiority or legitimacy. On the contrary, it is the proof only of the economic, political, tech-nological, and military power of a particular democratic state or group of de-mocratic states. In itself it has nothing to do with either freedom or justice, and thus nothing to do with democracy as such. A democracy, for example, no mat-ter how powerful or dominant—and precisely because it is economically and technologically powerful and dominant—that would hold itself up as *the model* of democracy, that would speak and act as if it embodied true democratic values in its struggle against tyranny and injustice (or "Evil"), according to the logic of Camus' argument would in fact not only be deluding itself but also constitute a threat to other democracies and to democracy itself. It would itself, no matter how violently antidemocratic its "enemies," be contributing to and profiting from the climate of terror it claimed to be attacking and using fear to silence those who oppose the actions it had taken allegedly to protect or spread democ-racy. By contributing to the climate of terror, it would itself constitute a form of messianism, another ideology, what could be called an antidemocratic form of democracy.

The paradox of democracy for Camus, therefore, is that when it is the most triumphant it is also the least democratic, and this also holds for individual polit-ical parties and groups within a particular democracy, as well as for democracies in general. For once "one party or group imagines itself to be in possession of the absolute truth" ("Democracy and Modesty," April 30, 1947), then a climate of terror exists and democracy is at risk. It is not surprising, then, that Camus' def-inition of a democrat is remarkably simple and straightforward: a democrat is "a person who admits that his adversary may be right, who therefore allows him to speak, and who agrees to consider his arguments. When parties and people are so convinced by their own arguments that they are willing to resort to violence to silence those who disagree with them, democracy no longer exists. Modesty is therefore salutary in republics at all times" ("Democracy and Modesty"). This may very well suggest that there have never been many true democrats or democ-racies, and that in spite of what is frequently claimed there are perhaps even fewer today than ever before. It certainly means at the very least that Camus him-self was suspicious and urges his readers to be suspicious of those who speak the loudest in defense of democratic ideals and absolutes but whose goal is to instill fear in opponents and to silence dissent. The silence that results from such ter-ror may very well signal, if not "the end of the world," then at least the end of democracy—in any case, it most certainly does not indicate its triumph.

It is not surprising, therefore, that Camus felt that the free press had an essential role to play in all democracies: that of refusing to choose either of the sides in ideological conflicts and thus continuing to provide a forum for dialogue across the ideological divides. In general, this means that the role of the press for Camus was to resist terror. An interesting aspect of Camus' *Combat* editorials is that they repeatedly question how well he and *Combat* in general have fulfilled this crucial democratic and critical function. He acknowledges that it was much easier to defend the honor of clandestine journalism during the Resistance, since its very existence was "proof of [its] independence, because it involves a risk" ("The Profession of Journalist," *Combat*, clandestine no. 58, July 1944). But when *Combat*, like other Resistance newspapers, was published openly after the Liberation and it was no longer true that "writing an article can land you in prison or get you killed," for Camus it was still the case "that words have value and need to be weighed carefully," and that "the journalist's responsibility to the public" should not be taken lightly ("Critique of the New Press," August 31, 1944). Independence and "honor" were obviously much more complicated issues in postwar France than during the war.

Camus makes one of his most interesting assessments of *Combat* a year after the Liberation. In one year, Camus claims, France has "turned a corner," and even if "justice has not yet arrived, . . . we have at least emerged from an abject condition in which injustice reigned" (September 1, 1945). The same could be said for the press as a whole, since he states that even if the press was not yet what it should be, it was also most definitely no longer the abject agency of collaboration of the official press of the war period. But if one of the goals of *Combat*, which Camus argues should also be a goal of a France striving to ensure freedom and achieve justice, was "to create a climate in which the various tendencies of French political life could confront one another without clashing" and thus "to make dialogue possible by pointing out differences and highlighting similarities" among different political groups from the moderate right to the revolutionary left (Camus mentions explicitly Christians and Communists), then, in his evaluation it had definitely come up short. Or, as Camus bluntly puts it: "In this respect, our year of work has ended in abject failure." The press fails when rather than being a vehicle for dialogue it provokes polemics and thus reduces opponents to silence rather than encouraging ongoing discussion. Democracy fails as well.

In September 1945, Camus still claims to be cautiously optimistic, however, concerning the possibilities for both *Combat* and French democracy. And even if he admits that "French public life will no doubt continue to be what it is, namely, an arena in which powerful orthodoxies confront one another while a few solitary voices try to make themselves heard," he is still sufficiently confident that *Combat* has learned from the failures of the previous year and that "tomorrow will be better." But in fact "tomorrow" turned out not to be better at all. Not for the press, because newspapers like *Combat* became even more dependent on financial interests and more closely connected to political parties. But not for democracy either, because officials of the government increasingly closed their ears to criticism and dissent and transformed the Fourth Republic into what Camus calls "a deaf and dumb republic," that is, not a democracy at all: for "there is no democracy without dialogue" ("The Deaf and Dumb Republic," March 17, 1947). When a dominant political party or the government as a whole believes that "no one else serves the cause of democratic truth" and thus that it has no need to engage in dialogue with the opposition or the opposition press, democracy suffers and is even at risk. And it makes no difference if the government is on the left or the right.

During the time Camus was associated with *Combat*, it survived various crises: paper shortages, competition for readership from existing and newly created newspapers such as *Le Monde*, and even a general four-week printers' strike that shut down the entire industry. After the strike was settled, Camus ironically announces the return of *Combat*, in spite of rumors of its demise or of its having been purchased by a rich industrialist: "Poor but free before the strike, *Combat* is back, poorer than ever but still free and determined to stay that way. Just as it lived on the income from its sales and advertising a month ago, it continues today to rely solely on its readers" ("The Deaf and Dumb Republic"). As noble an idea as this might have been, the poverty of *Combat*, which is for Camus also the proof of its independence, would in fact eventually prove to be fatal.

The experiment in a radically independent form of journalism did not and could not last forever. A newspaper born in the Resistance as a fusion of various political tendencies and that for almost all its existence was free from the control or influence of any investors or political party definitively lost Camus as its editor in chief and chief editorialist in 1947. Even if Camus would have been the first to say that no single journal, *Combat* included, was in itself essential to French democracy, its transformation and then demise were signs not just that the Resistance press no longer mattered in the same way it did immediately after the war. They were also signs that the free press was being "bought" and thus was not as free as it should be—signs that democracy in France was not what it could be either.

When the free press fails, democracy fails as well, and the result is an increasing climate of terror and the silencing of opponents and opposing positions—on each side of the ideological (or religious/cultural) divides. In 1947, Camus felt this was becoming or had already become the case in France. But all was still not lost, for to have the state of terror recognized for what it was would be a positive step—and one of the crucial functions Camus continues to assign to the press was to identify, analyze, and criticize the different "methods" of instilling fear and silencing differences of opinion and dissent used by different political parties and officials. Even if a journal that took on this critical task were read by decreasing numbers of people, its refusal to accept either polemics or silence would at least be a sign that in spite of the climate of terror, democracy had not been completely destroyed and silence was not total. This would be so as long as "a forum continues to exist far from the deafening tumult of partisan voices, a forum where independent minds can still bear witness without pretentiousness or fear. It is good that freedom can still be exercised, at least for a little while, and even if it must swim against the tide. . . . Here, at least, it is still possible to breathe, as lonely as the effort may sometimes seem" ("The Choice," April 22, 1947). Thus in his last editorials for *Combat*, Camus expresses only a very cautious hope that "for a while" more, at least, freedom will continue to be exercised in forums like *Combat*. It is not much, and certainly a far cry from the enthusiasm of his early articles. But it is still something.

Combating Terror

But on what could such hope, no matter how cautious, be based, given the incredibly bleak picture Camus paints in his last series of articles? It was certainly not a hope that sprang from a trust in or commitment to a particular political party or that was rooted in a faith in any ideology. The possibility of hope came, paradoxically, from the knowledge that things really *were* as bad as they seemed to be, that terror was indeed prevalent. For Camus this meant that people would soon have to face a dramatic choice, not between opposing political alternatives produced by competing ideologies but a choice of a more fundamental nature: between being either victims or executioners, losers or victors, in a war for the ultimate conquest and domination of the world. If this really was the only choice available, then compromise, dialogue, and cooperation would no longer be possible, because they would be considered signs of weakness rather than strength, of defeat and not victory.

But the purpose of Camus' last series of articles is to convince his readers that they in fact do have another choice: it is to refuse the choice of being either victim or executioner. It is to remind them that they still have the choice of opposing the ideological forces that divide the world between Good and Evil, infidels and believers, us and them, as well as the choice of refusing to accept, legitimize, or directly participate in the destruction of others in the name of any ideology—democracy included—or any set of religious, moral, or political principles, no matter how noble—freedom and justice included. For Camus, democracy could never come out of the barrel of a gun (or a bomb or missile), just as justice could never be achieved as the result of the mistreatment, torture, or execution of criminals or terrorists "Neither Victims nor Executioners" thus constitutes a powerful conclusion to Camus' contributions to *Combat* and thus to this collection as well.

After reading these editorials, it is impossible not to ask if we today live once again in an age of terror in which we are being presented with the stark choice between being either victims or murderers. If this is indeed the case, then the publication of Camus' editorials and articles could not come at a more propitious moment. To understand that it is possible to reject the choice of being either a victim of murder or responsible for the death of others is perhaps more necessary now than at any other time since the end of the Cold War itself. As is the need for forums such as those provided by *Combat* in postwar France and for editorials by writer-journalists with the literary talent, sensitivity, moral conscience, political convictions, and even the illusions of an Albert Camus.

Even though the following are not the last lines Camus wrote for *Combat*, or even the last of the series "Neither Victims nor Executioners," they are an appropriate and dramatic conclusion to his postwar political journalism. For freedom, justice, and democracy itself all ultimately depend on how these two very basic questions are answered:

> Oui ou non, directement ou indirectement, voulez-vous être tué ou violenté? Oui ou non, directement ou indirectement, voulez-vous tuer ou violenter? [Yes or no, directly or indirectly, do you want to be killed or assaulted? Yes or no, directly or indirectly, do you want to kill or assault?] ("The Century of Fear")

Camus' questions are simple and straightforward and of course meant to be answered with a resounding "no." For who would ever *want to* be killed or violently attacked by others? Who, except for the most fanatical or insane among us, would ever *want to* kill or violently attack others? But underlying the two questions is another, unarticulated question, which is whether one should accept in the first place that the only choice one has is to be either a victim of murder or a murderer oneself. That such a choice is unacceptable, that it constitutes no choice at all, and that even in an age of terror, alternatives always exist to being either a victim or a murderer are things of which it would seem we need to be reminded once again. For this reason, Camus' editorials could be considered as pertinent and necessary today as they were when they were originally published sixty years ago.

David Carroll

PREFACE

This edition is based on texts published in *Combat*. In the case of texts that Camus chose to reprint in the collections entitled *Actuelles* and *Actuelles III*, only significant variants (and typographical errors) have been noted. In general, Camus eliminated subtitles, reduced the number of paragraphs, and corrected punctuation. These strictly typographical changes are not indicated.

Works by Camus Cited in the Notes

Essays and articles others than those appearing in *Combat, Actuelles,* or *Actuelles III* are taken from Albert Camus, *Essais* (Paris: Gallimard-Pléiade, 1965), introduction by R. Quilliot and L. Faucon, referred to as *Essais.*

La Peste (Paris: Gallimard-Folio, 1987).

Articles from *Alger-Républicain* and *Le Soir-Républicain: Fragments d'un combat, 1938–1940, Alger-Républicain*. Cahiers Albert Camus 3. Edition established, introduced, and annotated by Jacqueline Lévi-Valensi and André Abbou. 2 vols. (Paris: Gallimard, 1978).

Carnets, mai 1935–février 1942 (Paris: Gallimard, 1962), referred to as *Carnets I.*

Carnets, janvier 1942–mars 1951 (Paris: Gallimard, 1964), referred to as *Carnets II.*

Camus éditorialiste à "L'Express." Introduction, commentary, and notes by Paul Semts. Cahiers Albert Camus 6 (Paris: Gallimard, 1987).

Journaux de voyage (Paris: Gallimard, 1978). Text established, presented, and annotated by Roger Quilliot.

Correspondence

Albert Camus–Jean Grenier, Correspondance, 1932–1960 (Paris: Gallimard, 1981). Preface and notes by Marguerite Dobreen.

Correspondance 1939–1947 Albert Camus–Pascal Pia (Paris: Fayard/Gallimard, 2000). Presented and annotated by Yves-Marc Ajchenbaum.

ACKNOWLEDGMENTS

I would like to offer my warmest thanks

To Catherine Camus, for her confidence and assistance,

To Robert Gallimard, without whom this edition would never have seen the light of day,

To Roger Grenier, who generously shared with me his memories and documents in his possession,

To Agnès Spiquel, for her help,

To Pierre Lévi-Valensi, whose historical knowledge and patience were invaluable to me.

INTRODUCTION

The eminent role that Camus played at *Combat* as editor in chief and editorial writer from August 1944 until June 1947 is well-known. It is difficult, however, to be certain which articles he wrote himself. There is obviously no doubt about those that he chose to reprint in *Actuelles: Chroniques 1944–1948*, published by Gallimard in 1950, or about those that bear his byline in the paper, as is the case for editorials published between December 13, 1944, and February 9, 1945, and for nearly all the texts that are not editorials, such as his reflections on journalism or his reporting on Algeria, which he reprinted in *Actuelles III: Chroniques algériennes* in 1958. Nor is there any uncertainty concerning those articles for which a typescript has been preserved in the Fonds Camus. It is hard to see why Camus would have saved typescripts of articles he had not written, particularly since many of these correspond to articles bearing his byline. These typescripts were made after the fact, based on the articles printed in the newspaper, as is shown by the text dated October 8, 1944, which reproduces a sentence with a missing line, just as it was printed in the paper. It is very likely that this version was prepared at a time when Camus was considering publishing a volume of his articles. Unfortunately, the typescripts in the archives end on January 11, 1945.

Those texts that pose no real problem of identification are therefore indicated as being certainly by Camus. The other texts included in this volume must obviously be regarded as simply "attributed to Camus," and in each case I have indicated the degree of likelihood in the notes. Some of these texts can be identified without much chance of error owing to the existence of objective evidence: an allusion in a letter by Camus himself, by Francine Camus, or by some other correspondent, or a specific memory recalled by a member of the *Combat* staff. Comparison with the anthologies that some of these staff members published, such as Albert Ollivier's *Fausses Sorties*,[1] made it possible to avoid some errors. This still leaves a substantial number of articles for which the only justification for an attribution to Camus is cross-checking and extremely scrupulous internal criticism of both form and content, and obviously any such attribution can be no more than a hypothesis. The task is made even more delicate by the fact that the members of the staff shared a common "tone," enforced by Camus and Pia, who were careful proofreaders, particularly where editorials were concerned. I hope that I have struck a proper balance between caution and a desire to be exhaustive.

This edition is not always in agreement with the incomplete list of articles that Roger Quilliot included in *Essais*,[2] which offered a selection of articles from *Combat* as "complementary texts" to *Actuelles* in addition to the list. The list is not entirely reliable, however, and some of the texts are published with a byline that was not included in the original article. This edition differs even more from

---

[1] Albert Ollivier, *Fausses Sorties* (Paris: La Jeune Parque, 1946).
[2] Albert Camus, *Essais* (Paris: Gallimard, 1965). Introduction by R. Quilliot, texts established and annotated by R. Quilliot and L. Faucon.

that of Norman Stokle, *Le "Combat" d'Albert Camus*, the errors in which have been noted for some time now.[3]

It seemed to me desirable to present these articles in chronological order of publication. This makes it possible to situate each article with respect to the news of the day on which it comments, and the period 1944–1947 was indeed fertile in news. It also allows us to follow, often on a day-by-day basis, the variety of subjects that Camus dealt with and thus to gauge the remarkable openness of his mind. Nevertheless, it also seemed necessary to me to propose a thematic grouping of the articles, so that their variety does not hide from view their coherence or the "obstinacy" of Camus' political convictions, to borrow a word that he often used. This grouping, which can be found at the end of the introduction, should make it possible to read all the articles on a given theme in a continuous fashion. This is the only purpose of the categories given here, and I have no intention of trying to impose a systematic classification on Camus' thinking. There are limits to any such grouping. For instance, the editorial of November 15, 1944, which deals with false information coming out of Germany, deals with the press, the war, and the situation in Germany all at once. Although it is possible to justify the distinction between domestic politics and international affairs, Camus himself noted on May 25, 1945, that "there is not a single domestic issue that does not also have global repercussions and that is not influenced in turn by international politics." In fact, all of his contributions to *Combat* could be included under the title of the longest section of *Actuelles*, "Morality and Politics."

Prompted by the news of the day, these editorials and articles are by definition "occasional texts." The events they comment on and the figures they describe—men involved in the making of history—were well-known to Camus' readers. The journalist knew that he could simply allude to matters that were part of the collective experience of his immediate contemporaries. Today's reader no longer shares this knowledge. In order to enable the reader to fully appreciate these texts, it was therefore essential to provide them with notes, often quite extensive, which are intended not as commentaries but merely as aids to preserve the clarity of the originals.

More than fifty years after the publication of these articles, and despite the fact that they were intimately linked to the historical events of their times, of whose hopes and disillusionments they offer a faithful image, they have lost none of their force or value. They still speak to us and still have much to say to us about freedom, justice, truth, and democracy. At times they seem to have been written for us, for our times, to spur us on to lucidity and vigilance. They attest to the importance and interest of Camus' work as a journalist at *Combat*, and to his astonishing resonance in contemporary consciousness.

---

[3] Norman Stokle, ed., *Le "Combat" d'Albert Camus* (Quebec: Les Presses de l'Université Laval, 1970). Apart from the errors in the notes, Stokle was very generous in his attributions and careless in the reproduction of the texts, so much so that the edition was not authorized.

THEMATIC CLASSIFICATION

The following attempt at a "thematic classification" of the texts collected in this volume is in no way intended to be authoritative or exclusive. Many of these texts fall under several headings and are therefore mentioned several times. All these articles were inspired by Camus' desire or determination to introduce morality into politics. The only purpose of this classification is to make clear the continuity of his concerns and the coherence of his thought.

In what follows, the letter "s" indicates texts signed by Camus; "a" indicates authenticated texts; and "p" indicates texts in which the attribution to Camus is most likely correct.

History in the Making

The Liberation of Paris

8/21/44: "Combat Continues" (a) 11
8/23/44: "They Shall Not Pass" (a) 15
8/24/44: "The Blood of Freedom" (a) 16
8/25/44: "The Night of Truth" (a) 17
8/30/44: "The Age of Contempt" (a) 20

The Continuation of the War

9/29/44: "We are emerging from euphoria." (a) 51
10/3/44: "The *Daily Mail* has just published . . ." (a) 56
10/6/44: "There was plenty of noise in the night sky . . ." (a) 61
10/19/44: "France's participation in the allied military
            government . . ." (p) 78
10/22/44: "The *Daily Express* . . ." (a) 85
11/14/44: "It is worth noting . . ." (a) 111
11/25/44: "Yes, our armies are on the Rhine . . ." (a) 123
11/29/44: "Only just liberated, Europe is in turmoil." (a) 126
12/13/44: "One reads almost everywhere . . ." (s) 138
12/15/44: "The Consultative Assembly . . ." (s) 141
12/20/44: "As von Rundstedt was launching his offensive . . ." (s) 147
12/22/44: "France has endured many tragedies . . ." (s) 149
12/31/44–1/1/45: *1945* (p) 159
1/2/45: "We have read . . ." (s) 160
2/17/45: "'Here, at least, we aren't living amidst lies.'" (p) 173
4/3/45: "What was being celebrated yesterday . . ." (a) 184
4/4/45: "As the end of hostilities draws near . . ." (a) 185
4/10/45: "The victories on the western front . . ." (p) 190
4/17/45: "With every step closer to victory . . ." (p) 194

5/9/45: "Who would think himself capable . . ." (p) 195
8/8/45: "The world is what it is . . ." (a) 236
8/17/45: "Now that the war is over . . ." (p) 240
9/1/45: "The postwar has begun." (p) 251

Domestic Politics

9/2/44: "The Democracy to Come"(a) 25
9/4/44: "Morality and Politics" (a) 27
9/6/44: "The End of a World" (a) 28
9/10/44: "The new government is constituted." (p) 34
9/19/44: "The National Liberation Movement . . ." (a) 41
9/26/44: "With the arrest of Louis Renault . . ." (a) 47
9/27/44: "Please forgive us . . ." (a) 48
9/28/44: "One can read the communiqué of the Council
          of Ministers . . ." (a) 50
10/8/44: "Yesterday, the National Council of the Resistance . . ." (a) 64
10/20/44: "We are not in agreement with M. François
          Mauriac." (a) 80
10/21/44: "Yes, the drama that France faces . . ." (a) 82
10/21/44: "Money versus Justice" (a) 83
11/3/44: "Governing is good." (a) 97
11/7/44: "For several weeks . . ." (a) 104
11/16/44: "The Government has decided . . ." (p) 113
11/23/44: "To judge by what one reads in the Paris press . . ." (a) 120
11/24/44: "The more one thinks about it . . ." (a) 121
11/30/44: "The ministry of information . . ." (p) 128
12/1/44: "The problem of the press . . ." (a) 130
12/5/44: "There is a sort of tacit agreement between M. Mauriac
          and us . . ." (p) 133
12/13/44: "One reads almost everywhere . . ." (s) 138
12/14/44: "Two days ago, the Consultative Assembly . . ." (s) 139
12/15/44: "The Consultative Assembly yesterday . . ." (s) 141
12/29/44: "Broad questions of policy . . ." (s) 153
1/2/45: "*Panem et circenses*" (Suetonius) 159
1/5/45: "Minister Tiberius" (Suetonius) 165
2/9/45: "To judge by what is being said about us . . ." (s) 170
3/9/45: "For two days, M. Teitgen . . ." (p) 174
3/11–12/45: "Yesterday we published . . ." (p) 176
3/18/45: "Breaking our general rule . . ." (p) 179
4/5/45: "'I am a teacher, and I'm hungry.'" (a) 187
4/6/45: "Those who look upon the resignation . . ." (a) 188
5/12/45: "We are waiting for a government shakeup . . ." (p) 196
5/25/45: "Yesterday, General de Gaulle . . ." (p) 218
5/26/45: "While awaiting the ministerial shakeup . . ." (a) 219

6/27/45: "M. Herriot has just made an unfortunate statement." (a) 227
8/23/45: "The Radical Party congress . . ." (p) 242
8/24/45: "At the Radical Party congress . . ." (p) 244
8/26–27/45: "We have proved to be excellent prophets . . ." (p) 246
8/28/45: "Many readers have asked . . ." (p) 248
11/15/45: "France is in a state of siege." (p) 253
4/22/47: "The Choice" (s) 285
4/30/47: "Democracy and Modesty" (a) 286

Foreign Policy

RECOGNITION OF THE FRENCH GOVERNMENT

9/30/44: "Mr. Churchill has just delivered a speech . . ." (a) 52
10/14/44: "Mr. Churchill said in his most recent speech . . ." (a) 71
10/15/44: "We beg our readers' indulgence . . ." (a) 73
10/17/44: "We must return once again . . ." (a) 75
10/19/44: "France's participation in the allied military government . . ."
          (p) 78
1/3/45: "The Agence Française de Presse . . ." (a) 162

EUROPEAN POLITICS

11/29/44: "Only just liberated, Europe is in turmoil." (a) 126
12/3/44: "General de Gaulle has had talks with Marshal
          Stalin. . . ." (a) 131
12/9/44: "Yesterday, before the House of Commons . . ." (a) 135
12/18/44: "The text of the Franco-Soviet pact . . ." (s) 145
2/17/45: "'Here, at least, we aren't living amidst lies' . . ." (p) 173
8/17/45: "Now that the war is over . . ." (p) 240

GERMANY

9/15/44: "In 1933, an eager, frenetic personage . . ." (a) 37
9/17/44: "What are the people of Germany doing? . . ." (a) 40
9/20/44: "We spoke the other day about the German people . . ." (a) 43
11/15/44: "There is something irritating . . ." (a) 112
12/20/44: "As von Rundstedt was launching his offensive . . ." (s) 147
6/30–7/1/45: "Images of Occupied Germany" (s) 229
5/7/47: "Anniversary" (a) 288

GREAT BRITAIN

9/23/44: "Four years ago . . ." (a) 45
10/3/44: "The Daily Mail has just published . . ." (a) 56
10/22/44: "The Daily Express . . ." (a) 85
5/31/45: "The Syrian affair . . ." (p) 221
6/1/45: "Mr. Churchill's ultimatum . . ." (p) 223

BELGIUM

11/19/44: "We need to look closely . . ." (a) 115
11/26/44: "This is what we have come to: Belgian blood has been shed in
Brussels . . ." (a) 124

SPAIN

9/7/44: "Our Brothers in Spain" 29
10/5/44: "We have said before in this space . . ." (a) 59
10/24/44: "We wish to protest . . ." (a) 86
11/21/44: "It is once again time . . ." (a) 116
12/10/44: "Yesterday, many newspapers . . ." (a) 137
1/7–8/45: "Spain is growing fainter." (s) 166
5/27/45: "The foreign affairs committee of the Consultative Assembly . . ."
        (p) 220
8/7/45: "General Franco has officially announced . . ." (p) 235
11/25/48: "Why Spain?" (s) 297

UNITED STATES

11/9/44: "Mr. Roosevelt's election . . ." (p) 106
4/14/45: "His face was the very image of happiness." (a) 192
4/15–16/45: "Mr. Truman has made no secret . . ." (p) 193

GREECE

11/29/44: "Only just liberated, Europe is in turmoil. . . ." (a) 126
12/5/44: "There is a sort of tacit agreement between M. Mauriac
        and us . . ." (p) 133
12/9/44: "Yesterday, before the House of Commons . . ." (a) 135

POLAND

1/3/45: "The Agence Française de Presse . . ." (s) 162

MIDDLE EAST

5/31/45: "The Syrian affair . . ." (p) 221
6/1/45: "Mr. Churchill's ultimatum . . ." (p) 223

SOVIET UNION

12/3/44: "General de Gaulle has had talks with Marshal Stalin." (a) 131
12/18/44: "The text of the Franco-Soviet pact . . ." (s) 145
4/10/45: "The victories on the western front . . ." (p) 190

International Politics

2/16/45: "Along with other difficult issues, the Crimea
        Conference . . ." (p) 171
6/1/45: "Mr. Churchill's ultimatum . . ." (p) 223

8/14/45: "We previously indicated . . ." (p) 237
8/15/45: "Yesterday the *Washington Times Herald* . . ." (p) 239
12/9/48: "What Is the UN Accomplishing?" (s) 301
12/25–26/48: "Responses to an Unbeliever" (s) 304

Colonial Politics

ALGERIA

10/13/44: "It is impossible to exaggerate . . ." (a) 69
11/28/44: "We get word from many quarters . . ." (p) 126
5/13–14/45: "Crisis in Algeria" (s) 198
5/15/45: "Famine in Algeria" (s) 201
5/16/45: "Algeria Asks for Ships and Justice" (s) 203
5/18/45: "Natives of North Africa Estranged" (s) 207
5/20–21/45: "Arabs Demand a Constitution and a Parliament for Algeria"
        (s) 212
5/23/45: "It Is Justice That Will Save Algeria from Hatred" (s) 214
6/15/45: "After being briefly traumatized . . ." (a) 225
8/4/45: "Many things have a claim . . ." (p) 233
3/14/49: "Only Privates Are Traitors" (s, Camus and Char) 309

INDOCHINA

2/17/45: "'Here, at least, we aren't living amidst lies . . .'" (p) 173
3/29/45: "Truth is a harsh master, allowing no time for rest." (p) 182
8/15/45: "Yesterday the *Washington Times Herald* . . ." (p) 239

MADAGASCAR

5/10/47: "Contagion" (s) 290

Political Line of Combat

8/21/44: "Combat Continues" (a) 11
8/21/44: "From Resistance to Revolution" (a) 12
9/2/44: "The Democracy to Come" (a) 25
9/4/44: "Morality and Politics" (a) 27
9/19/44: "The National Liberation Movement . . ." (a) 41
10/1/44: "People say, 'Tell us in a few words, what is it you want?'" (p) 54
10/7/44: "In Algiers on March 26, 1944 . . ." (a) 62
10/8/44: "Yesterday, the National Council of the Resistance . . ." (a) 64
10/20/44: "We are not in agreement with M. François Mauriac." (a) 80
10/21/44: "Yes, the drama that France faces . . ." (a) 82
11/10/44: "Yesterday, the Congress of the Socialist Party . . ." (a) 108
11/11/44: "Our friends from *Défense de la France* . . ." (a) 109
12/5/44: "There is a sort of tacit agreement between M. Mauriac
        and us . . ." (p) 133

12/14/44: "Two days ago, the Consultative Assembly . . ." (s) 139
12/15/44: "The Consultative Assembly yesterday . . ." (s) 141
12/16/44: "There is a belief in some quarters . . ." (s) 142
12/31/44–1/1/45: "1945"(p) 159
2/9/45: "To judge by what is being said about us . . ." (a) 170
6/5/45: "Henri Frenay is one of our comrades-in-arms." (p) 224
8/14/45: "We previously indicated . . ." (p) 237
8/23/45: "The Radical Party congress . . ." (p) 242
8/24/45: "At the Radical Party congress . . ." (p) 244
8/26–27/45: "We have proved to be excellent prophets . . ." (p) 246
9/1/45: "The postwar has begun." (p) 251
11/15/45: "France is in a state of siege." (p) 253
4/22/47: "The Choice" (a) 285
6/3/47: "To Our Readers" (a) 292

Morality and Politics

8/29/44: "Intelligence and Character" (a) 18
9/4/44: "Morality and Politics" (a) 27
9/6/44: "The End of a World" (a) 28
9/8/44: "Justice and Freedom" (a) 31
9/12/44: "You write us about the prisoners of war . . ." (p) 35
10/1/44: "People say, 'Tell us in a few words, what is it you want?'" (p) 54
10/6/44: "There was plenty of noise in the night sky over France yesterday."
          (a) 61
10/7/44: "In Algiers on March 26, 1944 . . ." (a) 62
10/8/44: "Yesterday, the National Council of the Resistance . . ." (a) 64
10/12/44: "There is much talk of order right now." (a) 68
10/29/44: "The day before yesterday, the minister of information . . ."
          (a) 92
11/2/44: "The Council of Ministers . . ." (a) 95
11/3/44: "Governing is good." (a) 97
11/3/44: "Pessimism and Courage" (s) 99
11/4/44: "Two days ago, Jean Guéhenno . . ." (a) 101
11/8/44: "The Consultative Assembly met yesterday . . ." (a) 105
11/11/44: "Our friends from *Défense de la France* . . ."(a) 109
11/23/44: "To judge by what one reads in the Paris press . . ." (a) 120
11/24/44: "The more one thinks about it . . ." (a) 121
12/1/44: "The problem of the press . . ." (a) 130
12/14/44: "Two days ago, the Consultative Assembly . . ." (s) 139
12/15/44: "The Consultative Assembly yesterday . . ." (s) 141
12/17/44: "When a revolution has broken out . . ." (s) 144
12/26/44: "The Pope has just delivered a message . . ." (s) 152
12/29/44: "Broad questions of policy . . ." (a) 153

2/9/45: "To judge by what is being said about us . . ." (a) 170
2/17/45: "'Here, at least, we aren't living amidst lies . . .'" (p) 173
3/9/45: "For two days, M. Teitgen . . ." (p) 174
3/11-12/45: "Yesterday we published . . ." (p) 176
3/27/45: "It is rather vexing . . ." (a) 180
4/3/45: "What was being celebrated yesterday . . ." (a) 184
4/17/45: "With every step closer to victory . . ." (p) 194
5/12/45: "We are waiting for a government shakeup . . ." (p) 196
5/17/45: "'Our food consists of one liter of soup . . .'"(a) 205
5/19/45: "The day before yesterday we protested . . ." (a) 210
5/25/45: "Yesterday, General de Gaulle delivered a speech . . ." (p) 218
6/5/45: "Henri Frenay is one of our comrades-in-arms." (p) 224
6/27/45: "M. Herriot has just made an unfortunate statement." (a) 227
8/8/45: "The world is what it is, which isn't much." (a) 236
8/17/45: "Now that the war is over . . ." (p) 240
8/23/45: "The Radical Party congress . . ." (p) 242
8/24/45: "At the Radical Party congress . . ." (p) 244
8/26–27/45: "We have proved to be excellent prophets . . ." (p) 246
9/1/45: "The postwar has begun. . . ." (p) 251
3/17/47: "The Deaf and Dumb Republic" (a) 280
4/30/47: "Democracy and Modesty" (a) 286
5/7/47: "Anniversary" (a) 288
5/10/47: "Contagion" (a) 290
12/9/48: "What Is the UN Accomplishing?" (s) 301
12/25–26/48: "Responses to an Unbeliever" (s) 304

Flesh

10/27/44: "It was difficult for us to speak . . ." (a) 90
12/22/44: "France has endured many tragedies . . ." (s) 149
1/2/45: "We have read . . ." (a) 160
4/17/45: "With every step closer to victory . . ." (p) 194
5/17/45: "'Our food consists of one liter of soup . . .'" (a) 205
5/19/45: "The day before yesterday we protested . . ." (a) 210

Neither Victims nor Executioners

11/19/46: "The Century of Fear" (s) 257
11/20/46: "Saving Bodies" (s) 260
11/21/46: "Socialism Mystified" (s) 262
11/23/46: "The Revolution Travestied" (s) 264
11/26/46: "International Democracy and Dictatorship" (s) 266
11/27/46: "The World Moves Quickly" (s) 268
11/29/46: "A New Social Contract" (s) 270
11/30/46: "Toward Dialogue" (s) 274

The Press

8/31/44: "Critique of the New Press" (s) 21
9/1/44: "The Reform of the Press" (s) 23
9/8/44: "Critical Journalism" (s) 32
9/22/44: "As everyone knows, newspapers are today subject . . ." (a) 44
10/3/44: "The *Daily Mail* has just published . . ." (a) 56
10/4/44: "It is no secret that the Underground Press Federation . . ." (a) 57
10/7/44: "In Algiers on March 26, 1944 . . ." (a) 62
10/11/44: "The situation of the press poses problems. . . ." (a) 66
10/20/44: "We are not in agreement with M. François Mauriac." (a) 80
10/24/44: "We wish to protest here in a firm and measured way . . ."
               (a) 86
10/31/44: "We can discuss the case of M. Stéphane Lauzanne . . ." (a) 94
11/5/44: "The *Officiel* has published . . ." (a) 103
11/15/44: "There is something irritating . . ." (a) 112
11/22/44: "It is time for some self-criticism." (a) 118
11/30/44: "The ministry of information is preparing a decree . . ." (p) 128
12/1/44: "The problem of the press . . ." (a) 130
12/10/44: "Yesterday, many newspapers . . ." (a) 137
12/23/44: "French Renaissance" (Suetonius) 150
3/9/45: "For two days, M. Teitgen . . ." (p) 174
3/11–12/45: "Yesterday we published . . ." (p) 176
3/16/45: "In *Témoignage chrétien* . . ." (p) 178
8/22/45: "The first National Assembly of the Press . . ." (p) 241
9/1/45: "The postwar has begun." (p) 251
3/17/47: "The Deaf and Dumb Republic" (s) 280
3/21/47: "Radio 47" [freedom of speech in broadcast media can be classed
               together with the written press] (s) 282
4/22/47: "The Choice" (s) 285
6/3/47: "To Our Readers" (s) 292

Justice

8/22/44: "Time for Justice" (p) 14
8/30/44: "The Age of Contempt" (a) 20
9/8/44: "Justice and Freedom" (a) 31
9/12/44: "You write us about the prisoners of war . . ." (p) 35
9/26/44: "With the arrest of Louis Renault . . ." (a) 47
9/27/44: "Please forgive us, but we are not yet done with the case of
               Renault. . . ." (a) 48
9/28/44: "One can read the communiqué of the Council of Ministers
               elsewhere." (a) 50
10/6/44: "There was plenty of noise in the night sky . . ." (a) 61
10/12/44: "There is much talk of order right now." (a) 68

10/18/44: "Let us say a few words about the purge." (a) 76
10/20/44: "We are not in agreement with M. François Mauriac." (a) 80
10/21/44: "Yes, the drama that France faces . . ." (a) 82
10/21/44: "Money versus Justice" (Juste Bauchart) 83
10/25/44: "We hesitated to respond . . ." (a) 88
10/31/44: "We can discuss the case of M. Stéphane Lauzanne . . ." (p) 94
11/2/44: "The Council of Ministers has just established a High Court of Justice . . ." (a) 95
11/5/44: "The *Officiel* has published . . ." (a) 103
12/30/44: "Judge Not" (s) 155
1/5/45: "The press has lately been preoccupied with injustice." (s) 163
1/11/45: "Justice and Charity" (s) 168
3/29/45: "Truth is a harsh master, allowing no time for rest." (p) 182
5/23/45: "It Is Justice That Will Save Algeria from Hatred" (a) 214
6/15/45: "After being briefly traumatized . . ." (a) 225
8/2/45: "Since the Court of Justice has acknowledged . . ." (p) 232
8/30/45: "We beg the reader's indulgence . . ." (a) 249
5/10/47: "Contagion" (a) 290

The Church

9/8/44: "Justice and Freedom" (a) 31
9/16/44: "A wire service report . . ." (a) 38
12/26/44: "The Pope has just delivered a message . . ." (s) 152
3/27/45: "It is rather vexing . . ." (a) 180
3/22/47: "No Excuse for This" (s) 283

Miscellaneous

12/24/44: "The Poet and General de Gaulle" (Suetonius) 151
12/31/44: "The Thirteenth Caesar" (Suetonius) 158
1/2/45: *"Panem et circenses"* (Suetonius) 160
1/17/47: "What do you think of American literature?" (s) 277

CAMUS at *Combat*

CHAPTER 1

Combat Underground: March–July 1944

Articles that appeared in clandestine issues of *Combat* can at best be classified as "probably" by Camus, and it is not out of the question that he wrote others. For obvious reasons, he kept no record of what he wrote, and no firm conclusions can be drawn from either the themes or the style of what was published, since everything that appeared in the paper constituted an act of resistance and reflected goals shared by everyone who wrote for it.

Combat, Underground No. 55, March 1944
Against Total War, Total Resistance[1]

Lying is never without purpose. Even the most impudent lie, if repeated often enough and long enough, always leaves a trace. German propaganda subscribes to this principle, and today we have another example of its application. Inspired by Goebbels's minions,[2] cheered on by the lackey press, and staged by the Milice,[3] a formidable campaign has just been launched—a campaign which seeks, in the guise of an attack on the patriots of the underground and the Resistance, to divide the French once again. This is what they are saying to Frenchmen: "We are killing and destroying bandits who would kill you if we weren't there. You have nothing in common with them."

Although this lie, reprinted a million times, retains a certain power, stating the truth is enough to repel the falsehood. And here is the truth: it is that the French have everything in common with those whom they are today being taught to fear and despise. There is one France, not two: not one that is fighting and another that stands above the battle in judgment. For even if there are those who would prefer to remain in the comfortable position of judges, that is not possible. You cannot say, "This doesn't concern me." Because it does concern you. The truth is that Germany has today not only unleashed an offensive against the best and

---

[1] As Roger Quilliot and Yves-Marc Ajchenbaum have suggested, it seems more than likely that this article was written by Camus.

[2] Goebbels, Joseph Paul (1897–1945). After joining the Nazi Party in 1922, he devoted himself primarily to psychological action, news, and propaganda. Named head of propaganda for the Nazi Party in 1928, he became Minister of Propaganda and Information in 1933. Loyal to Hitler to the end, he and his family committed suicide by poison during the final stages of the battle for Berlin.

[3] The Milice (Militia), created by Darnand in January 1943, was charged with supporting German efforts to suppress the French Resistance. [*Milice* is left untranslated throughout, but members of the Milice are referred to as "militiamen."]

proudest of our compatriots, but it is also continuing its total war against all of France, which is exposed in its totality to Germany's blows.

Don't say, "This doesn't concern me. I live in the country, and the end of the war will find me just as I was at the beginning of the tragedy, living in peace." Because it does concern you. Take note. On January 29, in Malleval in the Isère, a whole village was burned by the Germans on the mere suspicion that compulsory labor service holdouts[4] might have taken refuge there. Twelve houses were completely destroyed, eleven bodies discovered, fifteen men arrested. On December 18 at Chaveroche in Corrèze, five kilometers from Ussel, where a German officer was wounded in murky circumstances, five hostages were shot and two farms put to the torch. On February 4 in Grole, in the Ain, Germans, after failing to find the holdouts they were searching for, shot the mayor and two leading citizens.

These dead Frenchmen were people who might have said, "This doesn't concern me." But the Germans decided that it did concern them, and on that day they demonstrated that it concerned all of us. Don't say, "This doesn't concern me. I'm at home with my family, I listen to the radio every night, and I read my newspaper." Because they'll come after you on the pretext that somebody at the other end of France refused to go. They'll take your son, who also said it was no concern of his, and they'll mobilize your wife, who until now thought the whole business was for men only. In reality, it does concern you, and it concerns all of us. Because all the French are today bound together so tightly by the enemy that one person's act inspires all the others and one person's inattention or indifference can cost ten others their lives.

Don't say, "I sympathize, that's quite enough, and the rest is no concern of mine." Because you will be killed, deported, or tortured as a sympathizer just as easily as if you were a militant. Act: your risk will be no greater, and you will at least share in the peace at heart that the best of us take with them into the prisons.

That way France won't be divided. The enemy's effort is in fact intended to encourage Frenchmen to hesitate to do their national duty to resist the S.T.O.[5] and support the underground. It would succeed but for the fact that the truth stands in its way. And the truth is that the combined efforts of the assassins of the Milice and the killers of the Gestapo[6] have yielded risible results. Hundreds

---

[4] *Réfractaires*: the term refers to Frenchmen who refused to leave for Germany when ordered to do so as part of the Service du Travail Obligatoire, or S.T.O., the Compulsory Labor Service. I have translated it as "holdouts."

[5] The S.T.O. was established in February 1943 by the Vichy government acting under German pressure. The goal was to supply German factories with French labor. Many of the people drafted into the S.T.O. chose to go underground rather than depart for Germany, but 170,000 French "laborers" nevertheless answered the call.

[6] The Gestapo (short for Geheime Staatspolizei, or Secret State Police) was the political police force of the Nazi Party. Created by Göring in 1933 and later led by Himmler and Heydrich, it conducted a reign of terror in Germany and the occupied countries, employing the most horrific means to persecute opponents of the regime, resisters, and Jews. At the Nuremberg trials after the war, it was condemned for crimes against humanity.

of thousands of holdouts are still holding out, fighting, and hoping. A few arrests won't change that. And that is what the 125,000 young men whom the enemy plans to deport every month must understand. For all of them are in the enemy's sights, and the '44 and '45 drafts to which the enemy refers with admirable candor as "a labor reserve" stand for France itself, which in Germany's hate-filled eyes stands united.

Total war has been unleashed, and it calls for total resistance. You must resist because it does concern you, and there is only one France, not two. And the incidents of sabotage, the strikes, the demonstrations that have been organized throughout France are the only ways of responding to this war. That is what we expect from you. *Action in the cities* to respond to the attacks in the countryside. *Action in the factories. Action on the enemy's lines of communication. Action against the Milice*: every militiaman is a possible murderer.

There is only one fight, and if you don't join it, your enemy will nevertheless supply you with daily proof that that fight is yours. Take your place in it, because if the fate of everyone you like and respect concerns you, then once again, rest assured, this fight *does* concern you. Just tell yourself that together we will bring to it the great strength of the oppressed, namely, solidarity in suffering. That is the force that will ultimately kill the lie, and our common hope is that when that day comes, it will retain enough momentum to inspire a new truth and a new France.

COMBAT

Combat, Underground No. 56, April 1944
Outlaws[7]

What is the Milice? To go by the Paris press, it's our greatest hope, our last chance, and this last chance had better not be missed. This helps us to understand. Because the Milice is defending something, and that something has nothing to do with the order it claims to be upholding. It is defending the lives and the interests, the shame and the calculations, of a small proportion of Frenchmen who have turned against France and who face annihilation when victory comes. It enlists crime on behalf of cowardice.

But it also enlists crime on behalf of treason. For the past four years, the enemy has not let a single day go by without trying to turn some Frenchmen against

[7] In the view of Jacqueline Bernard, as reported by Yves-Marc Ajchenbaum in *A la vie, à la mort*, p. 80, it is unlikely that this article was written by Camus. Yet the article leads off with a question, a device used by Camus in several of his editorials (see, for example, "What Is an Insurrection?" August 23, 1944, or "What Are the Germans Up To?" September 17). The repetition of the phrase "it took four years" is similar to the repetition in the article "From Resistance to Revolution," August 21. And the mix of irony and seriousness is frequent in Camus' writing. Finally, if the Milice was obviously a frequent target of articles in underground newspapers, the attacks on these "outlaws" are quite similar to those contained in the July article, "You Will Be Judged by Your Actions," which was very likely written by Camus.

others. Everything was grist to its mill. Yet it is fair to say that it took the enemy
no fewer than four years to persuade a small number of disgraced Frenchmen to
bear arms against France herself and the best of her men. For during those shameful four years of madness, there were indeed among us heads of state, ministers of
government, and a police force that, consciously or not, out of cowardice or out
of weakness, in treason or inertia, played the German game. There were also
Frenchmen willing to fight on distant battlefields and to defend the cause of the
very people who were subjecting their own country to torture. But it took four
whole years to recruit a troop of murderous mercenaries resolved to lend France's
enemy a hand against France herself. It took four years of German propaganda to
dig up a "hero of two wars" prepared to sully his decorations in the most cowardly
and degrading police work.

But such men were found, and their very existence poses a problem of justice.
For as is always the case, Sganarella wants to outdo Don Juan, the lackey seeks
to go the master one better. On this point, convinced [*sic*] that the servants are
well trained. These self-appointed guardians of order courageously kidnap an
elderly couple, strip them naked in a field, and slaughter them with the most
refined methods of torture. Recently in Nice these exemplary French heroes had
the Germans hand over six Frenchmen arrested by the Gestapo (mostly for frivolous reasons) so that they could torture them, disfigure them, and put them to
death. They portray themselves as defenders of the law, yet they bring patriots to
trial before a court of bandits and send them to the firing squad a few seconds
after being found guilty in a parody of judgment. The "hero of two wars" claims
to be carrying on an admirable French tradition. Apparently it consists in taking
hostages, killing intellectuals and workers, and relying on a servile press to heap
lies and insults on the victims of torture and humiliation. In truth, however, we
know this tradition well. It was born on the other side of the Rhine in the heart
of another war hero. For M. Darnand,[8] what's involved is not tradition but
treason.

But all this explains why the problem of justice is easily resolved. For while it
is desirable in the case of other traitors that the forms of justice be respected, the
Milice has placed itself outside the law. It must be made quite clear that each
militiaman, in signing his enlistment papers, is ratifying his own death sentence.
By turning against France, these people exclude themselves from France. Rotten
branches cannot be left attached to the tree. They have to be lopped off, reduced
to sawdust, and scattered on the ground. That is the fate awaiting each of Darnand's murderers. Courts-martial would be pointless, moreover. The Milice is its
own tribunal. It has judged itself and sentenced itself to death. Those sentences
will be carried out.

[8] Darnand, Joseph (1897–1945) fought in World War I as a heroic commando and then became an active
militant in the extreme right-wing Action Française between the wars. A champion of collaboration with
Germany, he served as secretary of state for the interior in the government of Vichy and founded the Service d'ordre légionnaire and the Milice, which he directed for the purpose of combating the Resistance.
After fleeing to Sigmaringen with Pétain and later to Italy, where he was arrested, he was sentenced to
death and shot on October 10, 1945.

Combat, Underground No. 57, May 1944

For Three Hours They Shot Frenchmen[9]

The truth must be told: we are vaccinated against horror. All those faces disfigured by bullets and heels, all those crushed bodies, those murdered innocents, at first filled us with the revulsion and disgust we needed in order to know what we were fighting for. Now the daily struggle has colored everything, and although we never forget the reasons for it, we may at times lose sight of them. But the enemy is there, and as if to make sure that no one avert his eyes, he is increasing his efforts, outdoing himself, each time descending a little deeper into infamy and a little further into crisis. Today, in any event, he went beyond what anyone could have imagined, and the tragedy of Ascq reminds all Frenchmen that they are engaged in a general and unremitting struggle against a disgraced enemy.

What are the facts?

On April 1, 1944, during the night, two explosions severed a railway line and led to the derailment of two cars of a German troop train. The line was blocked. No one on the train was killed.

At around 11 that night, M. Carré, the station chief at Ascq, having been awakened at his home by night shift personnel, was on the telephone dealing with the situation when a German transportation officer entered his office screaming, followed by a number of soldiers who used their rifle butts to beat M. Carré along with M. Peloquin, a senior clerk, and M. Derache, a telegrapher, who also happened to be on the premises at the time. The soldiers then withdrew to the office doorway and from there fired on the three prostrate employees with submachine guns. Carré and Peloquin were gravely wounded in the stomach and thighs. Then the officer led a large contingent of troops into the town, broke down the doors of the houses, searched them, and rounded up some sixty men, who were marched to a pasture opposite the station. There they were shot. Twenty-six other men were also shot in their homes or thereabouts. Among the eighty-six people shot, some lay wounded.

The telegrapher, Derache, managed to alert district headquarters in Lille, which notified the Prefecture of the Nord. The prefecture called the Oberfeldkommandantur.

The executions did not stop until officers of the general staff arrived on the scene. The killing went on for more than three hours.

Whether it is possible to conjure up vividly enough an image of a scene described in such blunt language I do not know. But is it possible to read this report without being overcome by feelings of revulsion and disgust at the mere sight of the numbers: eighty-six men, three hours?

---

[9] Like the article of March 1944, this one is unanimously attributed to Camus (see Y.-M. Ajchenbaum, op. cit., p. 80). Indeed, the vigor of the style, the visionary realism, and, once again, the central idea of solidarity leave little room for doubt.

Eighty-six men[10] just like you, the readers of this newspaper, passed before the German guns. Eighty-six men: enough to fill three or four rooms the size of the room you're sitting in. Eighty-six faces, drawn or defiant, eighty-six faces overwhelmed by horror or by hatred.

The slaughter continued for three hours, a little more than two minutes for each victim. Three hours, the amount of time that some of you will have spent that day at dinner or talking quietly with friends, while elsewhere people watched a film and laughed at made-up adventures. For three hours, minute after minute, without letup, without a pause, in a single French village, shots were fired one after another and bodies fell writhing to the ground.

This is the image that must be kept in mind so that nothing is forgotten, the image that must be shown to any Frenchman who remains on the sidelines. For among those eighty-six innocents were many who thought that, having done nothing to oppose the German forces, nothing would be done to them. But France is one, there is but a single wrath, but a single martyr. And when M. de Brinon[11] writes to the German authorities not to complain about the massacre of so many Frenchmen but to whine that his work with the vice squad is being hampered, he is responsible for that martyrdom and guilty before that wrath. For the question is not whether these crimes will be forgiven; it is whether anyone will pay for them. And if we were inclined to doubt it, the image of this village soaked in blood and from this day forth populated solely by widows and orphans should suffice to assure us that someone will pay for this crime, because the decision is now in the hands of all the French, and in the face of this new massacre we are discovering the solidarity of martyrdom and the power that grows out of vengeance.

Combat, Clandestine No. 58, July 1944
The Murderers' Great Fear

On the walls and urinals of Paris, Darnand displays his prose. He addresses his own men, demands absolute obedience, and promises exemplary punishment for those who fail to comply. So there are disobedient militiamen! Will anyone be surprised by the news?

When the Germans burned villages and captured patriots, the militiamen carefully delayed their arrival until it was time to take charge of the prisoners. They stared at the silent captives and grew angry. Nothing is more irritating than the sight of a man to those who have deliberately ceased to be men. And then their work began. Their job was to prove that human dignity is a lie and that the idea of a self-conscious individual, master of his own fate, is but a democratic myth.

---

[10] The text continues on page two under the headline "Slaughter at Ascq."
[11] Fernand de Brinon (1885–1947). An active proponent of collaboration, he represented the Vichy government before the German authorities in Paris and later served as secretary of state. After the Liberation he was sentenced to death by the High Court of Justice and executed.

They heaped insults on their victims to whet their own appetites, to debase their prisoners with words and to debase themselves a bit further. Then they plucked out a few fingernails, stomped a few chests. The goal was to extract a cry of suffering from the gasping victim, a confession, a renunciation. If they succeeded, they breathed a little easier. They thought, We're all alike, those people won't be thumbing their noses at us anymore. They were happy to have transformed their silent judges into accomplices of their own degradation. Malraux says somewhere that it is impossible to aim a flamethrower at a man who is looking you in the eye.[12] So imagine, then, what a militiaman must be like to take pleasure in torturing a man whose eyes are open. These torturers have a very specific mission: it is to wipe out anything that isn't vile, anything that isn't cowardly, and to demonstrate by their own example and by making an example of others that man is made to live in chains and terror. If they were to succeed, there would be no more witnesses, and their own personal ignominy would be identified with the flaws of human nature.

Today, though, some would assign these people a new role. The Germans, occupied elsewhere, are no longer there to defend them. A resistance army has arisen out of the earth. The torturers are being asked to fight like men, rifle against rifle. And that is profoundly unjust. Where would anyone expect them to find the courage? They would need precisely those qualities that they were previously asked to destroy in themselves and others: confidence in man, confidence in the individual. Darnand[13] knows this. That is why he is making threats. But it is too late. There is no threat terrible enough to make a man out of a member of the Milice.

Combat, Clandestine No. 58, July 1944
You Will Be Judged by Your Actions[14]

Now that the final battle is getting under way, Pétain[15] and Laval[16] have raised their discordant voices and sought to gain favor for their common policy by seeming to speak in two different keys. Both addressed the country, and in

---

[12] In *L'Espoir* (*Man's Hope*), during the fighting in the Alcazar of Toledo, one of the republican fighters, the Negus, finds himself face-to-face with a fascist holding a flamethrower. Because the man hesitates "a quarter of a second" before aiming the flamethrower at him, the Negus has the time to fire a shot at him. Later he remarks: "It must be difficult to burn alive a man who's looking you in the eye." (*Oeuvres complètes*, vol. 2, Pléiade, Gallimard, 1996, p. 113.)

[13] See n. 8 above.

[14] The insistence on commitment through words and on justice; the use of expressions such as "the flesh of France," which anticipates a chapter title in *Actuelles*, and "the war has become total," which echoes the idea of the March 1944 article; and the very tone of this article, perfectly in line with those that went before, all argue in favor of attributing it to Camus.

[15] Pétain, Philippe (1856–1951). Marshal of France in 1918 and regarded as the victor of Verdun, he served as Minister of War for a few months in 1934. Close to Maurras and the Action Française, he became ambassador to Franco's Spain in 1939. He served as Vice-President of the Council of Ministers under Paul Reynaud in March 1940 and became President when Reynaud resigned on June 16, 1940, whereupon he asked for an armistice with Germany and became head of the French state—l'Etat français, which replaced the Republic after the vote of the National Assembly on July 10, 1940. He installed his

keeping with their traditional division of labor, Laval spoke of Germany, while Pétain pretended to speak of France. In truth, however, both spoke of treason, albeit in tones of sadness, as though that treason had suddenly become clairvoyant. This has been going on for years. Ever since Pétain laid the groundwork in Vichy for a regime that rationed everything it gave us except humiliation and shame, he has played what he takes to be a shrewd game, so that he remains our supreme symbol of compromise and confusion. When compromise reigns supreme, however, it suffices to speak plainly. We have reached a stage where there is no shrewd strategy other than courage and plain speaking. As usual, moreover, it is the French Resistance that speaks a language in which France can recognize herself. And since the hour for appeals is on us, the Resistance, too, is issuing an appeal to the people of this country. It is saying that there is nothing more to think over, weigh, or evaluate. Pétain's secret thoughts, if he has any, and Laval's tricks are of no importance: neutrality is no longer possible. The time is fast approaching when the people of this country will be judged not by their intentions but by their actions, and by the actions to which their words have committed them. That alone is just.

And the French Resistance is telling us clearly that for the past five years the words and actions of Pétain and Laval have done nothing but divide and humiliate France and kill Frenchmen. Pétain and Laval have been disgraced by the war. They will be judged for it.

The Resistance is telling you that we are now at a stage where every word counts, where every word is a commitment, especially when those words ratify the execution of our brothers, insult our courage, and deliver the flesh of France herself to the most implacable of enemies. When they call patriots terrorists and murderers, when they bestow the name "honor" on what is simply resignation, "order" on what is simply torture, and "loyalism" on what is simply murder, compromise is impossible.

---

government in Vichy. Adopting the new motto "Work, Family, Fatherland," he adopted a policy of active collaboration with Germany, although he had to share power with Laval and was further weakened when the Germans occupied the former Free Zone in November of 1942. After being evacuated to Sigmaringen at the end of the war, he returned to France in April 1945, where he was put on trial (July 23 to August 15, 1945). Sentenced to death, his penalty was immediately commuted to life imprisonment. He died on the Ile d'Yeu in June 1951.

[16] Laval, Pierre (1883–1945). Elected deputy first as a socialist and later an "independent socialist," Laval served several terms as a minister of the Third Republic and twice as President of the Council of Ministers. Forced to resign in 1936, he returned to power after the defeat of 1940. As minister of state under Pétain, he persuaded the Parliament to approve a revision of the constitution putting an end to the Republic and played a leading role in establishing the government of Vichy, in which he served as Vice-President. A passionate advocate of collaboration, he arranged the meeting between Pétain and Hitler at Montoire in October 1940. Arrested on orders from Pétain, who replaced him with Darlan from January 1941 until April 1942, he was freed by the Germans, who made him the strong man of the Vichy regime, in which he served simultaneously as Minister of the Interior, Information, and Foreign Affairs. He is known to have declared his preference for a German victory in the war. Toward the end of the war he left for Sigmaringen with Pétain, then went to Austria. Eventually he was arrested and sentenced to death and after a suicide attempt died before a firing squad on October 15, 1945.

The Resistance is telling you that you have no government on French soil and you don't need one. We are quite grown up enough to clench our teeth and bear what is surrounding and oppressing us; quite grown up enough to bear the thought of our imprisoned and tortured comrades, of whom we never speak, whom we leave enveloped in the silence of fraternity; quite grown up enough to endure hunger and murder. We don't need Vichy to settle our score with shame. We don't need hypocritical blessings. We need men and courage. We don't need to serve the cult of suffering; we need only to overcome it. Not alone, but with an entire people against a predatory nation and a few dishonorable traitors. We don't need a holiday from morality, we need soul, and we can't get it from those apostles who preached abdication of all our responsibilities.

Frenchmen, the French Resistance is issuing the only appeal you need to hear. The war has become total. But a single struggle remains. The flower of the nation is preparing to sacrifice itself, and now is not the time to be tempted by forgiveness. Anyone who isn't with us is against us. From this moment on there are only two parties in France: the France that has always been and those who shall soon be annihilated for having attempted to annihilate it.

Combat, Clandestine No. 58, July 1944
The Profession of Journalist[17]

"For the first time in history, the profession of journalist has become an honorable profession," M. Marcel Déat declared.[18]

M. Marcel Déat is right.

Clandestine journalism is honorable because it is a proof of independence, because it involves a risk. It is good, it is healthy, that everything to do with current political events has become dangerous. If there is anything we don't want to see again, it is the shield of impunity behind which so much cowardly behavior and so many underhanded machinations once took refuge.

Having become honorable activities, politics and journalism will be obliged one day to judge those who dishonored them. . . . For example, M. Marcel Déat.

---

[17] The liveliness, irony, and conception of journalism underlying this little sidebar leave little doubt as to its author's identity.

[18] Déat, Marcel (1894–1955). Socialist deputy, minister of the Third Republic, Déat became editor of the newspaper *L'Œuvre* in 1940 and founded the Rassemblement National Populaire, which favored collaboration. Appointed Secretary of State for Labor and Social Affairs in 1944, he proved to be a very active propagandist. After he sought refuge in Italy, he was sentenced to death in absentia.

August 21, 1944–November 15, 1945

Throughout this period, and until January 11 in particular, Camus' participation in the work of *Combat* was active and remarkably fruitful. After February 9 his contributions became somewhat less regular, although he remained quite active, as is clear from numerous editorials (which unfortunately were unsigned and for which no typescript remains in the archives), as well as the important series on the "Crisis in Algeria." After writing a final editorial in November, Camus left the staff of the newspaper.

August 21, 1944
Combat Continues . . .[1]

Today, August 21, as this newspaper hits the streets, the liberation of Paris is nearing an end. After fifty months of occupation, of struggle and sacrifice, Paris is rediscovering the feeling of freedom, even as bursts of gunfire erupt at street corners around the city.

It would be dangerous, however, to return to the illusion that the freedom that is the due of every individual comes without effort or corresponding pain. Freedom has to be earned and has to be won. It is by fighting the invader and the traitors that the Forces Françaises de l'Intérieur [FFI, or French Forces of the Interior] are restoring the Republic, which is the indispensable condition of our freedom. It is through struggle that freedom and the Republic will triumph.

The liberation of Paris is but one step in the liberation of France—and here the word LIBERATION has to be understood in its broadest possible sense. The fight against Nazi Germany continues. It will be waged unremittingly. But if this is the most difficult of the battles for which all France has mobilized, it is not the only one we must wage.

It won't be enough to regain the outward appearance of freedom for which France was obliged to settle in 1939. And we will have accomplished only an infinitesimal part of our task if the French Republic of tomorrow were to find itself, like the Third Republic, under the strict control of Money (*l'Argent*).[2]

Of course the struggle against the power of money was long one of the favorite themes of Pétain and his team. Yet it is also true that Money has never weighed more heavily on our people than in the period that began in July 1940, when it helped the traitors gain power and, in order to protect and expand its privileges, deliberately tied its interests to Hitler's.

---

[1] Editorial. Typewritten text. Until September 10 the editorials are generally titled and marked with the symbol X in lieu of a signature.

[2] This would remain a constant theme in the political attitude of both *Combat* and Camus.

It is no accident that men like Laval, Bouthillier,[3] Baudouin,[4] Pucheu,[5] and Leroy-Ladurie[6] succeeded one another in Vichy's ministerial councils.

It is no accident that the so-called "organizing committees" were headed by "organizers" whose relations with the proletariat in most cases were never anything but the relations of masters to servants.

Thanks to the fight we are waging with the Allies against Hitler's armies, all of French territory will soon be liberated. But it is up to us to secure our freedom.

The combat continues.

X

August 21, 1944
From Resistance to Revolution[7]

It has taken five years of obstinate, silent struggle for a newspaper born of the spirit of resistance and published without interruption despite all the dangers of clandestinity to be able to appear at last in the light of day, in a Paris liberated from its shame. It is impossible to write these words without emotion. The stunned joy that we are just beginning to read on Parisian faces is a joy we share, a joy we feel, perhaps, even more deeply than most. But the task of the men of the resistance is not yet complete. The end of the ordeal can now be glimpsed ahead. It is easy for us to make time for celebration. Joy now takes the place in our hearts that for five years was occupied by hope. There, too, we shall keep the faith. But the time that is now upon us calls for joint effort. The magnitude of the task that now awaits us obliges us to stifle our cries of joy and ponder the fate of the country for which we have fought so hard. Today, with the appearance of our first public issue, the men of *Combat* want to state as loudly and as clearly as possible what five years of perseverance and honesty have taught them about France's greatness as well as her weaknesses.

Those years were not wasted. The Frenchmen who entered this period with a reflex reaction of humiliated honor end it with superior knowledge, as a result of which they now rank above all else the intelligence, courage, and truth of the human heart. They know, moreover, that the insistence on these values, as general as they may seem, establishes certain daily obligations of a moral and political kind. To put it in a nutshell, just as they shared but a single faith in 1940, today,

---

[3] Bouthillier, Yves. Minister of Finance (1940–1942).

[4] Baudouin, Paul. Minister of Foreign Affairs.

[5] Pucheu, Pierre. A former director of the Steel Cartel, Pucheu served first as Minister of Industrial Production and then as Minister of the Interior (1941–1942). Sentenced to death in Algiers, he was executed in March 1944. Camus wrote an article about him entitled "Not Everything Can Be Arranged," which appeared in a clandestine issue of *Les Lettres françaises* in May 1944 (*Essais*, op. cit., pp. 1468–1470).

[6] Leroy-Ladurie, Jacques. Minister of Agriculture and Food Supply (1942).

[7] Article. Typewritten text. Reprinted the next day with an introductory paragraph underscoring the fact that it "sets forth the political line" of the newspaper and explaining the slogan.

in 1944, they share but a single politics, in the noble sense of the word. Having begun with resistance, they want to end with Revolution.

What We Know

We do not believe in ready-made principles or theoretical plans. In the days to come we will define, through our actions as well as in a series of articles, the content of the word "revolution." For the time being, however, this word gives meaning to our preference for energy and honor, to our decision to be done with the spirit of mediocrity and the moneyed interests and with a social state whose ruling class failed in all its duties and demonstrated a lack of both intelligence and heart. We want without delay to institute a true people's and workers' democracy. In this alliance, democracy will contribute the principles of freedom and the people will contribute the faith and courage without which freedom is nothing. We believe that any politics that cuts itself off from the working class is futile. The France of tomorrow will be what its working class becomes.

What We Want[8]

That is why we want immediate implementation of a Constitution that will restore full guarantees of freedom and justice; serious structural reforms, without which any politics of freedom would be a sham; merciless destruction of the trusts and moneyed interests; and a foreign policy based on honor and loyalty to all our allies, without exception. In the present state of affairs, such a program goes by the name "Revolution." This can probably be achieved in a calm and orderly fashion, but it is the price that must be paid if France is to regain the pure countenance that we loved and defended above all.

Many things in this shattered world are no longer in our power. But our honor, our justice, and the well-being of the humblest among us are ours to decide. And it is by upholding or creating such values, by unflinchingly destroying those institutions and clans that are bent on denying them, and by honoring the revolutionary spirit growing out of the resistance that we will define for the world and for ourselves the image and example of a nation saved from its worst mistakes and emerging from five years of humiliation and sacrifice with a youthful visage of grandeur regained.[9]

---

[8] This subhead repeats that of an article published in February 1944 in a clandestine issue of *Combat*, "Where Is the Resistance Headed?" It set forth the broad outlines of the "Fourth Republic," which was supposed to be created by new men and lead to the birth of a broad-based republican and revolutionary party as the heir to the Resistance. The style of this article did not justify attributing it to Camus, but it is not impossible that he had a hand in its writing, particularly since the same issue contained a short item entitled "The Short-Story Writer."

[9] That same day, a sidebar listed "the references of the newspaper *Combat*." The text offered a brief history of the paper, pointing out that fifty-eight clandestine issues had been published during the war and that the paper had begun as the official organ of the "Combat" movement led by Henri Frenay before becoming one of the newspapers of the Mouvements Unis de Résistance (United Resistance Movements)

August 22, 1944
Time for Justice[10]

The Vichy government has gone up in smoke.

With the first allied push against Paris and the first shock of insurrection, the men of Vichy, who governed against the nation for so long that in the end they forgot about it, thought they could go on deceiving the people. When the country turned on them, they failed to recognize France in faces distorted by excitement and rage. They left.

Those who had been the cruelest also proved to be the most cowardly. Darnand and Déat fled. But those who had deceived and lied constantly departed amid further deceit and lies. Laval and Pétain tried to make people believe that they had been forcibly spirited away. The President of Compromise and the Marshal of Confusion remained true to themselves, at least, even if they had not been true to France.

But confusion and compromise are no longer possible. This needs to be stated loud and clear.

There is no difference between Laval and Pétain, because in certain circumstances there is no difference between treason and resignation.

These men, who rationed everything except shame, who dispensed blessings with one hand while they killed with the other, who combined hypocrisy with terror, and who for four years treated us to an appalling mixture of sermons and executions, homilies and torture—these men could expect neither forgiveness nor indulgence from France.

We imagined what we needed to imagine when faced with countless stories of our brothers being arrested, deported, massacred, and tortured. Those dead children, kicked and beaten into their own coffins, remained in our hearts for four long years. We are not about to lose our memory now.

We are not men of hate. But we must be men of justice. And justice dictates that those who killed and those who permitted murder are equally responsible before their victims, even if those who covered up the murders speak today of "double-edged politics" and "realism." This is the kind of language we despise the most.

There are not two politics. There is only one, and it is the one that makes a commitment. It is the politics of honor.

In 1940 began an era in which all words and all actions made a commitment. And those who then seized control of what they called the destinies of France

---

and later of the Mouvement de la Libération Nationale (National Liberation Movement). The article then went on to say that "the journalists who took the initiative to turn *Combat* into a daily paper of news and combat were members of the editorial staff of the clandestine paper. This entitles them to say today that they know their responsibilities and will know how to find their words." The text ends with an homage to Vélin (André Bollier) and to the staff's deported comrades.

[10] The title, certain formulas, and the themes of this article suggest that it might have been written by Camus, but it is impossible to be sure.

simultaneously assumed responsibility for the heads that began to fall and for the faces disfigured by bullets. No "realism" can stand in the face of that simple truth.

To our comrades we took an oath that we never uttered out loud but nevertheless swore in the depths of our hearts—and we will keep it to the end.

August 23, 1944
They Shall Not Pass[11]

What is an insurrection? It is the people in arms. What is the people? It is that in a nation which refuses ever to bend its knee.

A nation is worth what its people are worth, and if ever we were tempted to doubt our country, the image of its sons on the march, brandishing rifles, should fill us with overwhelming certitude that this nation is equal to the loftiest of destinies and is about to win its resurrection along with its freedom.

On the fourth day of the insurrection, in the wake of the enemy's first retreat and a phony truce cut short by the murders of Frenchmen, the people of Paris will resume the fight and erect new barricades.

The enemy ensconced in the city must not be allowed to leave. The retreating enemy must not be allowed to reenter. They shall not pass.

To those few Frenchmen bereft of memory and imagination, forgetful of honor, heedless of shame, and cushioned by their own personal comforts who ask, "What good can any of this do?" we feel compelled to respond here and now.

A people that wants to live does not wait for its freedom to be delivered to it. It takes its own. And in so doing it helps itself even as it helps those who seek to help it. Every German who is prevented from leaving Paris means one bullet less for the Allied soldiers and our French comrades in the East. Our future, our revolution, depend entirely on the present moment, echoing with cries of anger and with the wrath of liberty.

The choice to kill was not ours.[12] We were placed in a position where we had either to kill or to bend our knees. And despite those who tried to put doubts in our minds, we know now, after four years of terrible struggle, that it is not in our blood to kneel.

Despite those who still wish to put doubts in our minds, we also know that we are a mature nation. And a mature nation takes charge regardless of its destiny, be it one of shame or pride.

[11] Editorial. Typescript. This title is obviously a translation of the Spanish Republican slogan "*No pasarán*," and Camus is known to have felt close to the Spanish Republican cause. He would later write a number of editorials and articles about Spain. See the thematic index.

[12] This sentence echoes one of the central themes of *Lettres à un ami allemand* (Letters to a German Friend).

We found the strength to bear the weight of our defeat, and we will not shrink from the burdens of victory.

On August 21, 1944, a battle began in the streets of Paris, a battle that will end in liberty or death for all of us and for France.[13]

X

August 24, 1944
The Blood of Freedom[14]

Paris is firing all its ammunition into the August night. Against a vast backdrop of water and stone, on both sides of a river awash with history, freedom's barricades are once again being erected. Once again justice must be redeemed with men's blood.

We are all too familiar with this war, and our flesh and our hearts are all too engaged to accept this dreadful condition without bitterness. But we are only too aware as well of what is at stake and where the truth lies to refuse the harsh fate that we alone must bear.

Time will tell that the men of France did not want to kill and that they went with clean hands into a war that was not of their own choosing.[15] Did it therefore take powerful reasons for them suddenly to grab their rifles and start firing without letup into the night at soldiers who for two years thought that war was easy?

Yes, and they have powerful reasons. Those reasons are measured by the immensity of their hope and the depth of their rebellion. They are reasons that point toward the future of a country that for so long some have sought to confine to morose rumination on its past. Paris is fighting today so that France can have a voice tomorrow. Tonight the people are in arms because they hope to see justice done tomorrow. There are a few who say that it isn't worth the trouble and that with patience Paris would be[16] delivered at little cost. This is because they have a vague sense of how many things are threatened by this insurrection— things that would remain as they are if events were to unfold differently.

Indeed, one thing must be made perfectly clear: no one can possibly believe that freedom won in the dark of night and with such bloodshed[17] will have the tame and tranquil face of which some are pleased to dream. These terrifying birth pangs signify a revolution.

---

[13] The same slogan was among those shouted by the revolutionaries of 1789.

[14] Editorial. Reprinted in *Actuelles*, untitled, in the chapter on "The Liberation of Paris," with some minor changes.

[15] Cf. editorial of August 23, p. 15, and *Les Lettres à un ami allemand*.

[16] In *Actuelles* the conditional *serait* was changed to the future *sera*.

[17] In *Actuelles* the words *dans ce sang* (with such bloodshed) were changed to *dans ces convulsions* (in such upheaval).

No one can hope that men who have fought for four years in silence and for days now in a din of thunder and rifle fire will agree to the return of the forces of resignation and injustice in any form whatsoever. No one can expect that those men—the best and the purest[18] that France has to offer—will again be willing to do what the best and the purest did for twenty-five years, which was to love their country in silence while silently despising its leaders. The Paris that is fighting tonight wants to assume command tomorrow. Not for the sake of power but for the sake of justice, not for political reasons but for moral ones, not to dominate their country but to ensure its grandeur.

Our conviction is not that this will happen but that it is happening today in the suffering and obstinacy of combat. And that is why the words that must be uttered above the moans of men in pain and despite the blood and the anger, despite the irreplaceable dead, despite the unjust wounds and blind bullets, are words not of regret but of hope—the terrific hope of men alone with their destiny.

Paris—this enormous, dark, sweltering city with its stormy skies and stormy streets—seems more illuminated now than the City of Light that was once the envy of the entire world. It is aglow with all the fires of hope and pain, with the flame of lucid courage, and with all the splendor not just of liberation but of the liberty to come.

X

August 25, 1944
The Night of Truth[19]

As freedom's bullets continue to whistle through city streets, the cannon of liberation are passing through the gates of Paris amid shouts and flowers. On this sultriest and most beautiful of August nights, the permanent stars in the skies above the city mingle with tracer rounds, smoke from burning buildings, and variegated rockets proclaiming the people's joy. This night unlike any other ends four years of a monstrous history and an unspeakable struggle that saw France at grips with its shame and its fury.

Those who never lost hope for themselves or their country are finding their reward tonight. This night is a world unto itself: it is the night of truth. The truth in arms, the truth in battle, the truth in power after languishing for so many years empty-handed and chest bared. Truth is everywhere on this night, which finds the people and the cannon roaring in unison. The truth speaks, in fact, with the voice of the people and the guns; it wears the triumphant and tired face of the fighters in the streets, beneath their sweat and their scars. Yes, this is indeed the night of truth, and of the only truth that counts, the truth that is prepared to fight and win.

---

[18] In *Actuelles* the phrase "and the purest" was deleted.
[19] Editorial. Reprinted in *Actuelles*, untitled, in the chapter on "The Liberation of Paris."

Four years ago, a few men rose up amid the ruins and despair and quietly proclaimed that nothing was yet lost. They said that the war must go on and that the forces of good could always triumph over the forces of evil provided the price was paid. They paid that price. And the cost was indeed heavy: it had the weight of blood and the terrible oppressiveness of prison. Many of those men died, while others spent years enclosed within windowless walls. That was the price that had to be paid. Yet those same men, if only they could, would forgive the terrific and marvelous joy that floods our hearts tonight like an inrushing tide.

For this joy is in no way unfaithful to their memory. On the contrary, it justifies what they did and proclaims that they were right. United in suffering for four years, tonight we remain united in intoxication; we have earned our solidarity. And on this overwhelming night we are stunned to discover that throughout those four years we were never alone. We experienced four years of fraternity.

Harsh battles still await us. But peace will return to this gutted earth and to hearts tormented by hope and memories. One cannot live by murder and violence alone. Happiness and righteous affection will have their day. But the coming peace will not erase our memories. And for some of us, the faces of our brothers disfigured by bullets and the great virile fraternity[20] of these years will never leave us. May our dead comrades rest in the peace that awaits us in the breathless night, the peace they have already won: our combat will be theirs.

Nothing is given to mankind, and what little men can conquer must be paid for with unjust deaths. But man's grandeur lies elsewhere, in his decision to rise above his condition. And if his condition is unjust, he has only one way to overcome it, which is to be just himself. Our truth tonight, the truth that hovers in the August sky, is in fact man's consolation. What gives our hearts peace, as it gave peace to our dead comrades, is that we can say before the impending victory, without scolding and without pressing any claim of our own, "We did what had to be done."

X

August 29, 1944
Intelligence and Character[21]

M. Bergery[22] has offered his services to General de Gaulle. He was not obliged first to withdraw his previous offer to Pétain, Pétain having withdrawn himself from the scene. M. Bergery was thus left with a surplus of services of no immediate use to anyone and only the best of intentions.

---

[20] The expression is borrowed from André Malraux (1901–1976), from the preface to *Le Temps du mépris*, a novel that Camus adapted for the Théâtre du Travail in Algiers in 1936. Cf. the editorial of August 30, which bears this title. Malraux was serving at the time as commander of the "Alsace-Lorraine" brigade, then fully engaged in combat in eastern France.

[21] Editorial. Typescript.

[22] Bergery, Gaston (1892–1974). A lawyer who served as a Radical deputy and chief of staff in Herriot's government, Bergery quit the Radical Party in 1934 and founded the newspaper *La Flèche*. He was one

Having pondered the situation, he came to the conclusion that it was immoral to let a mind like his go to waste, so he made a gift of his intelligence to General de Gaulle.

For M. Bergery is an intelligent man. Indeed, he wrote the one intelligent message that Pétain read on the radio. Before the war he published one of the few intelligent newspapers of the Third Republic. Its pages included a great deal of talk about purity and revolution, and trusts came in for some harsh words. All this intelligence led M. Bergery to become one of the thinkers of the Vichy regime. Now his oft-proclaimed purity has led him to offer his services to two different masters in quick succession without noticing what the gesture might lack in the way of tact. In short, M. Bergery is a practitioner of political realism.

This is uniquely a consequence of his intelligence. The faculty of intelligence is quick to grasp the relativity of all things. In examining a historical event, it usually comes to the conclusion that this too shall pass, hence that there is no reason to put oneself out. Having made the transition from the revolution to Pétain, why not go a step further and offer to work for the very people whom Vichy sought to dishonor.

If we were to reveal the pure essence of our thinking, namely, that political realism is a degrading thing, M. Bergery would be surprised, because intelligence alone is not enough to grasp this obvious truth. Character is also necessary, and M. Bergery has never shown any.

In one respect, however, he is not wrong. Character is indeed rare in this world, and it takes only a little intelligence to trim your course as circumstances might require, for who is there to point out your mistakes? Thus in politics realism is always right, even if it is morally wrong.

There are times, however, when morality comes back into politics, because men suddenly start paying for their politics with their blood, as some in France paid with their tortured bodies or their lives while others paid with secret sacrifices and unheralded nobility. And overnight realism becomes wrong, for when men of character set out to make history, history insists on character.

These are the moments when everything becomes clear, when every action constitutes a commitment, when every choice has its price, when nothing is neutral anymore. It is the time of morality, that is, a time when language becomes clear and it is possible to throw it back in the realist's face.

And this is what the language of morality has to say: M. Bergery failed to understand that in speaking for Pétain, he joined with him in his resignation,

---

of the founders of the "Common Front against Fascism" or "Frontist Party," which called for a realignment of left and right around a platform of pacifism and structural political and economic reform. On February 13, 1939, Camus published a rather favorable review of a Bergery lecture about this party in *Alger-Républicain*. See *Fragments d'un combat*, Cahiers Albert Camus 3 (Paris: Gallimard, 1978), vol. 2, pp. 623–625. In July 1940, however, Bergery was among those who believed that France ought to find its place in the new Europe, and he voted to grant "full powers" to Pétain. He was appointed Vichy's ambassador to Moscow and later to Ankara. The day before this article appeared, *Combat* had reported that Bergery had written from Ankara asking General de Gaulle for instructions. Tried by the High Court in 1949, he was acquitted of all charges.

and that in drafting a political message for Vichy, he also endorsed the execution of patriots and the acts of treason the regime committed.

M. Bergery, having discredited himself for four years, has now dishonored himself as well. And as long as men of character remain among the members of the Resistance, their role will be to point out to M. Bergery whenever and wherever possible that his intelligence was not enough to protect him from the unpardonable blindness that has cut him off from the nation forever.

August 30, 1944
The Age of Contempt[23]

Thirty-four Frenchmen tortured and then murdered at Vincennes: without help from our imagination these words say nothing.[24] And what does the imagination reveal? Two men, face-to-face, one of whom is preparing to tear out the fingernails of the other, who looks him in the eye.

This is not the first time we have had to confront such unbearable images. The year 1933 marked the beginning of an era that one of the greatest of our contemporaries has rightly dubbed the Age of Contempt.[25] And for ten years, whenever we heard the news that naked, unarmed human beings had been methodically mutilated by men with faces just like our own, our minds reeled, and we asked how such things were possible.

Yet such things were possible. For ten years they were possible, and today, as if to warn us that victory on the battlefield does not signify total triumph, we learn of comrades who had their guts ripped out, their limbs torn off, and their faces kicked in. And the men who did these things were men polite enough to give up their seats on the subway, just as Himmler,[26] who made a science and an art of torture, used the back door when he returned home at night so as not to wake his pet canary.

---

[23] Editorial. Reprinted in *Actuelles*, untitled, in the chapter on "The Liberation of Paris." Camus had previously used the title, which he borrowed from Malraux, for an article published in *Le Soir-Républicain* on December 14, 1939; see *Fragments d'un combat*, II, pp. 756–757.

[24] The news had been broken in *Combat* the day before under the title "Martyrs' Testimony": "In the trenches around Vincennes, the bodies of thirty-four Frenchmen tortured by the S.S. were found."

[25] Cf. editorial of August 25, above, p. 17. The great contemporary is André Malraux. *Combat* would later express anxiety when Malraux went missing and was presumed dead, and the staff offered him a warm welcome when he visited on September 23. On that day the paper published an often-reproduced photo showing Camus and Malraux together. Starting on October 4, the paper published excerpts from *La Lutte avec l'ange* under the title "May Victory Belong to Those Who Fought the War without Liking It."

[26] Himmler, Heinrich (1900–1945). Very close to Hitler, head of the Gestapo, and commander of all German police forces, Himmler became the Reich's Minister of the Interior in 1943. He bore major responsibility for the operation of the concentration and extermination camps. In 1945 he was sacked by Hitler after he parachuted into England in the hope of entering into negotiations with the Allies. The English arrested him, and he committed suicide later that year.

Yes, such things were possible, as we know only too well. But so many things are possible: why was this particular course of action chosen rather than some other? Because the point was to kill the human spirit and humiliate men's souls. Those who believe in force know their enemies well. They know that when a man believes in his heart in the justice of a cause, a thousand rifles aimed at him will not alter that belief. And if that man dies, other righteous men will say "no" until force exhausts itself. Hence it is not enough to kill the righteous man; his spirit must also be killed, so that the example of a righteous man renouncing human dignity may discourage all other righteous men and dishearten justice itself.

For ten years, one nation devoted itself to the task of destroying souls. It was sure enough of its strength to believe that the soul was the only obstacle still standing in its way and that it had to be taken care of. They set out to do just that, and, woe unto them, sometimes they succeeded. They knew that there is always some hour of the day or night when even the most courageous of men feel like cowards.[27]

They were always clever about waiting for that hour to arrive. And when it did, they sought the soul through the body's wounds, they reduced the body to exhaustion and madness and at times to treachery and deception.

Who in such circumstances would dare to speak of forgiveness? Since spirit finally understood that it could defeat the sword only by the sword, since it took up arms and achieved victory, who would ask it to forget? It is not hatred that will speak out tomorrow but justice itself, justice based on memory. And it is justice of the most eternal and sacred sort to forgive, perhaps, on behalf of those of us who died without talking, with the sublime peace of hearts that never betrayed, yet to strike a terrible blow for those of us who, though among the most courageous, were reduced to cowards by degradation of their souls, and who died in desperation, carrying in their ravaged hearts forever their hatred of others and their contempt for themselves.

August 31, 1944
Critique of the New Press[28]

Since we have been granted a brief interlude between insurrection and war, I would like to discuss today a subject I know well and which is close to my heart, namely, the press. And since the press in question is the new press that has emerged from the Battle of Paris, I want to speak of it with the fraternity and clarity that one owes to comrades in combat.

---

[27] The same formula occurs at the end of Tarrou's notebooks in *La Peste* (*The Plague*): "He ended by answering . . . that there was always some hour of the day or night when a man was a coward, and his only fear was of that hour." Folio edition, p. 254.

[28] This (signed) article is the first of a series on the press, continued on September 1 and 8 and November 22, 1944. It was reprinted in *Actuelles*, with its title, in the chapter on "Critical Journalism." Note that when Camus signed an article, he wrote in the first person singular and spoke in his own name, which he never did in his editorials, where the editorial "we" was always used.

When we were underground, we naturally wrote our articles simply and without declarations of principle. But I know that for all our comrades at all our newspapers, we did so with a great secret hope. We harbored the hope that these men, who had braved mortal dangers for the sake of a few ideas they held dear, would find a way to give their country the press it deserved and no longer had. We knew from experience that the prewar press had forfeited its principles and its morals. Hunger for money and indifference to grandeur had combined to give France a press that, with few exceptions, had no goal beyond that of aggrandizing the power of a few and no effect but that of debasing the morality of all. Hence it was not difficult for this press to become what it became from 1940 to 1944, namely, a stain on the country's honor.

Our desire, all the more intensely felt because it was often unspoken, was to liberate the newspapers from their dependence on money and give them a tone and a truth that would allow the public to discover what was best in itself. At the time we believed that a country is often worth what its press is worth. And if it is true that newspapers are the voice of the nation, we were determined to do our own small part to raise the country's stature by ennobling its language. Rightly or wrongly, it was for this ideal that many of us died in unimaginable conditions, while others endured solitude and coercion in prison.

In fact we merely occupied offices in which we cobbled together newspapers that we put out while the battle raged. This was a great victory, and the journalists of the Resistance deserve the respect of all for the courage and determination they showed. But—and I beg pardon for saying this in a time of general enthusiasm—this achievement pales because so much remains to be done. We have won the means to make the sweeping revolution we wanted, but we have yet to make it a reality. And to put it bluntly, the liberated press, to judge by the first dozen issues that have appeared in Paris, leaves a great deal to be desired.

I hope that what I have to say on this subject in this and subsequent articles will be taken in the right spirit. I speak on behalf of a brotherhood born of combat, and my remarks are not aimed at anyone in particular. These criticisms are addressed to the press in its entirety, including ourselves. Some will say that these criticisms are premature, that our newspapers must be allowed time to organize themselves before they are asked to examine their consciences. I disagree.

We are well aware that our newspapers have had to be put together in unbelievably difficult conditions. That is not the point, however. The point is that a certain tone could have been adopted from the beginning but wasn't. Indeed, now that the press is in the process of defining itself, of deciding what shape it will ultimately take, it needs to take a hard look at itself. It will then have a clearer idea of what it wants to be and what it will become.

What do we want? A press that is clear and virile and written in a decent style. When you know, as we journalists have known these past four years, that writing an article can land you in prison or[29] get you killed, it is obvious that words

---

[29] In *Actuelles* "and" was substituted for "or."

have value and need to be weighed carefully. What we were hoping to restore was the journalist's responsibility to the public.

Sin of Sloth[30]

Amid the haste, wrath, and frenzy of our offensive, our newspapers sinned by sloth. During the insurrection the body was so overworked that the mind let down its guard. Let me say here in a general way what I propose to examine in detail later on: many of our newspapers reverted to formulas that one might have thought outdated, and they did not shrink from the kinds of rhetorical excess and appeals to the shopgirl sensibility that filled the columns of our papers before and after the war.

The reason for the first fault is that we need to persuade ourselves [that we have won], although what we are doing is merely reproducing the occupation press with the roles reversed. The reason for the second is that we followed the path of least resistance and reverted to formulas and ideas that threaten to undermine the morality of the press and the country. Neither is acceptable unless we wish to abdicate our responsibilities and abandon hope of accomplishing what we need to accomplish.

Now that we have won the means to express ourselves, our responsibility to ourselves and to the country is paramount.[31] It is essential that we recognize this, and the purpose of this article is to make sure that we do. The task for each of us is to think carefully about what he wants to say and gradually to shape the spirit of his paper; it is to write carefully without ever losing sight of the urgent need to restore to the country its authoritative voice. If we see to it that that voice remains one of vigor rather than hatred, of proud objectivity and not rhetoric, of humanity rather than mediocrity, then much will be saved from ruin, and we will not have forfeited our right to the nation's esteem.

ALBERT CAMUS

September 1, 1944
The Reform of the Press[32]

Any moral reform of the press would be pointless if it were not accompanied by political measures intended to guarantee the newspapers real independence from the power of capital. Conversely, political reform would make no sense if it were not inspired by a searching examination of the nature of journalism by

---

[30] In *Actuelles* there was no subhead.

[31] The notion of "responsibility" is essential to Camus' conception of journalism: this programmatic text, which deals specifically with the press, complements the article of August 21, "From Resistance to Revolution," reprinted above, p. 12.

[32] Signed article, continuing the one published the day before, but not reprinted in *Actuelles*.

journalists themselves.[33] In this as in other respects, politics and morality are interdependent.[34]

The journalists of the new press were obliged to conduct just such an examination during the years of clandestinity, or so we believed. I still think this is true. But I said yesterday that questions of the sort we raised then are not much in evidence in the way the press presents itself today.

What is a journalist? He is first of all a person who is supposed to have ideas. This point deserves special scrutiny and will be dealt with in another article.[35] He is also a person who every day takes it upon himself to inform the public about the events of the day before. In short, he is a historian of the moment, and truth must be his primary concern. Yet every historian knows that even with distance from events, comparison of documents, and testimony from different witnesses, truth in history is an elusive thing. The only thing he can do about this state of affairs is to offer an ethical corrective in the form of a concern with objectivity and prudence.

How urgent these virtues become, therefore, in the case of the journalist, who is deprived of any distance from events and unable to check all his sources! What is a practical necessity for the historian becomes an imperious law for the journalist, a law he cannot violate without turning his professional activities into acts of wickedness.

Can we say that our press today observes the requirement of prudence and is concerned solely with the truth? Certainly not. It has reverted to methods born of the competition for news before the war. Any news is fit to print provided it appears to be a scoop (see, for instance, the false hope given to Parisians concerning the restoration of gas and electricity).

Since it is difficult always to be first with a major news story because currently there is only one source for such stories, journalists have been quick to jump on details thought to be picturesque. And even though war is still raging in Europe and our days are too short even to list the tasks that lie ahead and our memories too limited even to remember the names of all the comrades still in need of rescue, one newspaper has seen fit to publish a banner headline heralding the pointless statement of a public entertainer who has just discovered a vocation as an insurgent after four years of pusillanimous compromise. This sort of thing was already contemptible when *Paris-Soir*[36] set the tone for the rest of the press. But it's truly disheartening when it affects newspapers in which the hopes of the entire country are now invested.

---

[33] In "Examens de conscience" in *Le Figaro* of September 9, François Mauriac wrote that "the wish expressed by M. Albert Camus deserves our full approval."

[34] This formula sums up one of the essential principles of Camus' thought, one that explicitly or implicitly underlies all of his positions.

[35] See the article of September 8, 1944, "Critical Journalism," reprinted below, p. 32.

[36] Camus worked on the editorial staff of *Paris-Soir* in 1940, and for him the newspaper symbolized mediocrity, cowardice, self-indulgence, and sentimentality. It was a paragon of bad journalism.

Thus we see a proliferation of layouts intended to sell newspapers, with headlines in large fonts bearing no relation to the value of the information contained in the articles they introduce—articles written to flatter the public's taste for the simpleminded or sentimental. The newspapers shout right along with their readers and seek to please when they ought simply to enlighten. In fact, they give every sign of holding their readers in contempt, and in so doing journalists judge themselves more than they judge the public.

The argument for the defense is well known: "We give the public what it wants." But this isn't what the public wants. It's what the public has been taught to want for twenty years, which isn't the same thing. For the past four years, moreover, the public, too, has been mulling things over: it is ready to accept the tone of truth because it has just been through a terrible period of truth. But if, day in and day out, twenty newspapers fill the air with mediocrity and fabrications, the public will breathe that air and become dependent on it.

We have been given a unique opportunity to create a public spirit and to rise to the level of the country at large. Compared with that, what do a few sacrifices of money and prestige amount to, or the daily effort of thought and care that should suffice to maintain the quality of a newspaper? I merely pose the question to our comrades in the new press. Whatever their reactions may be, I cannot believe that they would take such a question lightly.

ALBERT CAMUS

September 2, 1944
The Democracy to Come[37]

As we have said before, a problem of government has arisen. This is in substantial measure our business, because it is everyone's business. But we have not yet taken a clear stand, because we were of the opinion that the men who have thus far represented France to the outside world deserved our confidence. We thought that when they consulted those who defended France on French soil, they would swiftly recognize the appropriate solution to this problem. We still think so.

But others have taken a stand, and their statements have surprised us. And since we cannot conceive of politics without straight talk,[38] we must take this opportunity to say what we think.

Our comrades at *Le Populaire*[39] have reported on a meeting between General de Gaulle and the Secretary General of the Socialist Party. The Secretary General

---

[37] Editorial. Typescript.

[38] Camus often called for "straight talk" (*un langage clair*) not only in politics but also more generally: "I grasped the fact that all of man's misfortune stemmed from avoidance of straight talk," said Tarrou in *La Peste* (op. cit., p. 229).

[39] Founded in 1916, *Le Populaire* became the official newspaper of the Socialist Party at the Congress of Tours in 1920. Léon Blum served for a long time as its political director, and Vincent Auriol often wrote for it. It ceased to appear during the Occupation and along with *Combat* numbered among the "patriotic

is said to have agreed to the formation of a government consisting of "a mix of experienced men, to ensure continuity of the Republic and doctrinal solidarity with yesterday's democracy, and new men, whose presence in the government will provide the injection of new blood that the country plainly wants."

We have fought side by side with our socialist comrades and shared their hopes often enough to feel that we have a right to say that this vocabulary in itself is not good. But, pending clarification, what it conceals troubles us even more.

We are perplexed by the mention of those "experienced men," whose policies, to put it plainly, were not so brilliant as to require us to affirm our solidarity with them today. Many of them betrayed France, either deliberately or out of weakness. Others, who did not betray their country, did not serve it well. They no longer have any business among us.

To be sure, we recognize that we must offer certain reassurances both at home and abroad. Order needs to be restored in France, for the sake of both France and her friends. But there must be agreement about that order.

An order that merely reflected the restoration of a regime, and of individuals, that proved incapable of withstanding the shock of war and of a Parliament that by a vast majority resigned its powers to Pétain;[40] an order that consecrated mon-eyed interests, behind-the-scenes intrigues, and personal ambitions—such an order would be nothing other than a form of disorder, since it would consolidate injustice.

Order means a consenting people. And unless the dreadful experience of those four years was in vain, unless our hopes be mere smoke and our faith foolish, the people cannot consent to the return of the very men who left when they should have stayed. In any case, the underground people—the anonymous men and women of the resistance—will not consent to their return.

The surest way of obtaining disorder is therefore to seek to restore that mediocre and corrupt order represented by men such as M. Chautemps,[41]

---

newspapers" authorized to appear after the Liberation. In its first free issue, it paid tribute to Léon Blum, and thereafter it reminded its readers daily that Blum had been "deported to Germany" (where he remained until May of 1945). Guy Mollet would succeed Blum as political director. On September 1, the paper published an account of the meeting between Daniel Mayer, Secretary General of the Socialist Party, and General de Gaulle, along with an editorial by Mayer focusing on the issue that Camus addresses in this article.

[40] On July 10, 1940, the two combined chambers of the legislature voted to grant full powers to Pétain by a vote of 570 to 80. On the attitude of the deputies, see the excellent work by Olivier Wieviorka, *Les Orphelins de la République* (Paris: Editions du Seuil, 2001).

[41] Chautemps, Camille (1885–1963). An active member of the Radical party, Chautemps held several min-isterial portfolios and even served as prime minister, particularly in 1937 and 1938. A member of Paul Reynaud's cabinet in 1940, he quit Pétain's government on July 10 and left for the United States. There he was among the group of immigrants who did not support de Gaulle and encouraged Roosevelt's suspicions of de Gaulle and his Provisional Government. Camus often attacked the Radicals in the wake of the "national unity" governments that drained the substance from the Popular Front, as can be seen in various articles that he published in *Alger-Républicain* (see *Fragments d'un combat*, op. cit.). After the Liberation, he saw the Radicals as typifying the prewar politicians whom he held responsible for the war and the defeat.

M. Chichery,[42] and so many others on the vain pretext of restoring democracy. It pains us to have to say it, but the old order that some would seek to revive today was not democracy but a caricature of democracy.

Democracy—real democracy—remains to be constructed. And we will do so in an orderly society—a truly orderly society, that of a united people determined to survive, in which each person will have the place he is due, hence in which those "experienced men" who today inspire nothing but indifference or contempt will always be able to spend their time writing memoirs destined to be read by no one.

September 4, 1944
Morality and Politics[43]

When we look at what is happening around us or, even more, when we ponder how we arrived where we are today, we see no need to rethink the scope of our last editorial or moderate our wariness of the political leadership that was swept away in France's defeat. On the contrary, further reflection has only made us more cautious.

There is no point in hiding from our friends around the world how profoundly uneasy the vast majority of patriotic Frenchmen felt on hearing of the political developments that followed the Allied landing in Algeria.[44] This uneasiness stemmed from the very nature of French hopes. And those hopes revolved around ideas of justice and rebirth.

That men already condemned by the people of France should return to the French political scene with innocent smiles on their faces was contrary to justice. And the rebirth of the country was seriously compromised by the fact that politicians determined to bring politics down to their own level of pettiness were

[42] Chichery, Albert. As president of the Radical Group in parliament in 1939, Chichery moved closer to Laval. He was executed by the underground on August 15, 1944.

[43] Editorial. Typescript, not reprinted in *Actuelles*. An important chapter of that book does bear the same title, however, although it is a title that could be applied to most of Camus' *Combat* articles.

[44] After the Allied landing in Algeria and in the wake of agreements signed at Cherchell between the United States and the local resistance, which had greatly assisted the landing, General Giraud was to assume leadership in North Africa. But the fortuitous presence of Admiral Darlan, who served as vice-premier from January 1941 to April 1942 and who remained the official successor to Pétain and head of the French armed forces, made it essential to deal with him. It was Darlan who signed the accords with General Clark as well as the cease-fire for North Africa on November 10. As Pétain's representative, he headed an Imperial Council consisting of prominent individuals and officials appointed by Vichy, while General Giraud had command of French troops. Faced with protests over this compromise with Vichy, Roosevelt spoke of it as a "temporary expedient." But nothing changed after the assassination of Darlan in December 1942. The Imperial Council simply put Giraud in charge of civilian as well as military affairs. Vichy laws—and officials—remained in place until de Gaulle's arrival in March 1943 and the formation of the French Committee of National Liberation in May 1943. Some saw this policy as one of American protection for "Vichyism."

permitted to speak and act as if they had the slightest idea of either the nation's grandeur or its suffering.

To come straight to the point, M. Chautemps has done us a great deal of harm—M. Chautemps and others like him.[45] They supplied our friends with information, but they who supplied the information didn't know what they were talking about. In fact, they never really knew what they were talking about, but they knew even less after France was plunged into an abyss whose depths their imaginations were too shallow to measure.

They spoke of France as of something dead or abstract, ignorant as they were of the land of blood and tears that went on living without them. Hence their words were false, and those words harmed us twice over, first because they were false and second because they drowned out our muffled cries. Today, it will take all our newspapers and all our voices together, and then some, to give a better account of ourselves.

If this history leaves us without resentment, it nevertheless stiffens our resolve. And we are resolved first of all not to open the doors of French politics to those who left at a time when the resistance was prepared to welcome them. In other words, the affairs of this country should be managed by those who paid and answered for it. In other words, we are determined to replace politics with morality. That is what we call a revolution.[46]

X

September 6, 1944
The End of a World[47]

For some time now our country has had only two real aristocracies, one of labor, the other of the mind. We now have a new definition of the word *aristocracy*: that part of the nation which refuses to be enslaved or to enslave others.

But the four years of defeat and resistance have only confirmed what was already clear before the war to all who loved France even as they judged her disconcerting failings. Plainly, the country's ruling class just gave up.

The French bourgeoisie had enjoyed a period of grandeur, but it had outlived itself. It could no longer rise to its duties and lived exclusively on the memory of its rights. When it comes to taking the full measure of any class, these are signs of decadence. What is more, the bourgeoisie was afraid. If the verdict against it had to be summed up in a few words, one might say that it did not love the people and would have accepted any bargain to save itself from them.

---

[45] See above, n. 41.

[46] The final sentences of this article sum up two points that Camus would make repeatedly: that France must be governed by men who had served in the Resistance, and that morality must ultimately govern politics.

[47] Editorial. Typescript.

It is fear that makes traitors. And many of those who subsequently betrayed their country did so only because they did not like the people, who always marched straight ahead with the blithe unconcern of those who know they are in the right. Whatever words Bergery[48] may have put in Pétain's mouth, the Vichy regime stood for revenge for the events of 1936. The cruelest were indeed the most cowardly.

Make no mistake: our condemnation is in no way abstract. Many representatives of the bourgeois class shared France's suffering and her struggles. They have their place wherever honor and fidelity have theirs. The point, however, is to see and understand the fact that the leading role of the bourgeoisie ended in 1940 and that its political representatives need only listen to and understand the great voice that is emanating today from a people concerned about its future.

We would have said exactly the same thing before the defeat. Today, however, we speak with memories of our humiliation still fresh in our minds. These memories do not incline us toward indulgence. When France is a happier and stronger country than she is now, there may come a time when we can look on calmly as a moribund class demonstrates through its political maneuvers that experience has taught it nothing.

Today, however, that is clearly impossible.

We have too much to do and too much to repair. What can one whose heart is still heavy with shame say to them besides, "Go away!" Yes, let them go away and leave us alone. They must recognize that France is no longer theirs to run. We are about to go to work. We are going to attempt, lawfully, honestly, day after day, to rebuild what they destroyed, to restore the incomparable and hidden face of the nation of which we dreamed throughout these past four years of darkness. To accomplish what we need to accomplish, however, we need to be alone. We must not be obliged to destroy still more before we rebuild.

None of us is asking this class to disappear. We know now that French lives are irreplaceable. But this class must understand, it must leave us at last after wearying us for so long. And having proved so wanting in courage and generosity, it must demonstrate enough basic intelligence to bear witness to a grandeur that it proved incapable of producing by itself.

September 7, 1944
Our Brothers in Spain[49]

This European war, which began in Spain eight years ago, cannot be ended without Spain.[50] Things are already changing on the peninsula. A ministerial shakeup has been announced in Lisbon. The voice of Spanish Republicans can once again

---

[48] See n. 22 above.

[49] Editorial. Typescript.

[50] Spain was Camus's "second fatherland." See J. Lévi-Valensi, "Camus et l'Espagne," in *Espagne et Algérie au XXe siècle* (Paris: L'Harmattan, 1985), pp. 141–157. His visceral attachment was not limited to "eternal Spain," however. He championed the Spanish Republican cause, whose case he pleaded first in

be heard on the airwaves. This is perhaps a good time to say a word or two about this country like no other, a country great by dint of the heart and pride of its people, who have never for a moment failed to merit the world's esteem despite the despair brought on by their defeat.

At the beginning of this war, the Spanish people were chosen to set an example of the virtues that would ultimately save Europe. In point of fact, however, it was we and our Allies who cast them in that role.

That is why since 1938 many of us have been unable to think of our Spanish brothers without a secret sense of shame. Indeed, we feel doubly ashamed, first because we allowed Spain to die alone and second because when our brothers, defeated by the same arms that were later to crush us, turned to us for help, we sent policemen to turn them away. Those whom we called leaders at the time invented names for this abdication of responsibility. They called it "nonintervention" one day and "political realism" the next. Compared with such imperious language, what could a poor little word like "honor" count for?

But the Spanish people, to whom the language of grandeur comes so naturally, having only just awakened from six years of silence, misery, and oppression, are already speaking to us, to deliver us from our shame. As if, being the very image of generosity, they understood that it was now up to them to reach out to us and had no difficulty whatsoever in finding the right words.

Yesterday, speaking on the radio in London, their representatives said that the French people and the Spanish people had suffered as one, that French Republicans had been attacked by Spanish Phalangists just as Spanish Republicans had been attacked by French fascists, and that because the two countries had been united in the past by their common pain, they should tomorrow be united by the shared joys of freedom.

Who among us could hear those words and remain unmoved? And how can we not say here and now, as loudly as possible, that we must not repeat the errors of the past, that we must recognize our brothers at once and liberate them as we ourselves have been liberated? Spain has already paid the price of freedom. No one can doubt that this fierce people is prepared to pay that price again. But it is up to the Allies to spare them the need to shed their own blood, of which they have been so prodigal but which Europe should take care to hoard, by granting our Spanish comrades the Republic for which they have fought so hard.

The Spanish people have the right to speak out. Give them but a minute and they will speak as one, they will shout out their contempt for Franco's regime and their passion for freedom. If honor and loyalty and the misfortune and nobility of a great people are the reasons for our struggle, let us recognize that that struggle transcends our borders and that we will never achieve victory as long as the cause of freedom continues to be crushed in long-suffering Spain.

Révolte dans les Asturies (1936) and later in articles published in various places, from *Alger-Républicain* to *L'Etat de siège,* and he often spoke out on the subject. A number of *Combat* editorials were devoted to the Spanish Republicans and to Allied policy toward Franco.

September 8, 1944
Justice and Freedom[51]

In yesterday's *Figaro*, M. d'Ormesson[52] commented on the pope's speech.[53] The speech had already caused a stir, but M. d'Ormesson deserves credit for stating in very clear terms the problem that Europe faces today.

"The problem," he said, "is to harmonize individual freedom, which is more necessary and sacred than ever, with the collective organization of society made inevitable by the conditions of modern life."

That is very well put. Nevertheless, we would suggest to M. d'Ormesson an even more succinct formulation by saying that for us the problem is to reconcile justice with freedom. To ensure that life is free for each of us and just for all is the goal we must pursue. Between those countries that have, with varying degrees of success, striven to give freedom priority over justice on the one hand or justice priority over freedom on the other, France has a role to play in seeking a superior equilibrium.

We must not hide from ourselves the fact that achieving such a reconciliation will be difficult. If what we read in history books can be believed, it has never yet been done, which suggests that these two principles are somehow contradictory. How could it be otherwise? Individual freedom means freedom for the banker and the ambitious businessman, hence injustice. Justice for all means that the personality of the individual must be subordinated to the collective good. In such circumstances what does it mean to speak of absolute freedom?

[51] Editorial. Reprinted in *Actuelles*, untitled, in the chapter on "Morality and Politics." This article initiated the dialogue with *Le Figaro*.

[52] D'Ormesson, Wladimir (1888–1973). French Ambassador to the Vatican from May to October 1940 and to Argentina after the war, from 1945 to 1948, and then again to the Vatican from 1948 to 1956, d'Ormesson was a writer who served after the Liberation as an editorialist at *Le Figaro*, where his editorials alternated with those of François Mauriac. On September 7, under the title "The Pope and the Social Problem," he asserted that only Christianity, "whose primary law . . . is the law of charity," could succeed in reconciling individual freedom with social organization. On September 11, d'Ormesson borrowed Camus' title with a slight variation: "Justice et la liberté" instead of "Justice et liberté." It is worth quoting its opening passage in full: "The newspaper *Combat*—whose editorials exhibit such a fine style—has recently devoted its attention to the article in which I commented on the pope's recent speech. The paper raised objections to the argument I was making, objections couched in such interesting terms that I thought there might be some point to continuing the discussion. How comforting it is in any case to be able at last to resume the practice of courteous debate! How marvelous it is to write what one thinks and arouse unfettered criticism!"

[53] The Pope in question was Pius XII, Eugenio Pacelli (1876–1958), who was elected Pope in March 1939. Having served as papal nuncio in Bavaria and later Berlin in 1920, he was no doubt influenced by his time in Germany. He tried to define the conditions of a "Christian peace." On December 26 Camus would point out that he had failed to denounce the dictatorships while they were still in power. His silence on the genocide of the Jews would become the subject of lengthy polemics in years to come. His condemnation of Marxism and the formation of two rival blocs in the Cold War led to a severing of relations between the Vatican and the East. In France, he would take steps to restrict the activity of worker-priests. On September 1, 1944, the Pope had broadcast a speech on "the gigantic effort needed to restore social life" and the need to restore "a moral law."

M. d'Ormesson, however, is of the opinion that Christianity provides a solution to this problem. Perhaps he will allow a person formed outside of religion but respectful of the convictions of others to express his doubts on this point. Christianity is in essence a doctrine of injustice (and that is, paradoxically, the source of its greatness). It is based on the sacrifice of the innocent and the acceptance of that sacrifice.[54] By contrast, justice cannot exist without rebellion, as Paris has just proven with a series of nights illuminated by the flames of insurrection.

Must one therefore give up on this effort to achieve what would seem to be an impossible reconciliation? No. One must simply appreciate the immense difficulty of the undertaking and make it clear to those who in all good faith would like to simplify everything.

Indeed, nothing else is worth living and fighting for in today's world. In the dispiriting conditions of the present age, the difficult and prodigious task we face is to establish justice in the most unjust of worlds and to save the freedom of souls destined from inception for servitude. If we fail, mankind will be plunged back into darkness. But at least we will have tried.

Last but not least, this effort calls for clear thinking and astute vigilance to warn us that whenever we deal with a social issue, we need to think about the individual, and whenever the individual claims our attention, we need to consider the good of all. M. d'Ormesson is right to think that Christians will manage to persevere in the face of such great difficulty because they are taught to love thy neighbor. Yet others who do not share their faith may yet hope to arrive at the same goal out of a simple concern for truth, a spirit of selflessness, and an appreciation of man's greatness.

X

September 8, 1944
Critical Journalism[55]

We also need to consider the journalism of ideas. Previously, we pointed out that the French press leaves something to be desired when it comes to its conception of news. Newspapers seek to inform their readers quickly rather than to inform them well. Truth is not the beneficiary in this setting of priorities.

Hence it makes no sense to complain that background articles take up space that would otherwise be wasted on news. One thing is clear: the news that is fed to our newspapers today—news which they print as they receive it—is useless without critical commentary. The press as a whole might do well to take this formula to heart.

---

[54] Without going into detail here about Camus' relation to Christianity, it is important to point out that care must be taken to avoid oversimplifying the problem, which touches on a theme of great importance in Camus' thought and work, namely, the theme of guilt and innocence.

[55] Article reprinted in *Actuelles* with the same title, which is also the title of the chapter containing four texts dealing with the press. It can be read as a veritable breviary for the journalist according to Camus.

For one thing, the journalist can help the reader understand the news by providing context aimed at defining the limitations of information whose source and purpose may not always be obvious. For example, he can lay out the news in such a way as to place contradictory dispatches next to each other, so that each can cast doubt on the other. He can enlighten the public as to the likelihood that a given piece of information is accurate in view of its origin with a particular foreign agency or bureau. To be more specific, it is clear that among the many bureaus maintained abroad by various news agencies before the war, only four or five could offer the kind of guarantees of accuracy that a press determined to play its proper role ought to insist on. It is the job of the journalist, who is better informed than the public, to indicate the extent to which news is based on sources he knows to be dubious.

In addition to this direct criticism within the text and in the selection of sources, the journalist might also try to explain the technology of news reporting to the public as clearly and accurately as possible. Since readers are interested in Dr. Petiot[56] and his swindles, there is no obvious reason why they should not be interested in the way in which an international press agency operates. This would have the advantage of awakening their critical faculties rather than appealing to their baser instincts. The only question is whether such critical reporting is technically feasible. I am convinced that it is.

There is another way in which the journalist can contribute to public debate, and that is by providing political and moral commentary on the news. The news reflects the chaotic forces of history, and it might be a good idea to record the daily thoughts of an informed observer or the common thoughts of a number of observers. Yet this cannot be done without scruples, distance, and some notion of the relative importance of things. Of course a predilection for the truth in no way prevents taking a stand on the issues. Indeed, if we have begun to get across the idea of what we are trying to do in this newspaper, neither truth nor commitment makes sense without the other. Here as elsewhere, however, there is a tone to be set, for without it nothing has any value.

When we look at today's press, it is clear that the astonishingly rapid progress of the Allied armies, the spate of news from abroad, the sudden shift from undying hope of liberation to certainty of victory, and, last but not least, the approach of peace have obliged all of our newspapers to delay no longer in stating their views of what this country is and what it wants. That is why there is so much talk of France in the articles they publish. But of course this is a subject that can be broached only with an abundance of caution and carefully chosen words. If we were to revert to the patriotic clichés and phrases that so annoyed the French

---

[56] "Doctor" Petiot was a swindler and murderer whose numerous crimes in the period 1942–44 were widely commented on by the French press in general, though not by *Combat*, which on November 3 remarked that "we are loath to magnify an affair that is disgusting from so many points of view. All too many distressing and urgent problems demand our attention for us to waste time on the scandalous details of sensational news. We only hope that our readers will be grateful to us for this choice." Petiot was sentenced to death.

in the past that they grew to detest the very word *patrie*, we would do nothing to clarify the definition we are after. But we are stripping away a great deal. New times call, if not for new words, then at least for new arrangements of words. And only the heart can dictate what those arrangements ought to be—the heart and the respect that stems from true love. This is the price that must be paid if we are to contribute in our own small way to the project of providing the country with a language that will induce it to listen.

Clearly, this comes down to insisting that substantive articles have substance and that false or dubious reporting not be presented as truthful news. These practices, taken together, are what I mean by critical journalism. And to repeat, the right tone is also necessary, and many things must be sacrificed. It might be enough, however, if people simply began to think about these things.

ALBERT CAMUS

September 10, 1944[57]

The new government is constituted. At first sight, it looks like any other government. It is a list of names. We are used to lists of names. So used to them that we no longer read them. To satisfy one's conscience, one is therefore tempted to say that the government will be judged by what it does rather than by what it is.

That would seem to be common sense. In fact, however, it would be to take the easy way out. Justice means judging men for themselves and not for their names or ideas. This ministry is not just a ministry. It is an assembly of living, breathing men, who have a certain way of shaking hands and of tying their ties. This government will be worth whatever these men are worth.

From this standpoint, certain men in today's ministry have already rendered a verdict on themselves by what they have done. Ministers were for far too long merely names or symbols for us not to rejoice at the sight of men of flesh and blood in their place, men who have paid a personal price. In the past, politicians took control of ministries, and only then did we try to persuade them to assume their responsibilities. Now, however, we have men who assumed responsibilities before taking over ministries, men who occupied jail cells before sitting down with green portfolios. France can thus take justifiable pride in having a minister who was only yesterday with the Breton underground[58] and another who is able to take up his duties only because he escaped from the train that was deporting him to Germany by climbing onto the roof of one of its cars.[59]

To be sure, this does not count as a revolution, but it is at least a revolution in our political mores. And that puts us in a good situation for the real revolution—the one we have begun, and which we are waiting quietly but vigilantly for the government to finish.

---

[57] Editorial. Probably by Camus. From this date on, editorials had no specific title, and the final X was replaced by the heading COMBAT.

[58] François Tanguy-Prigent, named Minister of Agriculture.

[59] Pierre-Henri Teitgen, named Minister of Information.

And of course having done good time in prison is no guarantee that one will make a good administrator. But it is at least a token that one is worthy of confidence at the outset.

We grant our confidence unreservedly to these men. They in turn must weigh the value of the capital that the country is entrusting to them with this confidence. They must not squander it. We see only one way for them to live up to their past, which is to bring the revolution that has begun in the streets into the institutions of government itself.[60]

But we shall have more to say on this subject.

September 12, 1944[61]

Comrade,

You write us about the prisoners of war and about your joy, mixed with sadness, at the arrival of Leclerc's victorious troops.[62] We would like to take this opportunity to respond.

Of men defeated in battle and now in danger of being forgotten you write that the thought of victory was never far from their minds. We know this. Those defeated soldiers have no need of anyone to plead their cause for them. They are men of our generation, we suffered defeat along with them, and after four terrible years we know that the brotherhood forged by defeat is more certain than that which is born of victory. No gulf separates us from them.

None of us liked war. Ten centuries of intellect and courage had made us civilized men. Hatred was not to our taste, and the idea of justice existed in our minds. So we asked ourselves if justice was on our side. And while we were asking ourselves that question, a thunderbolt struck and hurled us into the dirt.

We went into this war with the idea that it was absurd but that there was no other choice. Today we can say that we went into it to save our honor. What troubled us, though, was that honor spoke the language of M. Daladier,[63] and

[60] Camus and *Combat* generally would often return to this theme.
[61] Editorial, probably by Camus.
[62] Leclerc de Hauteclocque, Philippe (1902–1947). After escaping from a prisoner-of-war camp, Leclerc joined de Gaulle in London. He was named governor of Cameroon and military commander of French Equitorial Africa, which he aligned with Free France, and led his army from Chad to Tripoli. He participated in the D-Day landing in Normandy with Allied forces and entered Paris at the head of the Second Armored Division. He subsequently liberated Strasbourg and accepted Japan's surrender on behalf of France. He died in a plane crash in 1947 and was made marshal of France in a posthumous promotion.
[63] Daladier, Edouard (1884–1970). A Radical-Socialist, Daladier served several times as a minister or prime minister under the Third Republic and as vice-premier in the government of Léon Blum, whom he succeeded as premier from April 1938 to March 1940. His signature was on the Munich accords, and it was his government that declared war on Germany on September 3, 1939. Imprisoned by the Vichy government and put on trial at Riom, he was deported to Germany in 1943. After the Liberation he resumed his post as deputy. In Camus' eyes, he, like Herriot, symbolized those "right of center" politicians who exhibited little concern with social justice. Camus frequently attacked him in *Alger-Républicain* (see *Fragments d'un combat*, I, pp. 234–237, and II, pp. 668ff.).

the democracy we sought to defend had for some time been debased to government by executive order. While we were busy trying to resolve this contradiction, Germany smashed us in the face, while French traitors stabbed us in the back.

Since Munich,[64] in short, it has taken some time to articulate a consistent view. This basic need for coherence forced us to pay a tribute whose weight was measured in blood. But we ask if there is anyone in the world who can say that France did not enter this war with pure hands[65] or who would dare insult the defeated soldiers who paid the price that had to be paid for errors that were not only theirs but all of Europe's.

For you paid, and we paid. We know now that justice is with us. But our knowledge comes from executions at dawn and nights of agony, of frenzy, waiting, and terror.

What we say to you, however, is that there is no reason for regrets. It was better to perish with justice than to triumph with injustice. With patience and honor we have taken care that triumph should come only when justice itself comes.

Neither your suffering nor ours was in vain. In truth it was the same suffering, and what we shared in distress, today we must recover together in grandeur. For it was your refusal, coupled with our rebellion, that made us what we are. When you began your long and bitter meditation in June 1940, France meditated with you. We did what had to be done so that you would not be killed along with your thoughts, but you did what you had to do lest you die along with your dignity.

When our comrades come home, you mustn't be afraid that we will shun them. They are our brothers in arms and in victory, and their place is among us. Their fate seems harder than ours, for we at least were able to fight for the justice that suddenly became clear to us. So much solitude and loneliness, so much courage and helplessness—your fists clenched in idleness, you suffered long years in silence: our hearts sink at the thought. Our four years of war without uniforms are as nothing: you have our respect.

And should official France dare to forget you, you should know that we will link our fate to yours, since your fate is the fate of the entire country, which you and we have led from the most desperate of defeats to the most lucid of victories.[66]

---

[64] The accords signed in Munich on September 30, 1938, by Hitler, Mussolini, Chamberlain, and Daladier in an effort to save the peace actually allowed the Germans to occupy the Sudetenland in Czechoslovakia and then to invade the country.

[65] Like the editorial of August 24, 1944, "The Blood of Freedom," which also contains the phrase "pure hands," this one echoes themes from the *Lettres à un ami allemand.*

[66] On the same day, *Combat* began publishing a series of articles by Georges Bernanos with an introduction probably written by Camus:

"We are today beginning a series of articles by Georges Bernanos, which have not been published previously in France. These articles were passed on to us by a personal friend of the writer, who felt they belonged in this newspaper.

"This is an opportunity for us to affirm our deep solidarity with a spirit from whom many things might have separated us but for whom we have never felt anything other than fraternal gratitude.

"Our ambition is to speak as Bernanos does, but in our own voice. His is the only language capable of making the country aware of its greatness."

September 15, 1944[67]

In 1933, an eager, frenetic personage perched himself atop the ruins of the Weimar Republic[68] and announced to a delighted nation and an incredulous world that a magnificent new era had begun for his country and himself. Eleven years later, enemy armies have marched into the German fatherland and are about to deliver a final blow to a nation exhausted by ten years under arms and five engulfed by the flames of war. The experiment has proved conclusive.

A great many people believed in Adolf Hitler's genius: nearly all the Germans, many Europeans, and a few Frenchmen.[69] This was because, for many people, success is a law and brutality a temptation. It is by no means certain that such beliefs have altogether disappeared. Now that German territory has been invaded for the first time in more than a century by enemies determined to inflict upon it the marks and wounds of victorious force, it is time for a fresh look at the idea of Hitler's genius.

Hitler gambled everything on the ultimate success of his policies. Years without comfort; privations of every kind; the harshest of discipline; art, philosophy, and morality all enslaved to the common goal; Germany's material and spiritual resources mercilessly enlisted for one purpose only—never has a nation been subjected to such discipline or nursed such hopes. Acting in the name of the German people, Hitler made a fatal choice of power over happiness. Obedient to his word, eighty million human beings renounced ordinary well-being in the sole hope of someday achieving power.

One has to concede that, had Hitler succeeded, history would have acknowledged him as a great man. Some of us would no doubt have gone on denying this on the grounds that the word "man" had lost all meaning under the Nazi regime, thus debasing forever the very idea of "greatness." Yet all of Germany and much of the world would have forgotten the irredeemable mediocrity of this man consumed by his obsessions; the crimes hitherto unnamed but now bearing his name; and, finally, the misery that he trailed in his wake and caused to descend like night on so many desperate countries.

Today, however, faced with the result, History itself will recoil. It will weigh in the balance the sacrifices demanded of the German nation and the abyss of humiliation and suffering that will be its reward.

---

[67] Editorial. Typescript.

[68] The Weimar Republic refers to the German political regime from 1919 to 1933. It was a highly unstable regime and further weakened by economic crisis, which aided the growth of National Socialism and its eventual triumph. Hindenburg, the last president of the Weimar Republic, was obliged to appoint Hitler chancellor in 1933.

[69] Adolf Hitler (1889–1945) imposed the Nazi ideology on Germany and the occupied countries during World War II: totalitarian dictatorship, territorial expansion, supremacy of the Aryan race, persecution of Jews and opponents, etc. He became chancellor of Germany in 1933 and then "Reichsführer," chancellor and president, in 1934. He committed suicide on April 30, 1945, as the Third Reich was about to go down to defeat.

A nation that would have treated the happiness of a thousand peoples as nothing compared with the power of a great individual will be compelled to recognize that Germany sacrificed everything to obtain nothing. Deprived of happiness for ten years, it will not taste power for many years to come.

Yes, the experiment has proved conclusive. This man was no genius, this man who for ten years screamed his hatred above thousands of helmeted heads and who alone bears a weight of crimes and lies so great that no human forgiveness can ever lift it from his shoulders.

Order thus remains intact. For order insists that in the end realism does not pay. A lie may achieve victory when truth is afraid of its own strength. But there comes a time when truth refuses to die and takes up its sword. From that day forward, the lie is doomed, and realism is sapped of its strength.

What can spirits liberated from hatred as well as weakness learn from the terrifying example of Germany in agony? That in history as in other realms, genius never lies in falsehood but is contained entirely within truth aware of its own power. It took us ten years and millions of dead to recognize this obvious fact. Having paid so dearly for this lesson, at least we won't forget it.

September 16, 1944[70]

A wire service report that we published in our September 14 edition announced changes in the French episcopate. The issues raised by this announcement are general enough in their repercussions to call for further elaboration. The situation is clear, moreover. While many bishops, such as Msgr Saliège of Toulouse,[71] did honor to their faith and their country, a minority of Church dignitaries adopted attitudes during the Occupation that were incompatible with the interests of the nation. Cardinal Suhard[72] of Paris was one of the latter group.

Prior to 1940, many of us who respected Christianity as a prodigious spiritual phenomenon, nevertheless asked ourselves what blindness had led the Church to remain stubbornly aloof from the appalling problems that had plunged the century into turmoil. For years, many Europeans waited for leading spiritual voices to condemn what needed to be condemned. And for years those voices remained silent.

This determination to stand apart from the torment of nations in order to survive without having to take sides was the most unmistakable sign of a pervasive decadence in the Church. In 1936 the crisis became serious enough that one

---

[70] Editorial. Typescript.

[71] Msgr Jules Saliège (1870–1956), archbishop of Toulouse, publicly denounced the anti-Semitic measures of August 30, 1942, from the pulpit as well as in a "diocesan letter." He was named cardinal in 1946.

[72] Cardinal Emmanuel Suhard (1874–1949), archbishop of Paris during the war, never protested in any way against the persecutions.

major Catholic voice, that of Bernanos, was obliged to speak out and denounce the Church's lethargy.[73]

Since 1940, this issue has been laid to rest—and we say this all the more emphatically because we stand outside religion. Christians have once again embraced the life of the nation by embracing its risks. Doctrines, like nations or individuals, die only when they refuse to engage. Today we can say that for four years our Christian comrades proved that their faith was a living one.

This fact justifies our severity in judging those whose attitude risked separating the Church from the Nation. After all, if we show no mercy to the treachery of creatures whose business was to traffic in moral values under cover of politics, what awful accusation should we level against those whose business was to defend the spirit, to ennoble men's hearts, and to denounce evil?

We ask consistency of politicians who traditionally showed none. So how can we remain silent about the inconsistency of men who cloak themselves in one of the purest messages humanity has ever known? How can we not remind them that for a Christian, to be afraid is to betray one's faith?

The eternal vocation of these men was in fact to affirm that force is of no avail against spirit that refuses to recognize it. Their vocation was not to concede and temporize, it was to refuse and, if need be, to die. They betrayed their vocation.

It was more difficult for the Resistance to have martyrs than for the Church. Many of our comrades who are no longer with us went to their death without hope or consolation.[74] Their conviction was that they were dying, utterly, and

---

[73] The allusion is to Georges Bernanos's *Grands Cimetières sous la lune*, which condemned the Church's attitude in the Spanish civil war. Camus consistently showed his admiration for the Catholic writer, though the two were far apart in many ways. In 1939 he published a fine critique of *Scandale de la vérité* in *Alger-Républicain*. *Combat* printed articles by Bernanos on several occasions, some sent from Brazil, where Bernanos spent the war years, others given directly to the paper after his return to France.

On October 28, 1944, *Combat* reprinted Bernanos's article "Monseigneur Suhard et Jeanne d'Arc," which was written in January 1941, when Laval was recalled by Pétain. It is not out of the question that the short introductory paragraph was written by Camus: "When Pierre Laval was recalled by Pétain in January 1941 with the assent of the archbishop of Paris, Georges Bernanos wrote the following article, which reveals the full dimensions of Cardinal Suhard's attitude during the Occupation. This is an issue we have raised before. There has been no response. We therefore leave it to the greatest of Catholic voices to describe the true scope of this conflict of Catholic conscience."

Bernanos had this to say: "French Catholics will try to accept this latest blow to their conscience and to their honor with patience, but they will not forget it and will not forgive it. . . . This modern concept of passive obedience . . . must have its advantages, since dictators have made it the fundamental rule of totalitarian Morality. . . . The temporal salvation of France must have some importance in the eyes of the Almighty, since he deigned long ago to ensure it through the intervention of a Saint [Joan of Arc]. . . . The temporal independence of my country is also the guarantee of its spiritual liberty."

It is easy to see why a text like this would have captured Camus' attention.

On October 31, 1944, *Combat* published a response from Cardinal Suhard, claiming that he never intervened in politics and had resigned from the National Council established by Pétain. *Combat* did not wish to contradict Bernanos and said that it would await his return so that he could clarify his position. It added: "We reproach Cardinal Suhard for not having been Monseigneur Saliège at a time when all Christians should have lived up to the example set by the archbishop of Toulouse."

[74] Cf. "the conscious certainty of a death without hope" in "Le vent à Djémilla," *Noces* (*Essais*, p. 63), and of course *L'Etranger*.

that their sacrifice would end everything. They were nevertheless willing to make that sacrifice. How, then, can we not feel bitterness in judging the tepidness of men for whom death is but a way station and martyrdom a superior liberation?

For all these reasons, the problem is a serious one. It is politically serious, as the example of Spain, where the Church cut itself off from the people, ought to prove. But it is also morally serious. It is a problem of consistency and honor involving a person's whole attitude. Neither our friends at *Temps présent*[75] and *Témoignages chrétiens*[76] nor our Christian comrades at *Combat* will contradict us when we say that this problem must be resolved by Catholics without delay. It is up to Christianity itself to reject unrelentingly those who have demonstrated that they were Christians by profession only.

September 17, 1944[77]

What are the people of Germany doing? Sleeping. Their sleep is filled with nightmares and anxiety, but they are sleeping. We have awaited their awakening for so long, yet they continue to remain silent behind breached borders, stolid, stubborn, and silent as to the crimes committed in their name, resigned to the appalling destruction that is raining down on their cities.

People are asking about them almost everywhere: "They're about to wake up. They're going to redeem themselves in the eyes of the world and alleviate somewhat the awful responsibility they bear before History." But nothing is happening. German youths are falling in battle to preserve an honor that Germany's leaders have prostituted a thousand times over; a nation is about to die, a century of effort toward unity is about to culminate in the bloodiest of failures, but the German people remain unmoved. This enormous mass remains silent, as if the entire world and its own destiny had become alien to it. All observers, neutral as well as Allied, agree: the German people slumber on amid the twilight of their gods.

---

[75] *Temps présent* was a Catholic weekly whose literary editor was Stanislas Fumet. It ceased publication in June 1940 and resumed in late August 1944. On September 8, it published an article entitled "Justice for Truth," signed by "Synchrone," which paid homage to *Combat* and Camus: "One cannot fail to be moved by the rigor one finds in *Combat*'s editorials. We liked the following statements, which are more profound than what one reads elsewhere." [The article then quoted the final sentences of "Age of Contempt," from "It is not hatred that will speak out tomorrow but justice itself, justice based on memory" (see above, p. 21).]

"We believe that this editorial was written by Albert Camus. He deserves praise for it."

The article ended by pointing out that *Combat* and *Temps présent* shared the same conception of "morality": "It is public salvation, and purification of the air that the political spirit must breathe if it wants to live."

[76] Founded in November 1941 by Reverend Father Pierre Chaillet, a Jesuit theologian, to breathe life into the "spiritual resistance" to Nazism, the *Cahiers du témoignage chrétien* became *Témoignage chrétien* (singular; Camus erroneously used the plural) at the Liberation. Camus engaged in debate with Father Chaillet in his editorial of March 16, 1945. On the history of this weekly, see *Le Monde*, December 1, 2001, for an article by Thomas Férenczi marking its sixtieth anniversary.

[77] Editorial. Typescript.

In truth, the German people are true to their deepest vocation, the vocation of a country that did not want to think and that for years has been concerned only to avoid the burdens of thought. The unity that began with Bismarck[78] was not a harmonious and fruitful fusion of different individuals. It was unanimity from the beginning. And never was that unity as total as under Hitler. It was the indistinct and amorphous unity of a people content to have peace. Yes, this was a people that made war because it wanted peace of mind. And that peace of mind consisted in leaving to others the chore of thinking in its stead.

The German people do not love liberty, because they hate criticism. That is why they do not like revolutions that emancipate man and have made only legal revolutions, which reinforced state and nation simultaneously. And it accepted the Hitlerian regime, which deprived it of happiness and dignity, of honor and private life, because in the end it found the slumber of the spirit of which it had always dreamed.

That is why the Germans are sleeping today. Those who say that if the Germans rebel tomorrow, it will be out of despair and not under the impetus of constructive reflection, are right. They will succumb thereafter to the same old torpor and inertia, which will deliver them into the hands of the victors of the moment, concerned only with making their way slowly and obscurely back to that wonderful German warmth they cannot do without.

Then perhaps a new orator will come and offer some novel nostrum of his own to this unconscious unanimity. And we'll be back where we started.

Must we therefore give up all hope in Germany forever and take it upon ourselves to declare that eighty million Europeans will never be good for anything but denying the free spirit and killing people? We cannot accept that. But let us in any case admit our present uncertainty and disappointment. Even with the biggest heart in the world, who could plead the case of a people that refuses to speak out in its own defense?

September 19, 1944[79]

The National Liberation Movement[80] has held its first major public meeting. Men who spoke on behalf of no party and to no constituency that existed before the war were acclaimed by a fairly substantial number of Frenchmen. The novelty

---

[78] Bismarck, Otto von (1815–1898). As chancellor, Bismarck unified Germany and won the war of 1870 against France. He proclaimed the Second Reich at Versailles.

[79] Editorial. Typescript.

[80] The Mouvement de Libération nationale, or National Liberation Movement, replaced the Mouvements unis de la Résistance (United Resistance Movements) in January 1944. The importing meeting discussed in the article took place on September 17. *Combat* announced it by printing a communiqué that began, "The Resistance is calling you today, September 17." On September 19, the paper published a long report on the meeting.

of this may have gone unnoticed. It may also have gone unnoticed that these men, who for four years spoke of nothing but France, spoke yesterday of revolution.

Let us try to understand. What kind of revolution do they have in mind? The revolution that was discussed on Sunday at [the Salle] Pleyel was not like any of the revolutions proposed before the war by parties of very different kinds. For that reason they strike some people as vague. People are in the habit of relating words to the images they are most familiar with. For many people, "revolution" means 1789 and 1917. The rest is too tiresome to think about. It isn't even clear that the movements represented at yesterday's meeting have any precise idea of the revolution they have in mind. But they were speaking in the name of an inner force that transcends them, that has sustained them for four years, and that under certain conditions could tomorrow take on its true form.

Revolution is not rebellion.[81] What sustained the Resistance for four years was rebellion. In other words, total, uncompromising, initially almost blind refusal to accept an order that sought to put men on their knees. Rebellion begins with the heart.

But there comes a time when it moves on to the mind, when feeling turns into idea, when spontaneous enthusiasm culminates in concerted action. That is the moment of revolution.

The French Resistance in its original form began in the purity of total refusal. But four years of struggle have provided it with the ideas that were lacking at the beginning. At the end of its triumphant rebellion, it has come to the point of wanting a revolution. And if that rebellion doesn't run out of steam, it will make the revolution by providing it with what the country is waiting for, namely, a new theory specifically tailored to the situation. We here believe that it is already possible to lay down the preliminary features of this new doctrine, and we shall come back to this topic in the days to come.

For the time being, and despite the skeptics, we are pleased, leaving certain formal reservations aside, with this affirmation of will. We here do not believe in definitive revolutions. All human effort is relative. History's unjust law is that man must make immense sacrifices for results that are often paltry. Yet as slim as man's progress toward his own truth might be, we believe that it always justifies these sacrifices. We believe, in fact, in relative revolutions.

In any case, the amorphous thought that is coming to the surface today after four years of darkness should not be underestimated. It carries within it the seed of passions and rebirths of every conceivable kind.

Those who harbor doubts may be proved right in the future, but for the time being they are wrong, because they are giving in to mental sloth and cannot imagine how history might redeem itself.

---

[81] These reflections on rebellion and revolution would become central to *L'Homme révolté* (*The Rebel*). The evolution from rebellion to revolution figures here as an illustration of *Combat's* masthead: "From Resistance to Revolution."

Revolution does not necessarily mean guillotines and automatic weapons, or, rather, it resorts to automatic weapons only when necessary. Those to whom this new force seems vague or unimportant may be the same people who have already fallen to the rear and who, thinking they hold the truth of the moment, have forever lost the truth *tout court*, which is always the truth of tomorrow.

September 20, 1944[82]

We spoke the other day about the German people and their silence. Yet if the Germans do not speak, they nevertheless wish to listen. They wish to listen, in fact, to the man to whom they owe the dispensation from the need to speak for themselves. In Germany and above all in the Rhineland, people are waiting for a Hitler speech. But they wait in vain.

Hence the newspapers are speaking for him. Thus the *Kölnische Zeitung* explains in its editorial that Hitler will not say anything because the time is not right: "The Führer's silence speaks today to the German nation, and this silence is more eloquent than any words could be."

It is true that this silence is eloquent. It coincides with the silence of all Germany, and it is the silence of a man who has also given up on thinking. Hitler was of course not a thinker. But he was a man for whom words took the place of ideas. His meditations were screamed out to hundreds of thousands of Germans at the top of his lungs. For him to remain silent is no longer to exist.

Insufficient attention has been paid to the fact that Hitler never spoke as much as he did between 1938 and 1942. Those were his years of victory. After 1942 he was heard less and less, and in this summer of 1944 the great silence began. And the German people, who had renounced everything for the gruff voice of one man, ceased to exist even as its leader ceased to speak.

From this history one can draw a lesson that ought to discourage dictators around the world forever. People can speak only when they think they are right. Germany consented to be right or wrong with Hitler. And for Hitler might made right. Germany consented to be right or wrong depending on its might. The deep conviction of the German people was that Hitler would always be mightier than fate. But no man can ever subdue fate by force except in the silence of his heart or through the power of love. The type of force on which Hitler relied made fate laugh.

Today, the Germans' extraordinary imprudence in linking their fate to one man's ideas and speeches is reaping its reward. A people that so detested individualism has taken up individualism's basest aspect: the elevation of one man above all others in contempt of all conscience. If that man is wrong and falls silent, that suffices as a sign of expiation.

Expiation will be terrible for this unhappy nation. But it cannot be alleviated. Behind its silent leader it is about to embark on a bloody and desperate adventure whose end cannot be foretold.

---

[82] Editorial. Typescript, follow-up to the editorial of September 17, p. 40 above.

For Hitler has not fallen silent because he was wrong; he has fallen silent because he has lost. And continuing to identify his own person with that nation he has drenched in blood and shame, he will maintain his silence until it reaches its natural conclusion, which is death.

This man and this nation are about to die in a dreadful silence. But those who can no longer speak can still strike poses. Hitler can be counted on to see to it that Germany's attitude is bloody and theatrical. The coming days will not be happy ones. History will see this time as one in which a nation and its leader consented to collective suicide.[83]

September 22, 1944[84]

As everyone knows, newspapers are today subject to military censorship—which they have willingly accepted, moreover. We all understand the need to avoid giving anything away that might aid the enemy. So well do we understand this that whenever possible we censor ourselves. Every night, moreover, we are told with inexhaustible good will that the regime to which we are subject is not one of censorship but rather of military control. How can we not bow to such restraint and unwavering courtesy?

Now, however, a dispute over interpretation has erupted. We thought that "military control" dealt, as the term suggests, with control of military news. And we believed that military news dealt with information of potential interest to military operations. The control agency has a different interpretation, however. "Military news" is any news in which military people are mentioned. Since the most recent communiqué of the National Council of the Resistance alluded to certain armed formations, any mention of it by any newspaper was censored.[85]

---

[83] Hitler would indeed commit suicide in April 1945, but Camus' idea of the German people was to be contradicted by what he discovered in Germany at the end of June 1945: see "Images of Occupied Germany," below, pp. 229–231.

[84] Editorial. Typescript.

[85] *Combat* had already protested the day before against the censorship of the NCR communiqué under the title "A Bad Method": "In the course of its Tuesday meeting, the National Council of the Resistance adopted a resolution whose text was communicated to us Tuesday evening.

"There is no need to point out that this text contained no indiscretion that might have put the nation in danger. Publication was nevertheless prohibited by the military control authorities.

"Having no wish to create an incident, *Combat* respected this ban. For that reason it feels all the more comfortable in stating that the method of silencing the National Council of the Resistance by keeping its texts out of the public eye is a bad method of government."

These lines may have been written by Camus. He had already been involved in friction with the censors in his days with *Alger-Républicain* and even more at *Soir-Républicain*, and he had protested on numerous occasions, often in a jocular tone. See, for instance, in *Fragments d'un combat*, II, p. 750, a formula that is rather close to the present text: "We believe that the censor has opted for a bad method in attempting to sustain the 'morale' of the country in this way." See also, in the same work, pp. 720–725, "Notre position" (November 6, 1939), "Mise au point" (November 7, 1939), pp. 752–757, and "Pétrone et les ciseaux" (December 18, 1939), pp. 708–710.

And if for some reason we wished to describe the celebrated saber of Joseph Prudhomme,[86] we would have to submit it to the censor.

The result is clear. The military control authorities were yesterday subjected to ridicule in the French press. No one has anything to gain by this. And we would point out to the authorities that it is best to avoid becoming the butt of ridicule in a country that has just barely seen the end of its humiliation.

It is understood that the press is free. Without being military men in the sense in which military men understand the term, we proved for quite some time that we enjoyed our liberty. Liberty, whatever one may think about it, can coexist quite well with certain constraints, but only on condition that those constraints are freely accepted and clearly defined. Since the competent authorities have not proved capable of providing a clear definition, we must do it for them. Here, then, are our explanations:

We freely accept military censorship on news that might be of use to the enemy. We do not accept political censorship in any form. Above all, we do not accept that a control agency known by a specific name be used in furtherance of a policy that has no name.

In particular, we do not grant the military censorship the right to control the thought and actions of the leading Resistance organization.

If the authorities are prepared to understand these guidelines, we assume that things will proceed smoothly. If they are not, it will be up to the newspapers to meet in a plenary assembly to defend the freedom of the press in their own way. And we say this with calm assurance: one way to do this is to go underground to publish the political news and commentary that the authorities seek to censor. This is a kind of work with which we are, in the broadest sense, well acquainted.[87]

September 23, 1944[88]

Four years ago, on September 15, 1940, to be exact, Germany lost the war when it lost the Battle of Britain. Although Hitler believed himself to be riding a crest of victories, 185 German bombers fell around London, and Great Britain remained in the fight.

This is perhaps a good time to pay our English friends their due, namely, our somber friendship and our indelible memory of what they did, which will stay with us forever. That memory was born in the summer of 1940, when people brought together by retreat and exodus mingled in exhaustion in the cities of the

---

[86] Joseph Prudhomme was a character invented by Henri Monnier to symbolize the smugness, conformism, and stupidity of the petite bourgeoisie in the age of Romanticism.

[87] This statement provoked a reply from François Mauriac in *Le Figaro* for September 24–25. Mauriac wrote ironically of the extreme reactions of certain newspapers, and in particular about the call "to return to the underground with a clandestine press"—though he did not mention *Combat* by name. This was no doubt the first crack in the mutual understanding that had prevailed until that point between Mauriac and Camus.

[88] Editorial. Typescript.

south, abandoned all hope, and prepared for the desperate history that lay ahead. Those people had their doubts about England. They thought that England, too, would capitulate. But she did not, and despite all that followed, and the painful tragedies that failed to separate us, that is what we will never forget.

Of course we are not laboring under any illusions. Germany would never have been defeated without the incalculable sacrifices of great Russia, without the formidable blows struck against German forces by the Red Army. Germany would not have been defeated without the endless flow of matériel that America poured into Europe, without the industrial genius that managed to win the most desperate of battles with the least possible bloodshed.

But we cannot forget that England stood alone for a year, that she gritted her teeth for all that time but never gave up hope. We cannot forget that not a single Englishman entertained the idea of capitulation even for a minute.

We should add, moreover, that this heroism and calm determination would not have been so admirable had they not been accompanied by such modest reserve. Even today most Frenchmen are unaware of the seriousness of the wounds that Germany inflicted on Great Britain because the superb people of Britain forgot to complain. They suffered in silence and concerned themselves solely with winning the war. It was this inner strength and tranquil courage, moreover, that paved the way for a miracle: a country faced with extinction that nevertheless left intact the democracy on which it had thrived.

Many things could have separated or may yet separate us from our English friends. At times we have a hard time understanding one another. We often exasperate them, and they sometimes disconcert us. Yet come what may, some of us will never forget the astonishing spectacle of a nation that combined a courageous heart with a courageous tongue and, alone in a world gone mad, defended its freedom without once raising its voice.

In the article we published, the great writer Charles Morgan asked the French to forgive England for its victory and its might.[89] We forgive her with all our heart. We would not be a great nation if we did not know how to recognize nobility wherever it is found. Greatness must be given its due, and the British people have demonstrated their greatness. Despite what is being written all over France today, we are under no illusion that France has regained its former strength. We know that much remains for us to do, and we will try to do it with fidelity and clear thinking. Yet our pained and proud concern for our own country will never be allowed to make us ungrateful or cause us to forget that month of September when the humane truth that was being crushed in France scored its first victory in free England.

---

[89] Charles Morgan (1894–1958) was a novelist, playwright, and critic whose best-known novels were *The Fountain* and *Sparkenbroke*. Camus included a short note about him in his *Carnets II*, p. 21 (1942).

On September 20, *Combat* reprinted an article by Morgan entitled "Forgive Us Our Victory" that had appeared in *La France libre* at the end of 1943. In it, Morgan recalled his vain attempt to create the "United Powers" and stated his loyalty to England and love of France, and he then addressed the French in these terms: "When by dint of blood, sweat, and tears we have won the war, forgive us our victory. . . . Forgive us our strength. There will be times when we lack tact. . . . Forgive us our sins."

September 26, 1944[90]

With the arrest of Louis Renault, French big business has been put on trial.[91] The problem is complex because the interests involved are not simple. There is no hope of resolving it in a few lines. But if ever it were possible to reconcile objectivity with energy, one would want to do so in this case because of its importance for the national morale.

There is first of all a fact: French industry—and Renault along with it—worked for the enemy.[92] This is the plain truth, which immediately strikes the simplest souls, those who in one respect are never wrong. But explanations are readily offered. The French government had signed an armistice, which had every appearance of being legal. And under the terms of that armistice, French factories were obliged to work for the occupying power. French industrialists were merely obeying their government.

They can also demonstrate (as will become fairly clear in the Renault trial) that they did so against their will. They have compiled figures to prove that work was slowed and that Renault's output during the four years of the war attained barely a quarter of its prewar level. The profits they earned are more embarrassing. But it is no secret that certain industrialists can prove that they passed this money to the defenders of the good cause, though not always through direct channels.

Let us not close our eyes to the fact that this is a strong defense. Apparently there is no law under which firms can be condemned for saying that they had no choice but to respect the terms of an armistice that had the force of law. What can we adduce against this argument? The simple intuition that, in this instance, one of the most sacred duties of man and citizen was violated. But traditional judges will only laugh at this. Nevertheless, this is the intuition that needs to be fleshed out with content.

One could obviously contest the slowdown in production by attributing it to Allied bombing. One could point out that a substantial number of Renault factories were used not for production but for repairing German vehicles. But we prefer to say that these facts are beside the point.

Note, moreover, that a hasty revolutionary tribunal would not even argue the case. It would simply find the defendants guilty. That is not the course we have

---

[90] Editorial. Typescript.

[91] Louis Renault (1877–1944) was a French industrialist and founder of the Renault automobile firm. He had worked for French aviation in World War I. Under the Occupation, his factories worked for Germany. On September 23, *Combat*, along with other papers, published a report from Madrid stating that "the well-known industrialist [Louis Renault], allegedly wanted by the French government for his collaborationist attitude, has left France." The report was contradicted the next day: "The industrialist Louis Renault is under arrest." Incarcerated at Fresnes, he was accused of having delivered more than 6 billion francs' worth of war matériel to Germany. He defended himself by arguing that his factories were occupied and that he had been obliged to produce in order to avoid the deportation of workers and machinery to Germany. He died, however, before he could be brought to trial.

[92] *Combat* would frequently return to the need to judge French industrial leaders who had collaborated with Germany.

chosen; we are preserving liberty even when it benefits those who always fought against it. If we want to find them guilty, we must therefore substantiate the charges against them.

We must not be ashamed to say that those charges have a moral basis from which there is no appeal. To put it in a nutshell, the problem is one of responsibility. A captain of industry who enjoyed every privilege cannot be judged in the same way as some minor official who obeyed Vichy because he was in the habit of obeying. Men must bear responsibility for their privileges. Louis Renault, who before the war enjoyed a degree of power for which he was widely detested, had an opportunity to justify that power and make it bearable by demonstrating that he was aware of the duties that went with it.

For in the end obedience to the government is not among the necessary virtues of a captain of industry. In 1936, French industrialists proved that they were perfectly capable of disobeying the law and of putting themselves above the government. The same men cannot claim that when the moment to assume great responsibilities arrived, they passed theirs on to a government of their own choosing.

For us, nothing could be clearer: in 1940 the leading French industrialists had a duty to place themselves above the law and the government, this time in the name of the true interests of the nation. They will respond that their factories would have been taken over by the Germans. But they did say that already, and the results were lamentable. Production reduced to a quarter of its prewar level is still production. Construction slowed is still construction, and the sharing of profits was nothing but a sordid bargain.

Meanwhile, others did place themselves above the law. They had no papers and no money. What was a simple duty for them, a duty they found in their hearts, should have been an imperious and ineluctable obligation for Louis Renault. To put it plainly, he should have rebelled before the people did.

To speak in such terms is new and lends itself to ridicule. There would be less laughter if these ideas became law and if proportional responsibilities found some juridical translation. During these four dreadful years all Frenchmen were witnesses to a crime not foreseen by any law (and in saying this we are weighing our words carefully): the crime of not doing enough. French big business is guilty in our eyes because it refused to risk anything. It separated itself from the nation forever by calmly ignoring the nation's rebellions. And those men who invoked the law to evade their duties should hand over their places to others, to those who, though they cared nothing for honors, nevertheless saved their country's honor.

September 27, 1944[93]

Please forgive us, but we are not yet done with the case of Renault. The problem transcends the individual accused. It is no exaggeration to say that it bears on the country's future in that it will demonstrate whether or not we have the

[93] Editorial. Typescript. Continuation of the preceding article.

weapons necessary to destroy the legal fiction with which Vichy covered its treachery.

Indeed, the charge against Louis Renault has painful consequences. As we pointed out yesterday, French industrialists have tried to shift responsibility for their actions onto the government of Pétain and have tried to hide behind the armistice. If we condemn them, we will therefore have to condemn the host of others who also obeyed. And we will then cut ourselves off from the majority of the French.

That is not what we want, and that is why we tried yesterday to delineate the specific responsibility of French industry. Put simply, we had to show that that responsibility might not have been a matter of law.

It remains a responsibility nonetheless. We live in a time when politics has to be conducted on a moral plane, as a matter of sacrifice and responsibility, which is why it touches our emotions.[94] For four years, we judged not in the name of the written law but in the name of the law we carry in our hearts. The law of the law books was of use to no one but the executioners. Yet those who acted outside the law knew full well that they were acting within the truth. Hence there are cases in which law and truth do not coincide. Big business errs by hiding behind a law already rejected by truth, while for us the difficulty is to judge big business in the name of a truth that has yet to be embodied in law.

This situation is hard because it is general. It is not entirely new, however. In daily life we are all familiar with offenses that fall outside the strictures of the law. In such cases people sometimes resort to tribunals of honor. Hence we ought to appeal to a law of honor that would allow these cunning industrialists to be judged. Such a proposal may seem strange. But it comes down simply to saying that our country will never regain its greatness unless it punishes breaches of honor and duty as the gravest of offenses.

Even if all the courts in the world were one day to absolve Renault and recognize his defense as irreproachable in the eyes of law, on that day we would still maintain that his actions fall within the jurisdiction of a higher law, a law as clear in the popular mind as in the writings of specialists, a law whose dictates are imperative. That law, which the war industries violated, commanded them to ignore the law and to recognize that the era of responsibility had begun.

In 1940 an era began in France in which men were called upon to judge themselves one by one, in solitude, and deprived of all traditional support. From that moment on, for the next four years, French industrialists who produced for Germany judged themselves. We have only to ratify that judgment.

The government, which has taken the bold and novel step of setting the law to one side for the sake of this higher justice, deserves to be thanked. To it falls the task of fashioning its own new law around the permanent truth in the name of which Louis Renault stands condemned. But it is up to us to maintain clarity as to the moral nature of the difficult problem it is proposing to solve.

---

[94] Note Camus' insistence on dealing in moral terms with a problem that has not really been solved even fifty years after the fact.

September 28, 1944[95]

One can read the communiqué of the Council of Ministers elsewhere. We simply want to say here why we consider the government's decisions to be important.[96]

Without misplaced vanity, we want to say that these decisions reaffirm the principles we set forth in our discussion of the Renault case yesterday and the day before. More importantly, they translate those principles into practice.

The notion of "consorting with the enemy" (*indignité nationale*) as defined by the minister of justice corresponds to what we called the law of honor. It concerns those who were clever enough to betray their country without breaking the law. They will lose both their civic rights and their property. No justice could be more deserving of respect in our eyes. For liberty demands that it be extended to the enemy, and that demand, as difficult as it is to honor, is respected here: the guilty are not touched in their person.

Who can object if men who neglected all conscience in favor of money are deprived of what they held most dear, namely, the very same money that led them astray? This measure, at once implacable and well calculated, seems to us so invaluable that we hope it will be extended to any number of other cases in which men of liberty and justice are bound by their own principles and would be prevented from acting unless they decide once and for all to derive the new law they need from their own consciences.

Indeed, one of the first consequences of this measure can already be seen in the decision regarding the Renault factories. They have been requisitioned. The nation is taking them over because for four years they took care of Vichy and the occupying forces. In the eyes of the law it may be impossible to convict Louis Renault of cooperating with the enemy. But in the eyes of the nation he is accused of not having lived up to his privileges and his function. In the great economy of the French nation, people will henceforth need to have proved that they deserve what they own.

These decisions have started us down a necessary path. They are aimed at protecting the safety of the public. We will never approve them emphatically enough. The government has just demonstrated that it knows what the real

[95] Editorial. Typescript.

[96] The communiqué did indeed announce a number of important measures:

F. de Menthon, the minister of justice, won approval of an order to speed up prosecutions for "consorting with the enemy" (*indignité nationale*) and confiscation of the property of those found guilty.

R. Lacoste, the minister of production, announced measures to purge industry of collaborators, and the government approved the requisition of the Renault factories and the nationalization of coal mines in the Nord and Pas-de-Calais, as well as the confiscation of illicit profits.

P.-H. Teitgen, minister of information, issued temporary regulations governing the press and defining the provisional status of the Agence Française de Presse and the Entreprise des Messageries des Journaux Français.

It is easy to imagine that these measures, which paralleled Camus' calls of the previous several weeks for morality and justice, would have received his full approval, as well as that of the *Combat* team generally.

problems are and that it can deal with them. Acts of this kind will ensure that it enjoys the cooperation of the entire country. We have given enough proof of our independence to be able to say today that we unequivocally grant our full support to the spirit and will just demonstrated by the Council of Ministers.

September 29, 1944[97]

We are emerging from euphoria. In a legitimate access of enthusiasm, all of France believed that the liberation ended the whole ordeal and that Paris once again enjoyed peace the moment its flags were raised anew. This was not a clearly formulated thought but rather a natural inclination on the part of people who had suffered and fought a great deal and who had formed the habit of confusing their hopes of freedom with their hopes of ultimate victory.

Freedom has arrived, and little by little we are discovering that it has its pressures and burdens and will continue to have them as long as the war is not over and its consequences have not been overcome. Freedom has ended nothing. It is a beginning. Freedom is not peace. We have enjoyed our victory but have yet to see the victory of all. And we now know that all we have won is the right to go on fighting.

Of course we haven't forgotten the internal war against money and resignation, which we must continue to support. But for the time being it's a matter of war *tout court*, the war that flattened us, the war from which we picked ourselves up, the war that we must join anew.

In the enthusiasm of the liberation, and with help from a few overly hasty war correspondents, the French people came close to believing that Germany would be crushed in two weeks. At least we, for our part, never shared this illusion. And whenever we had occasion to speak of Germany, we expressed our conviction that it would hold out to the bitter end.

We hope we're wrong. But it seems to us that Hitlerian Germany is determined to end it all in the most tragic and theatrical of suicides and that it will impose a heavy price in blood for the victory that is not yet in hand. If we were inclined to doubt this, Mr. Churchill's recent predictions would provide food for thought.[98]

We must resign ourselves to the fact that the war is going to last longer than we expected. Even if we are fortunate enough to be proved wrong, we must live and act in the meantime with the conviction that the war will go on. This amounts to saying that the freedom we have just won commits us as much as it delivers us.

---

[97] Editorial. Typescript.

[98] Churchill, Winston (1874–1965), served first as a Liberal MP, then as a Conservative, and received his first ministerial portfolio in 1917. On succeeding Chamberlain as Prime Minister in May 1940, he organized Britain's resistance to the Nazis and became its symbol during the Battle of Britain and the threats of German invasion. He played a leading role in the war against Germany and its allies, coordinating the war effort and laying plans for the postwar period. He was defeated by Labor leader Clement Attlee in the July 1945 elections but returned to power from 1951 to 1955.

We say this without pointless zeal. No war is ever short enough. The world we are hoping for has already exacted too high a price. If more blood and more pain are needed, then that blood must be shed and that pain endured. Yet not a single European can contemplate this prospect lightly. In any case, in this country, where we have just experienced the full extent and full absurdity of human misery, no one can be expected to look forward to it.

As bitter as our situation is, our resolve must be no less firm. Not all Frenchmen recognized in 1939 that the war made sense.[99] They know now that it does. Indeed, it has taken on a higher meaning for them, since their task is now not just to destroy an enemy but also to banish the idea of France that four years of official treachery have created abroad. We no longer have a place to defend, but we do have a place to regain. As harsh or even at times unjust as this fate may seem, it must be accepted initially so that in the end it can be laid to rest.

We have put ourselves in the difficult position of a people who must once again demonstrate that we possess a nobility and grandeur that used to be taken for granted. That we must do this with the lives of the best among us is the dreadful tragedy of our new history. We have begun this revolting and necessary demonstration. We carried it on through four years of thankless struggle still too often ignored. Now we must continue it on the field of battle.

Some abroad may be aware of the difficult destiny with which we are faced. But we mustn't wait for others to express their gratitude. We must be silent and go to work. We must convince ourselves that the war is going to last and accept the sacrifices of victory as courageously as we assumed the burdens of defeat.

Victory itself will not be the end of it. Nothing is more difficult than to regain grandeur once it is lost in the eyes of the world. Yet we shall be on our way to rebirth and consecration if we can show the world the image of a nation generous to others and hard on itself, manfully resigned to the necessary sacrifices yet never oblivious of its own honor or of the happiness of others.

September 30, 1944[100]

Mr. Churchill has just delivered a speech whose force stems wholly from its clarity.[101] That is why reading it is so comforting. For resolute minds, truth is always the best news.

---

[99] Camus may have had himself in mind. See the passages of *Carnets I,* esp. pp. 165–182, in which he questions what the war is about.

[100] Editorial. Typescript.

[101] In his speech to the House of Commons, Churchill said that he hoped to see France take its place as soon as possible in the Allied high command. Expressing "sympathy" and "compassion" for France and paying homage to the French people, he added that he hoped to see the new French government recognized as soon as possible. This implied that the National Liberation Committee (the name initially adopted by the Provisional Government) would be responsible to an expanded "Consultative Assembly" approved by the people of France. See the editorial of October 14, 1944, p. 71 below.

But this same reasoning persuades us that truth remains the only valid means of diplomacy. And we speak the language of truth when we say that the only part of the speech that isn't clear is the part that deals with France.

Of course we know that Mr. Churchill cannot be clear. He could speak clearly in one of two ways: either by refusing to recognize the French government or by recognizing it. But he does not wish to do either, or at any rate he cannot do either alone. It is no secret that certain quarters of American officialdom are opposed to recognition.

Although this issue is painful to our pride, and French sensitivities are still raw, we want to discuss the subject without bitterness yet with the frankness that, while necessary, has not always been apparent in this matter. The fact is that there seem to be two reasons for this wariness of recognition. The first is opposition to General de Gaulle personally.[102] The second can be summed up as stemming from a certain reserve with respect to the Party of the Resistance, which some pretend to believe is entirely communist. From this comes the idea that nothing can be done before the legislative elections, in which the assumption is that Gen. de Gaulle might be rejected or that reassuringly safe political parties might return to the surface.

It will be evident that we are speaking frankly. But since this is the impression that we have in France, we have no reason to hide it. There is no other way of reaching a legitimate agreement. Having thus frankly acknowledged the wariness that some people outside France feel toward us, we must be equally forthright in stating our response.

Which is that France today is unified. It has internal issues to deal with, but these are nobody else's business, and if it deals with those issues with the requisite

---

[102] Charles De Gaulle (1890–1970) fought in World War I, was captured by the Germans, and made several attempts to escape. After the war he wrote books on political history and military strategy and in 1940 was named brigadier general ("temporary status"). As undersecretary of defense in the government of Paul Reynaud, he rejected the armistice and went to London, where on June 18 he issued an appeal to the French to continue the fight. He organized the Free French Forces with resources from the French colonies. In 1943, at the instigation of Jean Moulin, he created the National Resistance Council, which sought to coordinate resistance activities in France. After the Allied landing in North Africa, he overcame opposition and won Anglo-American recognition of his authority as replacement for Gen. Giraud. He also created the French National Liberation Committee. At the Brazzaville conference in January 1944, he proposed a new colonial policy under the auspices of the French Union. As head of the provisional government of the French Republic, first in Algiers and then in Paris as of August 1944, he became the incarnation of free France, restored the authority of the state, and reconstituted the French army, which fought alongside the Allies. Elected president of the government by the first constituent assembly in November 1945, he resigned in January 1946. In April 1947, he created the Rassemblement du Peuple Français (RPF). He returned to power in May 1958 in the wake of events in Algeria and proposed a new constitution, which became the basis of the Fifth Republic, of which he was elected president by universal suffrage. After eight years of war, he recognized Algeria's independence in 1962. Following failure of a referendum on regionalization and reform of the senate, he resigned in 1969.

Combat fully supported de Gaulle as liberator and head of the Resistance, but some journalists, including Camus, had doubts about his political activities and reserved the right to criticize him as they saw fit. A real split developed in 1947 between supporters of de Gaulle's RPF (Ollivier, Pia, Chauveau) and the rest of the staff.

clarity of mind, it will emerge greater than ever. This is our affair, and we are giving thought to it. But for all external matters, France is unified. And it must be treated as unified, including both Gen. de Gaulle and the communists.

Because Gen. de Gaulle, the parties of the resistance, and the communists have forged in shared combat a fraternity that they will not repudiate. They are not obliged always to have the same ideas about everything. We are not obliged to approve of Gen. de Gaulle in every instance or to share all his views of the Communist Party. On this or that issue we may even oppose each other strongly. But today there is only one France, the France of hope and of danger. Those who hoped together, who suffered, succumbed, and triumphed together, cannot allow themselves to be disunited just because certain foreign circles may hold one French party or another in suspicion.

Our allies must understand this and must choose either to recognize France or not. To postpone recognition until legislative elections that cannot be held before the end of the war is neither generous nor reasonable. If our American friends want a strong and united France, dividing France from outside is not a good way to go about it.

Some say, of course, that the French people have not spoken for five years and must be heard. This is not news to us. We fought to restore to the French people the right to speak. But the fact is that the people have just spoken. They spoke with their rifles and grenades from many barricades. Their voice, gruff and excited, was not of a sort to please everyone. But we swear to our friends that it was the voice of freedom itself.

We have lost many things in this war, but not so much that we are willing to resign ourselves to begging for what is rightfully ours. If we must keep silent and go to work by ourselves, we will do so. But that is not what we want. We want to be able to love our friends freely and to prove that there is no bitterness in our gratitude. We believe that we are not asking for much. And if that is still not convincing, then we ask that steps be taken to ease our difficult task in view of our long history of teaching the very name of freedom to a world that knew nothing about it.

October 1, 1944[103]

People say, "Tell us in a few words, what is it you want?"[104] This is a good question because it is direct. It calls for a direct answer. Of course that can't be done in one or two articles. As we return to it from time to time, however, we should strive to clarify our thinking.

---

[103] Editorial. Text probably by Camus, which picked up ideas expressed in the August 21 article "From Resistance to Revolution" and helped to define what might be called *Combat*'s political line.

[104] This text seems to be an indirect response to an article that appeared in *Défense de la France* on September 28. Like *Combat*, *Défense de la France* was a newspaper that came out of the underground. "Founded during the Occupation on July 14, 1941, former underground newspaper of the Resistance,"

As we have said more than once, we hope for a reconciliation of justice with liberty. Apparently this isn't clear enough. We shall therefore define "justice" as a social state in which each individual is granted every opportunity at the outset and in which the majority of the country's population is not kept in a shameful condition by a privileged minority. And we shall call "liberty" a political climate in which the human person is respected as to what it is and what it expresses.

That much is fairly basic. The difficulty has to do with the balance that is struck between these two definitions, as is shown by historical experiments with both. History offers us a choice between the triumph of justice and that of liberty. Only the Scandinavian democracies have come close to the necessary reconciliation of the two. But their example is not entirely convincing on account of their relative isolation and of the limited framework within which they have operated.

Our idea is that the reign of justice must be ensured in the economic sphere while liberty is guaranteed in the political sphere. Since we are making statements about fundamentals, we will say that what we want for France is a collectivist economy and liberal politics. Without the collectivist economy, which takes privilege away from money in order to grant it to labor, liberal politics is a fraud. But without constitutional guarantees of political liberty, the collectivist economy risks absorbing all individual initiative and expression. A constant, carefully balanced equilibrium between the two is a necessary and sufficient condition, not for the happiness of mankind, which is another matter, but for each individual to bear sole responsibility for his happiness and destiny. It is simply a matter of not adding a purely human injustice to the profound miseries of our condition.

In short, and we beg pardon for repeating what we have said before, we want to establish a true people's democracy without delay. Indeed, we believe that any polity that cuts itself off from the working class is pointless and that the France of tomorrow will be what the working class becomes.[105]

That is why we want the immediate implementation of a constitution in which liberty will be granted its guarantees and of an economy in which labor will be granted its rights, which are primary. It is impossible to go into details here. We shall do so whenever necessary. For those who know how to read us, we have already done so on any number of specific points.

A word also needs to be said about method. We believe that the difficult equilibrium we are seeking cannot be achieved without unremitting intellectual and moral honesty, which alone can provide the necessary clarity of mind. We do not

---

as the paper billed itself, its first open issue appeared on August 9, 1944, in Rennes. Only on September 17 did it begin to give a Paris address: it shared quarters at 100, rue Réaumur with *Franc-Tireur* and *Combat*. It used the same printer as *Combat* and was also produced by unionized workers. Its first Paris edition appeared on September 22. As of November 8, 1944, the paper took the name *France-Soir* while retaining *Défense de la France* as its subtitle. On several occasions the two papers engaged in polemics, in a friendly tone at first but more aggressively later on.

Robert Salmon's article reproached "some of our best friends" for engaging in systematic criticism of the government, said to reflect the "intellectual's taste for hypercriticism, degenerating into sympathy for anarchy . . . a priori suspicion of a minister because he does not belong to the same tendency they do."

[105] In fact, this paragraph repeats verbatim phrases used previously in "From Resistance to Revolution."

believe in political realism. Lies, even well-intentioned lies, separate men from one another and relegate them to the most futile solitude. We believe that, on the contrary, men are not alone and that when faced with hostile conditions, their solidarity is total. Anything that serves this solidarity and reinforces this communion, hence anything that involves sincerity, is just and free.

That is why we believe that political revolution cannot take place without moral revolution, which goes hand in hand with it and establishes its true dimension. This may help to explain the tone that we are attempting to give to this newspaper. It is simultaneously a tone of objectivity, of free criticism, and of energy. If only people made the effort to understand and accept it, we are foolish enough to believe that for many Frenchmen a period of great hope would begin.

October 3, 1944[106]

The *Daily Mail* has just published an interesting article on the French press by Allan Forbes.[107] It goes without saying that this article is well-disposed toward France. It simply sets forth the views of a perceptive colleague, who is surprised that the French press in general devotes more space to domestic politics than to news of the war. The English journalist is glad that this is not the case in his country.

He is right to be glad. This fact is proof that England is in good health. That is not the case with France. We have criticized the shortcomings of the French press often enough not to take exception to objective criticism courteously presented. But objectivity requires us to set Mr. Forbes's observations in context.

To begin with, why don't we devote more space to the war? The answer is simple: we don't receive any more information than we publish. All our war news comes from one source: the Agence Française de Presse,[108] which, incidentally, has been doing its job competently. Unlike our British colleagues, we do not have the two or three national and foreign agencies and foreign bureaus we need. No French newspaper today is able to send a correspondent abroad, not even to Geneva. We can't even get a journalist out to the front at Saint-Nazaire.

Furthermore, English papers can add dispatches from their own war correspondents to their other sources of information. After more than a month of attempts, we have not managed to persuade the Allied armies to accredit ours. Clearly, in this case, our responsibility has to be judged in light of these circumstances.

As a rough estimate, we would guess that we receive about one-third as much war news as our British colleagues. It should therefore surprise no one that we

---

106 Editorial. Typescript.

107 The *Daily Mail*, founded in 1896, is an important British daily newspaper. In the 1930s it had the largest circulation of any newspaper in the world.

108 The successor to the Havas agency, which became the Office Français de l'Information during the Occupation, the Agence Française de Presse was established by an order dated September 30, 1944, which stipulated that "conditions [will be set] under which a cooperative news agency will replace the A.F.P." But Roger Stéphane, writing in *Combat* in 1947, remarked that this still had not been done and that the A.F.P. was operating as a state agency. In 1957 a new law was approved.

publish one-third as much. It is a mistake to believe that we wouldn't devote to the war all the attention it deserves, if we had the opportunity. The war is still the public's chief interest, and even from a purely professional standpoint we aren't so blind as to fail to see the implications of that.

That brings us to the matter of domestic political coverage. It is true that this is the original sin of the French. It is true that our press does not always discriminate between lucid criticism and sterile polemic. But our English friends mustn't forget that the French have good reason to put so much energy, and at times vehemence, into their domestic demands. England did not experience, as we did, the phenomenon of official treason.

For four years that treason poisoned national life in France, and it continues to distort the issues we find most painful. England has not had to deal with shame. No Englishman has been forced, as we have been, to refuse his hand to another Englishman. In Great Britain contempt is not obligatory.

No other nation has had to deal with treason such as we have endured, which is unique by virtue of its duration, its extent, and its efficiency. Obviously this creates certain problems, and there would be no point in postponing dealing with them until later. Indeed, some of us remain vigilant in regard to domestic problems precisely because we are thinking about the war. We know from sad experience that a country cannot wage war without being certain of its health. We were very sick. It isn't reasonable to think that convalescence is now a foregone conclusion and that we can wage democracy's war without simultaneously making democracy itself a reality.

Allan Forbes concludes his article with a plea for understanding between the two countries. We would not be so presumptuous as to speak on behalf of a majority of Frenchmen. But those we know feel a desire for an understanding with England that is deep and warm and without ulterior motives. To that end, however, we must admit our mutual weaknesses and make an effort to understand them. Ours are the most glaring today. We have no particular reason to be proud of them. But we have no reason to be ashamed of them either. All anyone can ask of us is to make a good-faith effort to remedy them. We have that good faith. And we hope our colleague will be kind enough to see a proof of this in the simplicity with which we have set forth our observations.

October 4, 1944[109]

It is no secret that the Underground Press Federation[110] has protested the ordinances published in the *Officiel* concerning the publication and operation of newspapers. The Federation has appealed to General de Gaulle against the Government. There are reasons for this seeming paradox.

---

[109] Editorial. Typescript.

[110] The Fédération de la Presse Clandestine protested on September 30 that it had not been consulted about the decisions taken by the Council of Ministers. Since the new ordinances had not yet been published in the *Officiel*, the Federation expressed the hope that the texts would conform "to the plan already

The public might find this baffling. But the problem is clear, and if we are reacting so vigorously, it is because the problem is also serious. What is it? The *Officiel* has just published the ordinances concerning the press. In regard to all matters of direct concern to the journalists of the Resistance—to wit, the eventual publication of new newspapers (art. I, par. 3), the composition of the credentials committee responsible for excluding collaborators (art. IX), and sales price, allocation of paper, format, and publication frequency of newspapers (art. XIII)—these texts grant all power to the relevant ministries with no provision for consultation with the newspapers of the Resistance.

We oppose these measures. We are not keen to go to war against the Government. Indeed, we hope that the Government will avoid wars of this sort. We are defending not a position but an ethos. And if those in official circles were willing to reason along with us, they would have no difficulty recognizing that ethos, which is now hidden from them by too many intervening advisers.

Let us lay down a principle. The Government at the moment is forced by circumstances to govern without Parliament. Indeed, the only ones left who don't see that it is forced to do so are foreigners. We assume, moreover, that the Government does not wish to govern alone. Hence it must rely on something.

Would we appear naïve if we proposed that, on every issue, it rely on specialists in dealing with that issue? What do we mean by "specialists"? Not just people who are familiar with the technical difficulties of a profession but those who are familiar with both the technical difficulties and the ethical difficulties. What we have just given is a definition of the journalists represented in the Underground Press Federation.

These are the journalists who denounced the treason of the French press and the unworthiness of its representatives. They produced the underground newspapers. Today, resistance seems easy. Everybody resisted, as everybody knows. At the time, however, it bears repeating that the journalists of the Resistance, no doubt poorly informed, felt rather alone. In their solitude, they thought things over. They noticed that the dishonor of the French press had as much to do with individuals as with institutions. They changed things by taking steps that made a veritable revolution in the press possible. The public is still not altogether aware of these changes. But the action of the Underground Federation allowed our papers to appear in the middle of the insurrection and allows them to thrive today in complete freedom, without financial or moral servitude of any kind.

That is one concrete result. But we need to keep an eye on this young revolution. And we want to be consulted. Not for the sake of pointless prestige but because of the thinking we did while underground and of the knowledge that came to us in the night, which we are determined to put to use. If the Government does not rely on us in this matter, it will rely on nothing. Or it will rely on a host of eager counselors with advice to give, because they were among those who at first

---

adopted in clandestinity, which was dictated by one desire only, namely, to wrest control of the press from the trusts." It asked that "no decision concerning the press be taken without the prior agreement of those who represented and still represent the French Resistance."

shrugged their shoulders and said nothing would change anything and were then dumbfounded to discover that something had been changed in the meantime.

We cannot believe that the Government wants to rely on nothing. But we do not want to believe that it prefers those who are giving it advice today over those who paid yesterday. We must therefore go over the head of those advisers to appeal to another man, who was the first to pay and who showed that he, at least, had a conception of honor. That is why, despite the seeming paradox, we appeal to Charles de Gaulle against his government.[111]

To be candid, we do so with no particular joy. We would rather not be obliged to say no. But we act with determination because of the secret oath that each of us took in the solitude of the resistance years and none of us can ever forget.

October 5, 1944[112]

We have said before in this space how much we owe to our Spanish comrades.[113] This needed to be said, we believed, because when fascism began to spread its oppressive doctrines throughout Europe in 1938, the Spanish were the first to experience the desperate silence that ensued. We still believe that our fight is their fight and that we cannot be either happy or free as long as Spain is brutalized and enslaved.

That is why we are astonished by the treatment that continues to be meted out to men who never failed in their duty to liberty. If we talk about the Spaniards, it is because we know them well. But the same treatment has been reserved for many antifascist émigrés, and we wish to support the protest that has been lodged with the appropriate minister by the Justice Committee of the C.N.R.[114] in regard to a particular instance of this treatment.[115]

What is going on? By virtue of a few simple regulations, the government is once again concentrating Spanish Republicans in a Parisian barracks or else shipping

[111] See the text of that appeal: "The threatened press appeals to de Gaulle": "The National Federation of the French Press, deeply disturbed by the series of ordinances published in the *Officiel* on October 1 and 2, 1944, has decided to ask for an audience with the president of the Provisional Government of the French Republic in order to submit to him its vehement protest against these measures, which it regards as directly contrary to the spirit of the Resistance, the freedom of the press, and the honor of France."

[112] Editorial. Typescript.

[113] See editorial of September 7, above, p. 29.

[114] The Conseil National de la Résistance, or National Resistance Committee (C.N.R.), was established in 1943 by Jean Moulin, whom General de Gaulle had assigned to federate and coordinate the various resistance movements inside France. After Moulin's arrest, Georges Bidault became head of the C.N.R. On Bidault, see the editorial of October 8, 1944, p. 64 below.

[115] *Combat* reported on the same day that "the Justice Committee of the C.N.R. is protesting the slowness of the purge [*épuration*]," referring to the purge of former collaborators.

"This Commission, received by M. de Menthon, is protesting the slow pace of prosecution and the fact that certain ministers (Monzie, Prouvost) and business leaders (Hotchkiss) are still at large. Members of the commission observed that these facts are all the more surprising in view of the fact that antifascist émigrés are hunted down and arbitrarily incarcerated every day."

them off to the provinces, where they are in danger of finding themselves defenseless. Before saying how this has come to pass, we would like to refresh the memories of those without imagination. In 1938, people for whom we found the name "refugees" (even though we still had no idea of how weighty a meaning this word would eventually acquire) were mostly housed in concentration camps. During the war, either they signed up voluntarily or we forced them into labor.

The Vichy regime did not stop at such noble tactics. It asked these men to choose between slavery and death. Spanish Republicans had either to work for Germany or return to Spain. Most of our comrades joined the underground and fought for our freedom, which, with a tenacity deserving of a better fate, they persisted in thinking of as their own. Others, in the cities, obtained false work certificates. And still others worked for the occupier.

Today, all this is being sorted out. Republicans who used fake or real German work certificates to regularize their situation are now being concentrated in the Kellermann Barracks or shipped outside the *département* of the Seine. Meanwhile, those who fought with the underground find themselves in the most awkward position because they failed to apply for a place in the order established by the Germans. As a result, they can be, and in some cases are, arrested at any time.

For six years they have been on the run. These men have endured not only defeat and exile but also six years of humiliation and disappointment. Meanwhile, propaganda from certain quarters has harmed our comrades' reputation in the minds of some Frenchmen.

But we want to say as forcefully as possible that, on the contrary, these men were the first to set an example of courage and dignity for us, and we ought to be proud to reach out to them.

Against this elementary sentiment, bureaucratic arguments have been raised. But the issue is not a matter of bureaucracy. It is a matter of the heart. And if the bureaucratic regulations fail to correspond to these deeply felt desires, the solution is quite simple: the regulations must be changed before we forget one iota of the debt of gratitude we owe to Spain.

These thoughts came to mind yesterday as we were leaving a showing of *Sierra de Teruel*, [André] Malraux's overwhelming film about the war in Spain.[116] We would have liked everyone in France to see the faces of those warriors and of that

---

116 On the same day *Combat* published an unsigned review of this film, which Camus surely at least read over. Its text reads as follows: "*Sierra de Teruel*, a film by André Malraux. Only a few viewers enjoyed the privilege of attending a showing of *Sierra de Teruel*, the film that Malraux based on his novel *L'Espoir* (*Man's Hope*). A still from the film appears on page 1. But what we cannot reconstitute for our readers is the overwhelming truth of this film, which was shot with no resources other than poverty and courage. The simple story of these few men who join a squadron and die on a mountaintop achieves grandeur without any sense of effort or strain. For that, the note of truth was enough, along with the Spanish faces, whose presence, naturalness, and pride grip the heart when you think about what fate held in store for them. There is also the leitmotif of the film, in which all these men, confronted with the most heroic tasks, say simply that they will do what they can. And indeed, the whole world has seen what they could do. This film will no doubt be shown to the public. It is a miracle, by the way, that the sole copy survived, for the Germans thought they had burned it when in fact they only destroyed a copy of *Drôle de drame*."

matchless people joined together in heroic sacrifice. If we are to lay claim to the title of "great nation," we must be able to recognize grandeur and salute it wherever it exists. And there isn't a man worthy of the name who would not have felt a twinge in his heart yesterday at the sight of those images of a battle that was unequal from the outset yet never given up for lost.

We are well aware that it is impossible to receive Franco's ambassador while at the same time doing justice to the men he insults. We say that a choice has to be made. In any case, it is not possible to evade an imperious duty by pretending to abide by absurd regulations. And if the bureaucrats persist in ignoring this fact, then the bureaucracy will have to be destroyed to prevent them from landing us once again in the wretched situation of a country that extols republican freedom while persecuting its proudest defenders.

October 6, 1944[117]

There was plenty of noise in the night sky over France yesterday.[118] The sound of explosions and destruction, the very voice of death. At regular intervals the war thus reminds those who would otherwise be quick to forget that it is still raging.

At the same time we are told that the Allies may some day be obliged to announce an end to hostilities without having signed an armistice, because Hitler wants no end to the war. And Dr. Goebbels[119] has declared that every house in Germany will be defended to the death. At regular intervals the war thus stokes otherwise deficient imaginations.

The point is that we can never have memory or imagination enough to rise to the level demanded by the destiny that is now ours. To repeat what needs to be repeated, liberation is not peace. It is only the hard-won right to deserve peace by winning the war. We were forced to fight this war.[120] The whole world knows that France did not want it and that the best of her sons were cut down while dreaming of peaceful futures. Now that we are at war, however, we know who our enemy is. In 1933, many Frenchmen measured only what we had to lose in war. Today, we know what we have to gain.

Hence we must fight the war. And our first victory, won at such great cost, is the knowledge that we can make war without giving up any of our past faith, that we can win without hatred, fight while holding violence in contempt, and choose heroism while retaining our taste for happiness. But this victory is only the first. We need another, a definitive one, so that we can do something to make people happy without making them shed blood.

---

[117] Editorial. Typescript.

[118] More than 7,000 bombers took part in a gigantic attack on Germany, and the city of Saarbrücken in particular.

[119] On Goebbels, see the March 1944 issue of underground *Combat*, n. 2, p. 1 above.

[120] Once again, Camus reverts to one of the major themes of *Lettres à un ami allemand.*

But how are we to make war? Every country wages war as it can. The world must not forget that France, in order to wage war, must liquidate treason. Some say that we can make war only if we are united. That is true if people are willing to understand one another. It is true that personal quarrels, sterile polemics, and bad faith must be banished. But the experience of the war of 1939 teaches us that one cannot wage democracy's war abroad while suppressing democracy at home.

We have no personal quarrels to pursue, but we do have questions of principle to explore. That is where France must bring its youthful vigor to bear. Great countries are those that can endure history's convulsions without abandoning their efforts to solve their problems at home.

Great Britain has set an example for us to follow. To be sure, we must be sparing in our criticism. But we must also be that much more energetic in making those criticisms that we judge to be vital. Strength of character lies in saying no as clearly as we say yes, and strength of character is what we must aim for. This country wants to wage its war in conditions of total transparency.

To wage war, France requires not only unity but also truth. There is now but one war for all of us, and that is the war of truth. For many years to come, falsehood will make us feel weak, and only the harsh light of sincerity can give us strength.

Only under these conditions, then, can we associate this country in its entirety with a war that there is every reason to expect will go on for quite some time. If the people of France are granted their full rights, they will acknowledge their duties unbidden. No future is possible for this country unless it is capable of striking a disciplined balance between force and justice, in which each compensates for and reinforces the other. We want no justice without victory. But we have spent four years learning that a victory disdainful of all justice would be only a mockery of victory.

October 7, 1944[121]

In Algiers on March 26, 1944, the Congress of *Combat* declared that the "Combat" movement subscribed to the following statement: "Anti-Communism is the first step toward dictatorship." We think it worthwhile to remind people of this and to add that not a word of this statement needs to be changed today, as we seek to explore with some of our Communist comrades certain misunderstandings that have arisen recently. Indeed, we are convinced that nothing good can be done in secrecy. And today, in broaching one of the most difficult of all subjects, we want to try the language of reason and humanity.

The principle set forth above was not adopted without reflection. It was the experience of the past twenty-five years that dictated this categorical proposition. This does not mean that we are Communists. But neither are the Christians,

---

[121] Editorial. Text reprinted in *Actuelles*, chapter entitled "Morale et politique."

who are nevertheless prepared to countenance united action with Communists. Our position, like that of the Christians, amounts to saying that while we are not in agreement with the philosophy or practical ethics of Communism, we vigorously reject political anti-Communism because we know what inspires it and what its unavowed aims are.

So firm a position should leave no room for any possible misunderstanding. Yet this turns out not to be the case. Hence we must have expressed ourselves awkwardly or just plain obscurely. Our task now is to try to comprehend those misunderstandings and explain them. There can never be enough candor or clarity in dealing with one of the most important problems of the century.

Let us begin, therefore, by stating clearly that one possible source of misunderstanding is a difference in method. Most of our comrades' collectivist ideas and social program, their ideal of justice, and their disgust with a society in which money and privilege occupy the front ranks, we share. But as our comrades freely recognize, their adherence to a very consistent philosophy of history justifies their acceptance of political realism as the primary method for securing the triumph of an ideal shared by many Frenchmen. On this matter we very clearly differ. As we have said many times, we do not believe in political realism.[122] Our method is different.

Our communist comrades can understand that certain other people, not in possession of a doctrine as firm as theirs, had a lot to think about these past four years. And they did their thinking with an open mind, amid a thousand perils.

As countless ideas were swept aside and countless unblemished souls were sacrificed amid the ruins, they felt the need for a new doctrine and a new life. For them a whole world died in June 1940.

Today they are looking for that new truth with the same good will and open-minded spirit. It is easy to understand, too, that these same men, reflecting on the bitterest of defeats and conscious of their own deficiencies, found that their country had sinned by confusion and that in order for the shape of the future to emerge, considerable effort must be devoted to achieving a new clarity and vision.

That is the method we are attempting to apply today. We hope that others will grant us the right to make such an attempt in good faith. The intention is not to reinvent the country's politics from top to bottom. It is to undertake a very limited experiment: to introduce the language of morality into the practice of politics by means of simple, objective criticism. What this comes down to is saying yes and no at the same time, and saying both with the same seriousness and the same objectivity.

If you read us carefully, and with the straightforward goodwill that you would accord to anyone who acted in good faith, you will see that we often give with one hand what we seem to take away with the other, and more. If you concentrate

---

[122] Recall that the notion of "political realism," already denounced in connection with Spain, is here opposed to the frequently repeated wish to introduce morality into politics. This text is particularly important in defining the position of Camus—and *Combat*—with respect to the Communists in 1944.

solely on our objections, misunderstandings are inevitable. But if you balance those objections against our oft-repeated declarations of solidarity, you will see clearly that we are trying not to give in to futile human passion and consistently endeavoring to do justice to one of the most impressive political movements in history.

At times it may be difficult to see what the point of our method is. Journalism is not noted as a school of perfection. It may take a hundred issues of a newspaper to state a single idea clearly. But that idea can help to clarify others, provided that the same objectivity that went into formulating it is employed in scrutinizing its implications.

It may also be that we are mistaken, that our method is utopian and impossible to apply. Nevertheless, we believe that it is wrong to decide this in advance, before anything has been attempted. What we are doing here is conducting an experiment as honestly as men concerned with nothing other than honesty can do.

We ask our communist comrades only to ponder this as we ponder their objections. At the very least we will both gain by clarifying our positions, and we, for our part, will benefit by learning more about the difficulties inherent in our project and its likelihood of success. That is why we address our comrades in these terms. That, and our acute sense of what France would stand to lose if our mutual doubts and suspicions were to lead us into a political climate in which the best people in France would refuse to live, choosing solitude over polemic and discord.

October 8, 1944[123]

Yesterday, the National Council of the Resistance [hereafter: NCR] introduced itself to the people of Paris for the first time.[124] Hence it was possible to hear at last the representatives of what M. Georges Bidault[125] called "the political and spiritual families that contributed to the grandeur of this free country."

---

[123] Editorial. Typescript.

[124] On the National Council of the Resistance, see the text for October 5. On October 7, a press release was issued announcing a meeting of the NCR at the Vél' d'hiv' (or Vélodrôme d'Hiver, a bicycle race track): "For the first time since the liberation of Paris, the members of the NCR are today going to meet directly with the people." In fact, the NCR had apparently lost some of its authority following the formation of a government on September 9. (It is worth noting that no newspaper at the time made the slightest allusion to the fact that the same venue, the Vél' d'hiv', had been used as a temporary prison for foreign Jews rounded up by the French police on July 16 and 17, 1942.)

[125] Georges Bidault (1899–1983) was a member of the "Combat" movement and president of the National Resistance Council. After the arrest of Jean Moulin, he played an important role in relations between the internal resistance and General de Gaulle. He became minister of foreign affairs in September 1944 and continued to serve in that capacity in several Fourth Republic governments. He was also a founder of the Mouvement Républicain Populaire.

We are not sure that all of France has a clear idea of what the Resistance was and what role the NCR played in it. True, there has been a lot of talk about it since the liberation. But it takes imagination to see beyond the words to the everyday truth, the harsh suffering, and the feverish hours that filled these past four years. Nor is it clear that all of France properly appreciates the intentions of the men of the Resistance.

It is true that the NCR and the newspapers have often said that they felt they had a right to be consulted. It would be a serious mistake, however, to conclude from this that they wished to exclude others or that the Resistance entertained an exaggerated notion of what it was due.

Some readers may have noticed that yesterday's speeches, taken together, outlined a firm and well-developed program that would have surprised many of its defenders before the war.[126] But the ordeal of defeat and struggle proved decisive for these men of honorable intention.

Some on the right, who had never given any thought to the social problem, understood that a nation could not live cut off from its own people, and that what was given to the people would in the end redound to the benefit of the nation. Some on the left, whose ideal of justice transcended their native land, realized that no ideal could be sustained in a subjugated country, and that whatever one did for an unjustly humiliated nation would ultimately redound to the benefit of justice itself.

Here we touch on what is most significant about the Resistance. Through a rebellion of the heart, it brought together certain truths of the intellect. Because the men of the Resistance have a precise idea of what they have to teach, they felt it was their duty to continue by way of speech and action what they began in silence. That is why the NCR spoke yesterday, and why it daily asks to be consulted. But the very reasons for its action, the common understanding through which so many ideas once thought to be hostile to one another have been reconciled for the sake of the nation's grandeur, guarantee that the action of the Resistance will continue to transcend personal prejudices and ambitions.

We here deeply believe one thing: the Resistance does not wish to impose itself but wants only to be listened to. Many of us are conscious of having done no more than what duty required. Doing one's duty requires no reward or publicity and need not result in special prerogatives.[127] If nothing else, maybe it gives the

---

[126] Speaking to a crowd of some 15,000, one speaker after another protested against the Allies' failure to recognize the French government. They insisted on punishment of traitors and confiscation of the property of collaborators. They called for nationalization of important firms, denounced the insurance companies and large lending institutions, touched on social security, and declared that a free press was essential for guaranteeing free institutions. They called on people to be wary of anti-Semitism and insisted on equality for all citizens, including citizens of the colonial empire. Georges Bidault, minister of foreign affairs and former president of the NCR, said, "We cannot isolate ourselves from all the political and spiritual families that contributed to the grandeur of this free country."

[127] At this point in the text, a line was omitted, replaced by another line that repeated a previous one. This is true of both the published article and the typescript, which proves that the typescript was prepared from the published article. It was not difficult to restore the few words that were omitted, however.

right to do it again on occasion. The Resistance did what it could to restore this country's freedom. But that meant giving the people their sovereignty. The Resistance knew that, and that was the end it sought. It paid for what it did with suffering that is hard to contemplate and deaths that some of us will never be able to forget. But that was the price that had to be paid so that the French people could emerge from their silence. That has now been accomplished.

In a few months, perhaps, the people will decide what politics and what government they desire. No one can understand what the Resistance was and remains until he has fully grasped the meaning of this gravest and most important of truths.

If the people of France are someday allowed to express themselves freely and choose to disavow the politics of the Resistance, the Resistance would bow to their will, and those men who believed it was their duty to continue their service to their country would return home to resume the private lives and enjoy the less demanding gratifications on which they turned their backs for a while, in the midst of defeat, because they felt, at the time justifiably, that there were things to be done that could not be done without them.

October 11, 1944[128]

The situation of the press poses problems. Those problems have in fact been discussed in the press. And the public has tried to understand, at times impatiently, at other times anxiously. Apparently the discussion looked a bit like a family quarrel, and everybody knows we should be giving more space to dispatches from our war correspondents, even though they still haven't been accredited. But if newspapers are to deal with the war, one first has to have newspapers—real newspapers, that is. Obviously the issue is still the same, since we are convinced that what is at stake is the very existence of the new press.

Why not try to explain to the public, in measured terms, the reasons for our worry? And why not say clearly, for example, that there will soon be a clash between the new press and the old. There is in fact talk of reviving old names. Having thought it over, we are generally opposed to this. Why?

What the public is not sufficiently aware of is that journalism is the only area of our national life to have been fully purged, because during the insurrection newspaper staffs were cleaned out from top to bottom. This purge was carried out in one day. Its advantage over others is that it was more radical. The newspapers being published today may have their faults but at least they are supported solely by the proceeds from their sales. France now has a press liberated from the power of money for the first time in a hundred years.

We admit that we're keen on this revolution. And, admittedly, we are generally suspicious of the old titles. There are distinctions to be made in this regard.

---

[128] Editorial. Typescript.

There are papers that saw nothing wrong with resuming publication during the Occupation, whether in the northern zone after June 1940 or in the southern zone after November 1942. As far as those papers are concerned, pardon us if we say simply that we no longer want anything to do with them.

There are other papers that did not resume publication during the Occupation. Two cases need to be distinguished, however. There are those that courageously scuttled themselves and never forfeited their honor. They include *Le Figaro*[129] and *Le Progrès de Lyon*.[130] They have their place among us, which they occupy with such competence and dignity that we can always benefit from their experience. What is more, we did not wait for any official decision to welcome them back, and we did so gladly.

But there are other newspapers that did not publish during the Occupation because they were not authorized to do so, despite their negotiations with the German authorities.

And there are still others that did not resume publication but rented their equipment and offices to the occupiers and profited from a situation from which they could no longer derive prestige. We are on firm ground in saying that the verdict in their case is a foregone conclusion.

Some say that these old names could resume publication with new personnel. We see no point, however, in adding to the confusion. The reason given for this proposal is that the public is used to the old names. The response to this is that the public will get used to the new ones. If there are people who absolutely must read a newspaper that did not originate with the underground, they can buy *Le Figaro*, which is quite good. What is more, this argument starts from the premise that the public is naturally inert. That opinion was current before the war, precisely in the old newspapers, but over the past four years it has gone out of fashion. The first condition for becoming a good independent journalist is to learn not to be automatically contemptuous of one's reader.

Last but not least, there will no doubt be some who say that we take the position we do for fear of the competition. In this instance, in other words, we are the ones who are supposed to be contemptible. Let us simply say this: we have paid dearly for what we have won. We hope that the price paid by journalists in the cause of freedom will earn them if nothing else the esteem of those who take an interest in them. We know in the bottom of our heart that we will always accept, and feel grateful for, the competition of talent. What we no longer want is the competition of money. We are prepared to listen to reason, to whatever is in the national interest. But we see nothing in the arguments that have been raised against us worthy of anything other than regret and disdain.

---

[129] *Le Figaro* abandoned Paris for Lyons in May 1940. It ceased publication in November 1942, when the previously "free zone" was occupied. It surfaced again when Paris was liberated, with Pierre Brisson as editor.

[130] *Le Progrès de Lyon* ceased publication from November 1942 until the liberation of Lyons. Several of its journalists, including René Leynaud, joined the Resistance. See the editorial of October 27, 1944, p. 90 below.

If we cannot have understanding, then we ask to be shown a little patience. Allow the new press time to prove itself, notwithstanding the faults of which it is well aware. We make so bold as to point out that there is some basis for granting a reprieve in what the new press accomplished after June 1940.

October 12, 1944[131]

There is much talk of order right now. This is because order is a good thing, and we have sorely felt its lack. The fact is that the men of our generation have never known order at all, and the nostalgia they feel for it might make them do many imprudent things if they weren't also convinced that it ought to be indistinguishable from truth. This makes them somewhat suspicious and careful when it comes to choosing among the samples of order that have been proposed to them.

For order is also an obscure notion. It comes in several kinds. There is the order that continues to reign in Warsaw,[132] there is the order that hides disorder, and there is the order that Goethe loved, which stands opposed to justice.[133] There is also the higher order of hearts and minds that goes by the name of love, and the bloody order in which man denies himself, and which draws its powers from hatred. We hope to distinguish the good order we have in mind from all of these.

Clearly the order under discussion right now is social order. But does "social order" mean nothing more than quiet in the streets? There is reason to doubt it. In the heart-wrenching days of August, in fact, we all felt that the first shots of the insurrection marked the beginning of order. As disorderly as revolutions may seem, they are pregnant with a principle of order. That principle can prevail if the revolution is total. But if the revolution fails to come off or stops halfway, years of oppressive and monotonous disorder follow.

Well, then, does order mean government unity? Unity is essential, to be sure. But the German Reich achieved such unity, and still we cannot say that it brought true order to Germany.

Maybe it would help if we looked simply at individual behavior. When do we say that a man has put his life in order? When he is in accord with what he does and his conduct is consistent with what he believes to be true. The insurgent who dies in the chaos of passion for an idea he has embraced is in fact a man of order,

---

[131] Editorial. Text reprinted in *Actuelles*, chapter "Morality and Politics."

[132] There are several allusions here. The first is to statements made by Marshal Sebastiani to the Chamber of Deputies in 1831 when a Polish uprising was crushed by the Russians. This led to the publication in the newspaper *La Caricature* of a celebrated lithograph depicting a Russian soldier standing among bodies, with a caption that read: "Order reigns in Warsaw." Finally, at the time Camus wrote, Warsaw was still under German occupation; it would not be liberated until January 17, 1945.

[133] Goethe, Johann Wolfgang von (1749–1832). Obviously Camus is not attacking the author of *The Sufferings of Young Werther, Faust, The Apprenticeship of Wilhelm Meister*, or the *Conversations with Eckermann*, whom he quoted frequently in his *Carnets*. He is rather attacking the Goethe who said that he preferred injustice to disorder.

because he has organized his conduct entirely around a principle that he regards as self-evident.

But no one can ever make us regard the privileged individual who all his life eats three square meals a day and owns a fortune in blue-chip securities but locks his doors whenever there is a disturbance in the streets as a man of order. He is merely a man with fear in his heart and money in the bank.

If order in France meant fainthearted caution, we would be tempted to regard it as the worst form of disorder, since indifference licenses injustice of every kind.

Which leads us to the conclusion that there is no order without equilibrium and harmony. As far as social order is concerned, this means equilibrium between the sole government and the people it governs. And harmony must be based on a higher principle. For us, that principle is justice. There is no order without justice, and the ideal order lies in the happiness of the people.

Hence one cannot invoke the need for order to impose one's wishes. To do so is to tackle the problem the wrong way around. One mustn't insist on order as a condition for good government; rather, one must govern well in order to achieve the only kind of order that makes sense. It is not order that reinforces justice but justice that bestows its certitude on order.

No one is keener than we are for the higher order characteristic of a nation at peace with itself and its destiny, in which each individual shares in both toil and leisure, in which workers can do their jobs without bitterness or envy, in which artists can create without being tormented by man's misery, and in which each person is at last free to meditate in silence upon his own condition.

We have no perverse taste for a world of violence and tumult in which we squander what is best in ourselves in hopeless conflict. But since the contest has begun, we believe that it must be played out to the end. Thus we believe that there is an order that we do not want because it would commit us to resignation and mark the end of all hope for humankind. As determined as we are to help found at last a just order, we are therefore equally determined to reject once and for all the celebrated remark of a great man[134] by declaring that we prefer disorder to injustice, eternally.

October 13, 1944[135]

It is impossible to exaggerate the importance of the statements made by the Minister of Colonies regarding the imperial problem. After remarking on the important role the Empire played in the Liberation, M. Pleven[136] added: "The loyalty of the native populations places large responsibilities on our shoulders. . . .

---

134 Goethe.

135 Editorial. Typescript.

136 René Pleven (1901–1993) joined the Free French Forces in London in July 1940. As Commissioner for Colonies for the NLC, he presided over the Brazzaville conference of January 1944, which laid the groundwork for political reform in Africa. In September 1944 he became Minister of Colonies in the

A new phase of our colonial life must therefore begin. Our goal will be . . . to conquer hearts."

These formulas are of course still vague, but we think we perceive a clear intention behind them. In any case, this statement deserves closer examination.

For those of us who were familiar with French colonial policy, it was dismaying to see how ignorant and indifferent most Frenchmen were to their Empire. Not for the first time, a small elite of administrators and bold adventurers gave its compatriots riches that they neglected. Today, though, France is too diminished in Europe not to attend to all her possessions. As we undertake a necessary review of our gains and losses, it would be inexcusable to continue to overlook our imperial territories.

Yet to do so is to raise any number of difficult and painful issues. These problems cannot be resolved unless we tackle them head-on. "The goal," M. Pleven declared, "is to give each colony as much political identity as possible." That's fine, and the question is relatively simple when it pertains exclusively to the native populations.

But let us take a specific example, North Africa, where we find ourselves dealing with both a French population and a native population.[137] Now, while it would be desirable to extend still further the political emancipation that the Provisional Government has granted to the natives of North Africa,[138] one must bear in mind that the most serious obstacle to this lies within the French population.

It would be stupid indeed to hide the fact that much of this population supported the policies of Vichy. And that they did so for precisely the same reasons that caused them to oppose any form of political emancipation for native people.

What people there call, rightly or wrongly, the colonial spirit has always resisted innovation of any kind, even when the most elementary sense of justice demanded it. And if the government wants to implement its policy of friendship and protection for Algerians, it must first persuade or overcome this resistance.

This is of the utmost importance. We must not ignore the fact that our defeat cost us prestige in the eyes of a virile people like the Arabs. Hence the French might be tempted to make a new show of force in order to regain what they lost through force.[139] No policy could be more blind. We will not find real support

---

Provisional Government and in November became Minister of Finance, replacing Aimé Lepercq, who had been killed in an automobile accident. He left the government in January 1946 and became one of the founders of the U.D.S.R. He later served both the Fourth and Fifth Republics in several different ministerial positions, including two stints as prime minister. He sat in parliament as a deputy from the Côtes-du-Nord from 1945 to 1973.

[137] There is no need to emphasize the clarity of Camus' thinking in this area. His commitments are known from his support for the Blum-Violette plan in 1937 and his reporting on "Misery in Kabylia," *Fragments d'un combat*, I, pp. 267–335.

[138] In an order issued on March 7, 1944, General de Gaulle's Provisional Government, then in Algiers, abolished all exceptional measures applicable to Muslims, granted them access to all civilian and military positions, and increased their representation in local assemblies (from one-third to two-fifths).

[139] A timely warning in view of the May 1945 riots in Sétif, which were followed by repression. See below the articles on the "crisis in Algeria," pp. 198ff.

in our colonies until we convince them that their interests coincide with ours and that we do not have two policies: one granting justice to the people of France and the other confirming injustice toward the Empire.

The only purpose of these reflections is to underscore the enormous difficulty of an issue that touches on so many national and international problems. Their sole point is to remind ourselves that in the war especially there is an imperial problem that we must first address rather than ignore and then resolve in the spirit of generosity that should be ours.

October 14, 1944[140]

Mr. Churchill said in his most recent speech that he hoped at last to see the French government recognized when our Consultative Assembly convenes.[141] But it is true that he was speaking only for himself. His expression of hope stood as proof that the decision was not solely his to make. That is why we have waited, in a spirit of goodwill, for an American voice to confirm that hope in one way or another. America has remained silent, however.

Faithful to our policy of sincerity, we will therefore address our comments to the Americans. The point is not to lash out or to speak as if we wielded a power we no longer possess. It is simply to reason.

We know exactly how things stand with us. What we are about to write may be painful for a Frenchman to say, but we are well aware that with our economy in ruins, our army without arms and without a munitions industry to back it, our farms without machinery, and our good intentions without the means to implement them, we are dependent on our Allies. Everything that we can place on the other side of the scales—our sacrifices, our past grandeur, our resistance— counts for nothing when it comes to the cold calculation of policy.

So today, at least, we must calculate coldly. We have already noted that American policy reflected an obvious wariness of General de Gaulle personally. And we said that we stood in solidarity with him. So much for our position, but our opponents in fact raise some rather different arguments, which seem to have some merit.

The one we wish to take up today is the assertion that the French government has not been recognized by the people of France and that recognition cannot be granted until the people of France have made their choice. Let us first point out

---

[140] Editorial. Typescript.

[141] See the editorials of September 29 and 30 above, pp. 51 and 52. The Consultative Assembly, which General de Gaulle set up in Algiers in September 1943 and which consisted at the time of representatives of the various resistance movements, was to be expanded to include representatives of the various political parties. Churchill mentioned this in his speech of September 28. The composition of the assembly was decided by a decree issued on October 12. It was to have 248 members, with 148 seats reserved for representatives of the metropolitan Resistance and 60 for members of parliament, pro rated among the parties represented in the National Assembly in 1939. All the parties would thus be represented along with the various resistance organizations.

to our Allies that this argument presented no obstacle on their side when it came to recognizing Franco.[142] American diplomacy today finds itself in a paradoxical situation. It is waging war against fascism while maintaining official relations with the most dictatorial of regimes and refusing to recognize a government born of the struggle against the Hitlerian oppressor.

Nor did the argument that the people must choose prevent the United States from recognizing the government of Vichy.[143]

The paradox is even more glaring in view of the fact that the United States at war recognized the government that collaborated with its enemy only to refuse to recognize the men of that same country who helped to destroy that enemy.

The logic of this policy is thus intermittent. It is understood, however, that it is a question not of logic but of realism. Some will say that America needed to maintain relations with Vichy in order to lay the groundwork for the North Africa landing and needed to stay in touch with Franco in order to keep him in line. What better proof could there be, then, that it makes no difference whether the government of France is recognized or not, supposing that French support is no longer needed.

There is a temptation at this stage of the discussion to point out that France's support was needed not so long ago and is still needed even now somewhere in the neighborhood of Belfort. Apparently, these would not be arguments based on reason. We might speak the language of reason, however, if we pointed out to the Allies that they cannot afford to neglect a nation whose geographical position and desire to rise from defeat give it a place in Europe whose importance cannot be denied. Others will respond that since the French people have yet to declare themselves, it is not the French people who are being alienated.

On this point, it should suffice to point out that France is now a country in which free expression is possible. The few conflicts that have arisen in regard to domestic issues that we shall soon consider give proof of this. Indeed, the independent attitude of the press allows us to use the press as an example. It has been unanimous in calling for recognition of de Gaulle's government. Not a single French voice has sought to oppose recognition. What America is hesitating to recognize today is all of France.

---

[142] Francisco Franco (1892–1975) became a Spanish general in 1926 and was appointed head of the Spanish Army in 1934. He made his mark by putting down a miners' strike in Asturias in 1934 (this became the basis of the play *Révolte dans les Asturies*, produced by Camus and his comrades at the Théâtre du Travail). He led a nationalist coup against the Spanish Republic in July 1936, and in January 1938 he became head of the Spanish state, government, and army. Following the nationalist victory in 1939, he assumed the title of El Caudillo and established an authoritarian police state with backing from the Church, the army, and large landowners. Having received support from the Germans and Italians during the civil war, he declared his neutrality in World War II. Some thought that the Allies would intervene in Spain after the surrender of Germany on May 8, 1945, but this did not happen, and the Franco regime endured until 1975. Franco's government was recognized in 1939.

[143] The United States did indeed recognize the government of Vichy. Diplomatic relations were not broken off until the Allies landed in North Africa on November 8, 1942. The United States did not grant de facto recognition to the Provisional Government of the French Republic until July 11, 1944. De jure recognition was not granted until October 23, 1944.

This much needed to be said. Simply, without bluster or obsequiousness, free Frenchmen are asking free Americans to treat them no less well than they treated Franco's toadies or Vichy's handmaidens. Free Frenchmen are assuring the people of America that political "realism" cannot be the future of Europe and that America will lose the peace even if it wins the war. The language of free men is the language of clarity. If our American friends are hiding their thoughts, let them say openly what they think, and we will then have to take this into account. That will do more for the world's peace and honor than years of secret diplomacy or calculated silences.

October 15, 1944[144]

We beg our readers' indulgence for returning to the issue of granting recognition to the government of France.[145] We are indeed obliged to consider our position in the world ourselves, since others remain silent on the matter. To be sure, President Roosevelt[146] made a statement on Friday. But he failed to dispel any ambiguities.

He did indeed note that the provisional government of France was a "de facto" government. In precise terms, that means that it is not recognized as the "de jure" government of France.[147] Mr. Roosevelt simply acknowledged that de Gaulle's government exists in fact, that it is there, that it has, in short, a historical reality but no juridical existence, and that, when all is said and done, it is not legal.

The situation is therefore unchanged, and we must return to cold reasoning and to our argument of yesterday. If we must rely solely on ourselves and not on the benevolence of others, we should at least demonstrate that we did nothing to deserve our isolation before resigning ourselves to it.

De Gaulle's government would be illegal only if the conditions for legality existed and it had nevertheless ignored them. To be sure, it needs to be approved by the people. But voting is impossible for millions of our fellow Frenchmen, who are still in concentration camps or prisons, dreaming of their faraway homeland. We need to wait for them.[148] It is out of respect for the heart—more legal than the law itself—that we reserve their right to speak.

No legality is possible in French institutions in the sense in which the word *legality* is understood by professors. We can't do anything about that. But there

---

[144] Editorial. Typescript.

[145] Continuation of the previous day's editorial. Camus devoted several editorials to the question of recognition of the French government by the Allies (September 29 and 30; October 17 and 19; pp. 51, 52, 75, and 78).

[146] Franklin Delano Roosevelt (1882–1945) was elected president of the United States for the first time in 1932. He played a key role in World War II, which the United States joined after the Japanese attacked Pearl Harbor on December 7, 1941. Camus would devote two editorials to Roosevelt: November 9, 1944, when he was reelected, and April 14, 1945, when he died.

[147] See n. 143 above.

[148] This insistence on awaiting the return of prisoners would be repeated when a date was set for elections.

is a legality higher than any other in honor and rebellion, which for four years formed the basis of our law and which the government of de Gaulle was the first to define. This remains our law, and will so remain until popular sovereignty is reestablished, the sovereignty of the people being the ultimate source of legality in this country, as the French government has consistently maintained.

To say that we have no legal existence amounts to saying that we are wrong to be in the situation we are in. This is tantamount to punishing us in our misfortune with indifference and disdain. If it came to that, however, might we not prefer such plain talk to the ostensibly legal argument that is raised against us now?

We are also told that there have been clashes between the French government and various resistance organizations.

Some say that this poses the risk of a dual political authority and ambiguity of command in regard to the army.

It is true that there have been conflicts. Indeed, they are the proof that this country is now free and that it has the government it needs. Those conflicts have been openly reported in the press and rapidly resolved. The enormous task we have taken on cannot be completed in a day. It calls for both the power that comes from unity and the power that comes from free criticism, both of which are characteristic of strong democracies.

We have never believed that the war of words between Mr. Roosevelt and Mr. Dewey[149] was a sign of American anarchy. Yet the candidates express themselves in terms never used in the French press. Such clashes of opinion are good and healthy as long as they don't become an automatic reflex. They are at once the seed and the fruit of liberty.

Those who assert the contrary seem to be asking us to sentence ourselves to a period of abject, quivering silence while submitting to a leader who, once chosen, should be allowed to rule as a dictator. Our government would presumably not be recognized until we renounced all freedom of expression. By means of this stunning logic, the allied democracies would then recognize only dictatorial governments. The Franco and Pétain episodes might suggest that this is what they want. But we refuse to believe this and prefer to ask our Allies to examine their argument.

If none of our arguments proves effective, we will speak as General de Gaulle spoke to the nation yesterday.[150] His language was superb. We cannot be suspected of indulgence, and we have already given proof of our independence. But we must say frankly that it has been years since France has heard such lofty and uncompromising language. In it we recognize a stubborn desire for truth and honor, disdain for artifice, and lucid courage. Let our friends have no doubt: this

---

[149] Roosevelt, a Democrat, was running for reelection against John Dewey, Republican. The election was set for November 7, 1944.

[150] *Combat* printed the complete text of the speech broadcast by General de Gaulle, in which he told the French that they must rely on themselves above all and called upon them to work together and to forge a "real, sincere, fraternal" union to "beat the enemy, assert ourselves to other countries, and reconstruct and repair our nation."

voice is the voice of France. It is telling them, and we join in telling them, that we will accept isolation if we must, but we cannot morally accept ambiguity. Let others tell France that they do not want her to participate in peace conferences, and let them tell her why. Whatever people of other countries may think, we will then prove that France is now strong enough to live without illusions, if nothing else.

October 17, 1944[151]

We must return once again to the recognition of the French government.[152] This will be the last time. But there is no truth without a little obstinacy, and sound reasoning is nothing if not accompanied by stubborn determination. Since we began by being frank, we have no choice but to persist in our candor.

We may be wrong; indeed, we hope we are wrong. If the nonrecognition of the provisional government stemmed from a deep commitment to the logic of democracy, we would accept it, even though we have shown how absurd the consequences of that logic are in this case. We believe, however, that behind the logic lurk certain ulterior motives.

Ulterior motives are common in any political climate, but they make it impossible for humans to breathe. For four years now, we have been learning that our chief desire in life was to be not just voters but human beings. As Lawrence put it, we want a revolution not to give power to a class but to give human life a chance.[153] So we don't like ulterior motives. What can we do about them? It will suffice to speak plainly.

The ulterior motive that concerns us right now is the following: it appears that some people do not want France to participate in the conferences that will lay the groundwork for peace and shape the future. Or at any rate they do not want France to have more than a consultative voice. In framing this thought, are we giving in to bitterness and a sense of persecution? Apparently not. For what we say is not presumption but fact.

There have in fact been two conferences, one at Dumbarton Oaks,[154] the other in Moscow.[155] We were not present. Yet the question of peace was discussed at both. At Dumbarton Oaks, Germany was discussed without consulting the

---

151 Editorial. Typescript.

152 Continuation of the two previous editorials.

153 Thomas Edward Lawrence (1888–1935), also known as "Lawrence of Arabia," fought to establish an Arab empire and created a literary oeuvre that includes *The Seven Pillars of Wisdom*. Camus quotes him several times in his notebooks and lectures; the phrase in the text is similar to one quoted in *Carnets I*, p. 183: "Lawrence: 'The Revolution should be made not to give power to a class but to give life a chance.'"

154 An important conference involving American, British, Chinese, and Russian representatives was held at Dumbarton Oaks near Washington, D.C., from August 21 to October 7, 1944. It laid the groundwork for international institutions to replace the League of Nations and culminated in the creation of the United Nations in June 1945.

155 Immediately after the end of the Dumbarton Oaks conference a meeting was held in Moscow on October 9, with Churchill himself and American representatives in attendance.

only nation with full knowledge of the German problem. As we have said on several occasions, moreover, the Moscow conference was a peace conference as much as a war conference.

This is where we see the true magnitude of the problem of nonrecognition. For according to the official argument, it was only our government that was not represented. But this is a silly argument. It is obvious that those who excluded the French government have it in mind to exclude the entire French nation from the future of Europe.

We are not megalomaniacs. It is quite possible to imagine a peace from which France would be excluded. For various reasons for which we do not bear sole responsibility, our strength is sufficiently diminished that others may refuse to hear our voice. But the question remains: What kind of peace is being sought?

On this point, we are uncompromising.

It is not possible to opt for a democratic politics at home while engaging in action that denies the very principles of democracy abroad. In other words, to fight a democratic war, one must seek a democratic peace. And our point is simply this: a democratic peace cannot do without our vote, any more than it can do without the votes of any of the other nations that will constitute the Europe of tomorrow.

The League of Nations that some are seeking to revive will be a League of Peoples if it is to be anything at all.[156] We say this without exasperation or anger, because we have no doubt that eventually it will become clear to our allies themselves. But they will take their time about it, and in the meantime it is they and not we who will be judged. France is not all of Europe, not by a long shot, but there surely can be no Europe without France. That is why we remain unperturbed.

As the months go by, moreover, we are losing interest in this question. France and its government can live perfectly well without recognition. We are satisfied to have demonstrated the absurdity of the policy that has been adopted toward us and to have made clear the logic and justice of our position. That is enough to secure our continued peace of mind and allow us to pursue our recovery with determination.

October 18, 1944[157]

Let us say a few words about the purge.[158] We have dealt with this subject often. This is not only because it is a difficult one but also because it calls for sangfroid, and sangfroid in such matters is not always possible.

---

[156] This concern can be seen in Camus's support for Garry Davis, as is attested by the positions he took in November and December 1948.

[157] Editorial. Typescript.

[158] The purge (*épuration*) of collaborators would be the subject of long and passionate polemics, not only in the immediate postwar period between proponents of justice such as Camus and champions of charity such as the writer François Mauriac but also today, among historians, who argue about its legitimacy and extent. Camus here lays down principles to which he would frequently revert later on.

Let us begin by saying that the purge is necessary. This is not as obvious as it may seem. Some people in France would like to leave things as they stand, and those who feel this way do not always do so for disreputable reasons. The only answer to this objection is the following: if we are to leave things as they stand, we must know that everything that needs to be done has been done. In fact, however, some of what needs to be done has been done, but not everything.

The point is not to purge a lot but to purge well. But what does it mean to purge well? It means to respect the general principle of justice without failing to make allowances in individual cases.

What is the general principle of justice in this case? It lies in proportion. It is ridiculous to make an example of some bureaucratic department head who remained faithful to his habit of obedience while leaving important industrialists and opinion-makers untouched.

To every privilege correspond certain duties, and that is why the purge of government bureaucracies, which can be left to local committees,[159] cannot proceed without a purge at the national level, to be conducted in strict accordance with certain well-defined principles.

The state is bound to punish those functionaries who forgot that before being servants of the state they were servants of France. It must also judge the guilt of state agencies whose prestige derives from the prestige of the nation.

To purge the government may be a good thing, but the instruments of justice should also be applied to other institutions such as the banks and major industries. The only way to do this, moreover, is to clarify the notion of proportional responsibility to which we alluded earlier.

As inclined as we may feel to show indulgence to the feckless Frenchmen who acted with no clear idea of the national interest in mind, we are just as inclined to show no mercy to those responsible for this country's leading interests.

The case of M. Sacha Guitry can easily be settled by banning him from the stage for life.[160] People should be punished by striking at their most vital interests—in this case, vanity. But such mild measures will not do in dealing with men whose lives were based on the respect and privilege they were accorded by the nation. To put it bluntly, the notion of "consorting with the enemy" (*indignité nationale*) is useful.[161] Or, rather, it must be put to use. Furthermore, if it is indeed the case that the application of this higher moral law involves the assertion of principles of punishment incompatible with the spirit of democracy, a corrective is nevertheless available: namely, to impose a temporal limit on the exercise of what might be called moral justice.

Hence if the purge is to be short-lived, it is a good idea that it be rapid and judicious. When General de Gaulle recommended indulgence for those who

---

[159] By an order of October 10, 1944, departmental liberation committees under the National Resistance Committee were granted the power to establish investigative commissions and juries. In May 1945, however, they were barred from taking part in the purge of the economy.

[160] Sacha Guitry (1885–1957) was a writer and actor who continued to perform during the Occupation.

[161] In his editorial of September 28, Camus had already remarked on the importance of the offense of "consorting with the enemy," which was instituted on August 26, 1944.

made mistakes, he was right in principle.[162] But the applications of this principle need to be examined closely. There are social situations in which error is possible. There are others in which it is simply a crime.

If the law cannot cope with these subtleties, the law must be modified when appropriate, and for a precisely delimited duration. As difficult as this may be for souls that cherish justice and liberty, we must resign ourselves to it for a brief period. If we are resolute in this decision, its dangerous consequences will be eliminated, and its effectiveness at the national level will be maintained.

October 19, 1944[163]

France's participation in the allied military government that will occupy Germany until peace returns is incontestably great news.[164] One of our most legitimate expectations has been answered. We are now, in regard to this issue, in exactly the position we wanted to be in. But now that our rights have been recognized, our duties begin. And we must be as careful in gauging the latter as we were persistent in defining the former.

Readers can learn from other sources what the occupation of Germany will be like.[165] Suffice it to say for now that it will be harsh and pitiless. For an indefinite period the German people will be ruled by a foreign military government and deprived of all means of expression. Their cities will be isolated from one another and forced to submit to rigid laws laid down by the conquering powers in order to ensure as total a victory as possible. Hence increasingly large swaths of German territory are about to be subjected to the darkness of occupation, which so many European nations endured at the hands of the Third Reich. Only the Germans will have to do without something we never lost, not even in the darkest days of defeat, namely, hope.

The extreme harshness of the coming occupation therefore seems justified by the responsibility that Germany must bear for Europe's woes. The law of

---

[162] In a speech delivered on October 15, de Gaulle called for unity among the French and said: "Many may have made mistakes at one time or another. . . . Who has never committed an error?" Mauriac fully approved this remark in his article of October 17, entitled "Straying from Honor."

[163] Editorial. Text most likely by Camus.

[164] This was the form of recognition that Camus had advocated in his editorials of October 14, 15, and 17. But the news was premature. On the following day, October 20, *Combat* published a correction: "An official bulletin from the Ministry of Information states that 'no agreement has yet been reached between the French government and allied governments or between the French government and the joint allied military command.'" *Combat* went on to state that it had received its information from the Agence France-Presse.

[165] The documents reveal that until Germany is finally defeated, it is to be ruled by a military government under the command of General Eisenhower. This government will be in charge of maintaining law and order, dealing with prisoners and deportees, and rooting out the Nazi Party. Germans engaging in guerrilla actions against Allied forces are to be subject to the death penalty. Any interference with the progress of the Allied armies through Germany is a "capital crime." Civilian activities are to be limited and monitored, postal and telephone service interrupted, and newspapers banned.

occupation will be harsher than that to which France was subjected in 1940, though less harsh than that imposed on Poland. Indeed, the Third Reich will be in much the same position as Poland was in 1940. Germany will become a "General Government" administered by the Allies.

The difficult task of overseeing this occupation is what we have been invited to participate in. Our real duties begin with the work of government. At least two of those duties seem essential to us. First, we must never forget that while Germans ruled France with an outward show of tolerance, the occupier constantly violated his own laws. Indeed, what was so revolting about the occupation was the incessant contrast between the courteous language of the Germans and the abject cruelty of their actions. We must never forget this German example so that we are never tempted to imitate it.

It is just that the law imposed on Germany should be harsh. In any case, it can never compensate us for the moans and the silence of our tortured comrades. But once that harsh law has been clearly set forth, we must observe it strictly in order to show the misled Germans that strength can indeed be joined with justice.

Temptations will arise that might be understandable but cannot be excusable. The German people allowed their masters to mutilate and degrade men's souls, but for that very reason we must respect what is left of the German soul.[166] Not out of an idea of weakness or empty charity but in order to give the Germans another chance to do something someday for the good of humankind.

Our second duty is not to forget that this military government is provisional. We mustn't get used to it. Of course the occupation may be lengthy, and four years of such a regime can be difficult to bear, as we are well aware. But no reasonable person in Europe can believe that millions of individuals can be held in servitude indefinitely. Germany must one day resume its place. We can well imagine the look of defeat and bewilderment she will wear on that day. It is nevertheless for that moment that we must lay the groundwork.

We have shown that no defeat is definitive. Let us have the wisdom to foresee that no victory is definitive either.[167] We must never think of the occupation of Germany as our vengeance. We must use it to come to know the German people better and to reawaken in them whatever may still serve the interests of Europe. It would in any case be pointless to have insisted that we be given this challenging role unless we intended to bring to it a clear awareness of what we potentially represent, namely, justice.

We have never advocated a sentimental policy toward Germany. The goal for us has never been to answer insults with smiles. It was rather to employ all the energy needed to repair the insult of defeat and to begin with a show of strength so that we might be in a better position later on to show our generosity. When one who is weak cries out for justice, no one will believe that he does so for

---

[166] In the fourth of his "Letters to a German Friend," written in July 1944, Camus wrote: "We want to destroy your power without mutilating your soul" (*Essais*, p. 243).

[167] Cf. the final thoughts of Rieux at the end of *La Peste*: "But he knew that this chronicle could not be one of definitive victory."

disinterested reasons. We needed to be stronger before others would believe in our sincerity. Today we have that opportunity. If France in Germany lives up to the spotless standards of the mission it has taken upon itself, something at least will have been saved in a Europe torn apart by murder and madness.

October 20, 1944[168]

We are not in agreement with M. François Mauriac.[169] We can say this without embarrassment because we have supported M. Mauriac in the past, whenever we thought our support was warranted.

Many things in his article in *Le Figaro* warrant our approval now. We do not believe that it is necessary to gun down our fellow citizens at street corners or to diminish the authority of a government that we spontaneously recognized. But these justifiable feelings do not incline us to disparage our own actions or renounce our most cherished hopes.

Many Frenchmen surely are troubled, but not for the reasons that M. Mauriac believes. There may indeed be people in our country today who are afraid. If they are afraid for a few months, let us say simply that their anxiety won't amount to much and may even contribute to their salvation in this world. But there are also other people who worry that France may not yet have understood that it cannot resurrect itself unless it mercilessly destroys those interests that betrayed it.

Contrary to what M. Mauriac believes, this malaise, which stems from a variety of causes, has surfaced in the press that he complains speaks with a "unique" voice. This is the point on which we truly part company with him, because one can read of both fear and indignation in that press, and the voice of the self-righteous is louder than we in our ingenuousness would have believed. It is in any case to avail oneself of a dubious logic to accuse the new press, after two articles, of wasting its effort in pointless quarrels while at the same time alleging that it speaks with only one voice.

That voice is not as unique as it may seem. M. Mauriac complains that it represents only the Resistance, but we were foolish enough to think that the Resistance was identical with France. If we need a paper to represent something other than the resistance of the French people, what should it represent?

In other words, M. Mauriac's argument comes down to saying that there is something in France other than the Resistance. We had no doubt that this was the case back when our comrades, assembling for battle at the appointed hour, contemplated the lines outside the movie theaters and stared as the

---

168 Editorial. Typescript.
169 In *Le Figaro* of October 19, Mauriac published an article entitled "Justice and War" in which he argued that the French were uneasy and "increasingly resistant not to the demands of justice but to a system" characterized by "disorder," "confusion," and "arbitrariness." He added that the French could not be enlightened by the press, which was reduced to a "unique" voice, "that of the resistance."

stewards of their government passed in their automobiles. We assume, however, that M. Mauriac was not suggesting that we heed the voices of those who enjoyed themselves or betrayed their country while others faced enemy bullets.

Let no one accuse us of exploiting the Resistance. We have repeated often enough that the Resistance has more obligations than it has rights, and someday it will judge its own actions. Nor can anyone suspect us of complacency toward our press. We have a predilection for the truth, even when it goes against us. Nevertheless, we are certain that truth was not on M. Mauriac's side yesterday.

To be sure, there are things that are not right in the way the politics of this country is being conducted. Yet the sins are as much sins of weakness as of excess. Our duty is to denounce both simultaneously and to point the way to the right path, where the force of revolution joins with the light of justice. M. Mauriac speaks only of the excesses of the revolution. Our effort here has been to point out its weaknesses at the same time. This constitutes proof that the press is not as uniform as has been alleged. But that is not the important point. The important point is to maintain objectivity, and usually M. Mauriac has a keen sense of this, as he has demonstrated lately through his persistent and honorable concern with peace at any price.

Regardless of our desires and reactions, there can be no doubt that France has a revolution to make as well as a war.[170] That is indeed the drama it faces. But we cannot escape from this drama by evading the questions it raises. We can escape only by enduring it to the bitter end and drawing from it whatever truth it contains. We are convinced that there are times when each of us must argue with himself and sacrifice his emotional tranquillity. This is one of those times, and it is pointless to contest the terrifying fact that we will be obliged to destroy a living part of this country in order to save its soul.[171]

---

[170] Camus and *Combat* had made this essential point about the political and moral future of France several times since August 21.

[171] Mauriac replied to this editorial at length in an articled published in *Le Figaro* of October 22–23 under the title "Response to *Combat*." In particular, he wrote: "I would not swear that the editorial writer who refuted my recent article on 'Justice and War' in *Combat* really understood my thinking. I am even less sure that I understand his. . . . And since I have reason to believe that the author of the article is a younger colleague of mine for whom I feel the utmost admiration and sympathy, and whose faultless style I usually like a great deal, I find myself in an embarrassing position, which I avow with my usual simplicity and naïveté." After quoting the previous two sentences, Mauriac notes: "There is not a word here that does not wound me. . . . May the gentle not deprive the world of their gentleness! . . . There will always be enough cruelty in this world. . . . Would the legal revolution be impossible if there were no more innocents in French prisons? Does my naïveté make you smile? What can I do? My generation grew up in a Europe anxious and divided because a Jewish officer was serving time for a crime committed by another man.

"But I am well aware that the judicial system that has wrought havoc in France for the past two months probably won't disturb a man resolved "'to destroy a living part of this country in order to save its soul.' . . . My young colleague is more spiritualist than I imagined—more than I am, in any case. . . . The young masters of *Combat* have yet to flush certain scraps of Christianity entirely out of their system."

Declaring himself unable to understand "what this theological language conceals," Mauriac asked this opponent to "kindly light his lantern." Which Camus did in his editorial of October 24, p. 86.

October 21, 1944[172]

Yes, the drama that France faces is to be obliged to make a revolution while it simultaneously makes war.[173] We are not inclined to take this situation lightly. Some would like to devote all our resources to waging war, while justice is suspended. Others would like to pour all our resources into the revolution, so that justice is served while force is starved. But we cannot forget either the power we have to restore or the purity we must recover. In reality, moreover, we know full well that the two must coincide. But we also know that their reciprocal requirements may be contradictory.

Nor can we forget that in both cases the lives of Frenchmen are at stake: the best of us will have to die in the war, and we will have to destroy the worst of us in the revolution. One cannot be nonchalant about such a terrible drama, which will demand still more blood from a country that has already given of its marrow in two wars. And how can the best of us fail to ask themselves at times whether they have the right to add to this nation's pain and to the dreadful misery of this war?

We do not approach this matter lightly. This the whole world must know. To approach such a matter lightly would be to approach it with doubts. It is good for us to experience doubt from time to time, because this lends the appropriate gravity to our task. We are wary of judges who never have doubts and of heroes who never have the shakes.

When doubt is pushed as far as possible, however, a choice has to be made. We know full well that on the day the first death sentence is carried out in Paris, we will feel repugnance. At that moment we will need to remember the countless other death sentences imposed on men who were pure and will have to recall so many cherished faces now buried in the ground and so many hands we once loved to shake. When we are tempted to prefer the generous sacrifices of war to the dark duties of justice, we will need to remember the dead and the unbearable image of those whom torture turned into traitors.[174] As hard as that will be, we will know then that some pardons cannot be granted, and some revolutions are necessary.

But conversely, when we find ourselves exasperated by the spectacle of an entertainer acclaimed again by the very people who ought to despise him, or we are driven to inconsequential rebellion by the sight of mediocrity and stupidity honored anew, or we feel at times tempted to confound thoughtlessness with crime, as any just man might, we must remind ourselves of the exhausting daily effort that the quest for victory entails. We will know then that some violence leads nowhere and that some wars are inevitable.

What does all this mean? It comes down to saying that a nation that has chosen to live with such wrenching contradictions can save itself only by openly

---

[172] Editorial. Typescript.

[173] Continuation of the previous day's editorial, from which these key terms are borrowed.

[174] Camus returned to this idea several times. See, in particular, his article of December 30, 1944, p. 155.

dealing with those contradictions, only by making the immense effort required to balance justice with force, only by making the revolution and making war together, with equal lucidity and courage, because it can no longer distinguish between the two. A great nation is one that rises to confront its own tragedies. If this country is incapable of achieving victory and truth at the same time, if it agrees to make war while consecrating cowardice and treason at home, or, on the other hand, if it gives in to the violence of its passions by neglecting its position in the world and its duties in the eyes of others, then we would have no choice but to conclude that we are lost. We must do everything at once or accomplish nothing at all.

Is this harsh, impossible, and inhumane? Yes. We are aware of this. That is why we do not approach the matter lightly. Yet we have faith that no human task is beyond man's reach. What we need, purely and simply, is men. Men: in other words, hearts accustomed to boldness as well as prudence, souls that are sensitive and wills that are firm and minds that are capable of selflessness as well as commitment. And if someone were to object that this, too, is inhuman, our answer would be that for that very reason we must make the attempt, we must seize the last hope we have of restoring this country's grandeur.

October 21, 1944
Money versus Justice[175]

A monetary problem exists in France. Without being an expert, the average Frenchman can detect that something is wrong in this area at the present time. He knows that the value of his hundred-franc note varies considerably depending on whether he spends it on the black market or the white market. In a broader sense, this same Frenchman is unfortunately well aware of the dizzying rise of some prices compared with the relative stability of his wages. In other words, France is currently suffering from a gross injustice, which allows a few privileged individuals to thrive while starving and draining the majority.

The magnitude of the injustice makes this an urgent issue. The monetary problem is one of the first that needs to be resolved. We have touched on it before, but since then nothing has been done. To be sure, reasons for this inaction have been given. But the public does not understand them. We are neither financiers nor ministers. But we may be able to do something for the country by raising the issue and for our readers by attempting to clarify it.

In economics there exists a law of supply and demand, the effects of which were never more obvious than during the four years of occupation. A product for

---

[175] The signature on this article, "Juste Bauchart," is one of the pseudonyms that Camus used in the Resistance. Hence it is more than likely that he wrote the article or at any rate participated in drafting it. Although he was not an expert on economic issues, the opposition between the rule of money and the rule of justice is one of his themes. The pseudonym allowed him to adopt an unaccustomed style.

which there is little demand will decrease in price in order to attract buyers. But it will increase in price if demand is heavy. So much is obvious. But when all commodities become scarce throughout a country, all are demanded with increasing urgency, and all prices rise with the implacable regularity we have come to know. Add to that the massive quantity of unbacked banknotes placed in circulation by the government of Vichy, and the purchasing power of money falls to absurd lows as prices soar. This economic phenomenon, with which we are forced to cope, is called inflation.

Are there remedies for inflation? An obvious one would be a rapid increase in the quantity of goods offered for sale to the public, but in the short term that is unrealistic. In any case, the large quantity of paper money in circulation means that there is too much cash chasing too few goods, so prices will remain at their current unreasonable levels. Hence what needs to be curtailed is the circulation of banknotes.

Where are those banknotes? More or less everywhere, of course, but above all in the hands of those who had scarce commodities to sell, to whom money flowed. The problem of monetary circulation thus leads directly to the problem of scandalous fortunes.

We at *Combat* indicated what urgent measures needed to be taken to identify these illicit profits without delay. All banknotes needed to be marked, and securities should have been registered, so that all French wealth could be monitored. These measures were not implemented. Material difficulties were part of the reason for this. Problems of communication apparently made it impossible to impose these measures throughout France. But political reasons also played a part. The most publicly discussed of these was the fear of alienating farmers, who are currently holding large numbers of banknotes.

It is not our place to resolve these questions, but it is appropriate for us to say that these measures cannot be effective unless they are implemented rapidly. For some time now, people with illicit profits have been trying to regularize the status of their wealth. If one were to consult the Registry, we imagine that it would emerge that many banknotes were converted into real estate in recent years. Today they are being transformed into collectibles. The only way to stop this further fraud is to move quickly, and in the meantime all sales of real estate should be prohibited.

In any case, the responsible ministry must be convinced that the issue is urgent. It is because the circulation of money has not been regulated that price increases have not abated. It is because scandalous fortunes have not been confiscated by the state that the price of bread has risen. A quintal of wheat now sells for 450 francs instead of 410. The British magazine *The Economist* informs us that this is double what it would cost to import Canadian wheat into France. And that is not all. At that price, bread should sell at 6 francs per kilo. The actual price is only 4.9 francs. The reason for this is that the government makes up the difference, which costs it, and costs all of us, 5.3 billion francs per year.

Thus mere delay in the implementation of these measures in the public interest is a disservice to both the government and the people of France, while it simultaneously consolidates the position of a few privileged individuals and places a seal of approval on their criminal maneuvers. The situation is so absurd that it undermines the calls for amnesty that have been raised in various quarters. Neither justice nor liberty is possible so long as cash is still king. And one cannot speak to people of forgiveness when nothing has been done to assure them of their daily bread. If it is true, as François Mauriac says, that there is no justice in opposing France,[176] we want to assure him that there is no justice, either, in opposing the people of France, and yet it is this unjust justice that is now being consecrated owing to the lethargy and distraction of the ministries.

JUSTE BAUCHART

October 22, 1944[177]

The *Daily Express*[178] has just published a commentary on General de Gaulle's speech that is nothing short of stupefying.[179] This is the first time since the Liberation that a newspaper has taken this tone with us. It is of course not the first time that we have been criticized, as is only proper. But it is the first time that France and its representative have been impugned so vehemently and with such unparalleled crudeness of style and thought.

The *Daily Express*, which sees nothing in de Gaulle's October 14 speech but "inopportune nonsense," believes that the general was motivated solely by a desire to make himself popular in France by displaying anti-British sentiments. The paper points to Great Britain's wartime efforts, remarks that France lived comparatively well through the past four years, adds that French forces are of little use in the battle for Aachen,[180] and ends thus: "Some people think that the only hope for France is for Allied troops to continue to occupy the bulk of its territory until tempers have cooled."

It is hard to know whether France lived better or worse than its Allies during this war. But it is not possible, if one wishes to remain within the bounds of decency, to assert that it lived well. To be sure, it enjoyed a full ration of shame, and for four years not a single morning passed without the crack of some firing squad's rifles. In that respect we had more than we asked for. But we swear to our British colleague that all this still was not enough. For some Frenchmen, the only way to live well was to do what had to be done to obtain the boon of dying well.

---

[176] Mauriac ended his article "Justice and War," to which Camus replied in his editorial of the day before, by stating that "there is no justice in opposing France."

[177] Editorial. Typescript.

[178] The *Daily Express* (British) is a conservative, mass-circulation daily newspaper that was founded in 1900.

[179] On de Gaulle's October 14 speech, see Camus' editorial of October 15, p. 73, which was full of praise.

[180] There had been heavy fighting around Aachen. The offensive, which began on October 1, continued for several weeks.

It is also true that we are not useful in Aachen, although we may be in the Vosges.[181] But since we are speaking sincerely, we have to add that our twenty-five-year-old soldiers are still waiting for the weapons that would enable them to hasten into battle and that, not having received them, some have turned their efforts to living well again in the sense to which our colleague alludes. Those young men are fighting in Metz with their bare breasts and what few weapons the Germans were kind enough to give them during the Battle of Paris.

As to the need for Allied troops to occupy France, we would like to think that in putting the matter this way, our colleague was simply unaware that he was insulting this country while insisting on its greatness.

We know what an occupation is, as the reporter for the *Daily Express*, who had the good fortune to live badly these past four years, does not. We know this so well that we want no more of it, and the very word is enough to arouse our deepest wrath.

Allied troops in France are in a friendly country that has been willing, for the sake of our common victory, to lend them various bases temporarily. They cannot claim to maintain an order in France that is being maintained without them, and the mere supposition that they might have a political role to play represents a serious insult both to France and to her allies.

It is hard to say whether General de Gaulle would be popular if he exhibited anti-British and anti-American sentiments. In any case, the suggestion is somewhat at odds with the assertion in the same article that "the British are almost idols for the people of France." What is certain, however, is that General de Gaulle will always be popular for insisting as he has that France be respected as a country that did not acquire a taste for servitude as a result of her misfortune. In any case, we wholeheartedly accept the idea that we can be judged and criticized and simply ask our friends, whoever they may be, to make sure that their texts and speeches never forgo the restraint and respect that we believe we have a right to insist on.

The *Daily Express*, which is so prompt to point out our uselessness, may then see that, if nothing else, we are useful for reminding it of the rules of polite society and the true law of friendship.

October 24, 1944[182]

We wish to protest here in a firm and measured way against the methods of press censorship.[183] Our protest will be measured in its language but firm in its decision to publish our political commentaries, and this editorial if need be, against the wishes of the Censorship Office.

---

[181] In the Vosges, where the fighting was also heavy and protracted, the French First Army fought under the command of General de Lattre de Tassigny, as did the Alsace-Lorraine Brigade commanded by "Colonel Berger," also known as André Malraux.

[182] Editorial. Typescript.

[183] On censorship, see the editorial of September 22, p. 44.

Relations between the press and the Censorship Office have been governed since September 24 by an edict acknowledging the legitimacy of censorship in regard to military operations while declaring that all other matters should be exempt from oversight.

We subscribed to this agreement and respected our obligations under it. But the Censorship Office has failed to honor this basic commitment. We therefore declare that the censorship is illegal if it violates the agreement to which both parties have freely subscribed. And we believe that illegality in this instance is equivalent to nonexistence. In other words, we will ignore the decisions of the censors whenever they deny the very principles that define their right to exist.

In our Saturday issue we commented on news from a Francoist source concerning the activities of Spanish Republicans at the border.[184] Our commentary displeased the censor. For the reasons we have just indicated, we are going to reformulate it, but this time in even stronger terms than before.

Yes, there is a Spanish problem, even if there are some who are not happy about it. We warned our readers to be wary of news stemming from a Francoist source. This news in fact did a disservice to the French government in the eyes of foreigners by suggesting that the south of France was in chaos. It also sought to prod that government into taking steps to restore what is commonly called law and order. Reports in the Madrid papers alleging that Franco proposed to General de Gaulle that Spain send troops into southern France to restore order stem from the same motive.

With respect to the situation in our southern regions, these reports risk reinforcing deliberately spread rumors that our provinces have been plunged into anarchy—rumors that have impressed even some distinguished minds. On this subject, we are today publishing the first article by a British journalist who has visited the regions in question and who has favored us with an objective account of her journey.[185]

In other respects, we want our readers to be aware that the problem is even more serious than they may be aware. The case of Spain is not of interest to us solely because we owe the Spanish Republic an infinite debt. It also interests us because France's war effort is in danger of being compromised by Franco's policy.

What people in France still do not know, and we are determined to say whether the censor likes it or not, is that a large number of Germans (which we

[184] On October 22, an article originating in Perpignan indicated that Radio Madrid had reported that fighting had broken out in France between the army and the "reds," that is, Spanish Republicans who had managed to infiltrate France, and that the weapons used had been taken from the French underground. In a violent diatribe against the Republicans, Radio Madrid claimed that "Perpignan and Pau are under the control of a committee dominated by Spanish Republicans." A note from the editor added: "This news should be greeted with caution. Its source is the Franco-controlled radio. In other words, it is dubious." This was followed by a blank: "Political commentary censored."

[185] Under the title "An English journalist discusses the men of the Resistance and what they did in the region of Toulouse," Vera Lindsay noted that, contrary to "gossip" in Paris and London about "a sort of revolution" supposedly taking place in Toulouse and the Languedoc region, and despite the activities of members of the Milice [the Vichy paramilitary militia] still at large, order and calm prevailed.

estimate to be around 40,000) who came to Spain as refugees have now been organized into a veritable army of fully equipped soldiers. These are the people who are pressuring Spain to adopt the policy we have described, and these are the people whom Radio Madrid wishes to help with its slanted reports.

We ask one simple question. What would happen if these troops attempted to relieve the German garrisons in the southwest and came up against unarmed units of our F.F.I.? Such an attempt might appear desperate, but it would not be irrational, because it would allow Germany to buy a little time. It would aid Hitler's policy of resistance at any cost, of merciless struggle, which the dictatorships hope will delay their ultimate defeat. An operation of this kind would give the German resistance the time it is asking for while increasing the likelihood of bloodshed in some parts of France.

To recap, then, Franco is trying to convince the world that part of France is in chaos. We are today publishing information needed to contradict that propaganda. In doing so, we are doing our duty as journalists. The Germans in Spain are a threat to France, and all we have to stop them is the courage of our people's army, which includes some Spanish Republicans among its ranks. The democratic governments must therefore do their duty.

And that duty is not to blindfold and muzzle the press or conceal the truth. It is to arm the troops who will guarantee security and order in our *départements*. What we said on Sunday we will repeat today despite the obstacles that have been placed in our way: the war policy of France and the Allies carries an obligation to arm our units in the Pyrenees. In the present case, the political problem is perfectly clear: it is Franco who must be silenced, not the French press.

October 25, 1944[186]

We hesitated to respond to the invitation courteously extended to us by M. Mauriac in Sunday's *Le Figaro*.[187] The issues he raised seemed less urgent to us than some others. But many letters from readers have persuaded us that these concerns are shared by many Frenchmen and that the discussion could benefit from some additional clarity.

We might as well begin by admitting that the editorial challenged by *Le Figaro* was written with some irritation. François Mauriac's allegations against the resistance press wounded us because we considered them profoundly unjust. That is the real disagreement. And we regret that M. Mauriac said nothing about this problem in his response. But he did so because he preferred to go straight to the essential issue, which is the matter of justice. So let us deal with that.

---

186 Editorial. Typescript.
187 Continuation of the polemic with François Mauriac. This editorial replies to Mauriac's "Response to *Combat*," published in the October 22–23 issue of *Le Figaro* (see Camus' editorial for October 20, p. 80 above, and note 171, p. 81). This polemic, which focused initially on the resistance press, had since turned to the concept of justice and the purge.

What shocked M. Mauriac was our assertion that today we must learn to deny a part of ourselves. Obviously this doesn't mean that we should say things we don't believe. Nevertheless, it is true that the problem of justice essentially comes down to silencing what M. Mauriac calls "mercifulness" when public truth is at stake. This is difficult, to be sure, but one doesn't have to be a Christian to believe that sacrifices for justice are necessary.

Let's talk about a specific case. It is easy to get lost in abstract debate and the calculus of responsibilities. Some look for cases where judgment was arbitrary, while others cite cases where legal forms were respected. But this just creates confusion. So let's look reality in the face: this discussion began because a head was about to fall. On Monday, the first death sentence was issued in Paris.[188] It is with this dreadful precedent still fresh in our minds that we must take a position. Will we approve of this sentence or won't we? That is the heart of the issue, and it is a terribly difficult one.

M. Mauriac will say that he is a Christian and that his role is not to condemn. But we, precisely because we are not Christian, have decided—and here we ask him to pay close attention to what we say—to face the problem squarely in all of its ramifications. How do we propose to do this?

We have no taste for murder. The human person embodies all that we respect in the world. Our instinctive response to this sentence is therefore one of repugnance. It would be easy for us to say that our business is not to destroy men but simply to do something for the good of the country. In fact, however, we have learned since 1939 that we would betray the good of the country if we acted on this impulse. France bears within herself, like a foreign body, a small minority of men who were the cause of her recent woes and who continue to be the cause of her woes at the present time. They are guilty of treason and injustice.

It is therefore their very existence that raises the problem of justice, since they form a living part of this country, and the question is one of destroying them.

A Christian may believe that human justice is always supplemented by divine justice, hence that indulgence is always preferable. But we invite M. Mauriac to consider the dilemma of those to whom the notion of divine judgment is foreign yet who retain a taste for man and hope for his grandeur. They must either hold their peace forever or become converts to human justice. This cannot take place without distress. But after four years of collective suffering in the wake of twenty-five years of mediocrity, doubt is no longer possible. And we have chosen to

---

[188] The death sentence was meted out to the journalist Georges Suarez, a member of the Parti Populaire Français (Doriot's fascist party), who headed the collaborationist newspaper *Aujourd'hui*. He was accused of consorting with the enemy and treason. During his trial, sentences from his editorials were cited. "Denunciation is a duty," he wrote, or this, on the execution of hostages: "Those responsible for these executions are not occupying troops but killers in the pay of Jews and communists." Despite depositions in his favor attesting to his interventions with the Germans to save arrested resisters, he was sentenced to death and executed on November 9, 1944. In *Le Figaro* Wladimir d'Ormesson wrote, "We lose no sleep over the execution of the likes of Georges Suarez." Camus refused to comment on this execution (see editorial of October 31, p. 94).

embrace human justice, with its terrible imperfections, while seeking anxiously to correct it by clinging desperately to honesty.

We have never called for blind or precipitous justice. We detest arbitrary judgment and criminal stupidity, and we would prefer that France keep her hands clean. But to that end we want justice to be prompt, and we want all prosecution for crimes of collaboration to end at some fixed date. We want the most obvious crimes to be punished immediately, and then, since nothing can be done without mediocrity, we want the errors that so many Frenchmen have indeed committed consigned to carefully considered oblivion.

Is this language as dreadful as M. Mauriac thinks? To be sure, it is not the language of grace. But it is the language of a generation that grew up as witness to the spectacle of injustice, alienated from God, in love with man, and determined to serve mankind despite a destiny that so often seemed devoid of reason. It is the language of hearts determined to assume their full duties, to live with the tragedy of their century, and to contribute to man's grandeur in a world of foolishness and crime.

As for the soul of this country, which has intrigued M. Mauriac, he knows it too. He saw it in the eyes of some of our comrades during the marvelous days of the insurrection. It is to keep that bright ardor burning in the faces of young Frenchmen that we must renounce that part of ourselves that would prefer the consolations of forgetfulness and tenderness. Four years ago we were forced to harden some parts of ourselves. Maybe that was unfortunate. But we do not see why tenderness should not be virile and why firmness should not be allied with clemency. In any case, this is the only chance we have left to prevent France and Europe from becoming a desert of mediocrity and silence in which we no longer want to live.

October 27, 1944[189]

It was difficult for us to speak, as we did yesterday, about René Leynaud.[190] Readers who may have seen the brief notice that a resistance journalist answering to that name had been shot by the Germans will have passed over quickly what was for us a dreadful, shocking piece of news.

---

189 Editorial. Reprinted in *Actuelles*, chapter "La Chair" (with erroneous date of October 28).

190 On October 26, *Combat* published a short article about René Leynaud:

"Our friend René Leynaud, who was one of the first militants to join the 'Combat' movement, was shot dead by the enemy.

"Yesterday, the Agence Française de Presse published the following information, which dashed all remaining hope of someday finding one of our dearest friends, René Leynaud."

Lyons, October 25.

Last June, nineteen men held prisoner at Fort Montluc in Lyons were taken to Villeneuve near Trévoux (Ain) and shot in a field.

Yesterday their bodies were identified. Among them was René Leynaud, a reporter for the *Progrès de Lyon*. After fighting valiantly in Norway and France, this young journalist joined the Resistance. Arrested and

Yet we must speak of him. We must do so in order to keep the memory of resistance alive, not in a nation that may well succumb to forgetfulness, but in those hearts capable of being moved by the character of a man.

He joined the Resistance in the first months of the war. The elements of which his moral life was composed—Christianity and truth to his word—drove him to take his place, silently, in the shadowy battle. As his nom de guerre he chose a word that spoke of the purity in his heart: to all his comrades in the "Combat" movement he was known as "Clair" [meaning clear, transparent].

The only personal passion to which he held fast, apart from modesty, was poetry. He wrote poems that only two or three of us knew. They possessed the quintessential quality of the man himself: transparency. When it became necessary to devote himself full-time to the struggle, however, he gave up writing, indulging himself only to the extent of buying the most diverse books of poetry, which he then set aside to be read after the war. Otherwise he shared our conviction that a certain style, an obstinacy in righteousness, would once again make the country whole. For months now we have held his place at the newspaper open, and with all the stubbornness of friendship and love we refused to believe the news that he was dead. That is no longer possible today.

The style that he believed essential can no longer be his. In this terrible misfortune the absurd tragedy of resistance can be seen for what it is. For men like Leynaud joined the struggle convinced that no man had the right to speak unless he was willing to pay with his life. Sadly, the war fought by those not in uniform lacks the awful justice of the other war. At the front, bullets strike everyone indiscriminately, the worst as well as the best. For the past four years, however, it was the best who volunteered and who fell, the best who won the right to speak but lost the power.

In any case, the man we loved can speak no more, yet France needs more voices like his. This most stouthearted of men, who for so long remained silent

---

wounded in a sweep by police and militiamen, René Leynaud was transferred to Fort Montluc, from which he and eighteen fellow prisoners were sent to Villeneuve and shot.

René Leynaud leaves a wife and child. This young journalist enjoyed the esteem of all his colleagues and all who knew the quality of his heart and the ardent patriotism that animated him.

"If René Leynaud had not fallen into the hands of the enemy, he would have been a member of this newspaper's team of journalists, since he had been one of the most loyal, ardent, and courageous militants of the 'Combat' movement since 1941.

"The article we quoted mentions the quality of his heart. And it is true that Leynaud was the most loyal comrade one could possibly have, but it would be to mistake the man to see only his heart. What made his friendship so precious was above all his absolute, uncompromising honesty, as well as a delicacy that hid gifts as a writer and moralist that made him blush whenever they revealed themselves.

"One of his friends, who had hoped to write about Leynaud in this morning's paper, was unable to do so. We are deeply saddened."

Obviously the "friend" was Camus, who was probably not the author of the editorial of October 26, about a speech of General de Gaulle's, even though the ideas contained in it are ideas about which he wrote elsewhere. He knew Leynaud in 1943 and recalled their friendship in the introduction to a posthumous edition of Leynaud's poetry (*Essais*, pp. 1471–1479), *René Leynaud: Poésies posthumes* (Paris: Gallimard, 1947).

in obedience to faith and honor, would have found the words that were needed, but now he has been silenced forever, while others, unworthy to speak in his place, talk of the honor that was his, and still others, whose reliability cannot be taken for granted, invoke the God he had chosen.

It is possible today to criticize the men of the Resistance, to note their shortcomings and indict their failings. Perhaps that is because the best of them are dead. We say this because we deeply believe that if we are still alive, it is because we did not do enough. He, at least, did enough.[191] And today, returned to this earth which for us is without a future and for him was but a fleeting home, diverted from the passion to which he sacrificed everything, we hope at least that he will find consolation in not hearing the words of bitterness and denigration that now envelop the miserable human adventure that brought us together.

Fear not: we will not use him, who never made use of anyone. He left the struggle as unknown as he entered it. We will keep him where he would have wanted to be kept, in the silence of our hearts, and cherish his memory along with the terrible sorrow of irreparable loss. But since we have always tried to banish bitterness from these pages, he will forgive us if we indulge bitterness for one moment with the thought that perhaps the death of such a man is too great a price to pay to restore to others the right to forget in word and deed what the courage and sacrifice of a few Frenchmen meant in the four years just past.[192]

October 29, 1944[193]

The day before yesterday, the minister of information delivered a speech of which we entirely approve.[194] One point deserves further attention, however, because it is by no means commonplace for a minister to address the nation in the language of virile morality and remind people of the essential duties of conscience.[195]

M. Teitgen has analyzed the mechanism of concession that led so many Frenchmen from weakness to treason. Each concession made to the enemy and

---

[191] In *Actuelles* this sentence has "Leynaud" in place of "he."

[192] Mauriac took this last sentence as an attack on him and responded vehemently in *Le Figaro* of October 29 under the title "Mise au point."

[193] Editorial. Text reprinted in *Actuelles*, in the chapter on "Morality and Politics."

[194] Camus and *Combat* appreciated the fact that Pierre-Henri Teitgen, a resister from the very early days of the war, was minister of information (see article of September 10, p. 182). They nevertheless kept a close eye on his decisions. In November 1944 Teitgen became one of the founders of the Mouvement Républicain Populaire, or MRP, a coalition of Christian Democrats. The minister had announced the banning of collaborationist newspapers, which had previously only been suspended, with these words: "What is serious is that from failure to failure, concession to concession, surrender to surrender, and repressed remorse to repressed remorse, they brought the country to the point of being unable to make the elementary distinction between good and evil. . . . They deformed the country's conscience." Asserting that a free press "independent of the great oligarchies of money" was essential, Teitgen concluded by insisting on the need for "structural reforms." It is easy to see why Camus approved without reservation.

[195] In *Actuelles*, the phrase "of conscience" is absent.

each decision to follow the path of least resistance led to another. The second offense was no worse than the first, but the one combined with the other amounted to an act of cowardice. Two acts of cowardice added up to dishonor.

This is the tragic dilemma the country faces, and if it is difficult to resolve, it is because every aspect of human conscience is involved. The problem it raises has the incisiveness of yes or no.

France used to live by shopworn maxims, which explained to younger generations that life required compromise, that one had to know when to make concessions, that enthusiasm was short-lived, and that in a world where craftiness was always right, one had to make an effort not to be wrong.

That was the way things were before the war. And when the men of our generation reacted against the injustice, they were told that it would be passed on to them. So, little by little, the morality of least resistance and disillusionment spread. Imagine the effect in such a climate of the discouraged and quavering voice that called upon the French to withdraw into themselves.[196] It's always a winning formula to appeal to others by asking them to do what comes most easily and telling them there's no need to put themselves out. To pursue the path of honor means making terrible demands on oneself and others. It is exhausting, to be sure. And some number of Frenchmen were already worn out in 1940.

Not all were, however. It was astonishing to discover that many who joined the Resistance were not professional patriots. This is of course because patriotism is not a profession, and there is a way of loving one's country that consists in not wanting it to be unjust, and in saying so.[197] But it is also because patriotism was not always enough to mobilize men for the peculiar kind of war they needed to fight. A certain delicacy was also required, a refusal to engage in any kind of compromise, a pride that did not count among the bourgeois virtues, an ability to say no.

What is great about the present age, which in other respects is so wretched, is that the choice became pure. This is because intransigence has become the most imperious of duties and sanctions have at last been imposed on the morality of concession. If the cunning were right, it was necessary to accept being wrong. And if shame, lies, and tyranny determined the conditions of life, it was necessary to accept death.

It is this power of intransigence and dignity that we must today restore throughout France at all levels. People must understand that every embrace of mediocrity, every surrender, every choice to take the easy way out harms us as much as the enemy's guns. After four years of dreadful ordeals, an exhausted France has come to know the extent of its tragedy, which has deprived it of the right to indulge its exhaustion. The first prerequisite for our recovery, the first condition of our country's hope, is that the very men who found a way to say no yesterday will tomorrow just as firmly and selflessly say yes, and that they will

---

[196] The allusion is of course to the voice of Marshal Pétain.
[197] Cf. the first of the *Lettres à un ami allemand* (*Essais*, p. 221): "I would like to be able to love my country and love justice at the same time."

ultimately find a way to extract from honor its positive virtues, just as they previously drew from it the ability to refuse.

October 31, 1944[198]

We can discuss the case of M. Stéphane Lauzanne[199] because he did not receive the death penalty, whereas in the case of M. Suarez it was hard to be anything other than silent.[200]

Lauzanne in himself is without interest, however. Although he dishonored an entire profession, he was not the only one to do so. Nevertheless, his case is instructive in that it can be taken as a symbol.

As a journalist he had no talent: you can take our word for it. He had no morality, either: this you can take on faith. He was nevertheless the editor in chief of a major newspaper, and what he wrote sometimes appeared in the foreign press. To some extent (and it is impossible to write these words without quaking with rage), he spoke for France. He spoke for France precisely when France ceased to speak for herself. Today, if everyone knows that France is in decadence, it is thanks to men like M. Lauzanne, who worked hard to accredit the idea.

Who should be put on trial, then? The man who involved himself in cowardly accommodation and compromise of every sort, or the society that allowed a journalist devoid of talent and utterly without scruples to guide public opinion and speak on behalf of his country?

To put it bluntly, society's responsibility is enormous. A world in which jobs can be had without competence or at the very least some kind of virtue is a world that carries within it the seeds of its own destruction.

But the individual's responsibility begins where society's ends. Even if we assume that it was a matter of course for a man of mediocre or debased intelligence to participate in the reporting of news, which ought to be a scrupulous and thoughtful business, it was the individual's responsibility to recognize the responsibility inherent in his position the moment he was appointed to it.

We may open ourselves up to ridicule by saying what we think, but we'll say it anyway. A journalist who rereads his published article and does not ask whether he was right or wrong, who experiences no pangs of doubt or scruples, and who on some nights does not despair of being equal to the absurd but necessary work that he does week in and week out—in short, a journalist who does

---

[198] Editorial. Probable text.

[199] According to Georges Altschuler, who reported on his trial in the same issue of *Combat*, Stéphane Lauzanne, the editor in chief of *Le Matin*, was a "man without character," who had been successively pro-English, pro-American, and pro-German. Seventy years old, he was accused of having advocated active collaboration in his editorials and broadcasts on Radio Paris between 1940 and 1944. He was sentenced to twenty years in prison.

[200] On Georges Suarez, see the editorial of October 25, n. 188 above, p. 89.

not judge himself daily—is not worthy of this profession and bears the heaviest of responsibilities in his own eyes and in the eyes of his country.[201]

Now there is no denying that M. Lauzanne, a man who spoke on behalf of France, never questioned what he was doing. The problem was not that he lacked delicacy, for we know that when he was criticized for taking money from the Germans, his excuse was that it was paid to him in French francs. Clearly, that took care of any problems, and M. Lauzanne's patriotism remained intact.

Meanwhile, however, certain other Frenchmen came to believe that additional requirements were in order, and today their wish is to see in every important post men who accept their responsibilities and who weigh carefully the consequences of what they say and do.

The day this country demands as much of its children as they demand of themselves will be the day on which a revolution more profound than any previous upheaval begins. It is truly unfortunate that Frenchmen are today obliged to try one of their own for the crime of mediocrity and spinelessness, but it is the harsh law of the day that requires us to condemn mediocrity invested with the privileges of virtue and talent.

To put it succinctly, M. Stéphane Lauzanne was sentenced to twenty years at hard labor for overlooking one subtle point.[202] Otherwise he would have known that the nationality of money is determined not by the color of the banknote but by the hands that distribute it. In June 1940 the reign of subtle distinctions began, but those subtle distinctions covered the entire gamut of conscience and had the power to kill or dishonor. We beg pardon for thinking that they are still a matter of life or death for this country today.

November 2, 1944[203]

The Council of Ministers has just established a High Court of Justice, which is to judge the members of the Vichy government.[204] It should be noted that not all the members of that government are currently in custody, so that the council's decision amounts to asserting their guilt before issuing the arrest warrants

---

[201] Cf. Camus' statements to *Caliban*: "The profession of journalist is one of the finest I know, precisely because it forces you to judge yourself." *Essais*, p. 1565.

[202] Cf. the first of the *Lettres à un ami allemand*: "We are indeed fighting over subtleties, but subtleties as important as man himself." *Essais*, p. 224.

[203] Editorial. Typescript.

[204] Camus had already dealt with the problem of the purge on October 18, p. 76, and October 25, p. 88. In the first days of the Liberation, military tribunals and later juries established by departmental committees judged collaborators. Special courts—Cours de justice, Chambres civiques, and finally the Haute Cour de justice—were established subsequently. The High Court of Justice, "intended to judge the members of the organism known as the 'Government of Vichy,'" comprised five magistrates and twenty-four jurors drawn by lot from a list of one hundred names provided by the Consultative Assembly. Those one hundred names included thirty-three deputies, thirty-three senators, and thirty-four resisters not drawn from the parliament. This was the prelude to the trials of Pétain and Laval, among others.

they deserve. Note, too, that the government has taken a clear lead over the Académie Française, which continues to look upon Marshal Pétain as a writer and a great Frenchmen, thereby committing two errors. Some may object that the government's advantage over the Académie is slim. We would agree.

The task of a High Court of Justice is generally to judge crimes of treason. To establish such a court to deal with the government of Vichy thus amounts to declaring the entire government guilty of treason. The general terms of this statement may fail to make an impression, but if we look beneath the surface, we see that it comes down to saying that Marshal Pétain is a traitor, along with Prime Minister Laval and his other collaborators.

We wish to make one simple point: the people who are loudly applauding the government's decision with respect to the Patriotic Militias[205] today are the same people who will shrink from the blunt assertion that Philippe Pétain was a traitor. This is doubly instructive. It ought to instruct the government as to the value of some of the approval it has received, while at the same time it ought to instruct those who are applauding the dismantling of the militias that even if the Provisional Government sometimes seems overly punctilious about maintaining order, it has yet to demonstrate that it is inclined to blur basic distinctions.

To insist that the decision of the Council of Ministers amounts to accusing Philippe Pétain of treason is to highlight the true meaning of that decision. Our task, however, is to substantiate that charge with all due care. Indeed, some Frenchmen still believe that Pétain's intentions were good and that he was not responsible for the atrocities committed under his government. All that further reinforces an old theme of Vichyite propaganda, namely, that Vichy was pursuing a double policy.

The answer to this is simple. Even assuming that Vichy's policy was double, it was still a crime. And the very fact that it sometimes seemed to be double made it a crime worse than ordinary treason. Today we are sill suffering the consequences of the vast confusion that the Vichy regime sowed throughout France. Even after the regime chose to decamp to Germany[206] in order to go on speaking about France, the equivocal situation it created perpetuates itself at home.

The fictional legality that Vichy created is forcing us to substitute moral justice for legal justice and supplying arguments to people who ought to hold their peace forevermore.

The period that began in 1940 was one in which it was no longer acceptable to play a double game. It was either fight or bend the knee, but it was impossible to imagine fighting on one's knees. If Pétain believed that, the results are clear for everyone to see. French heads rolled as a result of laws that he signed. Perhaps,

---

[205] The government had just decided to disarm the "patriotic militias" created by the C.N.R. early in 1944 to ensure law and order during the liberation of Paris. The C.N.R. argued that the militias ought to be converted into civic and republican guards, but General de Gaulle insisted that "no group should be allowed to subsist outside the army and police."

[206] Under German control the Vichy government (in the person of Pétain, Laval, and others) left Vichy for Belfort and then Sigmaringen in August 1944.

in signing them, he never imagined what would follow, but if he himself lacked imagination in that regard, others imagined the consequences for him. He has had to assume all the consequences of acts that he regarded as merely clever. His policy of realism, his feeble cunning, his old man's half-baked ruses, and, last but not least, his diplomacy, which once might have seemed merely puerile and vain, led to too many deaths and entailed too much suffering during the four years of the Occupation for us to decorate them with any name other than treason.

People need to know these things. And they also need to know that if France is prepared to pardon those who failed to notice that the halting speeches that came their way via the airwaves betrayed the very voice of resignation and decadence, she has not decided to forget that responsible officials are indeed responsible and that a man who governs must be willing to submit to scrutiny what his government does.

In any case, that is what the establishment of the High Court ought to signify. But it must move quickly—more quickly than the Académie and so many others in this country who are slow on the uptake. If there are some cases in which our duty is not clear or justice is difficult to define, in this case we take our stand without hesitation. The voices of the tortured and humiliated join with ours in calling for justice of the most pitiless and decisive kind.

November 3, 1944[207]

Governing is good. But it calls for method. Good principles are sometimes compromised by the way in which they are applied. We have just had an example of this, and it may be useful to point this out for the sake of the government itself.

To come straight to the point, the government's arguments for dissolving the patriotic militias were at least worth discussing.[208] And they were discussed in a lively debate, which saw the clash of a wide range of opinions. So far nothing out of order. It was possible to believe that the government was right or that it was wrong, and we expressed our point of view in these pages. In any case, one was dealing with a government decision framed clearly in terms of two or three principles that were worth considering closely.

After this discussion, in any case, the government maintained its position. By the same token, those who had criticized the steps taken by the Council of Ministers held to their main argument, which hinged on the existence of a fifth column and the need for a "people's police." Again, attitudes were clear, and the government's position, though contested, was certainly not disparaged.

Now, however, there have been incidents in Paris. There were warnings, and then some railway cars filled with munitions exploded, causing deaths and

---

[207] Editorial. Typescript.

[208] Camus had already touched on the problem of the dissolution of the militias in the previous day's editorial.

injuries. All this has stirred emotions. And since these incidents may well have some bearing on the issues in contention in the recent public debate, all who were involved have had to reflect on the implications for their positions.

As things currently stand, it is impossible to say whether the explosions were the result of an accident or an attack. Some hold that an attack took place. Others are awaiting further information before making up their minds.

What should the government's policy be in this situation? Whatever sages and skeptics may think, the only wise policy for any government is always to tell the truth. The government, we assume, never denied that attacks were possible. It knows better than most that a minority of collaborators and *miliciens*[209] remain in this country.

What is still more symptomatic is the fact that the government never rejected the argument put forward by its adversaries. It simply said that if a fifth column exists, it is up to the government to root it out.

The government could therefore choose to fully inform the public today by releasing all information in its possession, excluding matters of military security, and it could admit that an attack was just as likely the cause of the explosion as an accident. Instead, it has chosen to release contradictory communiqués and to censor any indication that an attack might have been involved.

This, to put it mildly, is not a rational method of government. We will not insist on the principle of truthfulness, according to which the government should always be open about what it knows, or on the foolishness of believing that incidents that took place so close to Paris could be covered up for long. But we would like to point out to the government what the results of its policy have been. In effect, it has allowed people to believe that the government knew there was an attack, that it recognized the power of its adversary's principal argument, and that it suppressed the publication of any information that might have supported that argument because it felt uneasy about its own position, which it saw as threatened.

Such a policy makes no sense. It does not strengthen the government's position at all but in fact weakens it. It casts doubt on its motives, which previously there was no reason to regard as anything but pure. Finally, it discredits what many were prepared to praise.

This is unfortunate in every respect. By contrast, what we want is for ministers and government bureaus to adopt toward domestic policy the attitude that General de Gaulle inaugurated in foreign policy with his diplomacy of truth. France needs to speak with one voice, and it must be clear. It needs one government, but it must be truthful. It was asphyxiated by lies and needs to breathe the very air of truth. The minute that air is lacking, the very life of the nation is at risk. This is a principle to which all governmental offices ought to adhere, and if it were ever to become clear that they will not embrace it, then it might become necessary to force them to do so.

---

[209] That is, members of the Milice, Vichy's paramilitary militia.

November 3, 1944
Pessimism and Courage[210]

For some time now, articles have been appearing about works said to be pessimistic by critics bent on showing that this leads to servitude of the most abject kind. The argument is simple: a pessimistic philosophy is in essence a discouraged philosophy, we are told, and those who do not believe that the world is good are destined to serve tyranny. The best and therefore the most effective of these articles was the one by M. George Adam, which appeared in *Les Lettres françaises*.[211] In a recent issue of *L'Aube*,[212] M. Georges Rabeau responded to this indictment in an article whose title is impermissible: "Nazism Not Dead?"

I see only one way to respond to this campaign, which is to do so openly. The problem is not just mine, for Sartre, Malraux, and others more important than I am have been targeted, yet it would be hypocritical of me not to speak in my own name. I will not deal with the central issue of the debate, however. The idea that a pessimistic philosophy is necessarily a discouraged philosophy is silly, but it would take too long to refute it. I will therefore confine my discussion to the philosophical method that inspired these articles.

Let me begin by saying that it is a method that ignores the facts. Each of the writers under attack has proved in his own way that even without philosophical optimism, he knows his duty as a human being. An objective observer would therefore agree that a negative philosophy is not incompatible in practice with a

---

[210] Article signed by Camus and published under the rubric "Letters and Arts." Reprinted in *Actuelles*, in the chapter on "Pessimisme et tyrannie," with the erroneous date of "September 1945."

[211] *Les Lettres françaises* was established underground by Jacques Decour, whose execution delayed its publication. It reappeared in September 1944 under the leadership of Claude Morgan. It welcomed writers from the Comité National des Ecrivains, or National Writers Committee, of which it published a list, which included Camus. On October 7, 1944, under the title "Out of Season," George Adam published a critique of Jean Anouilh's *Antigone*. He showed that Antigone's desire for purity had led her to scorn men and life and culminated in what was nothing less than suicide and concluded that Anouilh's "individualistic pessimism" was "out of season."

[212] The article by Gaston (not Georges) Rabeau (the error is repeated in *Actuelles*) appeared in *L'Aube* on October 21, 1944. *L'Aube* was a Christian-Democratic paper born before the war, which ceased publication from June 1940 until August 23, 1944. With Francisque Gay as editor, it frequently published Georges Bidault and in fact became the official organ of the M.R.P. Rabeau argued that insufficient notice had been taken of Nazi ideology and that the universities had even contributed to its spread. He took philosophical ideas that interested Camus and caricatured them in a way to which Camus obviously could not remain indifferent: "It was our own universities that taught Nietzsche, and Nietzsche was one of the earliest sources of Nazism. . . . Then came the doctrine of nothingness and despair. This philosophy of nothingness and despair in the face of the world's absurdity and the futility of existence came from Martin Heidegger. With great originality and depth M. Sartre quite recently planted it in French soil [with the success of *Being and Nothingness*]. But many novels and plays have been spreading nihilist doctrines for some years now. . . . I hope that the celebrated authors I have mentioned will not continue their deadly work in this country." He ended with an appeal to readers of *L'Aube* to save France from the abyss into which these writers threatened to plunge it. It is worth noting that Sartre was mentioned by name but not Malraux.

morality of freedom and courage. He would simply see an opportunity to learn something about the human heart.

That objective observer would be right. For the fact that a philosophy of negation coincides in some minds with a positive morality actually points up the great problem that has caused such painful intellectual upheaval in recent times. To put it succinctly, it is a problem of civilization, and the question is whether man, without help from the eternal or from rationalist philosophy, can create his own values.[213] This project is larger than any one of us. What I believe is this: France and Europe today have either to create a new civilization or perish.

But civilizations are not made by rapping knuckles with a ruler. They are made by the clash of ideas, by blood and spirit, by suffering and courage. Themes that have been discussed in Europe for a century cannot be judged in an instant, in *L'Aube*, by an editorialist who does not hesitate to call Nietzsche lustful or say that Heidegger believed that existence is futile. I do not much relish the all too celebrated existential philosophy, and, to be blunt, I find its conclusions false.[214] Existentialism is nevertheless a great philosophical adventure, and it is difficult to see it subjected to criticism of the most constricted and conformist variety by M. Rabeau.

The problem is that existentialism's themes and projects are not now being judged in an objective manner. They are judged not according to the facts but in the light of a doctrine. Our Communist and Christian comrades lecture us about doctrine in lofty terms, and we respect them. Their doctrines are not ours, but it has never occurred to us to speak of them in the tone in which they have just spoken about us or with anything like their assurance. Let us continue with our experiment and our philosophy. M. Rabeau criticizes us for having an audience. I think he is exaggerating. What is true, though, is that the malaise that preoccupies us is the malaise of an entire era, from which we do not wish to separate ourselves. We want to think about our history and to live in history. We believe that the truth of this century cannot be discovered unless its tragedy is explored to the bitter end. If the age is afflicted with nihilism, it is not by ignoring nihilism that we will discover the morality we need. True, not everything can be summed up by the words "negation" or "absurdity." We know this. But negation and absurdity must be posited as ideas because our generation has encountered them and must learn to live with them.[215]

---

213 In an interview with *Servir* on December 20, 1945, Camus put it this way: "What interests me is to know how I ought to behave. And more precisely, how one can behave when one doesn't believe in God or reason." *Essais*, p. 1427.

214 Camus was of course often called an "existentialist," a judgment based more on a misleading comparison with Sartre than on his own writings and despite his repeated denials. See "No, I Am Not an Existentialist," an interview published in *Les Nouvelles littéraires* on November 15, 1945 (*Essais*, p. 1424). Nietzsche was an important source of Camus' thinking. He devoted a chapter of *The Rebel* to "Nietzsche and Nihilism." Although he was less familiar with Heidegger, he clearly was not unaware of his ontological reflections or his phenomenology.

215 These sentences shed historical light on the shift in Camus' thinking between *The Myth of Sisyphus* and *The Rebel*.

The men attacked in these articles have tried diligently to resolve this problem in their work and in their lives. Is it so difficult to understand that one cannot dispatch in a few lines a question to which others have devoted their entire lives without any certainty that they have found a satisfactory answer? Shouldn't they be granted the patience that we accord to any project undertaken in good faith? Shouldn't we address them more modestly?

I shall end this protest here. I hope to have dealt with it in a measured way. Yet I hope that readers will sense the indignation in these paragraphs. Objective criticism is something I prize, and I have no difficulty accepting the idea that work can be dismissed as bad or a philosophy as not good for the destiny of mankind. It is just that writers should be responsible for what they write. It makes them think, and we all desperately need to think. But to draw from such principles judgments about this or that intellectual's willingness to accept servitude, especially when one has proof of the contrary, or to conclude that this or that philosophy must inevitably lead to Nazism, is to paint an image of man that I prefer not to characterize, and it offers precious little proof of the moral benefits of optimistic philosophy.

ALBERT CAMUS

November 4, 1944[216]

Two days ago, Jean Guéhenno[217] published a fine article in *Le Figaro*, and we are loath to let it pass without saying that it ought to inspire sympathy and respect in all who are concerned about man's future. The article is about purity, a difficult subject.

To be sure, Jean Guéhenno probably would not have taken it upon himself to write about purity had a young journalist not reproached him in another article, intelligent but unjust, for his moral purity, which the writer feared Guéhenno conflated with intellectual detachment.[218] Guéhenno very properly replied by

---

[216] Editorial. Text reprinted in *Actuelles*, chapter on "Morality and Politics."

[217] Jean Guéhenno (1890–1978) edited the review *Europe* and later *Vendredi*, whose cessation Camus deplored in an article he published in *Alger-Républicain* in November 1938. A humanist and pacifist convinced that culture could contribute to man's progress, he wrote an essay on Michelet and a journal of the Popular Front years, entitled *Journal d'une révolution*. In 1946 he published his *Journal des années noires, 1940–1944*. His modest background only increased Camus' sympathy for the man and his ideas.

[218] In an article entitled "On Purity," published in *Le Figaro* on November 2, Guéhenno responded to criticism from a Communist journalist named Gilbert Mury, who had attacked him for his "noble soul," his "purity," and his "taste for eternity." These are reminiscent of the criticisms that would be directed toward Camus after *The Plague* and *The Rebel*. In particular, Guéhenno wrote: "The highest form of purity is to be pure among the impure, in the world, at the head of a great newspaper or at the podium of an assembly; it is to challenge men, sects, and parties, to conceive at every moment of what is possible and to undertake to do it, and yet to remain on the straight and narrow path. And that purity . . . is neither ineffective nor futile. There can be no doubt that the ends do not always justify the means."

arguing for purity maintained in action. And of course the problem of realism came up: the question was whether the ends justify the means.

We are all in agreement about ends but differ as to means. Rest assured that we all bring a disinterested passion to man's unachievable happiness. But there are some who think that any means of achieving that end are proper, while others disagree.[219] We belong to the latter group. We know how quickly means can be mistaken for ends, and we do not want just any kind of justice. This attitude sometimes provokes realists to irony, as Jean Guéhenno has just found out. But he is right, and we are convinced that what seems mad in his position is in fact the only wisdom open to us today. For what is at stake is indeed man's salvation. And this is to be achieved not by taking a position outside the world but through history itself. The point is to serve man's dignity by means that remain dignified in the midst of a history that is not. The difficult and paradoxical nature of such an undertaking is clear.

Indeed, we know that man's salvation may well be impossible, yet we say that this is no reason to stop trying and, furthermore, that it is not permissible to call it impossible before making a genuine effort to prove that it isn't.

We have that opportunity today. This country is poor, and we are poor with it. Europe is miserable, and its misery is ours. Lacking wealth and a material heritage, we have perhaps acquired a freedom that allows us to indulge in that folly called truth.

On a previous occasion we stated our conviction that we have been given one last chance. We truly believe it is the last. Deception, violence, and blind human sacrifice have been tried for centuries, and the experience has been bitter. Only one thing is left to try, and that is the plain middle course of disillusioned decency, scrupulous fairness, and steadfast support for human dignity. We believe that idealism is futile, but our idea, simply stated, is that as soon as some men are willing to serve good with the same stubborn and indefatigable energy with which other men serve evil, the forces of good will be in a position to triumph—for a very short time, perhaps, but still for a time, and that triumph will be unprecedented.

Some may ask, Why pursue this debate? There are so many more urgent issues of a pragmatic sort. But we have never shrunk from discussing such practical matters, as is obvious from the fact that when we do discuss them, not everyone is happy.[220]

In any case, the debate has to be pursued because no other item on the agenda is more urgent. Why pursue the matter? So that when realist thinking once again rules the world, men like Guéhenno will remember that they are not alone and know that purity, regardless of what others may think, is never deserted.

---

[219] This idea is central to *The Rebel* and the play *The Just Assassins* (*Les Justes*).

[220] In *Actuelles*, the final clause was reworded to read, "we don't please everyone."

November 5, 1944[221]

The *Officiel* has published the text of an executive order requiring newspapers to reveal their production figures[222] and inform the Minister of Information of their sales so that their paper allocations can be decreased or increased as needed.

This order is inspired by logic. The publication of circulation figures will someday be a way of allocating resources among newspapers, and clearly the workings of the press should be open to public scrutiny. As for the statements of circulation, certain difficulties arise, and some injustice may result for some of our sister papers, which do not sell all the papers they print and may not be allowed to try their luck much longer, yet it is obvious that the requirement was instituted in a spirit of fairness and rationality. Our point is simply that the logic of the measure must be pursued to the end.

Indeed, the order states that in case of fraud, the paper allocation for the subsequent two-week period will be reduced by an amount corresponding to the number of undeclared or concealed copies. We believe that this brief paragraph, which deals with a seemingly minor matter, poses a problem of political morality of the highest importance.

What does it literally signify? That fraud is to be tolerated, and that its only sanction will be a reduction in the quantity of paper allotted equal to the amount wasted in the previous allotment. This is not a punishment but an adjustment, a bargain struck between the thief and his victim.

That being the case, this brief text rests on untenable principles. It is tantamount to admitting that fraud is both inevitable and venial. If it is true that every punishment is proportionate to the crime, then this measure amounts to granting fraud a pardon or indulgence that in the end bestows upon it the status of a natural custom.

This is not the way to begin. If we want to establish new relations among citizens, if we want decisions made in a spirit of fairness like this one to bear their fruit, then we must call a spade a spade and punish fraud for what it is.

We will not say much about the danger of such a policy for the new press. It is not a good idea to tempt people to do wrong, and if the only risk of cheating is to have one's fraud rewarded rather than punished, that is a great temptation indeed. There is no need to point out how quickly the virtuous would at first be left in the dust and eventually dismissed as naïve.

What is more, to accept fraud so calmly and benevolently is in fact to legitimate it. We are not proposing to erect virtue as a principle. Virtue seldom rules in human affairs, and no one should make the mistake of assuming that we are naïve. Nevertheless, fraud should be punished diligently and severely enough to make it clear that we will no longer tolerate it. A newspaper that tampers with its books in the hope of achieving a larger circulation has no right to speak to the

---

[221] Editorial. Typescript.
[222] *Combat* regularly stated its circulation figure, which was roughly 180,000.

people of France: that much is clear. The least fraud in this regard should be punished by cancellation of the entire paper allocation for a period of time long enough to ensure that the benefits of honesty become clear.

We beg the indulgence of the minister of information[223] for taking up his time with an issue that may well be looked upon as minor. Our duty, however, is to ensure that values are restored to their proper place and to point out that the very idea of fraud is invariably among the causes of national decadence. If the *Officiel* neglects to treat this matter as seriously as it ought to, it is up to the press to do so and to uphold the necessary principles of firmness and dignity.

November 7, 1944[224]

For several weeks, some in France have been waiting with apprehension, others with eagerness, for draconian decisions to be made in regard to various financial matters. On Friday it was learned that the Government was about to act.[225] That evening, a bulletin of the Agence Française de Presse[226] announced a bond issue paying 3 percent in perpetuity. This bond issue was presented as an important financial initiative and a political act of real importance. To put it bluntly, we refuse to look upon this as a creative initiative, though we readily admit that it is an instructive political act. We cannot, however, subscribe wholeheartedly to the policy it represents.[227]

We beg our readers' indulgence if we say once again what is in our hearts, and say it unambiguously. The principal objective of this bond issue seems to be to prove to those with capital that their fears are unfounded and that the Government intends to reinstitute the so-called "politics of trust." In financial matters, this means assuring the moneyed interests that they will not be threatened and that the government seeks their support. In other words, the Government is proposing a "pause"—to use a term that is not easy to explain in regard to an area where it is impossible to say that much work has yet been done.

The bulletin mentioned above confirms this suspicion when it says that "the country will approve the decision to forgo any coercive measures. . . . There can be no doubt but that this appeal, which is in keeping with the French democratic tradition, will resonate well among peasants and other strata of society."

What this means is clear to us, but we are not sure that everyone understands it. It is indeed surprising that there has thus far been no reaction in quarters from which a reaction might have been expected, and especially from the editorial pages of our newspapers.

Make no mistake about our intentions: our point is not to criticize the bond issue but to point out its true political significance. No one will be upset if the

---

[223] Pierre-Henri Teitgen.

[224] Editorial. Typescript.

[225] The announcement was made on Friday, November 3, 1944.

[226] On the AFP, see n. 108 to the article of October 3, p. 56 above.

[227] Camus' observations are more moral than economic in nature.

Government feels the need to float a bond issue. But at least refrain from pre-senting as a bold initiative a measure of the sort that has allowed French govern-ments to avoid taking the kind of energetic decisions in regard to finances that the country has awaited for so long. In politics as in finance, measures are not good or bad in themselves. But they must be adapted to the situation and the time. And in the current period of dissension and chaos, the idea that so many ills due to the moneyed interests can be remedied by adopting a policy of confi-dence toward those same interests is either foolish of misbegotten.

In any case, the Ministry of Finance should know that it does not have our approval. We will do what needs to be done, on our part, to make sure that the bond issue is successful.[228] But we want to say in advance that we deem this mea-sure to be insufficient and that it has all the earmarks of a shortsighted policy, which, if pursued, will ultimately destroy the very interests it is meant to defend.

November 8, 1944[229]

The Consultative Assembly met yesterday for the first time.[230] There was every reason to stress the symbolic charge of this day and the consolations it afforded. Even in the most difficult moments, we ought not to neglect the grounds for sat-isfaction that the world is still capable of giving us. Whatever else can be said, France is today liberated from her shame. The value of that is beyond all measure.

But it would be a serious political mistake to suggest that the Consultative Assembly is beginning its work in a climate of optimism. In every corner of France, and in any number of scrupulous and disinterested hearts, worry and anguish are obvious. The country has not been saved just because it has been lib-erated, and we are in danger of losing in liberty what we were so overwhelmed to have discovered in nights of oppression.

The fate of France, and consequently the values that we respect, depend on its politics. And knowing as we do the vileness and temptations of politics, we can-not write these words without apprehension. Indeed, little that we see around us is comforting. The country is caught between two distinct approaches to poli-tics, both equally regrettable. One is the politics of reaction, and the Govern-ment has just given two or three indications that this is the course it is in the process of choosing. The other is the politics of outrageous demands, and the editorial pages of our newspapers offer a sufficient number of examples.

As often happens, the very blindness of the politics of reaction reinforces the demands from the other side, and the excessiveness of those demands serves as an additional reason for pursuing the politics of reaction. Those in France who wish to maintain the arduous dedication to human truth that became their hope

---

[228] Like other newspapers, *Combat* published advertisements inviting readers to purchase bonds, and the bond issue was in fact successful.

[229] Editorial. Typescript.

[230] On the Consultative Assembly, see the editorial of October 14, 1944, p. 71.

during the four unforgettable years just past feel caught between these two contrary forms of irrationality, with only the lamentably inadequate weapons of scrupulous language and obstinate objectivity to defend themselves.

For the best of us, this political climate, in which error and impatience lend each other support, is difficult to endure. The first meeting of the Consultative Assembly took place on the very day that François Mauriac professed himself to be tired of all politics and expressed his wish henceforth to address himself exclusively to men's souls.[231] This coincidence is instructive because it is bitter.

It should at least inspire this country's new representatives to think about what they are doing.

We say this with no illusions, but it needs to be said: each member of this first Assembly should reflect on this issue and ask himself whether it is possible to close his ears to the clamor of special interests and the shouts of partisan groups in order to find the words that France ought to speak if the country wishes to survive.

If the Consultative Assembly fails to steep itself in this essential spirit, its work will come to naught. It begins its labors under the aegis of liberty, which is a heavy honor to bear. It must know, however, that liberty does not exist without freely accepted constraints, that there is no such thing as general efficacy without particular sacrifices, that there is more than one way of loving and serving one's country, and that not all ways of loving and serving it are good.

Nothing great or fruitful will be accomplished in France or in the world if we do not do what we must to contradict the bitter words spoken 150 years ago by one of the purest lovers of liberty: "Everybody wants the Republic, but nobody wants poverty or virtue."[232]

November 9, 1944[233]

Mr. Roosevelt's election is good news.[234] For the sake of all it is best that the same men who led the war effort reflect upon the problems of peace. The ideal would be for peace to be made by the nations and individuals who suffered most from the war. But that, of course, is an unrealistic notion.

---

[231] In *Le Figaro* of November 7, Mauriac published an article entitled "Impure Politics": taking up the question of "purity" in the wake of Guéhenno and Camus, he said that the attempt to "introduce it into what is most impure in the world, namely politics, amounts to a hopeless struggle against some very venerable lies." He deplored the "ruse" and "fraud" by which the slogans of a party leader were passed off as the voice of the people and added that "ultimately this is what drives people accustomed to the free exchange of ideas (such as we had here with *Combat*) out of politics." Mauriac concluded by recalling Lacordaire's statement that in the end the soul is the only object of interest.

[232] The quote is from Saint-Just, about whom Camus would later write at length in *The Rebel*. It comes from his "Speech of November 29, 1792, on the hoarding of food supplies."

[233] Editorial. Text very likely by Camus. The attribution is indirectly authenticated by Roger Grenier's comments on the article of April 14, 1945 (see n. 461, p. 192) on Roosevelt's death, which repeats a sentence from this article.

[234] Franklin D. Roosevelt had just been reelected to a fourth term as president of the United States.

It is a good thing that America is now assured of being represented tomorrow by the same man who was able to persuade it that the European conflict was also its conflict.

Mr. Roosevelt's personality is not the issue. To be sure, he has an appealing face. Compared with the anxious, proud, ravaged, or vacant faces of Europe's powerful men, his is the very image of happiness.[235] Yet while sympathy can help to achieve mutual understanding, it is not a sufficient basis on which to build an alliance.

Evidence for this can be seen in the fact that Mr. Roosevelt's personal policy in regard to French matters has not always been well inspired. But then the Atlantic is wide, and viewed from afar French politics are not always easy to understand. It would take a great deal of love not to go wrong, and it is impossible to imagine love in relations between nations. The essential thing is to identify a few shared moral values along with a small number of obvious common interests. In this respect our entente with the American people is perfect.

France is not the issue, moreover; the issue is world peace. We would not be misrepresenting what the people of France think, we trust, if we said that our country is prepared to do a great deal and to give a great deal to assure the world of a peace that is finally just and therefore lasting. In this respect, the election of Mr. Roosevelt satisfies all our desires.

Three years ago, Mr. Roosevelt proved himself capable of seeing that the war in Europe was everyone's business.[236] It would be a great misfortune if, tomorrow, America failed to understand that peace, too, is everyone's business. The man who recognized the first of these truths and who little by little persuaded the vast majority of satisfied and happy Americans to follow him is in the best position to understand the second and make it clear to his countrymen.

It is essential that the great issues of the future be dealt with by men of tested mettle, men who will remember well the horror and cruelty inherent in all war before they lay down the conditions for world peace. That is why it is good that Churchill, Roosevelt, Stalin, de Gaulle, and the others will still be around tomorrow. They have been obliged to learn the value of things and of human life. They must speak not only in the name of victory but also in the name of suffering.

That is why, despite our differences and mutual irritations, and beyond our various reasons for anguish and doubt, we Frenchmen can without hesitation salute President Roosevelt's election to a fourth term. To him we offer our gratitude and friendship as a free people who, though unbowed by servitude, take from the memory of their suffering and the remembrance of their misfortune a terrible hunger for justice and peace.

France, too, voted for Mr. Roosevelt, not out of self-interest but out of concern for the future of the world and of mankind.

---

[235] This sentence would be repeated in the article of April 14, 1945.

[236] This was of course a major theme of *The Plague.* "From that moment on, . . . the plague was everyone's business." Op. cit., p. 67.

November 10, 1944[237]

Yesterday, the Congress of the Socialist Party held its first meeting.[238] To judge by the texts of the speeches, much of the time was devoted to harsh self-criticism. This was a promising beginning, and the upcoming sessions of the Congress deserve the closest attention. The idea of socialism is a great idea. And the Socialist Party is one of the great hopes of the France of tomorrow, but only if it can translate into reality the principles of renewal that were laid out before the Congress yesterday.

Ultimately, the reconciliation of justice and freedom, the simultaneous pursuit of a collective economy and liberal politics, the good of all combined with respect for each—these ideas, which so many in France find urgent today, are socialist ideas. Anyone who read carefully the basic tenets of the programs set forth by the Christian Democrats or the Movement of National Liberation would see clearly that any socialist activist could have subscribed to them. Why then did those who came out of the resistance without belonging to any party not immediately join the Socialists?

We put this question frankly because it is a question that many of us have been asking. Let us try to answer it just as frankly, encouraged to do so by the courageous way in which the Socialists themselves confronted the issue at their Congress.

What no doubt prevented many new people from joining the Socialist Party was its past. Its image was not an appealing one. We knew it when it was weak and helpless, more prodigal with words than eager for action, and as estranged from the socialist values of unselfishness and self-denial as religious bigots are estranged from true Christianity. In short, we were deterred by some of its adherents and most of its methods.[239]

Although any number of sentiments and ideas drew us to the party, to us it never seemed quite up to the challenges of these difficult times. In the past, moreover, the Socialists sometimes confused the realization of their doctrine with the winning of a majority in the National Assembly.

Our critique of socialism also included, and still includes, an element of nostalgia and regret born of seeing a great idea reduced to petty practices and a calling practiced as if it were a trade. We lost our confidence.

It would be misleading to suggest that all these doubts have evaporated. But the underground existed, and Socialists played their part in the struggle—a good and important part. Today, they speak with firmness and energy. Their loyalty seems resolute, and that in itself is of the utmost importance. There is no denying that if the Socialists are able to renounce individuals and methods that are today discredited or outmoded in order to rebuild a great party, they will be the

---

[237] Editorial. Typescript.

[238] Many members of the *Combat* staff, including Camus, were close to the Socialist Party in their thinking.

[239] Camus frequently gave voice to his wariness of the men and methods of the Third Republic.

major political force in the France of tomorrow and will become the focal point of much of the energy stemming from the resistance. But they have a great deal of work to do, work that calls for determined effort and clear thinking. They have to do the impossible, which is to overcome the force of habit. They have to find a new style and a new inspiration born of purity. They have to recover their youth. How difficult this will be becomes clear when one compares Daniel Mayer's[240] excellent presentation to the Congress with Félix Gouin's[241] speech to the Assembly.

Gouin's eloquence strikes us as unfortunate. No member of the resistance would have taken any pleasure or felt any emotion at hearing the resistance celebrated in such a pompous tone. We need truer, more direct language. We are tired of repeating that what we need is the truth and nothing but the truth. If we are certain that M. Mayer has a better understanding of this devouring hunger for the truth, it is because he, at least, has no habits to overcome.

Nevertheless, for all these reasons the Socialist Party Congress is an important event. We who serve only this country and a few overarching human values hope that socialism will find its expression among the Socialists and not be forced to look elsewhere and exhaust itself in the process. For if France needs men to serve it and it can be served only by those who are disinterested and armed with a few clear ideas, it also needs to be served very quickly, and the best road to the country's rebirth is also the shortest and straightest.

November 11, 1944[242]

Our friends from *Défense de la France*[243] are troubled by the editorial in which we denounced the damage done by a reactionary government policy in combination with extreme demands issuing from the public at large.[244]

They ask us not to use the word "reactionary" and to take a less negative attitude. Although they warn us of the danger of sowing discontent in people's minds, when we were merely revealing the discontent that is in our hearts, and

---

[240] Daniel Mayer, an early resister, was a close associate of Léon Blum's. He was the editor of the underground newspaper *Le Populaire*, founded Socialist Action Committees, and in 1942 advocated establishing a Council of the Resistance. After Léon Blum was deported to Germany, Mayer served as head of the S.F.I.O. in his absence and was in fact the party leader at the time of this Congress.

[241] Félix Gouin (1884–1977) was a Socialist deputy and one of eighty deputies who refused to grant full powers to Pétain in 1940. He joined Free France in 1941. In 1943 he helped to set up the Consultative Assembly in Algiers and continued to preside over it in Paris in November 1944. He later served as president of the Constitutive Assembly from November 1945 to January 1946 and as head of the Provisional Government after the resignation of General de Gaulle.

[242] Editorial. Typescript.

[243] On *Défense de la France*, see the editorial of October 1, 1944, n. 104, p. 54. Camus is responding here to an editorial by Robert Salmon on "The Political Future of the Resistance," which was published on November 9, 1944.

[244] See the editorial of November 8, p. 105.

against the possibility of reviving partisan conflict, when the parties are already in conflict over a wide range of issues, we know that their criticism is offered in a fraternal spirit, and we will respond in the same tone. In so doing we will avail ourselves of the opportunity to clarify our position.

Since our use of the word "reaction" followed our criticism of the recent bond issue, it was clear that the reactionary policy we had in mind was the government's financial policy.[245] On this point, we hope our friends will forgive us if we stick to our guns. We regret that no other paper except *Le Populaire* has yet taken a position on this issue.[246] Whether the Government likes it or not, a policy of trust in the moneyed interests at a time when those interests ought to be held in check serves interests which are not those of the nation. We call this policy reactionary because reactionary is the word for it. As everyone knows, we make it our business to call a spade a spade.

Our friends would also like us to go beyond criticism and offer some constructive proposals. But *Combat* was the first paper to take up the issue of scandalous fortunes, and we pointed out in a series of three fundamental articles what basic steps we thought needed to be taken.[247]

Our friends deplore the fact that we publicly questioned the Government's methods. It therefore behooves us to state our position with respect to the Government one more time. We have said in no uncertain terms that the Government has our confidence as a matter of principle. That is our loyal and considered judgment. But we believe that without frankness there can be no friendship and that sympathy cannot thrive on misunderstandings. We are therefore determined to remain vigilant and to speak out with equal clarity when we see things of which we disapprove and when we see things of which we approve. We do not know whether such an attitude will, as our friends claim, add to the country's malaise. But we are certain that that malaise would only grow deeper if we were to engage in a conspiracy of silence, ulterior motives, and concealment of our true concerns. Furthermore, the fact is that we make little use of our right to criticize.

When we do criticize, our friends can take it for granted that we have weighed our words carefully and that our comments are based on solid information.

In the end, *Défense de la France* wonders what we are after. But our friends know the answer perfectly well. We are trying to maintain the fragile truth that they and we have defended for several long months in the streets of Paris. To the freedom that we have already reconquered we are trying to add a justice not yet within our grasp. We won that freedom by dint of obstinacy and intransigence.

---

[245] See the editorial of November 7, p. 104.

[246] In a series of articles *Le Populaire* called for a financial policy that would free the state from trusts and man from capitalism.

[247] On September 11, *Combat* published an articled entitled "Scandalous Fortunes Should Be Confiscated," which indicated a number of measures to be taken immediately. On October 21, under the pseudonym Juste Bauchart, Camus published an article entitled "Money versus Justice," see p. 83 above. François Bruel commented several times on the need for a rigorous financial policy.

Justice cannot be had in any other way. No one should lie to the country, and no one should speak of political revolution while proposing reactionary measures. France can no longer stand for falsehood. We tell our friends this: it is time to call a spade a spade.[248] That is our job. The Government, the Assemblies, will deliberate as they see fit. But it is impossible to add silence to the falsehood that still lingers in France.

We know that a reactionary policy will be fatal both to the nation and to the interests that policy claims to defend. We know that he who blindly embraces the lesser evil ends up facing the greater one. And we know that he who refuses to give up any of his privileges ends up relinquishing them all, but only when it is too late. For all these reasons we insist that the government adopt a clear and decisive policy to organize the socialist economy that France needs and to shore up the political liberty without which France can no longer breathe.

November 14, 1944[249]

It is worth noting that the first issue to be debated in the discussions between France and Britain was the arming of French troops.[250] Other issues are no less important, and we shall have more to say about them in due course. But this one calls for a number of comments.

The production of weapons in a nation at war is indeed the primary problem. There is of course no other way to assure victory. But there is also no other way to minimize bloodshed among the nation's defenders. Modern warfare is so lethal that no country, no matter how numerous its population, can allow itself to go to war half prepared.

Modern war has greatly diminished the importance of courage compared to that of matériel. No matter how bold or determined a nation may be, it can be subjugated with a sufficient number of machines. And if it persists in fighting, its very flesh disappears along with it. Thanks to some notorious examples, the whole world now knows that it is impossible for a nation to sacrifice its youth and its elite without risking decadence of every variety. That is why the nations of the world have devoted so much effort to the production of weapons. They have learned to make war by sacrificing material wealth while economizing on men to the maximum extent possible.

This is even more true for France, which counts as one of the sad examples that give the world pause. France does not have enough men, for many reasons, no doubt, but primarily because it lost a great many. It has sacrificed the best of its men in the course of this long thirty years' war. At every level of our national

---

[248] Camus would use this phrase again in his editorial of November 30 and in *The Plague*, p. 45.

[249] Editorial. Typescript.

[250] Winston Churchill and Anthony Eden, the British minister of foreign affairs, came to Paris on November 11 to take part with General de Gaulle in a celebration of the 1918 armistice. The equipping of French troops by the Allies did indeed pose serious problems.

life we can measure the cruelty of their loss. Hence we must muster the courage to say that our young men must be spared.

In another respect, however, defeat has imposed unimaginable duties on us— this is the French tragedy. We have to regain our place, and we have to conquer and occupy Germany. We did not want this war, but we must wage it until it is won.

The violence that we detest has today become a necessity for us.

But we can no more throw unarmed men into battle today than we could during our four years of resistance. We have no war industry. We can produce only courage and sacrifice, with which we are restoring the honor of France even as we threaten what is most precious in French life. Every Frenchman who falls in the Vosges adds something to the country's grandeur but subtracts one unit from its most vital strength.

No crueler or more wrenching conflict can be imagined. Though it is hard for a nation to beg foreign powers for arms, France, faced with a choice between life and death, must save its life by asking repeatedly for what it needs to arm its soldiers and make use of their courage while preserving as many as possible of the lives it so desperately requires.

Of course anything that can be done to get our factories working again should be done. But everyone knows that this will not be enough. The problem would remain unresolved. If victory finds France exhausted and passive, the war will have achieved nothing for us or for Europe. Our Allies need to understand this. France is not asking for compassion; it is asking for arms. And if it asks for arms with feverish urgency, it is because it wants to be in a position to do its duty and save its future, and it knows that arms alone will enable it to resolve the most tragic dilemma that any nation has ever faced.

November 15, 1944[251]

There is something irritating about the many news reports that describe Mr. Hitler as either ill or dead. Some papers insist that these reports are true, and foreign news agencies fuel the flames with a spate of dispatches out of Stockholm that contain more question marks than credible information.

Given that a lid has been clamped on Germany, and given how difficult it is to get any accurate information, one wishes that the French press were less hasty to print reports that may be well-intentioned but are nevertheless of dubious authenticity.[252]

To be sure, it is impossible not to be struck by the fact that ordinarily prudent sources such as the Home Service broadcasts out of London are asking the question with increasing urgency. Nor can there be any doubt that Himmler has

---

[251] Editorial. Typescript.
[252] Camus discussed the need for vigilance in the reporting of news on several occasions. See the editorials of September 1, p. 23, and December 10, 1944, p. 137.

assumed an increasingly important role in Germany.[253] On that subject, clandestine German broadcasts, most notably the Volkssender, whose reports are never unreliable, have provided interesting details. When all the reports are examined carefully, however, the only things that seem certain are that Hitler has been keeping quiet and that Himmler is playing a central role in a Germany under siege.

Does it follow, as some frivolously maintain, that Hitler has been immobilized by madness or illness and that Himmler has taken his place? These reports may be true, but we have no way of knowing. What we do know is not enough to draw any conclusions. Hitler has been silent for a long time now, and for all that time Germany has fought with determination. Besides, when a country is under siege, police powers always increase in proportion to the danger. Hence Himmler's importance will continue to grow, but that in no way implies that Hitler has been sidelined.

If Hitler should be removed from the picture, we would rejoice. But given the current state of our information, we are not about to announce any such thing. In any case, whether or not the reports are true, our duties remain the same.

The constant circulation of these kinds of reports serves no purpose. Our morale needs no bucking up. These frivolous items serve only to distract.

If the point is to get Germany's attention, though, the effort is wasted. Germany is at a point where the morale of its people is of no consequence. A machine— devoid of soul, wound up as tight as can be, and set blindly on its way in a desperate last-ditch effort—has no need of morale. It keeps running until it is destroyed. And in fact the goal is to destroy it.

Finally, we want to put in another word in favor of serious news reporting. We want nothing to do with hypothetical dispatches or mysterious attributions. We need factual news, even if the facts are unpleasant. The French want to fight, and they know they can fight without sensational reporting. Indeed, they feel that some journalists have no idea of the change that has come over them and forget that this is now a different country. So they feel a bit neglected, and this may make them cross, because they no longer want to be neglected.

November 16, 1944[254]

The Government has decided to confiscate the property of Renault S.A.[255] Readers may recall that the Renault factories were initially requisitioned pending the disposition of charges against Louis Renault.[256] Louis Renault is now dead. Human justice has nothing more to do with him.

---

[253] On Himmler, see the editorial of August 30, 1944, note 26, p. 20. Camus had previously mentioned Hitler's silence in his editorial of September 20, p. 43.

[254] Editorial. Probably by Camus.

[255] On December 24, 1944, the Renault factories became a "national enterprise."

[256] On Renault, see the articles of September 26 and 27, 1944, pp. 47 and 48.

Yet the financial power that was his remains, and it was a power that could not be put to use for the benefit of the nation until the courts stripped Renault of his civil rights. Now that the courts can no longer do this, must that power remain in the hands of Renault's former stockholders?

The Government does not think so. It came to the conclusion that Renault's wealth had given rise to an abundance of privileges without corresponding responsibilities and must now serve the good of all. It thus rendered a moral verdict from which there is no appeal. We have given our views on this topic often enough that no purpose would be served by repeating them now. What needs to be pointed out, however, is that the Government, in coming to the conclusion it reached, publicly pointed to the responsibility of Renault's shareholders. It thus held responsible not only privileged individuals such as Renault but also money as such, in its most anonymous form.

A society based on money cannot lay claim to either grandeur or justice.[257] It has even less of a claim, however, when money retains all its privileges without accepting any of its responsibilities. By contrast, yesterday's decision signifies that money has duties, which are all the greater because its prerogatives were once so exorbitant.

We want to be clear. If the nation calls for confiscation of Renault's properties, it does not do so for reasons of envy. In some ways it is a matter of indifference to us that some people are wealthy and enjoy all the things that go with wealth. If our personal feelings are of any interest, we would add that the glittering lives of the wealthy strike us as impoverished and not terribly enviable.

Four terrible years have taught us the rudiments of a certain morality, however. We know now that those who have chosen to live for money can have no excuse unless they prove that they are willing to accept the responsibilities that go along with their privileges.

In 1940, French industrialists and their stockholders were called upon to measure the full extent of those responsibilities by paying the highest price. They were called upon to resist the enemy. They preferred to be paid instead.

When we discussed the Renault problem some time ago, some readers pointed out to us that certain workers also volunteered for work in Germany in exchange for high wages. That fact does not change our position in the slightest. True, these men were also guilty, but their leaders were more guilty, for the simple reason that they had been materially fortunate beforehand and lost their sole opportunity to justify the all too isolated good fortune they had previously enjoyed.

That is why we feel bound to say once again that we approve of the decision taken by the Council of Ministers. We have said enough about our opposition to, for instance, the Government's financial policy[258] to lend weight to the approval we offer today. We wish to add only one thing, namely, that while we are equally determined to criticize what needs to be criticized and to praise what deserves to be praised, we find the obligation to criticize a bitter one and would

---

[257] See "Money versus Justice," October 21, p. 82.
[258] See editorial of November 7, p. 104.

much rather be able to approve decisions such as the one taken today, which make our young democracy truer and stronger.

November 19, 1944[259]

We need to look closely at what has happened in Belgium. There are lessons to be drawn from any conflict between the government of a free country and the Resistance in that country, especially when the risk of Allied intervention looms on the horizon.[260]

It is clear that M. Pierlot favors a conservative policy.[261] More precisely, he is trying to maintain Belgium's traditional political face while making only those concessions that he believes are inevitable.

It is no less clear that, just as is the case in France, years of resistance in Belgium have produced men, and a body of opinion, hostile to any kind of conservative politics and eager to consolidate the liberation of the nation by introducing bold, just reforms.

Conflict was therefore likely. It has come about in connection with the disarming of resistance groups and in short order has grown serious. An already distressing state of affairs was brought to the boiling point by General Erskine's statement that he would intervene if disturbances posed a threat to military security.[262]

It is clear that initially M. Pierlot was opposed by the entire resistance, led by the Communists. Yesterday, the Socialists for all practical purposes disavowed the Communists by agreeing to remain in the Government. It is true, moreover, that the three ministers who have resigned, two of whom are Communists, joined General Erskine in signing a joint communiqué that has calmed things down somewhat.

It therefore seems likely that the crisis will be resolved, at least temporarily, and we are glad about this. We say "temporarily" because the resolution comes not from an agreement between the parties but from external constraint. The Pierlot government, which clings to power as a result of this compromise, finds

---

[259] Editorial. Typescript.

[260] *Combat* followed the Belgian crisis closely. It was perhaps not so much a matter of taking an interest in foreign policy for its own sake as one of seeking to draw lessons applicable to French politics.

[261] Hubert Pierlot (1883–1963) formed a Catholic government in a coalition with socialists. After Belgium's surrender, King Leopold III withdrew from public affairs and looked upon himself as a prisoner at Laaken (from which he would be deported to Germany in June 1944), and Pierlot went to London to head the Belgian government in exile. Upon returning to Belgium in September 1944, he formed a "national union" cabinet that was essentially a continuation of his London cabinet. Liberals, socialists, and Catholics had to cope with a strong Communist presence in the country, and Pierlot had to take Communists into his government. On September 30, the king's brother became regent. The royal question proved difficult to resolve, because Belgians reproached Leopold for meeting with Hitler in November 1940 and for his not very combative attitude during the war. Pierlot supported the idea that the king's powers ought to be restored once he was liberated. He resigned on February 7, 1945.

[262] General Erskine of the British army was in command of the Allied troops that liberated Belgium.

itself in a false position. Indeed, its weakness is now manifest, and it remains in power only because it has force on its side.

In other words, it governs with the threat of Allied intervention, which is the most distressing situation imaginable for the government of a country that has only just been liberated.

If a lesson must be drawn from this crisis, it seems fair to say that a government that places itself in such a position suggests that its policy lacks foresight. Some of M. Pierlot's ministers have taken some very bold steps. By contrast, others have dragged their feet. This unbalanced approach has been the worst failure of what is supposed to be a government of national union, although the union is due only to circumstances and has not been internalized. It is an approach that has only alienated all classes of society and satisfied none. In politics, one has to choose.

For instance, the Pierlot government adopted a financial policy that was destined to meet with opposition from important private interests. The right thing to do was to destroy those interests first with the support of the nation rather than stop halfway to the goal and then take steps to disarm the popular militias, thereby incurring the people's hostility. As things now stand, those powerful interests remain intact and hostile to M. Pierlot, who has also managed to alienate popular support.[263] This outcome is unpleasant to say the least.

In conclusion, we should add that the Belgians showed less discipline than we did in a similar matter.[264] The Allied viewpoint is readily comprehensible. Had M. Pierlot taken the trouble to explain his more clearly and more nimbly, he could have gotten his point across. The viewpoint of the resistance also has its legitimacy. Nevertheless, through political missteps alone, the Belgians today find themselves in an intolerable and scarcely imaginable predicament. We prefer not to think of what position we would have taken if the Allied armies had been obliged to turn against the French resistance. It is the painfulness of this situation that allows us to say that even if everyone involved in this matter behaved reasonably, M. Pierlot made an unforgivable mistake in putting his country into such a situation.

November 21, 1944[265]

It is once again time to update the situation in Spain.[266] Franco is still in power. He hopes to remain there, and since he no longer expects to do so with

---

263 The government had issued orders to disarm resisters. In reaction to this measure, three ministers resigned: two Communists and one former resister. They also demanded an investigation into collaboration by Belgian industrialists and called for nationalization of giant trusts.

264 On the disarming of the patriotic militias in France, see the editorials of November 2, p. 95, and November 3, p. 97.

265 Editorial. Typescript.

266 See articles of September 7 and October 5 and 24, pp. 29, 59, and 86.

his traditional friends, he is trying to do it with the support of the world's democracies.

To that end he has made certain advances.[267] He has spoken of Phalangist Spain as an "organic democracy" and floated the idea of a "Catholic bloc" with Spain as one of its members. With these proposals he believes he has made enough concessions to claim a place at the peace conference. He argues that nations that were able to remain at peace are better suited than others to deal with the problems of peace.

Meanwhile, negotiations are under way to create a transitional government in Spain. Franco himself has made offers to the monarchist party, but to date these have gone unanswered. In Paris, a M. Maura says that he has been sent by republicans in Spain to enter into talks with El Caudillo. But the Unión Nacional, which has its headquarters in Paris, has just denied this report, though without mentioning M. Maura by name.

Franco's opposition includes the Spanish Republicans and the Allies. The Allies have adopted an ambiguous policy. They maintain diplomatic relations with Spain. Msgr Spilmann[268] has used his credit in favor of Franco, and British conservatives waited until the dictator made his most recent proposals before rejecting his claim to a moral right to participate in the peace conference.

At the same time, the Allies have been encouraging the republican opposition. They greeted the notion of a "phalangist democracy" with incredulity. Governments have left it to the press and commentators to point out that Spain was never at peace, because its policy of nonbelligerence tied up several French divisions at its border, it fought against Russia, and it took advantage of the difficult situation in which Great Britain found itself to alter the status of Tangier by force.[269]

The Spanish Republicans, for their part, are on the road to unity but have not yet arrived. The most active organization is surely the Unión Nacional Española, which met recently in Toulouse.[270] But broad segments of republican opinion, including parliamentarians, movements of the democratic left, and especially union federations (the C.N.T. and U.G.T.), object to granting it the right to speak for all. Their chief complaint is that the Unión Nacional, though supported by the Communists, included prominent members of the old regime such as Gil Robles, who was involved in the repression in Asturias in 1934.[271]

---

[267] On November 16, Franco recognized the Provisional Government of the French Republic.

[268] Francis Joseph Spellman was the archbishop of New York. [Camus' "Spilmann" is a misspelling of his name.—Trans.]

[269] Under the terms of a 1923 agreement, Tangier was an international zone. France occupied it from 1940 to 1945.

[270] During this meeting, the Unión Nacional called for restoration of the Republic, a meeting of the Cortès in France, and constitution of a provisional government.

[271] Gil Robles was the leader to the extreme-right Ceda party, and it is true that his joining the government in 1934 paved the way for the bloody repression of the Asturian miners. In 1936, Camus and his comrades at the Théâtre du Travail wrote a play entitled *Révolte dans les Asturies* about these events.

Republican unity is more likely to be achieved, in any case, around men such as Prieto,[272] who is currently in Mexico, or Negrin,[273] who is in England. None of this prevents the republicans from working wholeheartedly together to bring about the downfall of Franco's regime or to deplore the ambiguities of Allied policy.

Clearly, the Pyrenees still exist, and while we are bound to hope that someday they will no longer stand in our way, that will not be possible until Spain is once again our friend. But we need to do something to make that happen. Some readers have asked us why we are taking sides in Spanish politics. The reason is that there are some situations in which one has to take sides, and if France must now wage war against fascism, it ought to wage war against all fascism or not wage war at all. We are doing everything possible to make sure that our reporting of the news remains objective. But when it comes to a conflict in which the honor of free peoples coincides with their interests, we should not remain neutral.

We do not have to intervene in Spanish politics. Indeed, we feel that the republicans ought to wait until the moment is ripe in order to ensure the success of their action. But we know that Allied diplomatic pressure would be enough to bring Franco down and avoid bloodshed among one of the most generous peoples in Europe. It would be cowardly not to do what needs to be done in order to bring that about by stating our urgent conviction here and now.

France will lose nothing by doing so. The only friends we have in Spain are republicans. But they are in the majority. There are 640,000 of them whom we will never forget. Six years ago they languished without hope in Franco's prisons. Like us, the Spanish Republicans have known misfortune and desperate combat. Like us, they forged a community of heart and spirit that will endure forever. We want no friends of whom we cannot be proud. And their friendship honors us as much as it obliges us. Republican France cannot have two policies, because it has only one voice.

November 22, 1944[274]

It is time for some self-criticism. A profession that involves daily judgment of breaking news in order to discern what common sense and basic intellectual honesty require is not without dangers. Wanting the best, you spend much of your time judging what is worst or even just what is less good. In short, you adopt the systematic attitude of the judge, the schoolteacher, or the professor of ethics. In this business, it is but one step from the presumptuous to the foolish.

---

[272] Indalecio Prieto y Tuero, who served as a minister in republican governments in 1936 and 1937, was sent on a diplomatic mission to South America and remained there after Franco's victory.

[273] Juan Negrin (1886–1956) served as minister and then head of the republican government during the civil war. In 1939 he sought refuge in France and later went to England, where he headed the republican government in exile until 1945. He died in Paris.

[274] Editorial. Text reprinted in *Actuelles* under the title "Autocritique" at the end of the chapter entitled "Le journalisme critique."

We hope we have not crossed that line. Still, we aren't sure that we have always avoided the danger of implying that we can see the future more clearly than others and never make mistakes. Of course we don't believe anything of the sort. We sincerely hope to participate in the common effort while abiding by certain rules of conscience that in our view have not been widely applied in matters of politics.

That is the extent of our ambition, and if we point out the limitations of certain ideas or political actions, we are naturally aware of our own limitations as well, and we try to make up for them by adhering to two or three basic principles. But reporting the news is a demanding business, and the boundary between morality and moralism is never clear. Sometimes one crosses it owing to fatigue or negligence.

How to avoid this danger? By means of irony. Alas, these are not ironic times. This is still an age of indignation. If only we can maintain our sense of the relativity of things, come what may, everything will turn out all right.

Of course we cannot avoid a certain irritation when we read, the day after the capture of Metz[275] and knowing what that victory cost, a story about Marlene Dietrich's arrival in the city.[276] Indignation about such things is always reasonable. But that does not mean that we believe our newspapers have to be boring. It's just that in wartime we don't think that the doings of movie stars are necessarily of greater interest than the suffering of peoples or the bloodshed of soldiers or a nation's determined effort to find its own truth.

All of these things are difficult. Justice is both an idea and a passion of the soul. We must learn to take what is human in it without transforming it into the terrifying abstract passion that has damaged so many men.[277] Irony is no stranger to us, and what we take seriously is not ourselves but the unspeakable ordeal that this country is going through and the bracing adventure upon which it has been obliged to embark. In the light of this distinction we can take the true measure of the daily task we face, as well as its relative importance in the great scheme of things.

We felt the need to say these things today for our own sake as well as for the sake of our readers, so that they may know that in everything we write, day in and day out, we are mindful of the duty to be thoughtful and scrupulous, which all journalists should adopt as their credo. In short, we do not omit ourselves from the critical scrutiny that we believe is needed at the present time.[278]

---

[275] Metz was liberated on November 20 after a hard-fought battle.

[276] Marlene Dietrich, the actress made famous by Josef von Sternberg's film *The Blue Angel,* left Nazi Germany for the United States in 1933. She put on a number of shows for Allied troops during the war.

[277] This would become the theme of *Les Justes.*

[278] According to Roger Grenier, Camus wrote the lines that follow his article on Synge's play *The Tinker's Wedding* under the heading "Stage and Screen": "Editor's note: the length of the column our critic has devoted to the work of Synge obliges us to postpone until next week a review of Turgenev's very fine comedy, *The Provincial Woman,* intelligently interpreted by Paul Oettly and Maria Casarès." [Casarès was Camus' mistress.—Trans.]

November 23, 1944[279]

To judge by what one reads in the Paris press, everyone in France is socialist, a phenomenon we've noted previously. From *Le Figaro* to *Le Populaire*, the collectivist economy enjoys a good press. M. Mauriac speaks of "socialist faith."[280] M. Jurgensen, writing on behalf of the M.L.N., characterizes the movement as "laborite."[281] The Christian Democrats use the same vocabulary.

This is less surprising than it may appear. And despite what some say, it is not only because France's slide to the left has accelerated. It is above all because in four years of forced meditation the men of the old right came to recognize that the social problem was real and that a nation could not enjoy youthful vigor without ensuring the welfare of all its children.

It is not this near unanimity that is surprising, then. For what is it, finally, that prevents such substantial segments of the public from joining together to form a powerful majority party capable of quickly enacting the structural reforms needed if France is to be reborn?

It certainly isn't the parochial quarrels that occasionally surface in the press. The idea that religious differences are somehow preventing the formation of a coalition of men of good will is silly. When the Socialists choose to focus on Voltaire's anticlericalism to the exclusion of everything else, they are simply being frivolous. And when M. Mauriac scolds them for it, he loses patience too quickly.

The problem that needs to be resolved is so important that all of us need to work at it. With the future of so many at stake, it is inconceivable that our efforts should founder on disputes about such an intimate matter as religion.

The real obstacle lies elsewhere. To begin with, it seems likely that not everyone is using the word "socialism" in the same way. What is clear is that everyone has a more or less confused intuition of the urgent need for social justice. Progress toward that end has already been considerable.

It is not yet enough, however. We need to clarify the political situation, which is at once so encouraging and so disquieting.

---

[279] Editorial. Typescript.

[280] As Camus had done in November, Mauriac wrote quite favorably about the Congress of the Socialist Party ("Le bilan de quatre-vingts jours," November 12). On November 16, he published an unusually long article on "Socialists and Christians," in which he expressed his hope that the two might join forces, with Christians giving up their opposition to secular education and freedom of teaching and socialists moving beyond their anticlericalism. On November 22, in a postscript to an article on "Criminal Cash" (the gist of which Camus would not have disavowed), Mauriac took exception to a sentence in *Le Populaire*, which hailed Voltaire as "the destroyer of primitive superstitions perpetuated in these climes by the Christian religion," and acknowledged that "I feel my socialist faith flagging in the face of this Himalayan peak."

[281] Jean-Daniel Jurgensen was one of the regular editorial writers for *France Soir (Défense de la France)*. On November 14, under the title "Entente Cordiale," he published an article in which he pointed out "how much closer England and France had become as both evolve toward socialism." He discussed the British Labor Party and hoped that France would take England as its model.

Our view is that it is possible to distinguish at least two kinds of socialism in the political philosophies that are currently seeking expression: a traditional Marxist socialism, represented by the old parties, and a liberal socialism, generous in spirit but not clearly formulated, which is reflected in the movements and personalities that have come out of the resistance.

The latter form of socialism, insofar as one can make out its content, tends to invoke a French collectivist tradition that has always made room for individual freedom and that owes nothing to philosophical materialism.[282] This is in fact what appears to prevent it from merging with the older socialist formations at the present time.

What we are witnessing, then, is a confrontation of two socialisms, and the problem of the moment comes down to figuring out whether this confrontation will result in a compromise doctrine and a broad coalition or simply force resistance socialism to clarify its program and find a novel form of expression. In our view, France has something to gain from this confrontation. But it seems that most people today want to move a little too quickly. Rather than seek quick unity, it would be better if people in both camps tried to clarify what it is they want to unite. Socialism is not a fashion; it is a commitment. Hence it is desirable that each of us try to understand what he is committing himself to. You can't be socialist in principle but conservative in finance, for example. Socialism is a permanent engagement on all issues.

If everyone who is sincerely seeking the formula that best sums up his or her aspirations were to ponder this matter carefully, a French socialism fueled by freedom's energy and uncompromising on matters of justice might at last emerge for the good of the country. It must be said, however, that there will be nothing new in this development, which will merely give historical reality to ideas already adumbrated by one Jules Guesde.[283]

November 24, 1944[284]

The more one thinks about it, the more convinced one becomes that some sort of socialist doctrine is beginning to take hold in a broad segment of the public. We briefly touched on this subject yesterday.[285] The subject is important enough,

---

[282] Isn't this what would decades later be called "socialism with a human face"? Camus' analysis is remarkably lucid, a rarity for the period.

[283] Jules Guesde (1845–1922), was a republican journalist who went into exile to escape imprisonment for supporting the Commune. Tempted by anarchy, he became an active participant in the creation of the Workers Party, which later became the Socialist Party of France and then the Section Francaise de l'Internationale Ouvrière, or S.F.I.O. He played an important role in making Marxism known in France and wrote many texts on collectivist themes. As a rival to Jaurès, he is seen as the leader of the revolutionary socialists, and, since his vision of socialism was essentially theoretical, he was regarded, rightly or wrongly, as the embodiment of socialist values in their purest form.

[284] Editorial. Text reprinted in *Actuelles* in the chapter on "Morality and Politics."

[285] This editorial expands on the topic broached the day before.

however, to warrant exploring it in greater detail. For in the end, nothing in all this is very new. Hostile critics might well express astonishment at the fact that the men of the resistance, and many other Frenchmen along with them, went to such lengths to arrive at this point.

But first let us say that it is not absolutely necessary for political doctrines to be new. Politics has nothing in common with genius (action is something else). Human affairs are complicated in detail but simple in principle.

Social justice can easily be achieved without an ingenious philosophy. It requires only a few commonsensical truths and such simple qualities as foresight, energy, and unselfishness. In such matters, to seek to innovate at any price is to work toward the year 2000, whereas we in France need to put our affairs in order immediately, tomorrow if possible.

Second, it is not novelty that makes political doctrines effective but rather the energy they embody and the sacrifices they inspire. It is hard to know whether the theoretical socialism of the Third Republic moved its adherents deeply, but today many yearn for a socialist politics because it gives their burning desire for justice a concrete form.

Finally, some may be tempted to believe that socialism won't accomplish much because their idea of socialism is a rather limited one. There is a certain form of socialist doctrine that we detest, perhaps even more than we detest the politics of tyranny. It is a doctrine that rests on optimism and invokes the love of humanity to exempt itself from serving human beings, the inevitability of progress to evade the question of wages, and universal peace to avoid necessary sacrifice. This kind of socialism relies mainly on the sacrifices of others. Those who preach it never commit themselves. In short, it is afraid of everything, especially revolution.

We have seen it before, and if all socialism meant was a return to *that* socialism, it is true that it wouldn't amount to much. But there is another kind of socialism, a socialism that is determined to pay the necessary price. It is a socialism that rejects both falsehood and weakness. It does not waste its breath with talk of progress, yet it is convinced that man's fate is always in man's hands.

It does not believe in absolute and infallible doctrines but in obstinate and tireless if inevitably halting improvement of the human condition.[286] It holds that justice is well worth a revolution. And if revolution is more difficult for it than for some other doctrines because it does not hold man in contempt, it is also more likely to demand only useful sacrifices. Can such an attitude of heart and mind be translated into reality? That is a question to which we shall return.

Today we want to clear up certain ambiguities. It is obvious that the socialism of the Third Republic did not meet the standards we have just set forth. Today it has an opportunity to reform itself. We hope it avails itself of that opportunity. But we also hope that the men of the resistance and those who agree with them continue to insist on those standards. Because if traditional socialism wants to

---

[286] This is one of the major ideas of *The Rebel.*

reform itself, it can do so only by reaching out to the new men who are beginning to appreciate the new socialist doctrine. It will need to embrace that new doctrine itself, and embrace it wholeheartedly. We now know that there can be no socialism without a full and faithful commitment of one's entire being. Indeed, that is precisely what is new.

November 25, 1944[287]

Yes, our armies are on the Rhine, Strasbourg is taken, and Alsace is nearly liberated.[288] We are well aware that this is what needs to be discussed today. But what words can describe a victory awaited for four years, anticipated in interminable silence, and heralded at last by the cannons' stentorian voice? How can we weigh our words properly when we speak of this moment, in which we cannot entirely rejoice, because it is a moment of joy only for the living and could not have come to pass without the sacrifice of so many?

Yes, we are looking at victory. Can anyone appreciate what this means for a generation that has never known anything but defeat? Now we must acknowledge, measure, and evaluate an overwhelming event that goes by a very different name: "victory." Of course some will say that this is the victory of equipment, of strategy, or of time. Forgive us for saying so, but none of these things has any very urgent meaning for us right now. What we see in all these banners, victorious communiqués, and outstretched hands is but one thing: the triumph of a people.[289]

That alone has meaning for us. For the spirit that drove the young French army to drive on past its assigned objective is the same spirit that made a success of the Paris uprising, which the sages had declared in advanced to be doomed. It is the same spirit that inspired a nation to refuse to give up, even in its most hopeless hour.

That, at least, we can be happy about. We have many reasons to be bitter or discouraged. It is not always easy to accomplish anything with human beings. They are not always agreeable or easy to live with. But a nation at war, a community in battle, our comrades determined to win because they know they are right—these will justify our existence. Whatever the future may hold, there are hours we will never forget.

By the same token, however, we must acknowledge that every victory wears a somber face. Because it paves the way for other victories and because it must be deserved, of course, but above all because no nation has ever won a victory without shedding the blood of its people. And because it took a long line of bodies

---

[287] Editorial. Typescript.
[288] Leclerc's Second Armored Division entered Strasbourg during the night of November 23.
[289] Camus has recovered the tone of his first editorials from the month of August, but the gravity—and profundity—of his reflection is somewhat at odds with the shouts of victory that filled much of the press.

riddled with bullets in prison yards and along the walls of France and the roads of Alsace before a cry of freedom hurled in the face of a German firing squad somewhere in central France in 1940 could make itself heard today in a Strasbourg draped with fresh new banners.

Yes, we must recognize that victory is not a happy word.

It is a word like all human words, which takes its meaning from sorrow as well as joy. That is our reason for welcoming it today with both the gratitude of hearts too long deprived of pride and the silence we owe to those who, from June 1940 to November 1944, justified the efforts of all who struggled to hold out for so long.

November 26, 1944[290]

This is what we have come to: Belgian blood has been shed in Brussels, even though the city has been liberated.[291] It took no particular acumen on our part to predict in our article on the Belgian crisis that the agreement, in place for only a short time, could not be anything but temporary.[292] It was reached under threat of allied intervention, and lasting agreements can come only of freedom, not of duress.

In any event, the arrangement worked out between the Pierlot government and the party of the resistance could have been followed up with mutual concessions. This would have allowed Belgium to wait until allied strategy had evolved to a less crucial phase. The country's political problems could then have been discussed in a climate of freedom, without which debate inevitably becomes strained.

At the present time there is no practical way of getting at the truth beyond the government's official statements. Yet even those statements reveal the Pierlot government's singular obstinacy in sticking to a policy based on force, which it is difficult not to regret.

Indeed, the official statements tell us that the Belgian resistance has already made significant concessions. The Socialists were unwilling to abandon M. Pierlot, the three ministers who submitted their resignations signed an agreement with General Erskine, and the various resistance movements urged their members to turn in their weapons.

In return, the government authorized demonstrations within a limited perimeter. At the same time, however—and still according to official statements— the Minister of War was granted dictatorial powers. He had the right to ban any

---

[290] Editorial. Typescript.

[291] On the same day *Combat* reported: "Bloody incidents in Brussels between police and demonstrators. Thirty-six wounded, some seriously." The demonstration was organized by the Independence Front, one of the most important resistance groups. It was authorized, but the demonstrators entered the ministerial zone, from which they had been prohibited.

[292] See the article of November 19, p. 115.

meeting, to censor or seize private correspondence, to impose administrative internment, and, finally, to censor any printed material deemed likely to damage the nation's morale.

These powers, owing to their broad scope and to the very terms in which they are expressed, recall realities still fresh enough in our minds that we can easily imagine the effect they must have had on the people of Belgium. Try to imagine a political situation in which M. Diethelm[293] suddenly found himself authorized to ban our meetings and open our mail and the press was prohibited from voicing any opposition. People who have just emerged from four years of struggle against tyranny might well lose their equanimity on finding themselves governed in such a tyrannical way by the government of their choice. If the forces of freedom are shooting at you, you begin to think you might have been better off facing the forces of tyranny, because then, at least, there is no mystery about why they are shooting at you. The actions of the Belgian demonstrators are even easier to understand when we recognize that, for strategic reasons they cannot fail to understand, they are condemned to silence, which leaves them seething with rage, as though a lid had been clamped down on a boiling cauldron.

Now the lid has been blown off. The police and the people have clashed. This distressing situation is more than regrettable. And all the noble minds will of course say that the people should have remained calm. Yet without resorting to polemic and without invoking arguments that will have weighed upon the heart of anyone who fought in the resistance at the announcement of today's news, it is nevertheless possible to think logically about what has happened.

What has happened is regrettable, yet we must grant that politics cannot be conducted with the idea that people should behave like saints. For the Belgian people to have chosen discipline and enforced silence, they would all have had to be stoic saints and heroes. Governing consists in putting people in a position where discipline does not seem beyond their capability. In this respect, the Belgian experience can serve as an example to any democratic government that forbids itself on principle to rely exclusively on force and must therefore limit itself to firmness guided by a just idea of man.

On this view of the matter, it seems difficult to say that M. Pierlot governed. Many of our comrades from the resistance will write that his policy was simply criminal, and it would admittedly take some effort to prove them wrong. But to keep our words measured, it will suffice to say that a policy condemns itself when, by dint of blindness and stubbornness, its result is to force a nation to resort to solutions that could not be more incompatible with its own interests.[294]

---

[293] André Diethelm, a military official in Algiers, was minister of war in the French Provisional Government.

[294] In December, Paul Bodin, *Combat*'s special correspondent in Brussels, reported that political agitation had ended but dissatisfaction remained, and Pierlot declared that he intended to remain in power since no one else wanted the job. He was forced to resign in February 1945.

November 28, 1944[295]

We get word from many quarters that many Algerian soldiers[296] have been made uneasy by the ignorance and incomprehension with which they have been greeted in the metropolis. Much of the misunderstanding apparently stems from the fact that the French think they are dealing with a professional army, and some go so far as to call the troops "mercenaries."

Things therefore need to be clarified, and memories refreshed. The army recruited in North Africa by the provisional government naturally includes some professional troops. They have proved their worth, and it would seem only fitting to give them their due.

But the vast majority of this army consists of reserve units that, after being mobilized, fought their way from Italy to Tunisia, Corsica, and the south of France and have now reached the Vosges.

The fate of these North Africans, whether they be French or Muslim, is of concern to all of us. Through two wars, these North African troops, fighting thousands of miles from home, have played a most important role in our shared battles.[297] Algeria, moreover, has always had a proper appreciation of what France owes it in this regard.

The people of the mother country would do well to keep this in mind. The soldiers they encounter in the Vosges are mostly civilians, who left their homes and families to defend a cause they have defended regularly. That should be enough for France to give them the welcome they deserve in full awareness of what they have done and are still doing.

No militant of the Resistance would think of slighting these men, because the Resistance today knows the meaning of courage and sacrifice. It knows how to recognize those qualities wherever it finds them. And we can attest that if there is one place they have always existed, it is the army of Africa, whose true face every Frenchman should know.

November 29, 1944[298]

Only just liberated, Europe is in turmoil. Belgium, Italy, Poland, and even, to a lesser extent, Greece[299] find themselves today facing problems that seem beyond their ability to deal with alone. And even if they could deal with them alone, they would not be allowed to. The domestic policies of these governments have so

---

[295] Editorial. Most likely by Camus.

[296] Note that the phrase "Algerian soldiers" includes both "French and Muslims," as Camus makes clear later in the article.

[297] See the article of May 13–14, 1945, "Crisis in Algeria," p. 198, in which Camus points out that "hundreds of thousands of Arabs have just spent two years fighting to liberate our territory."

[298] Editorial. Typescript.

[299] The Greek situation would quickly become critical. See the editorial of December 9, 1944, p. 135.

much influence on the conduct of the war that the belligerent powers cannot fail to take an interest in them.

Why close our eyes? The English high command is planning to take action against the resistance in Belgium.[300] England has laid down conditions for the formation of a new government in Italy.[301] Russia and Great Britain are intervening in the affairs of Poland, which the United States has abandoned to its fate.[302] Let us therefore say openly that these nations are not yet sovereign, though we should add that this state of affairs is temporary. Their servitude is legitimated by the state of war, but it would serve no purpose to call it anything but servitude.

When we look at the problem in this cruel light, we are better prepared to learn from it. For in the end, all the European crises are similar. When the old governing class regains power, it fails to adapt its policies to popular aspirations born of misery and oppression, but the old governing class enjoys the support of the Allied command. To put it succinctly, what we are witnessing in other countries is a latent conflict between the European resistance and the armies of liberation. That might seem a dreadful thing to write, but it is the truth.

Who, then, is right, and who is wrong? It is certainly possible to say that the resistance has been in too much of a hurry, that war has its laws, and that the war must be ended before undertaking a vast program of reforms. This is true. But the problems raised by the liberation of each country cannot wait, and it is those problems that are aggravating the conflict.

People need to eat right away, and the world needs justice now. The dilemma for France and for all of Europe is to be obliged to wage a war and make a revolution at the same time.[303]

The whole problem is to achieve success at the lowest possible cost. Those charged with running the world must never forget that this war is not a war of conquest or glory.

It is a European convulsion, which raises as many social problems as strategic ones. Anyone who wants freedom also demands justice. During the four years in which freedom was the sole bread of starving peoples, their craving for justice grew apace. Europe has exhausted its reserves of patience.

Europe must therefore be treated for what it is; its exhaustion and irritability must be taken into account. And the surest way to increase its impatience is to force down its throat men and methods it no longer wants any part of. Peacetime physicians cannot heal wartime ills. Victory is the primary goal but not the only one. And victory without justice would strike all these nations as a vast joke.

---

[300] See editorials of November 19 and 26, pp. 115 and 124.

[301] The Allies opposed the appointment of Count Sforza as Italian foreign minister.

[302] With the backing of the Soviet Union, the Lublin Committee had been established as a form of government in Poland, ignoring the existence of the Polish government in exile in London. See the editorial of January 3, 1945, p. 162.

[303] Starting with the very first articles he wrote in August 1944, Camus touched repeatedly on this key notion.

It is perhaps comforting to think that France has thus far avoided these point-less difficulties. But it would be dangerous for us to lull ourselves to sleep. France is sovereign because it is fighting. Other nations speak to her as an equal because Frenchmen are dying every day to win unmistakable victories. This is what allows us to solve our problems as we see fit. Yet those problems are still not solved, social justice remains to be achieved, and we can look forward to future disappointments if we do not draw the appropriate lessons from the crises that are tearing other countries apart.

The European resistance is expressing—at times ineptly to be sure—the hopes and demands of the peoples of Europe. Today those demands are being turned aside for reasons of military strategy. Since we are not subject to the same servi-tude as other nations, however, let us try to demonstrate, at least, that our demands are not opposed for any reasons other than strategic ones. The privilege we have won imposes an important duty on us, which is to give shape to the hopes of all these impatient peoples and in so doing to set an example.

November 30, 1944[304]

The ministry of information is preparing a decree that will reduce the print runs of Paris newspapers by 25 percent.

The threat of such a cut has been hanging over us for months now. And for months the Press Federation has been presenting the minister with evidence that his decision is unfounded. Shortages of pulp, coal, and transportation have all been invoked as grounds at one time or another. The Federation pointed out to the minister that there is pulp in Rouen, that mines in the north of France were holding coal in reserve for us, and that the national railroad (S.N.C.F.) has said that it had the means to transport that coal. Now we are told that there is a pro-duction shortfall of a thousand metric tons per month, though no mention was made of the five thousand tons purchased in Switzerland by M. Mendès France[305] in a clearing agreement.

At the same time, authorization to publish has been granted to some newspa-pers, and it has been announced that *Le Temps* is to return with a new name and

---

[304] Editorial. Very likely by Camus. The next day's editorial, which is a typescript, directly continues this one.
[305] Pierre Mendès France (1907–1982) was a Radical-Socialist deputy from the Eure who served as a sec-retary of state in the second Blum government in 1938. In June 1940 he was one of the French lawmak-ers who attempted to escape to Morocco on the *Massilia*. Treated as a deserter by the government of Vichy, he was arrested but escaped and joined Free France in London in 1942, where he served as an aviation officer. General de Gaulle appointed him commissioner of finance under the French Committee of National Liberation and minister of finance under the Provisional Government in Algiers. In Paris he became minister of national economy in September 1944. When his financial austerity plan was rejected in January 1945, he resigned. When Camus resumed his work as a journalist with *L'Express* in 1955, it was to support Mendès France's return to power in the hope that he might resolve the Algeria problem as he had negotiated peace in Indochina and Tunisian independence when he was premier from June 1954 to February 1955. See *Albert Camus éditorialiste à* L'Express *(mai 1955–février 1956)*, op. cit.

mysterious sources of financing.[306] Meanwhile, the government has proved incapable of regulating the provincial press. In Nice, the daily papers have ceased to publish for lack of paper, while in Toulouse no limits are imposed on press runs.

Our readers know that *Combat* has taken a moderate line in regard to the problems of the press. We have never competed for market share or cited our circulation figures to demand what the authorities did not wish to give us. We have disciplined ourselves to work within the imposed limits. But the cuts announced today threaten our very existence. And our moderation in the past entitles us to raise our voices today and call a spade a spade.[307]

Whether intentionally or not, such a measure amounts to depriving the resistance of its organs of expression. It can only have been recommended by interests hostile to the resistance and its desire for reform. This we will not tolerate.

Some whose judgment we respect will say that we are merely defending the interests of a faction. That is true. But we believe that that faction's interests are those of the country as a whole. A threat has been hanging over us for months, to be sure, but we are not alone. In France as throughout liberated Europe, the offensive against the resistance has begun. But that offensive is also an offensive of the forces of reaction against the people's will to reform. The men of the resistance have the bad taste not to want to be like those who fought in other wars, who returned home too tired to protect what they had defended. The resistance has committed the offense of ignoring its fatigue and taking an interest in a country from which some would prefer that it avert its eyes. That is why it is being attacked.

That is also why it will defend itself. We do not always agree with all of our colleagues, but on this point our solidarity is total.

To those who object that we are clinging to positions we have acquired, we will not take the trouble to correct them with the truth, which is that we would gladly give up those much-coveted positions to cultivate our own gardens. We do not speak the same language as our critics. Yes, we are defending the positions of the resistance, and we will do what we must to hold on to our means of expression until the people of this country have a chance to make their wishes known. Our fight did not end on liberation day. It continues,[308] and no one—not the forces of reaction, the moneyed interests, or the bureaucrats—will prevent us from having our say. Only the people of France, expressing themselves freely on election day, can tell us whether the time has come for us to keep silent. Meanwhile, we will indeed hold our positions, because that is the only way we can make sure that the lessons of the defeat and the victory are not betrayed, distorted, or falsified by interests we hold in contempt and seek to destroy.

If the Ministry of Information wants to break off relations with the press, it is sure to succeed. As we have said many times, the resistance never claimed to have exclusive rights. It's time to stop exaggerating. And we are getting tired of all the attacks on men who recognize no judges other than the people of France.

---

[306] This would become *Le Monde*, the first issue of which appeared on December 19, 1944.
[307] Cf. editorial of November 11 and n. 248, p. 111.
[308] Cf. Camus' first editorial, p. 11.

The resistance has given every possible proof of its patience, discipline, and moderation. It cannot go any further, however, without denying all that is purest in it. There are principles we will not allow to be tampered with. And when it becomes necessary, we will prove that objectivity is not incompatible with energy.

December 1, 1944[309]

The problem of the press, which we touched on yesterday, is only one aspect of the offensive against the resistance, which is something we cannot ignore. This offensive is less obvious here than it is elsewhere. But it is no less dangerous.

It is true that the men of the resistance are not saints, and that is fortunate, because we want nothing to do with a nation of saints. The resistance is open to criticism, and here, at least, we have always listened to such criticism with the respect that it deserves. When necessary, we have contributed to it, because we believed that the duties of the resistance outnumbered its rights and that it had everything to lose by becoming a sect.

What is at issue today, however, is not criticism, nor is it that exercise of mutual correction whereby the members of a community maintain a steady course to progress. It is a battle that is being waged at all levels against men and ideas whom some have come to regard as posing a threat to a certain concept of order.

To be sure, many Frenchmen knew nothing about the resistance, especially those who did nothing for it. When insurrection came to Paris, it is no secret that the calm that prevailed in the so-called wealthy neighborhoods was a calm of both ignorance and indifference. People who don't like the world to change when everything is in their favor were briefly of the opinion that the resistance was nothing more than a group of French patriots who had mobilized on their own. This brought smiles to their lips.

And indeed, the resistance was that. But it became something more than that: a force for renewal, which imagined a just France even as it was forging a free France.[310] People who don't like the world to change today feel that they were deceived. For them, the liberation of France meant nothing more than a return to traditional menus, automobiles, and *Paris-Soir*.[311] Let freedom come quickly so that we can at last be mediocre and powerful in comfort!

But the resistance insists that we mustn't rest, that everything remains to be done, and that the fight is still going on. It says that we must agree to be poor so that the country can be rich and agree to do without so that a people can at last get what it needs. But the resistance also calls itself socialist. That has been a source of misunderstanding.

Because of that misunderstanding, there are those who want to make the resistance pay. They want to rest,[312] they want to hold on to their privileges: the

---

309 Editorial. Typescript.

310 This text reiterates the main ideas of "From Resistance to Revolution," August 21, p. 11.

311 On *Paris-Soir*, see the editorial of September 1, 1944, note 1, p. 23.

312 Cf. the editorial of October 29, which drew a contrast between the desire for rest and "the thirst for honor," p. 92.

offensive has begun. We therefore have no choice but to fight. In fact, this challenge comes at the right time. We were beginning to get tired of the constant attacks on what some called "a faction," forgetting what the country owes that faction.

The resistance was beginning to get tired of hearing that it was doing too much one day and not enough the next and that it was a monolithic party yet crippled by divisions. It took all this criticism in good part, however, with a laudable desire for objectivity and youthful diffidence.

It was prepared to pardon mediocrity and self-interest, provided only that the mediocre refrain from being aggressive and the self-interested recognize that it is sometimes in their interest to keep silent and compromise when necessary. Little was required: we are not as eager to destroy as is rumored in certain quarters. On the contrary. When you passionately seek unity, you have to resign yourself to doing something for the mediocre and greedy, since everyone knows how many of them there are. But if the greedy are blind enough and stubborn enough to start a fight and stupidly try to stop what can't be stopped, then they will have to be crushed. We say that not as a matter of right but as a matter of duty, a duty that has not ended.

This is what the resistance is beginning to understand. And maybe it is a good thing that their adversaries have helped them to do so. Men who were passionate about freedom and justice for four years have now been reminded that while giving thanks, they mustn't forget the revolution that has yet to be made. A head of state who knew a revolutionary situation when he saw one had this to say after scoring a great political success: "First, never sing of victory. Second, liquidate the enemy, because he is only beaten, not exterminated. Third, never glorify yourself until you've reached your goal, and when you do, it becomes unnecessary."

We know now that the enemy must be exterminated, and we want to reach that goal where victory needs no song to celebrate it.

December 3, 1944[313]

General de Gaulle has had talks with Marshal Stalin.[314] The press has been unanimous: the Russian alliance is vital for France, because it makes possible a solution of the German problem.[315] All the commentators also approved the French

---

313 Editorial. Typescript.

314 Stalin (1879–1953) had been the uncontested head of the Communist Party and absolute master of the USSR since 1929, following the death of Lenin and the elimination of Trotsky. Despite the German-Soviet nonaggression pact (August 23, 1939), Hitler attacked the USSR in June 1941. Initial German victories ensued, followed by a long siege of Stalingrad (September 1942–February 1943), after which the USSR won back the territory it had lost, and Stalin, whom Churchill and Roosevelt recognized as an indispensable ally, participated in all the conferences concerning the postwar settlement.

315 The talks between de Gaulle and Stalin took place in Moscow between December 2 and December 6, 1944. Accords were signed by the ministers of foreign affairs of the two countries on December 10. See Camus' comments in his editorial of December 18, p. 145.

foreign minister's statement of opposition to the idea of a western bloc standing in opposition to an eastern bloc.[316]

Some commentators even went so far as to say that France might serve as a bridge between the USSR and the western democracies. But the Soviet press contradicted them, stating that the USSR needed no bridge to Great Britain and was mature enough to maintain on its own any contacts it deemed necessary. From this minor difference of opinion we conclude only that commentators must weigh their words carefully, especially when it is good will and enthusiasm that prompt them to write.

That aside, the situation is unambiguous. France has its own reasons for wanting the Russian alliance, since it has its own reasons for wanting Germany to be watched on two borders. There are also more general reasons for rejecting a policy of blocs in favor of a policy of European entente that seeks to reduce national rivalries as much as possible.

Despite all this, the Moscow talks do not seem likely to yield substantial surprises. General de Gaulle will express France's desire to achieve a full and lasting entente with the Soviet Union. If he returns home with elements of our future foreign policy, which will be based on a double and perpendicular alliance with the USSR and the western states, he will have solved a huge problem and thus met our immediate needs. We will all be able to rejoice in this.

May we say, however, that we are hoping for more? We hope that beyond these immediate successes, France will achieve other, more significant advances with broader implications for the future. We reject the policy of blocs because we repudiate the politics of balancing, of complicated interactions of alliances and interests, which have never led Europe anywhere but into war. Given this attitude, it would be logical to talk to Moscow not about a European federation, which will take time, but, more modestly, about the international aspect of the European problem.

Politics is impossible today without economics, and there is not a single economic problem at the moment that isn't international. In production as well as consumption all the countries of Europe depend heavily on one another. We know today that we are joined together in life as in death. We know that a neighboring people's hunger is a threat to us, and excessive economic power may be as well. An international economy cannot be dealt with by means of exclusively national policies.

Although such national policies are inevitable as things stand today, future European arrangements must reflect our newfound interdependence and solidarity.

To take a concrete example, if, not only in Moscow but in all the conferences at which the fate of Europe is being decided, it were possible to broach and then clarify the issue of raw materials, leading ultimately to an agreement on the need to internationalize them, it would mark a huge step toward world peace. Once

---

[316] The French foreign minister at the time was Georges Bidault.

the basis of an economic federation has been established in Europe, political federation will become possible.[317]

Of course these problems will not be resolved in a few hours of talks. But if France and the USSR could be the first to utter the words that alert minds in Europe have been waiting for so many years to hear, we would regard it as grounds for pride and confidence.

December 5, 1944[318]

There is a sort of tacit agreement between M. Mauriac and us: we provide each other with subjects for editorials. This may have something to do with the fact that what he is doing is similar to what we are doing, while our temperaments are surely different. In this, of course, we see nothing but advantages. Free debate allows us to correct and clarify positions all too often expressed in haste. We can all profit from this.

The question is whether exchanges of this kind are of interest to readers. Some well-meaning people have told us in no uncertain terms that the answer is no. At times we have doubts ourselves. Today, M. Mauriac's article in Sunday's *Figaro*[319] has drawn a considerable volume of mail concerning the Resistance. We must therefore explain our position.

M. Mauriac reproaches us for saying that an offensive against the Resistance is under way as well as for contending that the measures taken by two of our ministers are part of that offensive. In his view, we shouldn't be criticizing ministers drawn from the ranks of the Resistance. In contrast, we believe that we should. Indeed, the point is precisely that we are offering criticisms and not, as M. Mauriac maintains, making accusations.

Trust us: we will never stoop to allusions. If we ever conclude that M. Teitgen[320] and M. Lacoste[321] have become so intoxicated with power that they have turned their backs on their Resistance comrades, we will spell it out for everyone to see. We did not write that because we do not believe it. M. Mauriac should therefore refrain from putting words in our mouth.

---

[317] One cannot fail to be impressed by the lucidity of this remark, which remains current even today.

[318] Editorial. Very likely by Camus, continuing the exchange with François Mauriac.

[319] In *Le Figaro* of December 3–4, Mauriac published an article under the title "The Vocation of the Resistance." In it he cited "the editorial writer for *Combat*" who saw the measures taken by the ministry of information as "an aspect of the offensive against the Resistance," a phrase taken from Camus's editorial of December 1. Mauriac defended Teitgen and Lacoste by name, pointing out their recent past as resistance fighters, and he called upon the Resistance to trust statesmen recruited from their ranks.

[320] To this point, the decisions taken by Pierre-Henri Teitgen as minister of information had been treated quite positively by Camus and *Combat*. See the editorial of October 29, p. 92.

[321] Robert Lacoste was minister of production. A resister and member of the SFIO and Administrative Committee of the CGT, he would pursue a career in politics and serve as a member of several socialist governments, including that of Guy Mollet in 1956, in which he served as resident minister for Algeria from 1956 to 1958.

Nevertheless, it is still possible for ministers drawn from the Resistance to take measures that hamper the rebuilding effort that the Resistance has undertaken. M. Mauriac cannot be unaware that the ministries are still burdened with men whose only connection with the Republic is the posts they fill. These are the men whose way is blocked by the Resistance and its press. After weighing things carefully, we decided to denounce this state of affairs.

In any case, MM. Teitgen and Lacoste will not be frightened of rude language. They've heard it before. The knowledge that these harsh words are spoken by their own comrades may give them food for thought, however. A minister cannot be everywhere. He cannot imagine or keep an eye on everything that happens on his watch, and sometimes he may simply sign a document that is laid before him. So someone had better tell him what he ought not to sign. Comradeship in the Resistance was not a matter of mutual admiration. It had more to do with what M. Mauriac himself has well described as "lucid love." And it speaks the language of lucid love, which is the language of truth.

It is important, though, to note that the question is actually far broader than that. Simply put, the difference between us and M. Mauriac is that he believes the government has done enough in domestic policy and we do not.

We would simply remind our contradictor that in domestic politics, in certain circumstances, not doing enough leaves you vulnerable to the possibility that someday someone else might do far too much. That is our reasoning. To put it bluntly, if France, thanks to an energetic and farsighted policy, can avoid a Commune, M. Mauriac would agree with us that such a policy will have been for the good.

If he were to consider the current crises in Europe, and if he were to think about Greece,[322] he would recognize the threat we are attacking. Let him ponder this stark fact: yesterday, resistance fighters were shot in Athens for having protested against the government established by the Liberation. It was not to meet such a revolting end that they sacrificed everything, and for so long. How much more enviable the fate of their comrades killed during the occupation must have seemed to them, for they, at least, did not die by the hands of their friends.

We hope that M. Mauriac understands us better now. When we take up the defense of the men of the Resistance, he would be wrong to think, as some of our correspondents do, that we do so out of an exaggerated idea of their merits and rights. There is Resistance and Resistance. We know that today anyone can avail himself of the fact that the Resistance was clandestine to claim an impressive title and chase after a job. And we know that those in the best positions are not always the most deserving. But that's the way the world is, and mediocrity must be given its due. It is true, moreover, that not all resisters were heroes or saints. Is that a reason to condemn everything they did or to exaggerate their flaws and mistakes?

---

[322] Camus would return to events in Greece in his editorial of December 9, p. 135.

We know that M. Mauriac will not think so. That is why we are defending the Resistance not for what it did, which was natural, but for what it wants to do, which strikes us as just and good. That is what we want to preserve, because that is what will protect France from the worst misadventures. That is what makes us so bold as to criticize. What are a few harsh words if someday they prevent precious and innocent blood from being shed? The youthful face of France, of which M. Mauriac spoke with so much proper emotion, is one that we, too, know well: let there be no doubt of that. Indeed, it is to keep France from sinking into chaos and to protect it from wounds that cannot be healed that we call now for the intelligent severity that will make it worthy of respect for a long time to come.

December 9, 1944[323]

Yesterday, before the House of Commons, Mr. Churchill expounded his views on Greece.[324] His questioners pointed out that the British intervention was not justified either on strategic grounds or by concerns for constitutional legality. British army supply lines do not in fact pass through Athens, and the Papaandreou [sic][325] government was not elected in a regular election.

Mr. Churchill answered these objections by categorically affirming certain principles. He said that the right to represent democracy could not be granted to "gangs armed with lethal weapons who invade large cities and claim to lay down the law." He deplored the underground's assertion of its intention to govern the country.

His speech was vigorous and unambiguous. To put it in context, one should point out that it was in large part intended for American officials who have indicated their hostility to Britain's interventionist policy in Europe. Nevertheless, the principles affirmed by Mr. Churchill are applicable to all of Europe. We must examine them carefully.

Let us begin by saying that it is not without hesitation that we state our disagreement with a man who, for four years, was able to find the words that millions of oppressed people were waiting to hear. But the future of Europe is at stake, and tomorrow's history will depend on the principles adopted by the democratic countries today.

---

[323] Editorial. Typescript.

[324] After the evacuation of German forces from Greece (following the Russian offensive in Romania), the left wing of the resistance, organized in a national front under Communist leadership, opposed the Greek government back from exile and refused to lay down their arms. After declaring a general strike in Athens, they engaged in a battle with British forces that landed in Piraeus on October 14 to support the repressive measures taken by the authorities. From December 5 to December 10 *Combat* carried lengthy reports on events in Greece.

[325] George Papandreou (1888–1968) was the founder of the Greek Social Democratic Party. Exiled by the dictator Metaxas in 1938, he formed a government in exile in Cairon in May 1944. In October, in liberated Athens, he became prime minister in a national unity government. His decision to disarm the forces of the Resistance led to a veritable civil war. He participated in a number of subsequent governments, until he was forced to resign in the 1965 crisis that led eventually to the establishment of the "colonels' junta."

If Mr. Churchill's account of the state of affairs were accurate, much of his argument would be persuasive, but we doubt that reality is as he formulates it. He spoke in the name of a functioning democracy, a country without unrest or conflict, in a world without immediate problems. For the first time, perhaps, he did not speak for a continent devastated by four years of hunger and hatred and bearing wounds that can only be touched with great care.

To be sure, the men of the underground have not won the right to do as they please. Yet to tell them that they must wait at home for whatever reward the government deems wise to grant them is to give them a bitter pill to swallow. They have no need of a reward; their only need is for justice, and that the state must indeed give them. But it can do that only if it has a clear idea of what justice is.

British troops have fired on Greek citizens and killed men who only yesterday were their friends.

Mr. Churchill declared that this will continue. Maybe there is something persuasive about such stubborn determination, but we would hope that the fate of Europe could be decided in a less categorical fashion and that the whole issue could be considered in a more prudent manner.

People talk of communism and popular rage. We have too little information about the situation to debate its murkier aspects. But we know how easy it can be in similar circumstances for people to call us terrorists or communists and treat us accordingly. And, knowing this, we can imagine the situation of the rebellious people of Greece more easily than Mr. Churchill can.

The nations of Europe want a social order that takes their past suffering into account. Their demands are proportional to their miseries. The people of Greece have suffered longer and more atrociously than most during the past four years. The notion that they will be satisfied with the minister of a king imposed by two dictators, and with measures aimed at disarming the resistance and maintaining militias established by the Greek dictatorship is foolish.

But if that is difficult for some people to understand, there is also the importance that deserves to be attached to the demands of a people whose suffering was rivaled only by its pride. All we are asking is that the matter not be treated lightly and that the desperate cry that is being raised in Europe not be greeted solely with disdain and bullets.

As for democracy, perhaps the time has come to discuss it in a suitable way. Because the regime that rewarded a politician like Laval and gave power to a family like the Schneiders[326] is no more representative of democracy than the armed bands of which Mr. Churchill speaks. In any case, the point is not to choose one or the other. It is rather for those who govern the world today to adapt their methods to the distress of their people.

Mr. Churchill has declared that he wanted to guarantee order before changing the government in Greece. Mr. Cocks, who challenged him, suggested that British troops should first be withdrawn from Athens and then a British minister

---

[326] The Schneiders were a family of French industrialists, used here as a synonym for the power of money.

sent out to meet with representatives of the parties. This difference of method alone is instructive. We believe that true democracy means not allowing guns to speak before the people. This order is not the right order, in every sense of the word.

December 10, 1944[327]

Yesterday, many newspapers rather too hastily announced the resignation of General Franco.[328] When it comes to the news, it is better not to substitute one's wishes for the facts. Last night, a Reuters dispatch authoritatively denied the report. General Franco did not resign; he had gone hunting.

Nevertheless, the Phalangist regime on the peninsula is not on solid ground. France cannot turn its back on this problem. We have already said that our hearts and minds were on the side of the Spanish Republic.[329] Now that Spain is facing a problem of government that international diplomacy cannot ignore, we would like to add something to our arguments.

Many things in the Spanish situation recall our own. The big difference, however, is that Spain kept a constitutional government. The republican government of France abdicated in 1940 in favor of Vichy and the German. It handed over its powers and relinquished all its rights. By contrast, the Spanish Republic has never ceased to exist in law. It was expelled by force, but for the democratically minded, its legal existence has continued uninterrupted.

In theory, therefore, Spain should have no need of a revolution to form its government. It exists. It is awaiting the moment when it may resume its activity. Constitutionally, it would suffice for Señor Martinez Barrio, president of the Cortes, who is currently in Mexico, to return to Madrid and constitute the new government in order for the Spanish Republic to become once again in fact what it has never ceased to be in law.

If this war is indeed a war for democracy, the conclusion is obvious. We should recognize only one Spanish government, decided by a regular vote of the people, and this government should be the sole sovereign in peninsular affairs. If this war is indeed a war for democracy, Franco never existed, and we should ignore him.

This is the principle we hereby lay down, and we intend to stand by it. We wish that Mr. Churchill, who yesterday indicated his preference for regular governments, would also adopt this point of view. The day the Allies announce to the world that the Spanish republican government is the only government that represents Spain, a great malaise will be lifted, and the liberation of our neighbor will be halfway to becoming a reality.

[327] Editorial. Typescript.

[328] Camus had previously spoken out against the lack of vigilance in the reporting of the news. See his editorials of September 1, p. 23, and November 15, p. 112.

[329] Here again we see Camus's interest in Spain and consistent support for the Republic, in his view the only legitimate government. See his articles of September 7, October 5 and 24, and November 21, pp. 29, 59, 86, and 116.

But we also need help from the Spanish Republicans. What they need to do is to give substance to this legal government as soon as possible, so that the world can recognize it. They can do so by convening the Cortes without delay and by asking the Allies to respect and honor constitutional legality.

The Spanish Republic is not a work in progress. It exists. It survived defeat because it had the dignity never to accept it. Now, by its own efforts and with the help of its friends, it needs to claim the place it is due and bring the Spanish people the justice and freedom they have never ceased to deserve.

December 13, 1944[330]

One reads almost everywhere that we are at war. This is a manner of speaking. There are a hundred thousand Frenchmen fighting in the East; they are indeed at war. And then there is the rest of the nation, which is waiting. It is waiting, in fact, to go to war, and to finish it. It fully understands that there are no weapons. But it knows that peacetime can be brought closer even by those who are not at the front and that in modern war labor can help to avoid bloodshed.

Here, then, is a way of lining the rest of the nation up behind the troops at the front and at last uniting France in a common fight. It would be enough if France were producing again, if the factories were operating, and if the epic of reconstruction were at last begun. But even a quick look at what is happening makes us recoil in surprise and indignation.

Here are some facts. The glassworks of Courbevoie, Jérôme et Bonefoy, which employs more than four hundred semiskilled workers and which can be put to work on wartime electronics, is completely shut down. Although it has raw materials, there is no gas, which the gas company is unwilling to supply because the plant's owners owe a substantial penalty for excess consumption. An important factory is thus neutralized because the gas company insists on collecting its penalty, which the owners refuse to pay. Here, administrative obtuseness has combined with private obstreperousness to the detriment of the general interest.

But that is not the worst of it. It has been announced that the coal mines of the Nord will be nationalized.[331] The banks immediately dumped shares in these mines, creating a situation in which trading in these shares on the Bourse had to be halted.

What is more, the Ministry of Production has sequestered Francolor, a Franco-German consortium of chemical industries. The sequester administrator

---

[330] Editorial. This is the first text signed with the initials A. C. (A typescript exists, as is the case for all the texts signed with initials.) On December 8, *Combat* announced that it would publish editorials by different writers, who would sign their pieces. These include Henri Calet (H. C.) and Pierre Herbart (P. H.) in addition to Camus (A. C.). These three writers continued to publish at irregular intervals until February 9, 1945, when Camus signed with his full name an editorial affirming the solidarity of the editorial board. After that date, editorials once again became anonymous.

[331] The order took effect on December 14.

is unable to put the plant in operation, however, because the banks refuse to extend credit—credit they did not deny during the Occupation. So two industries of fundamental importance to the French war effort are paralyzed because capital is refusing to work with the nation in their exploitation.

Yet we will read again tomorrow that we are at war. No we aren't! For if we were, the state would requisition the Courbevoie glassworks to make the electronic parts our army needs. If we were really at war, the special interests would keep quiet and the banks would be held in check.

For that to happen, however, all the ministries must indeed go to war. When the Ministry of Production requisitions and nationalizes, the Ministry of Finance must not allow the banks to neutralize those measures. Everyone must feel responsible for how long the war lasts and how many French lives are needlessly sacrificed.

We would like to remain restrained and prudent. We are well aware that these are useful qualities today. But what outrage one feels at the thought of the precious blood being spilled today in the East while people at home are calculating what is in their own financial or political interest without worrying about what their stupidity may yet cost us.

Waging war most definitely does not mean allowing Frenchman to die every day because others suffer from a lack of imagination or a surfeit of greed! We have neither the right nor the power to waste lives. Blindness and venality are luxuries that we can no longer allow ourselves. There are interests that we must destroy.

I[332] scarcely dare quote the terrible words of a soldier in one of our most combat-tested units: "Here, at least, we are not immersed in lies." I scarcely dare quote him because it is impossible to accept that so much bitterness might be justified. If the men who are fighting are enveloped in truth, that truth must be extended voluntarily or involuntarily until it blankets the entire country, and until it is no longer permissible for Frenchmen to die with the unbearable sense that their deaths served no purpose.

A. C.

December 14, 1944[333]

Two days ago, the Consultative Assembly[334] opened debate on the constitution of works committees.[335] Although the subject is arid, the issue is of the utmost importance. No one, for or against, can deny that a measure that involves

---

[332] Camus allows himself to write "I," which he does not do when the editorial is unsigned, with the notable exception of his editorial of January 2, 1945, p. 159.

[333] Editorial. Text signed A. C.

[334] On the Consultative Assembly, see the editorials of October 14 and November 8, 1944, pp. 71 and 105.

[335] The works committees (*comités d'entreprise*) represented the interests of labor in industrial firms.

employees in the management of business is a reform whose repercussions are potentially considerable. What the Assembly debated the day before yesterday has significant implications for our social and political future.

We hoped that this would be obvious to everyone, and especially to our comrades in the Assembly. But an observer who tried to learn more about this difficult subject by sitting in the public gallery and carefully following the debate came away with the impression that this was not the case. During the main portion of the debate, he noted the presence of only about 40 of the 225 delegates. The rest were absent or wandering about the corridors.

Some will once again accuse us of asking for too much and of making a mountain out of a molehill. But in our current situation there are no molehills, or, to put it another way, every issue requires us to move mountains. What is true of the country at large is even more true of those who have taken charge of its politics. To put it bluntly, when only a fifth of an assembly's members bother to appear to debate a matter of national interest, that assembly is failing in its mission.

The Consultative Assembly is a child of the resistance. It has performed great services, and the work of its commissions is especially worthy of praise. We support it and believe that it serves a useful purpose. Its members have our sympathy and approval. Because they are our comrades, however, we cannot allow them to follow the path of least resistance.

We know that long, dry debates are difficult to follow. But those debates deal with our reality, a reality of rebirth tempered by heartbreak. No delegate is entitled to rest. The Consultative Assembly must not be an end; it is a beginning. It is not a shelter in which those worn out by past efforts can seek rest or play at being deputies; it is a place to engage in the only battle that matters to us today. And that battle demands all our vigilance and all our energy.

The Republic we want needs ministers and deputies for whom holding a ministerial portfolio or a seat in the assembly is not the be-all and end-all. Rather, each portfolio or mandate carries with it heavy responsibilities, which must be fully embraced. And foremost among those responsibilities is being there when the circumstances require it.

It seems that we are at war and that we are just beginning to make a revolution by legal means.[336] Yet I doubt that we can ever accomplish our goals if we have to stifle yawns the first time a dry subject comes up. I doubt that we can ever shake off the dreadful senility that afflicts our bureaucracies and customs unless each of us makes up his mind never to be tired.

We can do what we want to do. Our world will be tomorrow what we want it to be today. But our will must be firm and steady. The battles of the Liberation are just a foretaste of the battles to come.[337] We no longer have the right to be bored or distracted if we want France to breathe freely and deeply in the future.

---

[336] This is of course one of Camus' central ideas, but the words "it seems" signal the beginning of disillusionment.

[337] A reformulation of the notion that "the fight continues."

If we seem alarmed, it is because we know that the resistance is this country's last chance. That chance will be lost if France rejects the resistance. We shall see about that. But it will even more surely be lost if the resistance fails to recognize that its duties today are sacred, that peace is not at hand, that we are still at war, and that we are forbidden to indulge certain weaknesses. It is because we are determined to defend the resistance to the hilt that we will never hesitate to defend it against itself.

A. C.

December 15, 1944[338]

The Consultative Assembly yesterday took up the problem of transportation.[339] That issue in turn brings up the problem of supply. And one cannot discuss the problem of supply without touching on the black market. On this subject we would like to offer a few observations based on common sense.

Eating less is a price well worth paying in order to win the war. No one in France today would argue with that. But the sacrifices must be shared, and the burden of winning the war should not always be borne by the same people. For us, moreover, winning the war does not mean conquering square kilometers. It means giving France every available opportunity for survival. If we give a victorious France as a gift to an undernourished generation, we will not have accomplished much. The level of rations should at least be set at the minimum necessary to sustain life. Beyond that, we must be prepared to make all necessary sacrifices, and clandestine supply operations should count as treason.

Our English friends pride themselves on having stamped out their black market. They are right to do so. But they were helped by the fact that their rations are sufficient. It would obviously be a good thing if asceticism helped France achieve victory. But sobriety might serve just as well. Sufficient rations would deprive black marketeers of the one excuse they have left.

Still, the problem admits of no easy solution. In fact, it is likely that the current level of transportation could supply enough to meet our vital minimum. But a substantial quantity of food is siphoned off by the big restaurants and wholesale distributors. The first step in fighting the black market is to increase rations, but the black market makes this impossible. How can we escape this vicious circle?

The way out is to distinguish between the black market and the clandestine market. The threat to the overall supply system comes not from the fellow who climbs on his bicycle in search of a few eggs and a kilo of butter, nor is it from low-priced restaurants. It's the large-scale transport of foodstuffs and the thousand-franc restaurants that are contributing to the current crisis, the repercussions of which may be endless.

---

[338] Editorial. Text signed A. C.

[339] Note that Camus followed the work of the Consultative Assembly on a daily basis. See the previous editorial.

The crackdown must be aimed at these targets, and it must strike as one strikes in wartime. Selling essential medicines at fancy prices, storing tons of butter and meat to supply luxury eateries, and siphoning off the coal needed for the war effort are all things that must be condemned as sabotage is condemned in a country at war. The minister of supply[340] seems to be searching for solutions. Our opinion is that he isn't looking very hard. If he had been, he would already have found out, for example, that it takes no more than two weeks to close down a deluxe establishment (which may be disguising itself to look less prosperous than it is), confiscate its means of transportation, hit it with a heavy fine, and throw its owners in jail. Two weeks tops. And if that were to be done to one or two restaurants, it would give pause to the others.

If you want to accomplish anything, you have to demonstrate that you mean business. The measure we are proposing as a first step is an obvious one. We assure the minister that it would not be difficult to put into practice. A statement from him on this subject would be welcome.

To be sure, not all Frenchmen feel called to sacrifice to the same degree. But the vast majority of them will accept sacrifice if it is shown to go hand in hand with justice. Fine speeches are not enough if you're talking to empty stomachs and bitter hearts. Examples are necessary. And if you bring justice to the people, then you can ask them to make whatever sacrifice is required.

There is nothing new in any of this. What would be new, however, is a decision to act without delay, followed promptly by action.

A. C.

December 16, 1944[341]

There is a belief in some quarters that the new press seeks to grant itself a monopoly by preventing the publication of new newspapers.[342]

If that were the case, it would be essential, first of all, to point out that it has failed to achieve its goal. New newspapers are appearing. Still, if the allegation against the new press were true, it would be a serious matter. It could be accused of betraying the democratic spirit that it claims as its own.

Hence we must examine our own intentions. Do we want to limit the Paris press permanently to those newspapers that are being published today? Our

---

[340] Paul Ramadier (1888–1961) was a lawyer who became a mayor and in 1928 a Socialist deputy. He was one of eighty deputies who refused to grant full powers to Pétain, and he joined the Resistance early on. He served as minister of supply from November 1944 to May 1945, then as minister of justice in 1946, and as the first premier of the Fourth Republic in 1947. It was he who ended Communist participation in the government.

[341] Editorial. Text signed A. C.

[342] We have seen the degree to which the problems of the "new press" preoccupied Camus. See, among others, his editorials and articles of August 31, September 1 and 8, October 7 and 11, and November 22, pp. 21, 23, 32, 62, 66, and 118. *Le Monde* was soon to publish its first issue (December 19).

answer, in no uncertain terms, is no. Or, shifting to the other extreme, do we want the French press to revert to what it was before the war, namely, a public forum in which one man's opinion depended on another man's wallet? Again, no.

Between these two extremes, is it possible to imagine a position that would protect the right of free expression while at the same time limiting its abuse? Is it that difficult to imagine a democracy that would not be obliged to impose coercive rules yet would not be vulnerable to a variety of excesses? We do not think so. It is possible, moreover, to clarify our position in regard to the particular issue now before us.

We are in a provisional period, in which everything is permitted—ventures directed toward justice as well as ventures directed toward profit. We feel compelled to take positions in regard to matters of justice, but we feel compelled to do so only because the law is absent. Democracy presupposes law. A free press presupposes laws defining the status of the press. For a long time now we have been waiting for the government (in this instance, the Ministry of Information)[343] to set forth the rules governing the press, two or three of which are essential for protecting the press from the domination of money. What we want is not the right to publish ourselves to the exclusion of all other newspapers; it is the knowledge that all newspapers are free to publish without suspicions as to their motives and without running the risk that, while their intentions might be pure, they might end up serving interests we no longer want any part of.

While awaiting the promulgation of these rules governing the press, we protest the publication of new newspapers. But our protest is directed not so much against the papers themselves as against the conditions under which they are appearing. If this it the way things stand at the moment, it is not because we want things this way but because the new press law still has not been announced. The ministry has been slow to act, and, paradoxically, it is the ministry that is today compromising democracy.

The Ministry of Information may well respond that it wants to wait for the Legislative Assembly to act. In our view this would be unfortunate. But if that is the course to be chosen, the Federation of the Press will be justified in maintaining its hostility to the publication of new newspapers.

We do not believe that France's ideal is to have the press stemming from the Resistance as its only organ of expression. The moment we are sure that newspapers will be allowed to publish and express themselves clearly and honestly, we will be glad to see the advent of new competitors, even if they prove indifferent or hostile to the Resistance.

---

[343] The ministry was headed at this point by Pierre-Henri Teitgen, whose courage and uncompromising language Camus and *Combat* had praised on several occasions. Over the previous few weeks, however, as various problems went unresolved, the newspaper's tone had turned much more critical, which had provoked reactions from Mauriac, among others.

We are defending not positions but a principle. And we believe, in fact, that it is the principle of democracy. When the ministry finally relieves us of this rule of vigilance, we will believe that we've done our duty in our limited and specific domain. Today, each of us has his assigned task. We will carry out the mission that has fallen to us, which is to uphold the profound principle of democracy, until such time as the government gives democracy the concrete legal form that will allow us to turn our attention to other things.

A. C.

December 17, 1944[344]

When a revolution has broken out, what must be done to destroy it? Experience shows that it must first be applauded, and that the people must be praised above all for their generosity, unselfishness, and magnanimity. When the people begin to assert their will, the time has come to shout from the rooftops that were they to dare to profit from their victory, they would be dishonoring it and dragging it through the mud, that the only benefit they should derive from the revolution is the glory of having made it, but that any guarantees they might demand would be tantamount to stealing from their own renown.

Once the people have been lulled to sleep by unstinting praise of their disinterest, the coast is clear. The people must be made to feel that the arms they still have in their possession are a sign of disorder and that they will be setting a fine example of good behavior if they turn them over to certain designated individuals or authorized bodies, which will bear them in the people's name.

Once the people are disarmed, the lion must continue to be praised for its good nature. Immediately thereafter, however, one can begin to insinuate that the revolution, once thought to be so pure, was not unmixed with crimes, that lunatics mingled with its heroes, but that, fortunately, the twisted were few in number.

The day after that, these shackles can be thrown off. If nothing has stirred by then, it is time to announce that the revolution, which at first deceived everyone, turns out after all to have been nothing but a crime motivated solely by plunder, but thank God the country had not fallen into the clutches of its leading scoundrels. But all the rubble, all the thefts, murders, fires, and crimes of every sort, stand as witness to what the revolution would have wrought had it not been nipped in the bud.

Once this theme has been broached, experience shows that it cannot be repeated often enough, until eventually the people, blinded by the sudden storm of accusations, end up believing that they have just barely avoided plunging headlong into an abyss of crime. That is the right moment to profit from the people's fear, which leads to stupor, and launch a bold foray to the rear, stopping the victorious in their tracks.

[344] Editorial. Text signed A. C.

So said Edgar Quinet in 1868.[345] Clearly, little changes in this world. Greek historians tell us that when the aristocrats in certain Hellenic cities took up their posts, they were required to swear an oath always to blacken the name of the people. This two-thousand-year-old principle relied on methods that Quinet described and that we are witnessing in operation today. Here in France, for centuries now, oaths that have never been sworn are nevertheless being kept.

A. C.

December 18, 1944[346]

The text of the Franco-Soviet pact has now been made public.[347] Until the content of the treaty was known, we felt there was no point in commenting on it. Now that the terms have been published, however, a direct commentary seems no more urgent than before. The obligations of the respective parties are so clearly set forth that we could do no more than paraphrase them.[348] This pact is first of all an instrument of war, with a precise and limited objective. It aims to neutralize Germany in the present conflict and in the years to come. That is why it is both practical and necessary and sure to win the accord of both the French and the Soviet people. We therefore approve the treaty as published, fully and without reservation, in addition to which we wish to express our gratitude to the man who has led France to the place it occupies today.

Two additional observations are in order, however. The great importance of the published text should not be allowed to obscure the fact that the Moscow talks surely dealt with subjects other than the alliance. Soviet interests, like French interests, extend well beyond the German problem, paramount though it is. The Soviet zone of influence is vast, and the security of France does not end at France's borders. What was discussed in Moscow in this regard is therefore of great interest, and it is to be hoped that the government will inform the country about what was said.

---

[345] Edgar Quinet (1803–1875) was a historian and friend of Michelet, a professor at the Collège de France who gained fame for his participation in the Morée expedition and for his work *De la Grèce moderne et de ses rapports avec l'Antiquité* (1830). In 1846, his course was suspended by Guizot. In 1848 he became a deputy but was banished after the coup d'état of December 2, 1851. From exile in Belgium, he published historical studies of revolutions and *La Philosophie de l'histoire de France*. After returning to France in 1870, he again became a deputy and summed up his theories in *L'Esprit nouveau* in 1874. It is easy to see why the man and his work interested Camus.

[346] Editorial. Text signed A. C.

[347] General de Gaulle had visited Moscow from December 2 to December 6. Following up his discussions with Stalin, French foreign minister Bidault and Soviet commissar for foreign affairs Molotov signed an important "treaty of alliance and mutual assistance" on December 10. *Combat* published the full text on December 18.

[348] The pact dealt with (1) the common struggle "until the final victory over Germany" was won; (2) a commitment not to "enter into separate negotiations with Germany"; (3) a commitment to take "all necessary measures" to prevent "any new attempt at aggression on [Germany's] part"; (4) mutual aid and assistance in the case of German aggression; and (5) economic assistance for reconstruction of both countries.

Furthermore, the preamble to the pact gives us an opportunity to say more about an idea that means a great deal to us.[349] Indeed, France and Russia emphatically stated their desire to work together toward international security. They indicated that the alliance between them was not an exclusive one and in fact looked forward to integrating it into a more general system in which the interests of all countries could be reconciled.

That is what is important. At times—and today is one of those times—the system of international alliances can seem to be a necessity imposed by history. But it has never resolved the problems of more than two or three nations at a time, and then only for a limited duration.

Peace is the property of all nations. Today we know that the nations of the world share a common destiny, and when a Czech is slapped in the face in Prague, the repercussions are felt by the prosperous residents of Fontainebleau, the collective farmers of the Ukraine, and the cotton growers of Texas. We know that when one country experiences industrial growth, or when poverty increases in another, the effects are felt in the farthest corners of the globe. The organization of world security cannot therefore rely on international treaties and alliances, which are necessary but not sufficient stepping-stones to a more far-reaching structure of peace. Since wars can no longer be anything but world wars, peace today must be organized on a global scale.

These are not new ideas. No governments can be more sensitive to them than those of France and Russia. It should never be forgotten that Russia did not adopt its present national policy until its proposal for a system of collective security had been rejected, and that it was the only state to lay general disarmament on the table only to have its offer dismissed out of hand.

After so many failures, it would have to have been extremely naïve to continue in the same vein, and fortunately for us it has never been naïve. There can be no doubt, however, that in a different political climate, it will revert to its original position.

When we hear that there is suspicion in the United States concerning the Franco-Soviet alliance, we should not be afraid to remind our American friends that they bear their share of responsibility for the failure of international security policy. They turned their backs on it when they could have saved it. Europe thus fell prey to nationalism of one stripe or another. Things progressed rapidly to a head from there.

Today we must start all over again. The Franco-Russian alliance is the first step. But it is a sign of great political wisdom to have made it clear that the agreement was not intended to exclude others. Indeed, it is to derive support from complementary alliances, which will bring the united nations together in a solid yet flexible system. That will be the second stage. It would be foolish, however,

---

[349] The preamble asserted in particular that the signatories were "convinced that once the victory is won, the restoration of peace on a stable basis and its preservation for a durable future depend on close cooperation between them and the rest of the United Nations." The two countries agreed "to collaborate to create an international security system that will allow effective action to preserve world peace and foster harmonious relations among nations."

to deny that the final step—insofar as the word "final" can be applied to any-thing involving love and hatred among human beings—can only take the form of a world organization in which nationalisms will disappear so that nations may live, and in which each state will give up what it must of sovereignty in order to guarantee its liberty. Only then will peace be restored to this exhausted world. An internationalized economy in which raw materials will be shared, commer-cial competition will turn into cooperation, colonial markets will be open to all, and currency itself will achieve a collective status is a necessary condition for such an organization to exist.[350]

We are still a long way from that goal. Hatred has been aroused, hearts burn too hotly for justice, and Europe has scores to settle. But beyond the shouts and the violence, and despite our staunch determination to win a lasting victory, let us not forget the goal we seek. Only when we have reached it will the bitterness of so many sacrifices begin to abate.

Until then, we are pleased to hail this bright and solid alliance, which will allow France and Russia to play the leading role they must play in the vast effort of reconstruction upon which our hopes for the future rest.

A. C.

December 20, 1944[351]

As von Rundstedt was launching his offensive,[352] Hitler warned his people that they should not delude themselves. His words should be taken to heart by all nations currently involved in the war.

"No illusions" should indeed be our watchword. To begin with, it serves no purpose to minimize the German offensive by describing it as a "final push" or a good opportunity for the Allies to finish them off or a desperate attempt by the Germans to break out of the box in which they find themselves. Every offensive is dictated by tactical exigencies, and we do not yet know whether this opportunity will prove good for us or whether this push will indeed be their last.

Our point is a simple one: Germany exists, it has not been defeated, and the war is not over. This offensive has been in preparation for two months, and

---

[350] Camus' ideas about international organization remain current today, at least as far as the European Union is concerned.

[351] Editorial. Text signed A. C.

[352] On December 17, Marshal von Rundstedt launched a counteroffensive that *Combat* described as a "serious attack" in the Belgian Ardennes, between Montjoie and Trèves, and succeeded in capturing some territory on the border with Luxembourg. Very tough combat persisted for a month, and the situation became critical enough that the Americans considered withdrawing from Alsace. Von Rundstedt (1875–1953) had tried to distance himself from Nazism. After being sent away by Hitler in disgrace, he was later recalled. After the defeat of Germany he was arrested by the British and ultimately freed in 1949.

knowledgeable observers saw it coming. The fact that it was launched earlier than expected and not in the plain of Cologne as anticipated takes nothing away from its seriousness. On the contrary, we are facing a substantial attacking force executing a well-prepared battle plan. That is all we know for sure, and our decisions and efforts must be based on what we know.

The conclusion to be drawn is also simple: our duty is clear. It is not to try to estimate how far the Germans may advance. There is no point to that. It is to help stop that advance and transform it into a costly defeat. It is never to forget that we are at war, and that if we are fighting with American lives at Montjoie, we must fight elsewhere with French sacrifices.

This offensive can therefore be instructive and salutary if it awakens imaginations no longer able to distinguish between what is urgent and what is superfluous. What is urgent is to integrate all of France in the war effort—not only through appeals for unity but also by means of decisions and measures intended to assign each French citizen a specific role in the common struggle.

That offensive should teach us that it is not possible for a country at war to allow its young people to choose on their own between enlisting in the military and idling away their time at fashionable night spots. It should teach us that a country at war cannot tolerate treason, stupidity, or senility in its bureaucrats. A country at war strips down of its own volition to what is essential. What is essential today is intelligence on the one hand and courage on the other. What is essential is the needs of the army, the feeding of the people, and the needs of production.

It is not by underestimating the German offensive, moreover, that we will forge the determined will we need today and will need tomorrow. It is by saying quite clearly that Germany is far from defeated and that it will take many more months of effort to put it down for good.

Just imagine for a moment a German return to Paris. We know full well who would be standing shoulder to shoulder to continue the struggle. We know full well who would flee or lie low until the situation reversed itself again. This country is now collapsing under the weight of so many conversions. The Republic is suffocating from the crush of new friends. But if it should find itself alone again or in danger, it will discover who its true defenders are, even if today they seem to disagree among themselves. It is their faith and their stubbornness that freed France and will win the war. It is their faith and their stubbornness that will soon restore the country's youth and vigor. For the rest, I have no idea whether von Rundstedt's offensive will offer a good opportunity to finish Germany off or not, but I know that it is our last opportunity to rid ourselves of some of the lies that have done us so much harm[353] and cost us too much blood.

A. C.

---

[353] Allusion to a celebrated phrase in a speech delivered by Pétain on June 23, 1940: "I hate the lies that have done you so much harm." The author of that speech was Emmanuel Berl (see Patrick Modiano, *Interrogatoire* [Paris: Gallimard, 1976], pp. 88–89).

December 22, 1944[354]

France has endured many tragedies that have today reached an end. It will endure many more that have yet to begin. But there is one tragedy from which the men and women of this country have been suffering for five years now: the tragedy of separation.[355]

Nostalgic longing, broken loves, ghostly dialogues carried on across the plains and mountains of Europe or sterile monologues conducted in the mind of one person awaiting reunion with another—such are the signs of these wretched times. For five years French men and French women have been waiting for one another. For five years their aching hearts have waged a desperate battle against time, against the idea that their missing partner is growing old and that so many years of love and happiness have been lost.

Yes, the era is one of separation. No one dares utter the word "happiness" in these tortured times. Yet millions of people are seeking it today, and for them these years have been a time of constant suspense, which they hope will one day end, making happiness possible once again.

Who can blame them? And who can say they are wrong? What would justice be without a chance for happiness, and of what use would freedom be in misery? We know this well—we French who went to war not to conquer but to defend, in fact, a certain idea of happiness. But to put it bluntly, the happiness we sought was a fierce happiness, fierce enough and pure enough that we thought it worthwhile first to endure years of unhappiness in order to achieve it.

Let us therefore hold on to the memory of that happiness and of those who have lost it. That will make our fight seem less unfeeling, and it will remind us of how cruelly France suffered and how tragic was the lot of her separated children.

I will not say here what I really think about separation. This is not the time or place to write that separation seems to me to be the rule and reunion only the exception, or that happiness is an accident that persists. What is expected of all of us is a message of hope. Indeed, only one thing was asked of our generation: to prove ourselves capable of overcoming despair. Maybe that prepared us to speak of the ultimate hope, the hope that must be salvaged from the world's misery and that resembles a victory. This is the only hope that seems worthy of respect. The only thing over which we cannot triumph is eternal separation, which puts an end to everything. For the rest, there is nothing that courage and love can't accomplish. Five years of courage, five years of love: such is the inhuman ordeal to which French men and women have been subjected, the measure of their distress.

---

[354] Editorial. Text signed A. C. Reprinted in *Actuelles*, chapter "La chair" (The Flesh).

[355] The theme of separation is of course central in *The Plague*, and Camus noted its importance in his notebooks as early as December 1942. See *Carnets I*, pp. 67–72 and 90–91.

The idea behind the "Week of the Missing" was to commemorate all this.[356] One week is not a very long time. The difficulty is that it is easier to be ingenious in doing harm than in doing good. When we want to alleviate misfortunes, our means are limited, and we give money. I only hope that people will give a lot. Since we cannot do anything for the pain, let us do something for the misery. The pain will thus be liberated, and all these frustrated individuals will have the leisure to endure their suffering. For many, this will be a luxury they have been denied for quite some time.

Still, no one should think that giving money is enough to quiet all qualms of conscience; some debts are inexhaustible. To the missing men and women, the vast, mysterious legions of our brothers and sisters, we give the faces of those we know, who were plucked from our midst. Then we realize that we did not love them enough, that we did not derive from them all the benefit we could have when they were with us. No one loved them enough, not even their country, since today they are where they are. May this week, "our" week, not cause us to forget "their" years. May it teach us not to love them mediocrely, and may it bestow upon us the memory and imagination without which we can never make ourselves worthy of them. May it serve above all to help us forget the emptiest of our words and make ready for the silence we shall offer them on that difficult and wonderful day when they stand before us once again.

A. C.

December 23, 1944[357]
French Renaissance

A new illustrated weekly magazine recently appeared on the scene.

Rolls of paper were allocated so that it could print photographs depicting life in France and around the world. In the time it has been publishing, it has shown that it deserved the confidence placed in it.

The journalists who put it together hit right away on a brand-new formula well suited to the times. Of course they copied *Match*, because truth is eternal, and anyway it was much less exhausting to do what had been done before. But they went much farther.

---

[356] The "Week of the Missing," which included the collection of contributions on the streets, had been advertised by posters and articles in the media. It lasted from December 24 until January 1. The liberation of prisoners of war and deportees did not begin until April 1945.

[357] Note signed Suetonius. Possibly by Camus. The signature is reminiscent of certain articles that Camus wrote for *Alger-Républicain* and *Le Soir-Républicain* and signed "Nero" or "Petronius." Despite the temptation to attribute to Camus a pseudonym borrowed from a Latin author (70–125) who interested him enough that he took the theme of his *Caligula* from Suetonius's *Lives of Twelve Caesars*, one must bear in mind that not all the "Suetonius" articles were by Camus: Roger Grenier recalls having written some of them. For this particular article, the first of a series, the attribution cannot be certain. But the irony, the defense of the Resistance press, and the attack on newspapers that published sensationalistic images suggest that it might be plausible.

Readers may stumble across pages showing horrible scalped heads and bodies tortured by the Germans. Clearly, this is a magazine of strong sensations, direct and agreeable. Turn the page, however, and you come upon dancers in short skirts, who yield another sensation no less direct or agreeable.

Obviously this is quality work, done at last by professionals who have nothing in common with the apprentices of the resistance press—technicians, in other words, who have their own idea of the public and what it needs.

We welcome our new colleague, and we congratulate the Ministry of Information for finding a way to encourage a publication that does honor to France and will certainly help to raise its standing in the world.

SUETONIUS

December 24, 1944
The Poet and General de Gaulle[358]

M. Paul Claudel recently evoked the figure of General de Gaulle in *Le Figaro*. Since M. Claudel is a poet, he did so in verse.[359] He personifies France and invites her to address General de Gaulle. The result is appalling.

France asks the general to look her in the eye and says, "General, you who are my son." And the general replies, "Shut your mouth, woman!" The inspiration for the piece begins with Péguy,[360] continues with Déroulède,[361] and ends with the anonymous poets of *La Veillée des Chaumières*.[362]

For M. Claudel's great works we feel the admiration they command. For General de Gaulle we have the respect he is due. Clearly, however, this poem reduces both men to ridicule, and that is unfortunate. Since, moreover, General de Gaulle is obviously not responsible for this, we have no choice but to blame M. Claudel.

His responsibility is far more that of the citizen, however, than of the poet. M. Claudel previously confused the heroism of the underground with that of the

---

[358] Note signed Suetonius. The attribution to Camus is much more certain than for the previous note: Francine Camus sometimes sent her mother in Oran texts by Camus, and she sent her this one.

[359] Paul Claudel (1868–1955) was a Christian poet and diplomat. His occasional poems are not of the quality of his *Cinq Grandes Odes* or his plays, but they do attest to his successive loyalties, since this poem, "To General de Gaulle," which first appeared on the literary page of *Le Figaro*, appears in the collection *Poèmes et paroles Durant la guerre de trente ans* (Paris: Gallimard, 1945) immediately after a poem dedicated to Marshal Pétain.

[360] Charles Péguy (1873–1914). The comparison with, for example, the lines of "La Tapisserie de sainte Geneviève et de Jeanne d'Arc" is not out of place: "Still, says France, I am saved!" "Still, says France, the rest of you see that they've not done me in, and I am saved!"

[361] Paul Déroulède (1846–1914) remains the symbol of (bad) patriotic and revanchist poetry. After founding the Ligue des Patriotes, he supported General Boulanger (1837–1891) in his rejection of a parliamentary republic.

[362] *La Veillée des Chaumières* (or, more accurately, *Les Veillées de la Chaumière*), whether it refers to the book of that title published by Mme de Genlis in 1823 or the illustrated weekly magazine founded in 1860, stands for writing of an unctuous, moralistic, and edifying sort.

belt tighteners. That was an error of moral judgment. His error now is one of historical judgment. He is confusing the representative of the Resistance with General Boulanger.

Those two errors have led to a third error, of style. A writer may be capable of bringing biblical images to life yet lack the ability to render the commonplace.

Suetonius

December 26, 1944[363]

The Pope has just delivered a message in which he openly states his support for democracy.[364] This is good news. But we believe that this carefully worded message calls for equally careful commentary. We are not sure that we speak for all of our Christian comrades at *Combat*, but we are certain that the feelings of a great many of them are reflected in what we are about to say.

We would like to take this opportunity to say first of all that our satisfaction is not entirely exempt from regret. We have been waiting many years for the leading spiritual authority of the day to condemn dictatorship in no uncertain terms. I repeat: in no uncertain terms. For certain encyclicals do suggest such a condemnation, but only when properly interpreted. It is a condemnation formulated in the language of tradition, which has never been clear to the vast majority of men.

Yet it was that very same majority that waited all those years for someone to speak out and clearly identify the source of the evil, as the Pope has now done. Our secret wish was for this to be said when evil reigned triumphant and the forces of good remained muzzled. Obviously there is cause for rejoicing that these words have been spoken now, when the spirit of dictatorship is reeling. But we did not wish merely to rejoice; we wanted to believe and to admire. We wanted spirit to prove itself before force arrived to back it up and prove it right.

We would have liked to see the Pope disavow Franco in 1936, so that Georges Bernanos would not have had to speak out and curse the regime.[365] The voice that has just dictated to the Catholic world which side it ought to choose was the only voice that could have spoken out amid the tortures and cries, the only voice that could calmly and fearlessly have denounced the blind force of armored divisions.

We may as well say forthrightly what we think: we would have liked the Pope to have taken a stand at the height of that shameful period and denounce what needed to be denounced. It is wrenching to think that the Church left that obligation to others, to obscure individuals who lacked its authority, and some of whom lacked the invincible hope on which the Church thrives. For the

[363] Editorial. Text signed A. C. Reprinted in *Actuelles*, chapter on "Morality and Politics."
[364] Pope Pius XII's 1944 Christmas message contained the following statement: "True democracy, whether republican or royalist in form, guarantees the freedom to which peoples aspire, whereas in authoritarian states governed by political men, no one has the right to live his own life honorably." On the Pope's attitude during the war and Camus' "reservations" about him, see the editorial of September 8, 1944, and n. 53, p. 31.
[365] The allusion is to *Les Grands Cimetières sous la lune*. Camus called Bernanos "the great Catholic voice" in his editorial of September 16 (see n. 73, p. 39).

Church did not need to be concerned about surviving or protecting itself. Even in chains it would not have ceased to exist. In chains, moreover, it would have found a strength that we are tempted not to grant it today.

At least we now have this message. Catholics, who gave the best of themselves in the common struggle, know now that they were right and that they did well. The Pope has recognized the virtues of democracy. At this point the wording is subtle, however. Democracy is understood in a broad sense. It can encompass monarchies as well as republics, according to the Pope. This democracy is wary of the masses, which Pius XII subtly distinguishes from the people. It also allows for inequalities of social condition, albeit tempered by the spirit of fraternity.

Democracy as defined in this text has a paradoxical "radical-socialist"[366] tinge, which surprises us no end. Furthermore, the Pope makes no secret of what he really wants by calling for a "moderate" regime.

Of course we understand his desire. There is a kind of intellectual moderation that is useful when it comes to understanding social issues and even to promoting the welfare of all. But all the Pope's subtleties and precautions leave a great deal of room for the most detestable kind of moderation, namely, moderation of the heart. It is this moderation, in fact, that finds inequality tolerable and injustice bearable. These counsels of moderation cut two ways. Today there is a danger that they play into the hands of those who want to keep everything as it is and who have failed to understand that some things have to change. Our world does not need tepid souls. It needs burning hearts, men who know the proper place of moderation. The Christians of the first century were not moderates.[367] The Church today ought to make a point of not allowing itself to become mixed up with the forces of conservation.

We say all this because we want every well-known and well-honored institution to serve the cause of freedom and justice. There can never be too many of us in this fight. That is the only reason for our reservations. Who are we, after all, to criticize the century's highest spiritual authority? None other than common defenders of the spirit who believe that the demands on those whose mission is to represent that spirit are endless.

A. C.

December 29, 1944[368]

Broad questions of policy gave rise to major debates in the Consultative Assembly. Delegates took part in extensive discussions. Democracies are often criticized for being too much given to talk. To some extent that's true, but one needs to be

---

366 "Radical-socialist" is intended here in the sense of the French Radical-Socialist Party, which was "neither radical nor socialist" but very bourgeois and middle-of-the-road.

367 Camus took great interest in the early centuries of Christianity from the time of his master's thesis (see *Essais*, pp. 1224–1313) to the writing of *La Chute*.

368 Editorial. Text signed A. C.

careful in making such criticisms. Sometimes a great deal of talk is necessary in order to bring to light the two or three common principles without which action would be impossible. True, dictatorships can move into action more quickly, but on occasion they pay dearly for it. There is a choice to be made between economizing on words and economizing on blood.

Nevertheless, speeches must eventually lead to principles and ultimately to action. It would be too much to say that such was the case with the speeches that animated the recent debates of the Consultative Assembly. In the end, however, agreement seems to have been reached on one point: the government must govern.

To govern is to achieve harmony internally as well as with the nation. One speaker clearly demonstrated that the government is not governing to the extent that its policy is not coherent. The ministers who have succeeded one another in various posts have unfortunately not all shared the same ideas. Different ministries are not all following the same line, so that the Ministry of Finance has at times countered the Ministry of Production, while the Ministry of the Interior thumbs its nose at the Ministry of Justice. In short, government is possible only where there is a precise doctrine for governing and a plan that all ministers must follow.

It is this doctrine and this plan that we are interested in. From our reading of what was said in these debates, we believe that M. Jules Moch[369] set forth the outlines of the doctrine, while M. Gorse[370] defined its spirit and intentions in the loftiest terms.

Socialization of banks, insurance companies, and key industries; financial and fiscal reforms to do away with illicit products and limit legitimate profits; and systematic reconstruction: this is the program to which we, too, subscribe. As for its spirit and intentions, one has to be grateful to M. Gorse for uttering the youthful words *adventure* and *heroism* in the most venerable of surroundings.

The government has a free hand because it has the nation's backing, but it bears the burdens and responsibilities that go along with this freedom. Its actions will decide whether this country will be a land of senescence and resignation or a land of youth and grandeur. It will decide whether the French ideal is one of retreat or conquest. France nearly perished on account of the pettiness of its

---

[369] Jules Moch (1893–1985) was an S.F.I.O. deputy who served in Léon Blum's cabinet in 1938. After entering the Resistance, he joined de Gaulle in 1942. He served as a member of the Consultative Assembly in Algiers and later in Paris as well as of two Constituent Assemblies and held several ministerial portfolios under the Fourth Republic. He sided with Mendès France when the latter resigned from de Gaulle's government in April 1945.

[370] Georges Gorse (1915–2002) was a graduate of the Ecole Normale Supérieure who joined de Gaulle right at the beginning, in June 1940. As a member of de Gaulle's cabinet in Algiers in 1943, he played an important role in Free France and later served as deputy from the Vendée. He was placed in charge of Muslim affairs in 1946–1947. He also served in several governments of the Fifth Republic and later became France's first ambassador to Tunisia and, subsequently, Algeria.

interests and its enthusiasms. The task of the government is to prove to the country that the century ahead is one of great adventure, that a world is to be built, and that the era of somnolence and selfishness is at an end. Above all its task is to show the French that this is not a bad or hopeless thing and that this torn country, covered with wounds and scars, still has enough prestige for some people to seek to heal it and set it on a course to greatness.

Such fine things cannot be accomplished with mere words. It will take clarity of vision, resoluteness of will, the firm hand of leaders who refuse to prevaricate, and intransigence in the face misrepresentation. It can be done not by setting up a High Commission for Logistics but only by cracking down on the black market and confiscating hoarded supplies for distribution to a population that remains undernourished.

It can be done not by authorizing the publication of a pornographic magazine[371] but only by supplying the nation with a steady flow of information regarding the great trials that lie ahead. It cannot be done by allowing 600,000 unemployed workers to stand by and watch as houses fail to be rebuilt, or by borrowing money that would be better confiscated, or by pardoning deliberate treason at a time when some would condemn inadvertent treason, or by censuring what everyone knows, or, finally, by thinking that signing petitions is enough.

The government will govern. It will need to be harsh, tenacious, stubborn, ever vigilant, without illusions, immune to discouragement, disdainful of artful maneuvers, always concerned with efficiency, fair, yet energetic. That is a great deal to ask. Some will accuse us of asking for the moon. The answer is simple, however: if the government and the rest of us do not propose a goal that is extreme and immoderately ambitious, slumber will once again overtake the soul of France, plunging it back into that state which for any nation is akin to death.

A. C.

December 30, 1944
Judge Not[372]

Wherever I turn, I hear attacks on the Resistance and resisters. What scoundrels they are! They take credit for a liberation that couldn't have been achieved without the Allies, they're all clamoring for government jobs, and they thrive on hatred and injustice. I also see that they are not without defenders, people willing to admit that they deserve some credit and suffered a great deal.

---

[371] See "French Renaissance," December 23, p. 150.
[372] Article signed by Albert Camus.

All this was to be expected. No sacrifice has ever escaped calumny and denigration. Yet suffering and honor are hardly exceptional credentials in a world in which people were obliged to choose both simply to remain human.

Resisters have one additional credential, however, which has not to my knowledge been stressed enough. They made their choice in solitude. For the sake of those unaware of the extremes to which this could lead, I want to discuss today a terrible tragedy that remains a source of terrible chagrin to everyone who has heard about it.

Many men of the Resistance are acquainted with a comrade whose fight against the Germans began in 1941.[373] The course he chose was among the most difficult: to organize sabotage of railroads in the northern zone. When the authorities issued a warrant for his arrest in 1942, he was obliged to flee to the southern zone. After being arrested by Vichy, he spend thirteen months in prison and upon his release he took up an important post in the United Resistance Movements, where he was once again responsible for organizing acts of sabotage. In that position, he was not satisfied merely to issue orders; he personally took part in missions and exposed himself to every danger. Eventually he was arrested along with some very important Resistance leaders at a meeting near Lyons, the existence of which was known to very few people.[374] Because of the identity of those captured in that episode, the Resistance suffered a very cruel blow. Two weeks later, however, our comrade was back, saying that he had escaped. Because of this, some of his companions suspected him of cooperating with the Gestapo, but the majority continued to trust him. Why? It is hard to say, though at the time it was easy to feel: because of a certain quality of his handshake, his courageous acts, his honest gaze. Those who trusted him never had cause to regret it. From then until the liberation, this man, who could not help but be aware of the cloud of suspicion that hung over him and who suffered inwardly because of it, continued his efforts and admirably served his country's cause.

After the liberation he accepted an official post in one of our ministries. Nothing had changed, except that people close to him noticed a growing nervousness

---

[373] The man in question is René Hardy, an engineer with the French national railway system, who joined the Resistance early on and became a leader of Résistance-Fer, in which capacity he was in close contact with Henri Frenay and the Combat movement. Hardy was arrested by the Germans only to be released a short while later, and he said nothing about his arrest to his comrades. The circumstances surrounding his release have remained mysterious to this day.

[374] The meeting in question is now well known as the occasion at which Jean Moulin, sent by de Gaulle to unify the various internal resistance movements, was arrested at Caluire on June 21, 1943. Shortly thereafter, Moulin died after being tortured by the Gestapo, which had clearly been tipped off about the meeting. Klaus Barbie, head of the Gestapo in Lyons, seized papers that allowed him to identify "Max," as Moulin was known. Hardy's role in this arrest has been a matter of considerable controversy. After the Liberation he was arrested and charged with having been a German informant, but his undeniable service to the Resistance, attested by Henri Frenay among others, led to a not-guilty verdict in January 1947. A few months later, new documents casting doubt on his story were discovered, and he was arrested again, only to be acquitted a second time in 1950 "with a minority in favor." These verdicts remain controversial. See Frenay, *La Nuit finira*, pp. 483–490. Hardy died in 1987, a few months before Barbie was put on trial for crimes against humanity.

and sudden bouts of depression that left him close to tears. A month ago, this man was arrested by Military Security. His comrades were dumbfounded to learn that he had confessed to having revealed the location of the secret meeting to the Gestapo. But even before their initial anger could subside, they also learned that their comrade had been arrested shortly before the meeting, that his wife may have been in the hands of the Gestapo, and that he had been obliged to talk by either torture or blackmail. It was easy to reconstruct the story from that point. After years of irreproachable service, a warrior had momentarily given in to pain or anguish.[375] He then resumed his place, and no one can say whether it was out of despair or in the hope of repairing the wrong he had done. For endless months he lived with what he had done and with the thought that others had paid with lengthy suffering for his moment of surrender. For endless months he continued to do his duty though he no longer felt himself worthy of it. Now he has been arrested. Soon he will be judged.

I have little to add to this simple narrative. Nothing, in fact, but a question: Who would dare to judge? The men of the Resistance took a silent oath to hold out if tortured. That oath was necessary. If it was never openly pronounced, it was because everyone was aware that pain has its limits, and before being subjected to torture no man knows whether he will prove to be a coward or not. That is why this oath was one that each resister took in solitude, to himself alone.

Most held out. The torturers were defeated. Others weren't as strong. It would of course be easy to accuse them. Yet I want to say loud and clear that no resister would want to condemn them, for if they had done as so many others did and stayed home, if they had not chosen the more difficult path, they would be alive and respected today. To be sure, difficult paths demand superior loyalties. But there are times, and circumstances of suffering, in which a man is no longer himself, in which reason becomes madness and pride becomes supplication. Every resister lived in fear of that moment, not because of the pain it presaged but because it stood to bring them either self-contempt or the invincible peace of knowing that they remained loyal.

No, this man is not within the jurisdiction of our courts. He can only be his own judge. An official tribunal may soon find him guilty. But in the depths of our hearts we know he is innocent. If he ever returns to a life that he can no longer relish, we will offer him our hand and our silence. Not only because he endured an unimaginable ordeal while a host of others slept and enjoyed themselves in the midst of terrible suffering, but also because we all know that in the end, this implacable struggle, begun in solitude, brought him the most dreadful condemnation of all, the judgment each man makes of himself, in utter solitude.

ALBERT CAMUS

---

[375] See under the head "Peste" in *Carnets II*, p. 118: "But there is always an hour of the day or night when a man is a coward. It is that hour that I am afraid of." This note was in fact used in *La Peste*, p. 254.

December 31, 1944–January 1, 1945
The Thirteenth Caesar[376]

We Roman historians crave objectivity. That is why we are not out of place in this newspaper. Yet if we are Roman historians, we are nonetheless men.[377] Some things try our patience.

M. Georges Duhamel[378] is one of those things. At times I am aware of the injustice in my attitude, but there's nothing I can do about it: M. Duhamel tries my patience. In the first place because he published the most patience-trying book imaginable about America. When he came face-to-face with a new civilization, the only words he could find to express his sentiments were those of the timid retiree, the grumpy old duffer whose every grimace conveys the idea that in his day things were just fine.

He tries my patience because one can read him everywhere, because he is not modest, because he is sentimental, because his sentimentality is devoid of quality, because he is prolix, and because his prolixity makes me long for Tacitus, though Tacitus was of course one of my most formidable rivals.[379]

M. Duhamel has lately produced a series of articles that have exhausted my patience entirely. In them he lauds the kind of resistance he practiced, in broad daylight apparently, thus requiring more courage than the modest struggle in which 300,000 clandestine combatants engaged.

As a historian, I know that no conclusions can be drawn without critical evaluation of the testimony of witnesses. But since I am also a man, I know that no one should pretend to have been a hero who was merely a good, well-behaved servant and that functionaries should never speak louder than true warriors.

In studying the Caesars of the decadence,[380] I learned the value of one virtue they all lacked, namely, modesty. This note is intended to remind people of that.

---

[376] Note signed Suetonius. Very likely by Camus.

[377] This sentence parodies a line in *Tartuffe*, act III, scene 3: "Ah, pour être dévot, je n'en suis pas moins homme!" (If I am devout, I am none the less a man.)

[378] In one of regular columns in *Le Figaro*, Georges Duhamel (1884–1966) rather complacently described his attitude of passive resistance during the Occupation. Yet even "Suetonius" acknowledges his "injustice" toward a writer whose work, especially the *Chronique des Pasquier*, marked the interwar period and who did nothing discreditable during the dark years. Apart from his satire of American life in *Scènes de la vie future* (1930), Camus' critical attitude no doubt stemmed from Duhamel's status as a literary institution whose books were filled with respectable sentiments of the sort that Camus himself rejected. Shocked by this note, Mauriac responded to it (along with the important editorial of January 5) in a piece entitled "Contempt for Charity" on January 7–8, 1945. He says he does not wish to borrow the term "patience-trying," "which M. Camus uses in a very superior way, availing himself, I imagine, of the superiority of his future work, [when] he allows himself to judge the author of *La Vie des Martyrs, Civilisation,* the *Sulavin* cycle, and *La Chronique des Pasquier.*" It is very likely that this short text by Suetonius played a considerable role in the bitterness of the subsequent polemic between the two writers.

[379] Tacitus (c. 55–c. 120), Latin historian famous for his concise and suggestive style.

[380] Suetonius's masterpiece was *The Lives of the Twelve Caesars.*

It is only right to add that my twelve Caesars were nevertheless more amusing than M. Duhamel, who definitely tries my patience in ways no words can express.

SUETONIUS

December 31, 1944–January 1, 1945
1945[381]

It is customary at the beginning of the new year for a newspaper to address New Year's wishes to its readers. In this, our first year of open publication, it is easy for us to do this, because we know that our readers' wishes coincide with our own. Once upon a time, in a world where the appearance of prosperity reigned, misery could be a lonely affair. Today, except for a contemptible minority, suffering is common and loneliness shared. All our readers will therefore agree with us in wishing for an end to this war, so that the vast forces being expended on it can be applied to peacetime labors; so that loved ones can be reunited at last and so that the missing can be found and the dead freely mourned; and, last but not least, so that our hearts can be delivered from hatred.

We have proved that we could rise to the challenge of this most terrible of wars. We did not shrink from the ordeal. Hence we are entitled today to wish for it to be over in order to make room once again for human creativity and happiness. But we want the conquest and bold adventure to continue in peacetime, in which we shall maintain our vigilance to ensure that the grandeur of this country and the world's justice are never again separated.

January 2, 1945
Panem et circenses[382]

The government has just increased the taxes that have already imposed an oppressively heavy burden on the film industry.

The Caesars whose history I wrote adopted the opposite policy. They staged the games of the Circus for free. Bread was also free, but it's even less advisable to speak of that.

---

[381] Text published in the December 31, 1944–January 1, 1945 issue. It may have been written by Camus, but possibly in collaboration with others, most notably Pascal Pia. In some respects it is reminiscent of the New Year's greetings published in *Le Soir-Républicain* on January 1, 1940: "We have two wishes to formulate, precise, youthful, ardent wishes. We want and with all our strength hope to bring about a new world that will afford man every opportunity to achieve his dignity. . . . *Le Soir-Républicain* does not wish you happiness because we know that you have been battered in flesh and spirit. But from the bottom of our hearts we wish you to have the strength and clarity of mind necessary to forge your own happiness and dignity." *Fragments d'un combat*, II, pp. 735–736.

[382] Note signed Suetonius. Possibly by Camus.

They understood that such grandly staged spectacles, the distant forebears of our films, were what later came to be called an opium of the people. Film is not a delicacy for the rich. It is a weekly drug that the masses can no longer do without, and they are certainly entitled to forget the woes of the day for a few hours.

Some ill-intentioned people will say that this opium has indeed had a stupefying effect on the masses and that it deserves this crackdown. But the industry, which is actually an art, could easily be compelled to turn its product into an instrument for ennobling the soul rather than debasing it.

French filmmakers have made an effort in this direction, yet they alone are affected by this tax hike. Hollywood films, which so often forsake their cultural mission, come to France with their costs already recouped through their screening in America. The taxes may be heavy, but any money earned by these imported productions is still pure profit.

The Germans did not manage to kill off French cinema even though they subjected a conquered country to the oppression of an occupying force. Will the Minister of Finance succeed where the Germans failed?[383]

SUETONIUS

January 2, 1945[384]

We have read with the requisite respect and approval the letter from a soldier published yesterday by *Le Populaire*.[385] Its severity was legitimate, and its condemnations were for the most part well-founded. As for the consternation and bitterness evinced by the writer, we have said enough about this, and have often enough asked that the entire nation be placed on a war footing, that we need not dwell on these matters here.

Still, we cannot approve one aspect of our comrade's letter, namely, his condemnation of young people in the rear: "Emaciated, manipulated, foolish young people loudly mock anything that exceeds their grasp, be it Victor Hugo or courage."[386] Not that this view can be contradicted. Indeed, no argument for it is given. It merely reflects an intuition, which to a large extent we understand and approve of. But perhaps one should also give some thought to the young people of France, who, on reading this letter, might be tempted to doubt

---

[383] The Minister of Finance at the time was René Pleven. See the editorial of October 13, 1944, n. 136, p. 69.

[384] Editorial. Text signed A. C. and reprinted in *Actuelles*, chapter on "The Flesh."

[385] On *Le Populaire*, see the editorial of September 2, 1944, n. 39, p. 25. On January 1, 1945, under the headline "A Soldier at the Front Speaks to You," the paper published a letter signed A. F. (André Figuéras), introduced by M. B. (probably Marcel Bridoux). This letter, which referred to Léon Blum, describes the disillusionment of a soldier in Paris on leave: "All excited after waiting a year for leave, you say to yourself after two days that it's not worth going to the front to fight and that you're better off there than here. . . . Death is better than a thousand absurd lives."

[386] This is the final sentence of the letter.

themselves, to imagine that this is the way others see them, and to assume responsibility for giving their elders such a pathetic and dispiriting image of themselves.

The young people of France have not had an easy time of it. Some of them fought. It is no secret that on the day of the insurrection, there were as many children's faces on the barricades as there were adult faces. Others had no opportunity to fight or lacked the presence of mind to do so. Today, all are waiting to see what comes next. The legacy of two generations has left them wary of ideas and careful with words. Now they find themselves faced with immense tasks for which no tools have been given them. They have nothing to do, and everything in this world exceeds their grasp. Who can blame them for this? I recently saw many of these young faces gathered in an auditorium.[387] In them I saw only seriousness and attentiveness. These young people are truly attentive, which means that they are waiting for something and that no one has yet responded to their silent appeal. If they are isolated and passive, the responsibility is not theirs but ours, by which I mean the entire country and the government along with it.

Words of scorn will do them no good. What they need is a fraternal hand and a virile tone. This country, which has suffered from senility for so long, cannot do without its youth. But its youth need to be shown that people have confidence in them and are prepared to instill in them a spirit of grandeur rather than a sense of distress or disgust. France has endured a time of desperate courage. It was perhaps this courage that had no future and showed no tenderness that saved her in the end. But the violence of a soul alienated from all there is cannot serve indefinitely. Of course the French need no illusions. They are already too quick to harbor them. But France cannot live by suspicion and rejection alone.

In any event, its young people need to be provided with affirmations so that they can affirm themselves.

It is always difficult to truly unite those who fight with those who wait. The community of hope is not enough; community of experience is also necessary. Yet even if men who have suffered differently can never come together in spirit as one, let us at least do nothing to drive them apart. In the case at hand, let us not add to the anguish of young people in France a condemnation that would revolt them if they were aware of its injustice and reduce them to a situation of inferiority if they were to find the charge plausible. We have plenty of reasons to give in at times to bitterness. Insofar as possible, however, we should keep our bitterness to ourselves.

The truth is that these young people do not make fun of what exceeds their grasp. At any rate, the ones we have known never laughed at anything other than bombast, and they were right to do so. In battle, however, or when confronted with the spectacle of courage, they have always been silent. This was proof of their quality and evidence of an exigent spirit that asked only to be used, and which is in no way responsible for the solitude in which it has been left.

A. C.

[387] Francine Camus, in her letters to her mother, commented that students often asked Camus to give lectures. Note the use of the first-person pronoun, which as a rule Camus does not use in his editorials. Here, however, he is recounting a personal experience.

January 3, 1945[388]

The Agence Française de Presse has just published a communiqué, which as we have pointed out elsewhere originates with an unnamed government source.[389] This communiqué concerns the transformation of the Lublin Committee into a provisional government of the Polish Republic.[390] The question this raises is a delicate one, and in our reporting on the issues yesterday we spoke our minds. We have no desire to comment further on those issues today and will confine ourselves to a discussion of political methods.

In that connection our comment is essentially that the communiqué published by our agency lacks the elementary hallmark of courage that goes by the name clarity. In sum, the text states that France is not obliged to intervene in Poland's internal affairs, that it continues to treat both Polish governments with the same respect, and that it does not wish to take sides.

It would be impossible to shirk the duties incumbent on every government more completely. And in particular, it would be impossible to do more to make both sides unhappy. It is not our job to dictate to the government how it should behave or what policy it ought to adopt. We can say, however, that if situations arise in which one cannot take sides, it is better to remain silent than to issue an ambiguous statement in which for the first time France has abandoned the clear manner in which it has spoken since the liberation.

To assert that our country is not obliged to intervene in Poland's internal affairs is to avoid the real issue. To recognize a foreign government is not to intervene in that country's affairs. It is an act of international politics that every nation is obliged to perform or not to perform after carefully weighing the pros and cons.

To justify our neutrality by saying that we don't know enough about the political situation in Poland is to forget that the Allies used the same argument for years to block recognition of de Gaulle's government.[391] We criticized them enough for this to know that the only thing their reticence ever signified was the set of unstated assumptions on which it was based.

---

[388] Editorial. Text signed A. C.

[389] The text of the AFP dispatch was published in the same issue of *Combat* with the comment that "it seems to have been inspired by an unnamed government official." The pertinent portion of the text reads as follows: "The Lublin Committee's decision to transform itself into a provisional government of the Polish Republic came as no surprise in Paris. Responsible officials stress that this is essentially an internal matter in which France is not obliged to intervene. The decision of the committee, we are told, can in no way alter France's relations with the Polish government in London or its position with respect to the committee."

The text points out that France lacks information about "political realities in Poland" and that Christian Fouchet, who had been sent to Poland to look into the fate of French prisoners and deportees, would be able "to provide useful information."

[390] The Lublin Committee was established when that city was liberated by Soviet troops on July 24, 1944. Its legitimacy was contested by the English, who supported the Polish government in exile, established in London at the time of the German occupation.

[391] See the editorials of September 30, p. 52, and October 14, 15, 17, and 19, 1944, pp. 71, 73, 75, and 78.

The reasons for France's present position are not clear to us, and silence would have been less ambiguous. We believe, moreover, that a position like this can hardly serve our country's interests. What, in fact, are its consequences? On the one hand, we have disappointed the London government by sending a delegate to the Lublin Committee. On the other hand, by maintaining our relations with the London government, we run the risk of allowing a nation we have chosen to be our ally to think that our policy involves unstated motives.

Understand us well. We do not seek a political fight with the Ministry of Foreign Affairs. What we had to say about the issue we have said.

We are only discussing a certain method and a certain manner of speaking. We are arguing for a logical policy. Since we have chosen to ally ourselves with the U.S.S.R., it goes without saying that we have recognized the legitimacy of the Soviets' desire to have a friendly Poland for a neighbor. We cannot ignore the fact that the U.S.S.R. is supporting the Lublin Committee. France expects that in the near future this committee will become the real government of Poland. One can regret this fact or be glad about it, but one cannot pretend to ignore it without the risk of compromising the mission we have decided to undertake.

It is not politic to make everyone unhappy. Nor is it politic to deceive anyone. It is politic to choose after due deliberation and then to proceed directly toward the chosen goal. The governments of the Third Republic thought they could go to Munich and prepare for war at the same time. They were wasting their breath, whereas we, when we speak of the need for clear language and unambiguous political ethics and run the risk of being dismissed as visionaries, feel that we are expressing a deeper political reality that is better suited to the times in which we live. Rectitude is today France's ultimate talent. General de Gaulle has demonstrated this for five years. It would be unfortunate if this prodigious example were tarnished by two or three communiqués of the sort put out by ministries and bureaucracies bent on perpetuating traditions that are all the more disastrous for being so venerable. To put it in a nutshell, we would like to see French policy continue to be expressed in texts that we can read without the embarrassment we felt on reading the commentary that to our dismay the whole world can read in today's paper.

A. C.

January 5, 1945[392]

The press has lately been preoccupied with injustice. This is because it cannot talk about justice. A Catholic novelist, a woman, has written that there is no justice except in hell. Our courts are doing what they can to justify this unfortunate assertion. Columnists and editorialists can thus take their pick of absurd

---

[392] Editorial. Text signed A. C.

sentences and preposterous instances of leniency. In between, prisoners are snatched from their prisons and shot because they were pardoned.[393]

We want to say simply that all of this was to be expected and that it is probably too late now for justice to be done. The justice we called for was difficult to implement because it required reconciling the country's pressing need to destroy the treacherous part of itself with our insistence on due respect for the individual. Quick justice was essential to achieve that end.

We are told that this was impossible, and that a few weeks was not enough time to arrest those guilty of treachery, put them on trial, and punish them. But we know that. That wasn't the problem. The problem with quick justice was that it had to be clear justice. Explanation is in order, since our point was misunderstood.

In a defeated country, treachery sometimes weighs more heavily on the conscience of those who were saved than on the souls of those who did the saving, because thoughts must turn to punishment. This terrifying word has always repelled tender hearts. Yet we needed to get used to this idea, to assume responsibility for human justice and agree to decide what needed to be decided. And as if this task weren't difficult and disheartening enough, we also had to undertake to carry it out scrupulously, which meant in accordance with the law. Now, it bears repeating that there is no law that applies to the kind of treachery we have all experienced. The problem we had to solve is a problem of conscience, which arises with respect to a law that was never written. We live in a world in which one can fail to act honorably without violating the law.

What needed to be done, then, if not create the law we did not have? Here, too, however, we were held back by our scruples. The law that had to be created would have had to apply to crimes committed before it existed. Thus we were faced with an ex post facto law, which is the hallmark of every illegal regime and a stain on every dictatorship.

So, did we have to admit that we were helpless and judge with the laws at our disposal, which were in fact useless?

This is apparently what we did. The results are plain to see. It is in the light of those results that we say we should have embraced the contradictions in our situation and resolutely allowed ourselves to appear unjust in order to do real justice. There is no need to point out how the friends of the people who are being judged today would settle the matter if they were to return to Paris as masters. That is not the point. The point was to create the law we needed, to formulate it in clear and irreproachable language. And to make up for the fact that it would have been an ex post facto law, it would have been necessary to set precise time limits on its application. If we had done these things, it would have been possible to move quickly, because it would have been possible to speak clearly. The government could not arrest all the guilty parties in a few weeks, but it could

---

[393] The issue of the purge had come up several times in the month of October and had already led to exchanges with Mauriac. With this article, however, Camus' tone changes to one of bitterness and disillusion. Abuses of the kind described here did in fact take place. The purge remains controversial to this day.

have created a law of honor that would have been applied for six months or a year and would have rid France of a persistent shame.

Now it is too late. They will go on handing out death sentences to journalists who don't deserve as much.[394] They will go on half-acquitting recruiters with silver tongues. And the people, tired of their sick justice, will continue to intervene from time to time in cases that should no longer be their concern. A certain common sense will preserve us from the worst excesses; fatigue and indifference will do the rest. People can get used to anything, even behavior that is shameful and stupid. In the end, the French cannot ask for more than their minister.

All of this was indeed to be expected, but we cannot say this without bitterness and sadness. A country that fails to purge itself is preparing to fail to remake itself. The face that a nation wears is that of its system of justice. Ours ought to have something to show the world other than this face of confusion. But clarity and unsparing, humane righteousness cannot be learned. For want of clarity we are going to have to settle for paltry consolations. Obviously M. Mauriac was right: we are going to need charity.[395]

A. C.

January 5, 1945[396]
Minister Tiberius[397]

For a historian, there is no such thing as an insignificant fact. Had the price of a bushel of wheat in Rome been lower, the face of the world would have been different.[398]

That is why I find myself deeply interested in the increase in railway fares. Forty percent is quite a bit, and the government must have its reasons. "The government always has its reasons," Caligula said when he decorated his horse. I

---

[394] This may be an allusion to Georges Suarez (see the editorial of October 25, 1944, n. 188, p. 89) or more likely Henri Béraud (1885–1958), who had just been sentenced to death for "collaboration with the enemy." A novelist and reporter for *Gringoire*, Béraud wrote anti-English articles and books and strenuously opposed democracy. His sentence was commuted to forced labor. On January 4, Mauriac had denounced his death sentence in *Le Figaro*.

[395] The allusion is to Mauriac's article of December 14, "The New Alliance," in which he wrote: "Happy are those who believe that above the political order reigns the order of charity." Mauriac reacted very strongly to the closing sentences of Camus' article. On January 7–8 he published a new article entitled "Contempt for Charity," in which he took an ironic tone: "What a pity that our young master, who is clear about everything, did not deign to clarify the law for lack of which 'we are going to have to settle,' he says, 'for paltry consolations.' To which he added, one suspects with a superior smile, 'Obviously M. Mauriac was right: we are going to need charity.'" This is the same article in which Mauriac rose to the defense of Duhamel (see "The Thirteenth Caesar," January 1, p. 158).

[396] Note signed Suetonius. Attribution to Camus is very probable.

[397] Tiberius, emperor of Rome from 14 to 37 C.E., succeeded Augustus and preceded Caligula.

[398] An obvious parody of Pascal's famous line: "Had Cleopatra's nose been shorter, the whole face of the earth would have been different."

should add that Caligula did not give his reasons. It was enough if people believed in their existence.[399]

The world has made some progress since then. And our government has given its reasons. It has said that the increase was advantageous because it would decrease the number of passengers. As everyone knows, trains today find it advantageous if passengers don't take them. The government not only gave its reasons but also provided a demonstration of them. It pointed out that trains from western France were being used mainly by black-market traffickers, people whom we Ancients called "hunger-bearers," and who earned 10,000 francs per day with every trip. Now, if I understand correctly, their trips will earn them only 9,243 francs per day, which will obviously discourage them from resuming their activities.

Clearly the government is energetic. When Tiberius watched his moray eels eating his slaves, he said that no government can ever be energetic enough. Our ministers have grasped this point, and they continue to feed the slaves of the tax collector to the eels of the black market.

SUETONIUS

January 7–8, 1945[400]

Spain is growing fainter.[401] A good many false news reports have come to us from there.[402] Now it seems that everything is as expected, which is a roundabout way of saying that Franco is still in power.

In truth, things couldn't be simpler. The Phalangist regime has been in power as long as Hitler. Germany was on its last legs for a few months now, and the Franco regime was following suit. Then, a few weeks ago, Germany recovered some of its strength, and this spilled over into Spain, where the Hitlerian regime appeared to regain some of its former solidity. This sharing of misfortune and hope by the two countries, along with their common political alignment and parallel rise and fall in temperature, should open everyone's eyes. But some people are incurably blind.

Meanwhile, among Spanish Republican émigrés, efforts have been made to organize for more effective action. The Spanish Parliament has met in Mexico, and Dr. Negrín has been prevented from speaking in London.[403] It is true that he had the unbelievable audacity to assert that Spain was not asking for allied

---

[399] Camus' interest in Caligula is of course well known. His play of that title would be written in September 1945.

[400] Editorial. Text signed A. C.

[401] This sentence seems to echo the title of an article by Montherlant, "Barrès Is Growing Fainter," which was reprinted in *Aux Fontaines du désir* and used as the title of a section containing three texts about the writer Maurice Barrès. The (perhaps unconscious) connection with Spain can be inferred from a passage in one of these texts: "Toledo tells me that Barrès is growing fainter." See Henri Montherlant, *Essais* (Paris : Gallimard, 1963), p. 270.

[402] See the editorial of December 10, 1944, p. 137. Camus of course closely followed events in Spain.

[403] On Jan Negrín, see the editorial of November 21, 1944, and n. 273, p. 118.

intervention and want nothing more than an end to the united nations' diplomatic support for Franco. Obviously this offended common sense.

One has to believe, however, that M. Negrín had his reasons, because France now seems to want to get involved. We are told that M. Mateu will arrive in Paris on Wednesday with the rank of ambassador representing Phalangist Spain to the French government. M. Mateu, who has a major interest in the Hispano-Suiza Corp., whose German connections are well known, was indeed the man for the hour. But if the reports are true, we want to state flatly that while he may have been the best choice to represent a general who is serving the Germans, he is not the right man to shake the hand of another general who has never served any cause but that of France and freedom.

The French Republic has nothing in common with the dictatorship of Franco. Maybe it's true that we don't have to intervene in Spain. But to resume diplomatic relations is to intervene, and we grant recognition to force and injustice when we accredit their representative. We have other business to take care of. And if we are incapable of erasing the unbearable shame of the Vichy government's decision to hand Companys[404] and many others over to Phalangist firing squads, let us at least shut our mouths and maintain a scrupulously neutral silence. To do so will do us no honor but will at least spare us from indignity.

Some may object that we bring too much passion to our work when we write about Spain. Yes, we do write with passion, but we also write about justice with passion. Is this a way of saying that our idea of justice is mistaken? So much stupidity and cruelty, blindness in high places, politics mixed with human blood, so many countries subjected for years to bloody and ridiculous dictatorships—who can speak of such things without quivering with rage or passion? Some will say that there may be high political reasons—very high political reasons—for maintaining relations with General Franco. But we know no higher political reasons than honest words and human freedom. What political reasons could be high enough to induce us to shake the hand of a man who was an accomplice to everything we despised and everything we fought against?

America and England are not in a position to judge a humiliation they did not endure and silent suffering they were spared, but how can we ignore such things?

In all of free Europe only we are capable of speaking in such terms. Why, then, are we hesitating to state in no uncertain terms that we want nothing to do with General Franco and will recognize only the constitutional government of Spain, which the republicans are preparing to convene in a lawful assembly and with the highest of hopes? Passion is here supported by reason and truth. One can never be passionate enough, moreover, in defending a cause in which our reasons and our truth are so deeply invested.

A. C.

---

[404] Luis Companys (1883–1940) was president of the Generality of Catalonia in 1934. At odds with the central government, he aligned himself with the Republicans in 1936. After the civil war he took refuge in France, but the Vichy government handed him over to Franco. He was shot in Barcelona in 1940. Camus recalls these facts in his article "Why Spain?" published in *Combat* on November 25, 1948 (see p. 297 below) and reprinted in *Actuelles*.

January 11, 1945

Justice and Charity[405]

M. Mauriac has just published under the title "Contempt for Charity" an article that I find neither just nor charitable. In dealing with the issues that divide us, he has for the first time taken a tone that I do not wish to make an issue of but that I, at least, will refrain from adopting. I would not have responded to his article, moreover, had circumstances not conspired to oblige me to abandon these daily debates in which the best and the worst of us have engaged for months without clarifying any of the issues that truly matter to us.[406] I would not have responded if I did not feel that this discussion, in which our very way of life is at issue, was devolving into confusion. And since I am personally attacked, I would like to end by speaking in my own name and trying one last time to make clear what I have been trying to say.

Whenever I used the word *justice* in connection with the purge, M. Mauriac spoke of *charity*. So singular is the virtue of charity, moreover, that in calling for justice I seemed to be pleading on behalf of hatred. To hear M. Mauriac tell it, it truly seems that in dealing with these mundane matters we must make an absolute choice between the love of Christ and the hatred of men. Surely not! Some of us reject both the cries of enmity that reach our ears from one side and the tender solicitations that come to us from the other. Between these two extremes, we are searching for the just voice that will give us truth without shame. For that we do not need to be absolutely clear about everything; we need only to desire clarity with passion and intellect and heart, qualities without which neither M. Mauriac nor I are likely to do any good.

This is what allows me to say that charity has no business here. I have the impression, moreover, that M. Mauriac is misreading the texts he has taken it upon himself to contradict. Clearly he is a writer who works by feel rather than argument, but on these questions I'd prefer that we set feelings aside. He has completely misinterpreted me if he thinks that I'm smiling at the world we have been given. When I say that the charity that has been held up as an example to twenty nations starved for justice is paltry consolation, I beg my critic to believe that I do so without smiling.

As long as I respect M. Mauriac for what he is, I have the right to reject what he thinks. To do so, it is not necessary to feel the contempt for charity that he so generously ascribes to me. On the contrary, our respective positions seem clear to me. M. Mauriac does not wish to add to the hatred that already exists, and

---

[405] Framed article printed with headline and signed Albert Camus. This unusual presentation underscores the importance that Camus and *Combat* attached to this piece. Reprinted without title in *Actuelles*, chapter on "Morality and Politics."

[406] No doubt the fact that this article was the last published before Camus took a month's leave from his post (his first since August 21) played a part in its placement. Fatigue and illness (to which Camus refers as "circumstances" and about which we know from Francine Camus' letters to her mother) had made him more vulnerable to Mauriac's attacks, to which he here responds in his own name.

in that I am quite prepared to follow him. But I do not wish to add to the lies that already exist, and there I await his approval. Not to put too fine a point on it, let me say that I am waiting for him to say openly that there is today a need for justice.

To tell the truth, I don't believe he will: this is a responsibility he will not assume. M. Mauriac, who has written that our Republic should know how to be harsh, is meditating on the possibility of writing before too long a word he has yet to utter: pardon. To him I would simply say this, that I see for our country two ways unto death (and there are ways of surviving that are no better than death): the way of hatred and the way of pardon.[407] One seems to me as disastrous as the other. I have no taste for hatred. The mere idea of having enemies strikes me as the most tiresome thing in the world, and my comrades and I had to make the most strenuous of efforts to see the enemy as such. But pardon seems no better to me, and in today's circumstances it would look like an insult. In any case, I am convinced that it is not up to us. If death sentences horrify me, that is my business. I shall join M. Mauriac in granting open pardons when Vélin's parents[408] and Leynaud's wife[409] tell me that I can. But not before. Never before, so as not to betray, for the sake of an effusion of the heart, what I have always loved and respected in this world, the fount of man's nobility, which is loyalty.

That may be a hard thing to hear. I can only hope that M. Mauriac is aware that it no less hard to say. I stated flatly that Béraud did not deserve the death penalty, and I confess that I have no imagination left for the leg irons that, according to M. Mauriac, those found guilty of treason are required to wear. It took all the imagination at my disposal over four long years to conceive of the fate of thousands of Frenchmen who had honor on their side and yet were consigned to the worst tortures on the word of journalists whom some would now turn into martyrs. As a man, I may admire M. Mauriac for his ability to love traitors, but as a citizen, I deplore it, because such love will bring us a nation of treacherous and mediocre men and a society we no longer want anything to do with.

Finally, M. Mauriac has flung Christ in my face. I will tell him this, with all appropriate gravity: I think I have an accurate idea of the grandeur of Christianity, but some of us in this persecuted world have the feeling that if Christ died for certain people, he didn't die for us.[410] Yet we refuse to give up hope in man. While lacking the unreasonable ambition to save man, we are at least keen to serve him. While we are willing to do without God or hope, we cannot give up as easily on man. On this point I can indeed tell M. Mauriac that we have

---

[407] As early as May 1944, Camus declared himself to be "without hatred and without compassion" in regard to Pierre Pucheu.

[408] On Vélin, the pen name of André Bollier, see "A Newspaper in History."

[409] On René Leynaud, see the editorial of October 27, 1944, p. 90.

[410] Camus described his position with respect to Christianity in his editorial of September 8, 1944, p. 31. This sentence resonates with any number of passages in *The Plague* and *The Fall*, among other works.

not lost heart and will refuse to the end a divine charity that would frustrate men
of the justice they are due.

ALBERT CAMUS

February 9, 1945[411]

To judge by what is being said about us, it would seem that *Combat* has changed
its line and succumbed to a regrettable fever of opposition.[412] It is true that since
the Liberation many things and many people have changed. And I suppose that
is why the very people who have remained steadfast in what they were saying are
now accused of inconsistency.

In any case, I am bound to say that *Combat* has never changed its position.
Our team has remained united around the very things that united us in insurrection and that keep us together now in a time of great confusion. This paper's
editorial writers are jointly responsible for what the paper says.[413]

Careful readers are well aware of this. We have always said that liberation was
not liberty and that the fight against the Nazi enemy was for us identical with
the fight against the power of money. We have always maintained that alliance
politics was not enough and that our only goal was a world organization that
would at last bring peace among nations.

For six months we have championed the same program without wavering. For
six months we have called for a war–and-reconstruction economy what would
mark a break with the past, and for socializations (first of all in banking) that would
place production at the service of the collectivity rather than abandon it to the private interests whose dereliction of duty we have noted. For six months we have
called for the creation of a true popular democracy based on economic justice and
liberal politics. For six months, aware of the contradictions that are suffocating a
world caught between an economy that is now international and a politics that
remains stubbornly national, we have called for a world economic federation, in
which raw materials, commercial markets, and currency would be internationalized
and which would also lay the groundwork for a political federation that might prevent the nations of the world from slitting each other's throats every twenty years.[414]

---

[411] Editorial. Signed text.

[412] Probably an allusion to an article that appeared in *Le Monde*'s "review of the press" on January 25,
which expressed surprise at "the limited role that *Combat* is apparently inclined to allow for groups from
the Resistance," owing to its rejection of the national union advocated by Communist Party leader
Maurice Thorez, which according to *Combat* would become the only party in a one-party state.

[413] Camus, who had published nothing since January 11, had been back at the paper for a few days but
on a somewhat reduced schedule. He resumed his position and his full responsibility with this signed article, following which editorials once again became anonymous, as they had been in the first few months,
a move no doubt intended to serve as a guarantee of unity among the various editorialists.

[414] These two paragraphs succinctly summarize *Combat*'s political line prior to the emergence of ideological cleavages.

We were not alone last August in defending this program, and we were not all that original. Near unanimity existed then, and therein lay our greatest source of hope. Our government had accepted the principles set forth above. And it was for precisely that reason that we gave the government our support while vowing to remain vigilant and directing all our effort to defending the common hope in the language of objectivity. What has changed to occasion such surprise in some of our comrades? Let us be blunt: what has changed, it seems, is not our convictions but the intentions of the government.

The decisions taken over the past few weeks and the policies adopted by certain ministries are no longer consistent with the program outlined above. There are ministers who no longer have our confidence because they no longer have our approval. We are not the ones who are isolating ourselves at the present time; it is the government that is isolating itself. For we are not alone. The Socialist Party, the trade unions, and, last but not least, the C.N.R., have recently announced their positions. M. Cachin himself has published two articles correcting the latest declarations of the Communist Party and calling for needed socializations.[415] No, nothing has changed, except perhaps the goals of the government.

What else is there to say? The word "opposition" has been mentioned. I myself would find opposition unfortunate. I hope we can avoid it. But we will choose the path of opposition tomorrow without hesitation if the domestic political program that has been announced fails to prove that the government has kept its promises. For we too have promises to keep. We made them at a time when humiliation had become a religion and dereliction of duty a national pastime. We will keep our promises out of respect for ourselves and for the people of this country. That is our idea of honesty, in any event, and we shall stand by it.

ALBERT CAMUS

February 16, 1945[416]

Along with other difficult issues, the Crimea Conference had to decide whether the decisions taken by the future League of Nations would be taken by majority vote or unanimous consent.[417] A reader not well-versed on this issue might conclude that this was a matter of pure form. In fact, the whole future of the world hangs in the balance.[418]

---

[415] Marcel Cachin (1869–1958), a member of the SFIO, was one of the founders of the Communist Party at the Congress of Tours in 1920. He directed the newspaper *L'Humanité* from 1918 to his death and played an important role in the Resistance. After the war he became a deputy and was regularly reelected.
[416] Editorial. Text probably by Camus.
[417] The reference is to the important Yalta Conference, in which Stalin, Churchill, and Roosevelt met from February 4 to February 11. A prelude to the San Francisco Conference that established the United Nations, the Yalta Conference drew new borders in Europe, divided Germany into zones of occupation, and established that the Polish government would be open to Polish émigrés in London.
[418] The lucidity of this remark cannot be overstated. The Yalta Conference did indeed prove decisive for the future of the world, most notably by establishing spheres of influence for East and West.

What is really at stake? Imagine a political conflict between two members of the League leading to sanctions against one of them. The question is whether those sanctions can be enforced as soon as a majority of nations finds against one of the parties to the dispute, or whether sanctions must wait until unanimous consent has been achieved. If the latter, the power in danger of being punished by the world council would obviously have to approve the measures taken against it. Its veto would be enough to nullify any decision of the Supreme Council.

Clearly, the question of the veto comes down to this: either the future League of Nations will be a federal instrument that will strictly enforce the rules of an international democracy, or it will be an organization that will call upon the great powers to demonstrate the supreme virtue of sanctioning themselves for their own imperialist aims. Although we are widely reputed to harbor utopian inclinations, we have only moderate confidence in human virtue, hence we conclude that it is a question of choosing between international democracy on the one hand and recognition of imperialism on the other.

In this respect, the decisions of the Crimean Conference were decisions of boundless importance. The official communiqué stated that the problem had been resolved. The solution was disclosed today by The *New York Times*, which is generally reliable and whose report has yet to be contradicted. According to that paper, the veto power will be maintained, but its use on all major issues will be limited to the five great powers: the U.S.S.R., the United States, Great Britain, France, and China.[419]

If this report is accurate, it is of considerable importance, for it would effectively put an end to any idea of international democracy. The world would in effect be ruled by a directorate of five powers. The decisions they take will still be applicable to all other nations, but any one of the five could nullify a decision against its own interests by exercising its veto. The Five would thus retain forever the freedom of maneuver that would be forever denied the others.

We are well aware that it is flattering for us to be counted among the five powers. We are also well aware that this solution would resolve the German question for some period of time. But we are only too well aware as well of the reasons for five years of dreadful struggles and atrocious miseries not to say as simply as possible how deeply distressing we find decisions such as these. They bear on the fate of millions of people who expected that with victory would come certainty that the peace would last long enough for them at least to forget their pain. They expected that some kind of international law would protect small nations as well as great ones and punish imperialist projects. Instead, if the *Times* report is correct, what they are being offered is an ephemeral balance of power and inevitable struggles for influence. They expected the victorious countries to give up a portion of their sovereignty to an international organization. Instead they are confronted with a reinforcement of great-power sovereignty at the expense of the sovereignty of smaller nations.

---

[419] These five nations were to enjoy permanent seats on the Security Council.

To be sure, France retains her sovereignty. But the point is that it is incumbent on France to declare forthrightly that justice is not served by this decision and that the path that we are being asked to take in the name of "realities" fails to take account of two terrifying realities, war and conquest, which will eventually bring the world to a new confrontation with death. France, whose wealth today consists solely in her labor and her liberty, should say to the world that the only realistic course leads to economic federalism, to the sharing of wealth, and to the submission of all nations to the rule of international democracy. These were the purposes for which this country took upon itself for four years the burden of guns, deaths, and tortured bodies. And since some would speak to us of grandeur, let us continue to say that if our grandeur is to be built on the misfortune of others, we want no part of it.

February 17, 1945[420]

"Here, at least, we aren't living amidst lies," said a friend of ours who is fighting on the Alsatian front. When we first published these words, some found them bitter, others atrocious.[421] Unfortunately, events seem to justify them all the more with each passing day. But if we are to maintain the proper attitude and the proper detachment, it behooves us to distinguish between lying on the one hand and equivocation and confusion on the other.

It was a lie to declare, hand on heart, that France has always played a benevolently protective role vis-à-vis her colonies, yet we have no reason to doubt the sincerity of the words that General de Gaulle spoke on the occasion of the Annamite [Vietnamese] holiday Tet, or the munificent promise he held out to millions of people: "France intends to make the political, economic, social, and cultural development of the Indochinese Union one of its primary goals."

Such declarations can easily be negated, however, if we invoke a nonexistent tradition to support them. If we insist that none of the past can be repudiated, we seriously impair our chances of future success. As everyone knows, the General Government in Indochina balanced its budget by selling opium, just as it browbeat local "elites" and oppressed the people. If France wants to remain in control in the Far East, it must announce that it intends to renounce such methods.

A much more serious lie, and much more dangerous for the future, is to pretend to be working toward an international democracy when (according to a report published in yesterday's *New York Times*) the five great powers intend to reserve to

---

[420] Editorial. Text possibly by Camus.
[421] The repetition of a previously quoted phrase and the explicit reference to the editorial of December 13, p. 138, which Camus signed, suggest that this editorial was also by him, but a few days earlier Camus had noted that "the editorialists . . . answer to one another." The question cannot be resolved on internal grounds. Camus was not a specialist on Indochina. That role was filled by Colonel Bernard, who would later publish a number of key articles on that issue. But Camus was interested in colonial issues and in the relation of the nation to people and state.

themselves the veto power, a decision which, if confirmed, will lead to implicit recognition of various types of imperialism. In this connection, it is worth pointing out the persistent ambiguity of the terms people, nation, and state.

If our century is one in which economic and social realities have interpenetrated and the interests of peoples fit uncomfortably within the obsolete limits of the nation, the history of the past thirty years has taught us that the state has often worked against the nation. It has become a commonplace to maintain that no matter what the circumstances a country needs a strong state. But the heart of the issue lies elsewhere. A people either chooses or allows to be imposed on it a regime whose executive and ruling organs constitute the state. The less the doctrine that state champions in the nation and in the world is linked to the particular interests of the people it represents and to the general interests of the peoples that surround it, the more power it will seek, even to the point of becoming despotic.

The ill-fated Pétain, following an absurd logic of his own, tried to resolve the problem of the relationship between people, nation, and government by substituting the "French State" for the "French Republic," which strictly speaking made no sense. We should be careful not to confuse matters further by turning the state into a kind of superior entity that must be "served." It is the role of prefects to serve the state, but the role of the state in a regime like ours is to serve a policy that is well expressed, albeit incompletely, in the Charter of the Resistance, for example. A democracy needs a coherent and energetic state but not a "strong state" in the sense that the word has taken on. In our case, this coherence and energy should be used to accomplish needed reforms at home and defend the French people's desire for peace in the world.

We are of course aware that the French government is not responsible for the decisions taken at Yalta, but as General de Gaulle has said, France need not feel bound by any agreement to which it was not a party, and which it can approve only as the representative of the French people.

As distressing as it is not to live in a world of truth, let us not exacerbate our pain by allowing the best of us to die at the front in a climate of deceit.

March 9, 1945[422]

For two days, M. Teitgen,[423] the minister of information, has been under attack by the Consultative Assembly. Today he is going to answer. While his justifications may be clever and honest, we doubt that they will get to the heart of the

---

[422] Editorial. Text probably by Camus, who often defended the Resistance press against newspapers subject to the power of money. The vehemence of the attack on Pierre-Henri Teitgen may have been due to Pascal Pia, though Pia, it should be remembered, usually signed the few articles he wrote. Furthermore, the attribution of the article of March 16, which would respond to *Témoignage chrétien*'s attack on this piece, is almost beyond doubt.

[423] On Paul-Henri Teitgen, see the editorials (and notes) of September 10 and October 29, 1944, pp. 34 and 92.

issue. Why should they, since most of the criticism directed at him has concerned questions of paper and allocation, which are no doubt important but surely secondary?

In fact, what should have been challenged is the very existence of the ministry of information and its mission. On the face of it, there is reason to doubt the need for such a ministry. For if it were a matter of informing the public about government policy, each ministry has press attachés for that purpose, who, by the way, discharge their duties without giving the slightest thought to the ministry of information.

As for material difficulties such as the lack of paper, these were never enough to justify the creation of a special industry. They could have been dealt with by a professional organization such as the Press Federation or a department of the ministry of industrial production. Hence the real reasons for the existence of the ministry of information lie elsewhere.

M. Teitgen's mission and that of his ministry was clear: it was to effect a transition. M. Teitgen was supposed to file indictments against those newspaper companies that worked with the enemy for four years. He was supposed to oversee the confiscation of their property and make sure that the confiscated property was put to good use. He was supposed to grant authorization to publish to new newspapers provided that they satisfied certain clear and generally recognized criteria. And finally, he was supposed to draft rules that would protect the French press from the influence of financial and economic interests.

M. Teitgen has done none of these things—nothing serious, at any rate. In some areas he contented himself with short-term expedients, while in others he resolutely abstained from taking any action at all.

As far as authorizations to publish are concerned, they were awarded without rhyme or reason, other than an obvious inclination to favor the popular democrats.[424] A post of this kind calls for a man capable of remaining above the parties. M. Teitgen preferred to ensconce himself in his own.

This was a serious offense. More serious still was the fact that he allowed a new press regime to establish itself without reinforcing either its discipline or its freedom. For this is a matter that affects not only newspapers but freedom in general.

There are two ways of infringing liberty: by police power or economic power. The latter can be exercised either directly—in a material manner—or indirectly, by orienting the way people think, by addling their brains, by using the press to bias them in favor of special interests. The law of 1881, which still governs the press in this country, left the door wide open to the power of money. It has been amended only slightly. We now know the extent to which the moneyed interests used the press before the war.

In order for the Resistance press to see the light of day, how many men and women were killed, tortured, or deported? Must all that sacrifice have been in

---

[424] The last phrase should no doubt be read as "Christian democrats," since Teitgen was one of the leaders of the M.R.P., the Christian Democratic party.

vain? And today, because nothing stands in the way, must this or that newspaper be allowed to accept money from some well-heeled lender, abdicate its independence, and squander the fortune in courage and sacrifice that enabled it to become what it is? Is freedom truly served when such things are allowed to happen?

If the Resistance press, still vulnerable to pressure from the moneyed interest or from government, ultimately forsakes or betrays the national interests that justify its existence, some dishonor will attach to the failure to do anything to attempt to protect it from such pressure. It may already be too late.

If M. Teitgen does not intend to serve the free press, why is he waiting to say so? And if he cannot, why is he waiting to resign?

March 11–12, 1945[425]

Yesterday we published as objective as possible a report of M. Teitgen's speech. Truthfulness obliged us to say that the speech was clever enough to change the sentiments of a portion of the Assembly. It is also true, however, that the speech seemed clever only because the objections put to the minister were weak or incomplete. Once again, clarity is called for.

Let us start off by saying that M. Teitgen is quite right to call for a reform of political morality. We at *Combat* will not contradict him on this point, and we do not wish to pick a personal quarrel with him. All we are saying is that if journalists are expected to be impartial, a minister should not place himself above his office and should not be too sensitive to criticism. There was nothing modest about M. Teitgen's speech. M. Francisque Gay,[426] in his defense of the minister, also muddied the waters. The fact that M. Teitgen is a Catholic is of no importance, and we readily grant that he is a man of many merits who has suffered personally. But that has nothing to do with his office. The rules of politics in this case are rules of modesty.

Our role is to judge not what M. Teitgen is but what he does. In recent days he has received a wide range of criticisms of varying merit. But the one major criticism that takes precedence over all the others was made by M. Texier alone.[427] In a sense, it is of no importance that new newspapers were granted authorization to publish, and it was not inappropriate for M. Teitgen to summon all his "spiritual families" to speak at the same time. But strict legal statutes

---

[425] Editorial. Text probably by Camus, a follow-up to the previous one and included in the reply by *Témoignage chrétien*.

[426] Francisque Gay (1885–1963) was a Christian activist in Marc Sangnier's "Sillon" movement. He turned the publishing house that he directed into one of the centers of the Resistance. As director of *L'Aube*, he was one of the founders of the M.R.P. He served as a member of the Consultative Assembly and deputy from Paris and later as vice-premier or minister in governments headed by de Gaulle, Gouin, and Bidault. Some months after this article was published, he tried to arbitrate between *Combat* and Henri Frenay and Claude Bourdet.

[427] J. Texier, one of the first resisters, who became editor of a daily paper in 1944–45.

governing the press should have been issued first, in order to assure its champions that the children of Pascal and Voltaire of whom the minister spoke were not also the cousins of Messieurs de Wendel.[428]

The simple question is this: has M. Teitgen established a legal statute governing the press, or has he not? He knew the importance of such regulations, because he assented to them when the Resistance was still underground. But he has not issued them. The day before yesterday he said that he was about "to take the necessary preliminary steps." But the broad outlines of the statute were worked out underground, and the reform should have taken no time at all: all that was needed was the will to implement it. Apparently that will was lacking. That is how things stand today. Our proposals are treated as "advice," and the government's promises are deferred. Structural reforms have been put on hold, financial measures have been delayed, and the press statute has been postponed. Tomorrow, when the enemy has consolidated its position, the reforms will fail or will be seen as bad. We will be the utopians.

This is how things will go with the press if we are not vigilant. We of the underground press had confidence in ourselves. We knew the price of shame, and the memory of our comrades served as our guarantee. But other newspapers have emerged. We do not hold them in suspicion, nor are we accusing them of anything. We are simply saying that we haven't as much confidence in them as we have in ourselves. It is no doubt a good thing that they are publishing, but the press statute should have been announced first, before the authorization to publish was granted. This was not done. Now the gates are open. Regardless of what M. Teitgen may want, money will find a way in if it wants to and if it has not done so already. That is our case, and as you can see, it is a simple one. M. Teitgen has a pure heart and a guilty mind. He will forgive us if we withdraw our confidence in him.

The verdict is not ours to decide, but that won't stop us from stating our views. M. Francisque Gay, again defending the minister, said that if the "rotten press" returned, the blame would fall on the Resistance press and not on the minister. We will continue to protest against this view as long as we have an ounce of energy. The Resistance press did what was within its power: it occupied premises during the insurrection and published newspapers under conditions without historical precedent. Afterward, it was up to the minister to give a statutory definition of freedom of the press. Within its limited domain, the Resistance press made history. The minister was supposed to make law. He did not do so, and for that he is entirely responsible, whatever his intentions may have been.

Hence our conclusion is unambiguous. In politics, it is not possible simply to be what you were. You define yourself by what you do. On the one issue where there was something to do, M. Teitgen did nothing. Pardon us, therefore, for saying that in our eyes he is nothing. Or at any rate, he should be nothing from now on.

---

[428] The Wendels were a family of industrialists who for decades had been a major power in the steel industry as well as in politics and finance.

March 16, 1945[429]

In *Témoignage chrétien*, Father Chaillet was good enough to comment on our position in regard to the current minister of information.[430] His manner is courteous, but he manages to confuse a number of different things. In particular, we would like to assure him that it is perfectly possible to have an opinion about the press statute and the usefulness of a minister without necessarily invoking a philosophy of solitude and irony. It is in fact rather naïve to assume the opposite. Whatever our philosophy might be, assuming we all share one in common, we can assure *Témoignage chrétien* that we don't rely on it to deal with all of life's vicissitudes. We aren't that inspired.

The problem we are facing is a merely practical one. We are asking for a press statute that the minister has had six months to prepare and which he tells us is still only in the preliminary stages. We're afraid that it may be too late. Father Chaillet wonders whether the statute will be enough to prevent the moneyed interests from taking a hand in the affairs of the press. In our view, this is not the right question. True enough, there is no certainty that the statute will have the desired effect, and we are not so naïve as to believe that institutions, even well-wrought institutions, can by themselves vanquish interests. What is certain, however, is that money will have its way if an intelligently crafted statute is not adopted. Father Chaillet can take it on faith that we are certain of two or three things that have nothing to do with philosophy. If the regulation of the sale of paper were to end tomorrow, we would return to the press regime that existed before the war, and the independent press would cease to exist in this country. To cite just one example, any press baron prepared to make the necessary financial sacrifice for the required period of time could print newspapers of twelve pages and sell them for the same price as our four- to six-page editions, and the circulation of the paper published by Father Chaillet's friends would collapse within a few months, as would ours.

If a new statute does not prohibit these practices or force paper dealers to charge the publishers of twelve-page papers three times what they charge the

---

[429] Editorial. Text very likely by Camus, to judge by its content and tone; a follow-up to the editorials of March 9 and 11–12.

[430] On *Témoignage chrétien*, see the editorial of September 16, 1944, n. 52, p. 31. In the March 16, 1945, issue of that paper, Father Chaillet published an article entitled "Notes on an Important Debate," in which he defended Pierre-Henri Teitgen's speech to the Consultative Assembly against the criticisms of "the *Combat* editorial writer," from whose editorials he cited a number of passages and whom he praised in passing as a writer he "always profits from reading" despite their "metaphysical differences." In particular, he reproached the writer for "attacking the assembly born of the Resistance" and "putting weapons into the hands of those waiting for the right moment to attack publicly the press born of the same Resistance." He added: "We agree as to the corrupting virtue of money. . . . But is there any assurance that a statute will suffice to prevent the failure of the reforms?" He concludes by commenting on the final paragraph in the March 11–12 editorial: "It is peremptory, as if establishing despair as a standard. This judgment may well be appropriate for the solitude of a philosophy of irony. It does not have a useful place in a progressive revolution, where what one was has considerable influence on what one must become. It is not as easy to build a new world as it is to build a stage set." Was this allusion to the theater a reference to *Le Malentendu*?

publishers of four-page papers, our dead comrades will have sacrificed in vain. France will go back to the same old lies as before.

This simple example should be enough to justify our harsh criticism of M. Teitgen. In any case, it should show that we are inspired solely by a general concern for the public good. The personality of the minister in question is of little interest to us, but what he has done and above all what he hasn't done are of great interest. And contrary to the views of our amiable opponent, to judge the minister solely by what he has done is by no means a token of despair. In human terms, we readily acknowledge that what a man has done in the past should always be taken into account, but the actions of a minister cannot be judged on sentimental grounds.

Finally, when we say that journalists of the Resistance did what they had to do to bring about a revolution of the press, we are not thinking of what they have done since the liberation. We are in a good position to know that in that respect they have not always set a shining example, although they have done at least as well as the new non-Resistance newspapers. We are thinking only of what the Resistance press did during the insurrection, when it achieved every objective it was assigned. Since then, it has waited for the minister to consecrate its victory. But the minister's mind was elsewhere, and it is because of this distraction that we are withdrawing our confidence.

Our friends from *Témoignage chrétien* should therefore be able to see perfectly well that philosophy has nothing to do with our position. Yet a policy so obviously riddled with inconsistencies might well lead us to adopt a philosophy in which bitterness played too large a part were it not for our rational faith in man, which makes obstinacy a primary virtue.

March 18, 1945[431]

Breaking our general rule, we trust that we may just this once speak out in anger. Many sources tell us that the siege of Paris has not ended and that miserable Parisians who go to the countryside in search of food for their families are being arrested, searched, and threatened. After their contraband is confiscated, their meat ration is not increased by a single gram but is instead canceled for several weeks. They are threatened, while the black market, far from suffering as a result, is thriving as never before, since people have to pay seventeen francs for the same egg they bought for five francs only to have it snatched from the mouths of the children of Paris by the economic police.

The bounds of decency have been exceeded. M. Ramadier[432] has thus far distinguished himself by handling all logistical matters with perfect neutrality. In the most difficult of situations, this minister has chosen never to intervene. Instead, he contents himself with reporting to those under his jurisdiction about

---

[431] Editorial. Text possibly by Camus, in that Camus previously wrote of certain ministers in harshly critical terms, particularly those ministers who held positions of responsibility before the war, as Ramadier did.
[432] On Paul Ramadier, see editorial of December 15, n. 340, p. 142.

a situation that they are perfectly capable of assessing without his help. He breaks his silence only to announce what he has not been able to do. He does so courteously and objectively. As an informer he could not possibly do better.

For a time it was possible to believe that this minister was a disciple of Machiavelli.[433] He banned the consumption of meat so that our allies would give us corned beef. M. Ramadier had apparently decided to prick the honor of the Americans. Since he did nothing, they were forced to do something in his stead. But then our butter was also taken away, along with other things about which the Allies could do nothing. Hence this was not a policy; it was a system based on sharing and distributing a single commodity: statistics.

This system was just barely tolerable, but it depended on allowing each consumer the freedom to supply his own needs. Since the government was incapable of demolishing Vichy's system, the absurd autonomy of the *départements*, and the omnipotence of the prefects, Parisians concluded that it was up to them to go out and find the dozen eggs that the minister of supply took six months to fail to come up with. They did so, and their ingenuity is daily saving the lives of the children indispensable to our future.

Now M. Ramadier has decided to emerge from his lengthy period of slumber. And as if to deny the people under his jurisdiction the right to succeed where he failed, he has dispatched a swarm of zealous lackeys across Paris to persecute all who refused to die of hunger.

This we cannot stand for. For months now, M. Ramadier has demonstrated that he was incapable of meeting our needs. We will not ask him to resign, since everybody knows that ministers enjoy a longevity in office inversely proportional to their abilities, and everyone knows that stable governments are strong governments. Nevertheless, we can insist that he not shed the enviable beatitude that has enveloped him for many months.

All we expect of him is that he continue on his course while allowing private individuals to do what he was incapable of doing. M. Ramadier cannot be unaware that infant mortality rose by 40 percent this winter. We will allow him to welcome this news with serenity and admit that there is nothing he can do to improve the situation. But we will not allow him to stand in the way of people who feel less easy in their hearts when their own children's lives are at stake and who do for themselves what they waited in vain for the government to do for them.

March 27, 1945[434]

It is rather vexing and a bit ridiculous to be obliged today to take a stand on the issue of *laïcité* [the French tradition of secular education—Trans.]. This may seem like beating a dead horse, and we refrained from intervening in this

---

[433] Machiavelli, Nicolo (1469–1527), whose masterpiece *The Prince* describes a political doctrine based on cynicism.

[434] Editorial. Text authenticated by a letter from Francine Camus to her mother, which included this article.

polemic because we hoped it would be short-lived. Yet it seems that this is not to be, since the government itself is about to take a stand and since M. Capitant[435] on Saturday filed a bill that met with a certain indignation before being withdrawn yesterday.[436]

In any event, the issue cannot be avoided and must be dealt with. Our only regret is that it has been raised at all. Catholic activists, lacking foresight and prudence, have placed weapons in the hands of their enemies. Sure of receiving a favorable hearing in certain quarters of the government, they forgot the risk of offending the many Frenchmen who see secular education as the best guarantee of freedom of conscience. In this respect, to say that this debate is inopportune is also to offer an opinion on the issue it raises.

Freedom of conscience is far too precious a thing for us to attempt to regulate it in an atmosphere of passion. Restraint is essential. Christians and unbelievers should also note that with respect to education, freedom of conscience depends on freedom of choice. Since teaching is provided by the state, the state cannot teach or assist in the teaching of truths not acknowledged by everyone. Thus it is possible to imagine the state offering lessons in civics.[437] Here it is unchallenged. By contrast, it is impossible to imagine official instruction in religion, because contradictory views cannot be avoided. Faith can no more be taught than love. Those who are sure enough of their truth to want to teach it to others should do so with their own funds. They cannot reasonably ask the state to do it or help them to do it.

For nearly half a century, we have known only one peace in France, namely, religious peace. We have enjoyed peace because religious teaching was based on the principles set forth above. Why modify now the institutions that embodied this peace? They have been good for everyone because, we are happy to say, they made anticlericalism a thing of the past. Opening those institutions to question will surely harm the interests of religion more than it will serve them.

We have always treated religious issues with the respect and attention they deserve. That is why we feel justified in warning Catholics against carrying their convictions too far. No one wants to see a dialogue between Christians and

---

[435] René Capitant (1901–1970) was a jurist and among the first to join the "Combat" movement (along with F. de Menthon he was one of the founders of Liberté). A convinced Gaullist, he was a member of the National Liberation Committee and served as minister of national education in the Provisional Government. In 1968 he became minister of justice. He also wrote numerous political works, including *De la Résistance à la rénovation* (1945), a title that seemed to echo the subtitle of *Combat*. In October 1940 Camus published excerpts from Capitant's 1935 book on the doctrine of national socialism in *Le Soir Républicain*, along with an introduction of his own (see *Fragments d'un combat*, II, pp. 653–657).

[436] In 1940 the Vichy government instituted a policy of granting generous subsidies to private schools (including religious schools). Capitant proposed setting up a special fund to replace these subsidies. When the Consultative Assembly debated the issue a few days later prior to voting on the national education budget, Capitant defended the principle of secular education but argued that the subsidies could not be eliminated without first approving transitional measures. In fact, the appropriations were continued until the end of the school year and terminated as of July 15, 1945.

[437] Civics instruction now exists, but the problem of state aid to private schools, which now exists in France, still gives rise to passionate debates.

unbelievers more than we do, because we think both sides would benefit. But the lay school is in fact one place where such an encounter is possible. Even with all the objectivity in the world, the same cannot be said of private [religious] schools. Many of our university and high school teachers are Catholics and even priests, and there is nothing wrong with that. There is no reason why a similar collaboration cannot be established in the public elementary schools. By contrast, it is impossible, or at any rate very rare, for unbelievers to teach freely in religious schools. That is where we see advantages to objectivity. For us, that settles the matter.

Vichy had its reasons for ignoring these arguments and subsidizing private schools. Those reasons no longer exist today, and it is right for the state to reclaim its freedom. Beyond that, we have only the following to say. If we were Catholics, and if, as would only be natural, we wished to spread our convictions as widely as possible, we would favor eliminating private religious schools altogether, and we would participate directly, as individuals, in national lay education. Young Catholics would thereby gain precious experience of the people of this country and of a national reality which their sheltered upbringing all too often prevents them from seeing. It would thus serve a common goal, which it must be granted restores to its proper place the parochial dispute over subsidies to which we have just been treated.

March 29, 1945[438]

Truth is a harsh master, allowing no time for rest. Today we had intended to moderate our tentative approval of the government's Indochina plan. We intended to say that if the plan set forth by M. Giacobbi[439] marked a certain progress with respect to our traditional colonial policy, it nevertheless betrayed a timidity that would prevent it from achieving its stated goal. We wanted to show that the grant of unlimited powers to the governor-general, the vagueness of the proposed election procedures, and the emphasis on the military aspect of our undertaking—in short, everything about the plan—suggested a failure to understand that reform can be effective only if it is total.

All these things still need to be said. Yet even as we contemplated the best way to say them, the following dispatch from the Americans' United Press forced itself upon our attention: "Officials in Washington did not seek to deny reports that Allied strategy included no plans to supply weapons to French Resistance forces in Indochina, as General de Gaulle has requested."

---

[438] Editorial. Text very likely by Camus. The accent on "solitude" and "solidarity" in the last two paragraphs should offer sufficient guarantees of its authenticity. On Camus and Indochina, see the article of February 17, 1945, n. 421, p. 173.

[439] Paul Giacobbi, a member of the Radical Party and senator of the Democratic Left, was one of eighty deputies who refused to grant Pétain full powers in 1940. He served as minister of supply in the Provisional Government until November 15, 1944, and then as minister of colonies. In April 1947 he became one of the founders of the Gaullist R.P.F., only to quit the party a short time later.

So this is one of those times when it becomes difficult to report the truth. Do we have the right to make demands of our own country at a time when others are making judgments about it that they have no business making? Should we challenge French colonial policy at a time when it is being repudiated by foreign powers? If not, should we acquiesce in a degradation of our country's image on the pretext that anything likely to enhance that image runs the risk of serving its rivals? Should we renounce our sense of justice for the sake of our prestige abroad?

These are not questions to be treated lightly. Of course we know that many people in such circumstances would not hesitate to choose silence, setting their country's interests above the interests of justice. We intend to speak out, however, because we believe that the two are inextricably intertwined and that the face that France must show the world is the face of justice.

We begin by saying to all who oppose us that our reforms in Indochina will accomplish nothing if they are seen as concessions made necessary by events rather than as formal signs of a policy of emancipation. This is the basis on which we will be judged, and every one of our hesitations will become a weapon against us. Justice, full justice—therein lies our victory. Indochina will be with us if France leads the way by introducing both democracy and freedom there. But if we hesitate at all, Indochina will join forces with anyone at all, provided they are against us. Given the extremity of the situation in which we find ourselves, half measures are out of the question. The French government must understand this, and no matter what the situation, we must repeat it constantly.

At the same time, however, we say to the American people that their government's stated policy cannot possibly be what they want, that their boys cannot possibly be fighting so that French soldiers in Indochina can be sacrificed to nameless interests. All great nations make mistakes, and America has made its share.

True, France has not always done all it should have done. But there has always been a part of itself that was not taken in by its mistakes, and on two or three occasions it was able to do more than it was obliged to do. The Americans cannot be unaware of this.

They have never been our enemies. At no time in history have we ever not been brothers in arms and thought. And we know that the American people cannot want to see what is purest in that fraternity betrayed by the sacrifice of men fighting in enemy territory in our common cause.

The men who are addressing these words to their American comrades know what resistance in an occupied country means. It is above all an overwhelming sense of solitude. When that solitude goes without support, when arms do not fall from the sky, it turns into despair. And the ultimate sin in this world is to rob courage of hope.

National fortunes come and go, and man's struggles are ephemeral. What is not ephemeral, however, is man's solidarity in the face of suffering and injustice. Beyond governments, beyond the interests of a few, we know that the cause of the American people is also our cause and will continue to be so as long as freedom is interfered with anywhere in the world. It is this certainty that compels us, with clear awareness of our mistakes but also conscious of the justice of our request, to call upon the free people of America not to allow this sacrifice.

April 3, 1945[440]

What was being celebrated yesterday in the city's streets? The hope of imminent victory, premature armistice fever, the joyful union of nation and army, an enthusiasm that even empty stomachs could do nothing to dampen, and a people's insistence on hoisting its banners even though the world pays them no heed. There was a great deal to celebrate, many things that permeated the crowd itself and made it difficult to perceive from within it what was worth celebrating and shouting about.

Far from the areas where the crowd gathered and cheered, however, deserted Paris wore its historical face. For that, a few old stones and a river forever young were enough. The eerie silence of the abandoned city was perhaps the best place to grasp the reasons why so many people had come together in a vast outpouring of human emotion. For all those men and women had of course gathered to contemplate a military spectacle and applaud the hopeful promise of a power we do not yet possess. But they also knew that it was their city's holiday and that they were being invited to celebrate what Paris had once again done for freedom.

Yesterday was thus a celebration of hoped-for power and freedom already in hand, of the army and the people, of war and revolution. In the hearts of all the cheering people, moreover, there was no doubt that this marriage, impossible for so long, had been achieved without effort. No one distinguished between insurgents and soldiers. To celebrate Paris was to celebrate the city that had provided both fighters for the insurrection and soldiers for the front.

At this point we would like to express our emotions, as difficult as it is to do so and as out of place as it may seem. For this joining of the national spirit with the revolutionary spirit, which was and remains our greatest and only hope, was what needed to be revived. We hoped that the man who was the first to point this out and who exemplified it throughout the war would stress the lesson of Paris and join in weaving the two traditions together. General de Gaulle did not do as we had hoped.

To be sure, his speech was not without emotion, which in part we shared.[441] We listened to the portrait of historic Paris, of Saint Genevieve and Saint Joan of

[440] Editorial. Text authenticated by the fact that Francine Camus mailed a copy to her mother. The themes and tone here are reminiscent of the editorials of August 1944.

[441] General de Gaulle gave a speech at the Hôtel de Ville in which he stressed the "symbolic" aspect of Paris and the major myths on which it was founded. Beyond what is mentioned in the editorial, he evoked 1871 and the triumph of Prussia, 1914 and the taxis of the Marne, 1940 and the surrender. He magnified the role of Paris in the liberation of France, glorified the army, and after reminding his listeners of French "duties" and "losses," concluded with a call for reunification and courage: "Let parties and private interests silence their demands. Let us be people of few words! Let's get to work!"

Arc, of Henri IV and the Three Orders of the Constituent Assembly. All that was worth remembering. But we also expected General de Gaulle to call attention to 1830, 1848, and the Commune. To say that we expected this is to put it too mildly; we were sure that he would remember those dates. Yet not a word was heard to justify our confidence.

Yet these were days important in the history of Paris, and what would Paris be, in point of fact, without freedom's barricades and the nameless dead? They alone did not make Paris, of course, but in the end Paris could not have been made without them! Let there be no misunderstanding. We are not nostalgic for revolutions past, even though we surely lived through the purest of revolutions in August '44, and the unselfishness of those days is something we will never know again. But we also know the price of blood, and we know that the blood of France is too rare for us to wish to see any more of it spilled. We ask only for recognition of the fact that the blood of freedom[442] can no more be divided than grandeur can, because it is the essence of grandeur. The true power of this nation is its power of indignation, its force of renovation. When we come to doubt the one, it is because we have questions about the other.

It is not possible, in any case, to lead this country to power while ignoring its revolutionary virtue. This is a truth that was consecrated in four years of silent struggle and that should have left its imprint on this country's politics. Our chance for the future depends on the power of new ideas and rebellious courage. If General de Gaulle's often solitary voice had been able to harmonize momentarily with the voice of the people who cheered him, it would have expressed that chance. And once again, as in the days when he spoke to us from across the sea, he would have been the spokesman for the multitude who, because they never did set one thing apart from another, were bound to die on the cobblestones of Paris.

April 4, 1945[443]

As the end of hostilities draws near, the regulation of the peace grows more complicated with each passing day. There is no reason to be surprised or otherwise affected by this: it is a normal development of the situation. As the common discipline imposed by the war is eased, each state reverts to acting independently. It would be hasty and crude, however, to conclude that the Allies are divided because they have different views on certain issues.

What exactly is going on? Each nation wants its own conception of the peace to take precedence, and each wants to protect its own interests. That is only human. Recently and somewhat belatedly, it was revealed that under the terms of the secret agreements signed at Yalta,[444] Russia asked for three votes at the San

---

[442] An echo of the title of the editorial of August 24, 1944, p. 16.

[443] Editorial. Text authenticated by inclusion in a letter from Francine Camus to her mother.

[444] On the Yalta Conference, see the editorial of February 16, p. 171.

Francisco Conference.[445] The United States briefly considered making a similar request. Great Britain would not have objected, probably because it was counting on controlling the votes of the Commonwealth nations, which would have given it five. But some of those countries have already hinted that they intend to exercise their independence. In any case, much dismay greeted this news, not only among the smaller powers but in certain circles in America as well, so that in the end Washington abandoned its original plan. In the face of this opposition, the U.S.S.R. seems to have retreated somewhat. The Soviet delegation has dropped its most important member, Mr. Molotov,[446] and the press has bluntly stated that bilateral agreements are in its view likely to yield better guarantees of security than international councils, although the two are not incompatible.

We should add that there were other reasons besides the question of the voting procedure for this tepid attitude toward the San Francisco Conference. The Soviet Union had asked that the Polish government—that is, the Lublin government[447]—be invited, only to meet with a polite but firm refusal from President Roosevelt. Furthermore, the Soviets take a rather dim view of the idea that the future government of Germany should be drawn mainly from the Catholic center-left, which apparently enjoys solid backing from London as well as Washington.

All of these are issues that would no doubt be discussed in a preliminary conference of the "Three" or "Five Great Powers," if only such a meeting were envisioned.

The facts we have just rapidly summarized merit the attention of the French people. Not because we ought to be glad or sad about them but simply because they are facts. Two very great powers are going to emerge from this war at once weaker and stronger than they went into it, and because of that they have the right to insist that their voices be heard. The future of French foreign policy cannot avoid this glaring truth.

Nor should French policy try to circumvent this fact by clever maneuvering. It would be absurd for France to choose one camp and stick with it. In any case, we have before us the example of England, whose position is not so different

---

445 The San Francisco Conference, which would take place on April 25–26, 1945, was held to draft the United Nations Charter.

446 Vyacheslav Molotov (1890–1986) was close to Stalin and played a major role in the history of the Soviet Union. After joining the Bolshevik Party in 1906, he was deported and escaped several times. He was one of the founders of the newspaper *Pravda*, and after the October 1917 revolution served as a member of the Central Committee and later the Politburo and president of the Council of Commissars of the People. In 1939, he became commissar for foreign affairs and until 1949 negotiated all international treaties. From 1953 to 1956 he again served in this post. As a representative of the most hard-core Stalinist line, he was dismissed from the Central Committee and eventually expelled from the Communist Party in 1964.

447 See the editorial of January 3, p. 162.

from ours and which is managing fairly successfully to remain above the fray without becoming isolated.

Always mindful of people's concerns but uncompromising on its guiding principles, free of petulance, and capable of resisting its sentimental leanings and its wariness toward or preference for certain personalities or regimes as opposed to others: these should be the tenets of our foreign policy.

Because of the situation in which France now finds herself, her present condition, her role can only be one of mediation. Any narrowly continental or even European policy would be shortsighted. While contributing to the stability and organization of Europe with simple, straightforward treaties dictated by common sense, she must also stand between this continent and America not as an arbiter but as a conduit.

April 5, 1945[448]

"I am a teacher, and I'm hungry." Of all the letters we receive, how could we read this one without feeling a pang in our hearts? A sentence like this takes only a moment to write, but how many desperate days must have pre-ceded it?

It would be nice to be able to set those days alongside the many speeches, decisions, and bulletins with which we have been inundated. It would nice to be able to spur the imaginations of those whose actions have direct repercussions on the individuals for whose lives the government is responsible. But imagination, like food, is in short supply these days. The ministry of supply[449] continues to live in a world of abstractions, while hundreds of thousands of French men and women continue to suffer from everyday realities that could not be more discouraging.

Yet how can anyone fail to see that such a sentence constitutes the most damning of indictments of a society that, like it or not, is coming to an end. For how can anyone go on defending this crazy world in which a teacher with a graduate degree earns a tenth as much as the most underprivileged bartender and in which neither intellectual talent nor skilled labor is paid what it is due?

We are told that we need to be patient and trust in capital. But in this case it is the teacher who has to wait and not the minister, which tends to undermine the argument, and in the provincial restaurant where the teacher goes hungry every day, absurd income disparities mean that cutlets will be served at one table and boiled vegetables at the other. As long as money is free to invest in the black market, patience will remain impossible and trust unthinkable.

---

[448] Editorial. Like the previous pieces, this one is authenticated by the fact that it was included in a letter from Francine Camus to her mother, as well as by the reuse of the quote from Baudelaire.
[449] See the editorial of March 18, p. 179, which was highly critical of Paul Ramadier.

The minister of supply is a man whose leanings are well-known, so we will spare him our correspondent's conclusions. Impatience colors the tone of his remarks. One can't eat politeness. We would simply add that we cannot be altogether proud of this country as long as working people go hungry. To judge by the people assigned to it, the ministry of supply has been deemed to be a department of relatively minor importance. It would be impossible to overstate what a colossal error this is. This issue should be paramount among official concerns. Human lives, the value and common dignity of which we have learned to recognize, depend on what measures are taken. The sentence quoted at the beginning of this editorial brings shame to our country and our government. The government must be changed if the country is to be made respectable again.

Of course we have no illusions. Baudelaire said that two rights had been omitted from the Declaration of the Rights of Man: the right to contradict oneself and the right to disappear.[450] Although some of our ministers abuse the former, their discretion in the use of the latter is rather bewildering. M. Ramadier will not disappear, *the garbage collection system* will not be reorganized, inertia will assert its strength, and the teacher will still go hungry.

But we will not tire of issuing warnings or of repeating that there are no minor issues. The France of tomorrow will be what its workers and teachers are. If they go hungry, we should feel ashamed. But if they receive the bread and the justice they are demanding, our consciences will be clear. M. Pleven[451] will forgive us for thinking that this freedom is more important than freedom for capital.

April 6, 1945[452]

Those who look upon the resignation of M. Mendès France[453] as the outcome of a personal dispute are sorely mistaken. It is not only a man who has departed but a ministry, for with its annexation to the ministry of finance, the ministry of national economy loses its reason for existing, which was to oversee and coordinate

450 Camus here repeats this remark in the same terms in which he cited Baudelaire in *Carnets I*, p. 160. In *Edgar Poe, sa vie et ses oeuvres*, Baudelaire wrote the following in the introduction to his translation of *Tales of the Grotesque and Arabesque*: "Among the many enumerated *rights of man*, which the nineteenth century has in its wisdom revised so frequently and so self-indulgently, two rather important ones have been left out, namely, the right to contradict oneself and the right to *disappear*, but society regards the man who disappears as an insolent rebel."

451 René Pleven became minister of finance in November 1944. See the editorial of October 13, 1944, and n. 136, p. 69.

452 Editorial. Text authenticated by its inclusion in a letter from Francine Camus to her mother.

453 On Pierre Mendès France, see the editorial of November 30, 1944, n. 305, p. 128. As minister of national economy from the very inception of the government, he had already submitted his resignation to de Gaulle on January 18, but the general had asked him to reconsider. He resigned for good on April 5 when his recommendations for strict monetary controls and wage and price stability were not accepted.

industrial production, labor, agriculture, and supply. That is a change of some moment.

To be sure, the ministry of national economy has thus far done nothing to endear itself to us. But one has to recognize that its inaction was forced upon it and is clearly the primary reason for M. Mendès France's resignation.

There were two reasons for the ministry's inability to act. First, the refusal to grant the ministry of national economy control over the ministry of finance left M. Mendès France without the means to act. Second, it soon became clear that his control over the other departments of his ministry was merely theoretical. Sovereign ministers are no less touchy and jealous of their independence than sovereign nations. This is cause for regret at a time when, in order to save itself from shame, disorder, and misery, a country is obliged to make war and revolution, both of which demand concerted and disciplined action.[454] They also require the government to choose the means it intends to use and the doctrine it wishes to follow, and, finally, they require that it adhere to its decisions once taken. Only a policy capable of steadfastly pursuing its goals can hope to change the established order.

There is no need to point out that we are a long way from having such a policy. We don't know much about the measures advocated by M. Mendès France. We know that his proposed financial policy was energetic and utterly undemagogic, which is rare enough to inspire respect and esteem. But we also believe that strictly financial measures are unlikely to have much of an impact if they are not accompanied by economic and administrative measures. For us, even lacking knowledge of the specifics of his plan, that was enough to justify the ministry of national economy. It seemed like the instrument most capable of putting right a situation characterized by famine for the many and riches for a few. But if it was to accomplish anything useful, it needed to be granted the necessary powers.

What is the use of talking about the French community if that community cannot make its views known inside the government and if the government is not concerned with setting clear priorities among its ministers? Under these conditions, it should come as no surprise that responsibilities are parceled out, while the best ministers find themselves powerless against the great citadels of the bureaucracy. M. Mendès France's resignation is noteworthy because it sheds some light on the situation of the government and makes things a little less murky than they were. With the ministry of national economy moving to M. Pleven's control, we know what to expect from it in the future.

M. Pleven has stated his views in sufficient detail that we know who he is. Undoubtedly honest and sincere, he is also a resolute adversary of reform. Change dismays him; his tastes are conservative. He was therefore a poor choice for the new responsibilities that have been given to him. In view of his ardent

---

[454] Camus had made similar statements often since August 21, 1944.

desire to save and conserve, we are afraid that he may well conserve the black market, the trusts, and injustice.

As gentle as his grip may be, we also fear that the franc is slipping through his fingers and losing a little more of its purchasing power every day. For we are at a point in our history when even the most disinterested conservatism can't help being suicidal.

April 10, 1945[455]

The victories on the western front cannot account for the tranquil placidity with which the French are receiving the news of the prodigious successes that Russia is now scoring in the east. Of course it is well-known that our compatriots take no interest in changes that occur beyond their borders. But the world is moving fast, and what made us strong when we had our health and our tradition has been and will continue to be a source of woe if we aren't careful.

In this connection, the French need to correct their traditional indifference to and ignorance of Russia. For the past twenty-five years, French governments, along with the majority of the people, have refused to see or understand the fact that an astonishing experiment was under way over a vast expanse of territory, an experiment with which, like it or not, we will some day have to reckon. We began by refusing to accept the Revolution of 1917. We forced Lenin's Russia to surround itself with a thick cordon sanitaire through which no news could pass.[456] For want of news, people made things up. With help from thickheaded conservatives, France soon came to believe that the Soviet Union had been swept by anarchy. Suspicion breeds suspicion. Whatever we think of political realism, moreover, it has to be granted that the moral tragedy that the German-Soviet pact represented for so many decent people[457] is easily explained if one sees it as a consequence of Munich.[458,459]

---

455 Editorial. Text probably by Camus, similar to the editorial of December 18, 1944, p. 145, which Camus signed.

456 Lenin (1870–1924) went from revolutionary activist and theoretician to leader of the Bolshevik majority in 1903. Under his leadership, the Bolsheviks embraced the idea of socialist revolution and dictatorship of the proletariat. After being elected chair of the People's Soviets in 1917, he established the governmental structure of the U.S.S.R. and in March 1918 signed the treaty of Brest-Litovsk with Germany. This treaty, which freed up some German troops to join their comrades on the Western Front, endangered the Allied position in the final months of World War I. After the armistice of November 1918, the Allied powers organized a sort of diplomatic, economic, and political blockade of the U.S.S.R. Recognition of the Communist regime faced many obstacles and came only belatedly.

457 On August 23, 1939, the Soviet Union signed a nonaggression pact with Germany. This agreement was of course violated when Hitler attacked the Soviet Union in June 1941. The pact, which envisioned the division of Poland between Russia and Germany, put the French Communists, who on the whole approved the agreement, in a difficult position.

458 Note that appeared in *Combat*: "For convincing evidence of this, see M. Gafenco's remarkable book, *Préliminaires de la guerre à l'Est* (Libraririe de l'Université, Fribourg)."

459 On Munich, see the editorial of September 12, 1944 and n. 64, p. 36.

People still had their eyes shut in 1939. And, as presented by the press, the Russo-Finnish war[460] led to one of the greatest misunderstandings of all time. Not until the Germans attacked and the Russians resisted in '41, and then the Soviet victories of '42 and '43, did France and the world finally wake up to the fact that a formidable power had come into being on the fringes of Europe, a power that could claim supremacy in many areas.

Today we can see this even more clearly. Virtually every paragraph of the Czech government's first proclamation stressed the pro-Soviet orientation of its politics. We must recognize that Russia is taking the place in Central Europe that France traditionally occupied. This will not surprise the French who suffered in shame when Hitler entered Prague. For four years, we have had to cleanse ourselves of that shame. Today, as the hour of victory approaches, we must recognize that the same shame prevents us from taking a leading place among the victors. What could we even say without the Franco-British friendship that we seem to disdain so unreasonably?

That is why our first order of business should be to admit our errors. As everyone knows, moreover, we are not communists. Because of this we are that much more free to say that the French did the impossible by ignoring for twenty-five years a civilization that was being created before their very eyes.

It is indeed a civilization, despite any objections we might wish to raise against it. In America and Russia, the world has rejuvenated itself in different ways. We are better informed about America, but we need to open our eyes to Russia as well. So let us open our eyes and acknowledge that old cultures need to rejuvenate themselves too. The last thing that can be done with history is to turn up one's nose. For that reason (and many others besides), we must recognize that anti-Sovietism is a stupidity as awful as systematic hostility to England or the United States would be.

Does this mean that all Russian policy must be approved automatically? That would be another kind of blindness, and there are principles to uphold in everyone's interest, which Russia sometimes seems to neglect. The point is simply that we must own up to our illusions and accord the new Russia the place she has earned with her superhuman sacrifices.

In Europe, that place is the very one that we have given up. But whatever regret we may feel as Frenchmen, we must acknowledge that nations sooner or later pay the price for their failures. Today, our renaissance depends in part on our will, and that is of course exclusively our own affair. But it also depends on our lucidity. The first effort we need to make is to put things back in their proper places.

---

[460] The Soviet Union invaded Finland in November 1939. Without support from the West, Finland signed a treaty with Moscow that deprived it of a portion of its territory. Under pressure from Germany, Finland continued its war against the Soviet Union, with which it signed an armistice in September 1944. Under the terms of the Treaty of Paris in 1947, it once again lost Carelia. Though included in the Soviet orbit, it managed to maintain a degree of independence.

April 14, 1945[461]

His face was the very image of happiness.[462] For so many who knew him without ever coming near him, all that remains is the smile that for all those years he displayed on the front pages of newspapers, on movie screens, and amid cheering crowds of his countrymen. This is no doubt the reason for the emotion that was felt throughout the free world at the news of his death, even though it was but one of the many deaths that America has contributed to our common cause.

History's powerful men are not generally men of such good humor. Ambition's hallmarks are not often signs of joy. But it would never have occurred to anyone to associate Roosevelt with ambition. He was too much the expression of his country to have given any thought to dominating it. He was a great individual rather than a great man.

What, in fact, is a great individual if not a man who lends his face, his words, and his actions to a great civilization? In this respect, Roosevelt seemed to us the exemplary American. But it is the distinguishing characteristic of accomplished individuals to speak for their entire culture even when they seem to be speaking in the most personal of terms.

To be sure, we could not approve of all his policies. But whose policies can always be approved? His, at least, never bore the marks of greed or hatred. To the idealism that America has shown also has a place in reality he brought grandeur and efficiency. The greatest praise one can offer him is to say that he knew the value of life.

He also had to triumph over himself before triumphing over others. His laughter was praiseworthy. It was the laughter of a hard-won serenity, the kind that one finds after an infirmity has been overcome. His apparent happiness was not that of comfort, nor that of a mind too limited to perceive mankind's distress. He knew one thing: that there is no pain that cannot be overcome with energetic and conscientious effort. When we know this about a man, we know what he is worth, and we begin to like him.

But he is dead. Until now it was possible to talk about his accomplishments but not about his destiny. Today we know his destiny. He was the great leader of the free people that he led to the threshold of victory. On the verge of triumph, he suddenly changed course, as if he had been made to take charge of freedom's risks but not to endure the dissension that will come with victory. That is as it

---

[461] Editorial. Text authenticated by Roger Grenier, *Albert Camus, Soleil et Ombre* (Paris: Gallimard, 1987), p. 189: "In the middle of the night, after the paper had been put to bed, Pia sometimes invited some of us into his office, and he would read us the editorial by Camus that was to appear the next morning. He showed us how something like an allusion or personal confession could be included in a subject dictated by current events. For instance, when Roosevelt died, there were a few sentences about the illness against which he had struggled all his life, sentences that Camus could not have written without thinking about the tuberculosis that continued to threaten him."

[462] The same expression occurs in the editorial of November 9, 1944, p. 106.

should be. But there is not a single free human being who does not regret his loss and who would not have wished his destiny to have continued a little longer. World peace, that boundless good, ought to be planned by men with happy faces rather than by sad-eyed politicians.

But that is not to be. We are told that America was plunged into deep silence at the news. It is not difficult to believe that people felt such distress. Given a moment's thought, who among us would not share it? When one man succeeds to this degree, everyone succeeds. Despite all the distractions of the moment, people feel emotional enough to observe a moment of silence because this man has left this unreasonable world, whose only hope lies in the quality of its people.

April 15–16, 1945[463]

Mr. Truman[464] has made no secret of how heavy he finds his new responsibilities.

They are indeed overwhelming. He has to succeed a man of rare magnitude, while at the same time the unambiguous yet immensely tangled relationships born of world war are coming unraveled. It is his job to oversee the most perilous of transitions, from war to peace.

As American troops close in on Berlin, he must hastily master the detail of global issues and projects from the treatment of defeated Germany to the wealth and poverty of nations. The United States is now intimately involved in all these things. It is worth noting that Mr. Truman called a first meeting of his advisers to discuss European issues.

To be sure, the new president of the United States has explicitly stated that he intends to adhere to Mr. Roosevelt's policy. As to economic policy, however, the world remains totally in the dark. Until now, Mr. Truman has specialized in domestic politics, where he was no doubt a serious player but hardly an innovative one. He has always defended well-established ideas, and all we know is that in the last election he stood up for smaller countries.

Since he is not a man with a program or plans, it is possible, and even probable, that the cabinet and the Senate, which had labored somewhat in Roosevelt's shadow, will regain some of their former importance. Mr. Truman's intentions will no doubt become clearer in the upcoming congressional debates about whether the United States will join the Bretton Woods monetary agreements[465] and about the tariff question. Both are issues with important consequences for America and the world.

---

[463] Editorial. Text possibly by Camus, in that it is a follow-up to the previous one, but neither the content nor the tone settles the issue.

[464] Harry Truman (1884–1972), Roosevelt's last vice-president, succeeded him and carried on his policies. He accelerated work on the atomic bomb and made the decision to drop the first two on Japan, thereby ending the war. He presided over the San Francisco Conference and was reelected in 1948. He was responsible for the creation of NATO.

[465] The United States and forty-four other countries met at Bretton Woods in July 1944 to establish a new international monetary system to replace the gold standard.

One other thing will take longer to clarify itself: Mr. Truman's attitude toward international relations. Relations between nations are in the first place relations among men. The things that poison human relations—anger, incomprehension, and selfishness—more or less directly affect international relations.

We hear that Mr. Truman is a man of even temper and that he likes music. Let us also hope that he has the inclination and ability to think on a world scale, and to do so in a disinterested manner.

April 17, 1945[466]

With every step closer to victory, we all experience an intensification of hope and anguish. For us, victory does not mean simply putting an end to the enemy. It also means reunion with all whose return we are awaiting. We have suffered not only oppression but also separation. For many years now the world has reverberated not only to the sounds of exploding bombs but also to the futile cries of those who were lost.

All that is about to end. But the men and women of France, who have pined so long for their loved ones, are eager to know what the future will bring. Will their long suffering at last be compensated by a reunion that will make up for everything, or will it end with the ultimate separation? For if the enemy can no longer build anything, he can still destroy. That is probably why these days of victory do not find France as happy as she might be. Every man and every woman in this country has a more private victory to win, a victory that will remain uncertain until the day of the great reunion comes.

That is also why each report of a happy homecoming affects us even more than the announcement of a great military success. Of course we know that the homecomings would not be possible without the military successes, but the heart and its unjust wisdom remain. It is good to give in to them. Yesterday, a group of political deportees arrived in Paris after a long trail of woe.[467] These are our comrades, the ones of whom we are most proud, whose astonishing odyssey caused General de Gaulle to feel an emotion that he did not try to hide yesterday on the station platform.

Today comes news of the rescue of resistance journalists,[468] including our friend Claude Bourdet,[469] the son of Edouard Bourdet. We have never spoken of him so as not to reveal anything about him to the enemy. But under the name

---

[466] Editorial. Text possibly by Camus. Although the tone is not entirely decisive, Camus dealt with this subject in his editorial of December 22, 1944, p. 149, in terms somewhat similar to this piece. Furthermore, separation was of course an important theme in his work, especially in *La Peste*.

[467] The day before, General de Gaulle, Henri Frenay, and various political and labor leaders had appeared at the Gare de Lyon to welcome the first train bringing political prisoners home from Ravensbrück. Among them were the actress Rosine Deréan, about whom Jacqueline Bernard, who did not return herself until the end of May, was to write an article in 1946.

[468] A dispatch from the A.F.P. correspondent with American forces announced the liberation of 3,500 French prisoners from Buchenwald, including a number of political figures, journalists, and professors.

[469] On Claude Bourdet, see the introduction, pp. xxxi–xxxii.

Aubin he was one of the coordinators of "Combat" when it was underground and served as its representative to the C.N.R. A man of fragile health but cheerful character, he drew from his Catholic faith and his commitment to honor the strength he needed to take part in the arduous adventure known as the Resistance. After worrying about his fate for so long, what a joy it is to know that he is alive and on his way home to those who love him! His place on our team awaits him. There will never be enough of us to try to keep our judgment independent in these difficult times, when we must make the transition from disinterested combat to a political life in which it is not as easy to remain just.

There will never be enough of us throughout France to measure what we had hoped for against what we are doing, or to decide what we must change and what we ought to hold on to. That is why, in our eyes, the most moving sight of the last few days of an atrocious war has been the arrival every five minutes at the Gare d'Orsay of a new trainload of men who only yesterday were in chains but who today are free, back in a Paris radiant with sunshine and spring weather.

That is where one must go to join the crowds of people saluting these returning prisoners, if one wants to understand what victory means to a country that for four years was riven in its conscience and its affections.

May 9, 1945[470]

Who would think himself capable of describing this delirious day without getting it wrong?[471] Amid the mingled and exalted voices of an entire nation, what one voice could hope to impart to this great hurrah for freedom and peace its true meaning? Perhaps, as the memory recedes into the past, it will become possible to choose from among the cannons, sirens, and bells, the songs, flags, shouts, and laughter, the one special image that will capture every aspect of this moment with equal justice. For now, we can only immerse ourselves in it and try to express the immense human warmth, the overwhelming joy brimming with tears, and the wild excitement with which the streets of Paris were filled yesterday. Suffering need not be solitary, but joy surely never is. Yesterday's joy was everyone's. We must therefore speak for all.[472]

In the face of this great outpouring, the memory of so many pitched battles and hard-fought struggles took on its full meaning. Why did we fight so hard, if not to allow a people to celebrate its deliverance? In all the capitals of Europe and around the world, millions of people joined in celebration. Some laughed under warm May skies, while others basked in the heat of the night. What they all

---

470 Editorial. Text probably by Camus, harking back to the tone of his editorials on the liberation of Paris.

471 Germany surrendered on May 8, 1945.

472 These expressions are rather close to what Rieux says at the end of *La Peste*, which can be read as a continuation of these reflections, even in the sequence of ideas: "When he felt a temptation to add his voice directly to the thousand voices of those suffering from the plague, he was struck by the thought that no aspect of his suffering was not shared by the others, and that in the world where pain is so often solitary, that was an advantage. Surely he was obliged to speak for them all" (p. 274).

celebrated together, however, was the strength that free men derived from consciousness of their rights and fanatical devotion to their independence.

History is full of military victories, yet never before has a victory been hailed by so many overwhelmed people, perhaps because never before has a war posed such a threat to what is essential in man, his rebelliousness and his freedom. Yesterday belonged to everyone, because it was a day of freedom, and freedom belongs either to everyone or to no one.

For five years, millions of soldiers were obliged to witness scenes of carnage in order to prove that no one man could claim freedom for himself at everyone else's expense.

Once again this truth demanded its awful proof, as if history were nothing but the long and frightful record of the sacrifices men have had to make unremittingly in order to claim the freedom that some would just as unrelentingly deny them.

The years of subjugation were also years of silence. And so it is that this day of freedom was a day in which millions of voices repeatedly cried out. In a Paris teetering between spring and summer, the amazing roar of the crowd could be heard all night long. This we will never forget. It was the exultation of the free spirit embodied in an entire nation. This war was fought to the end so that man could hold on to the right to be what he wants to be and say what he wants to say. Our generation understood this. We will never again cede this ground. We will never allow ourselves to be muzzled.

All around the city, fountains deprived of water for so many years sprang back to life, shooting jets of water upward into the glowing skies. In the depths of our souls, all of us experienced a surge of new hope. It is this that we will have to preserve if this victory is to be made final and to remain our common possession.[473] Those of us who are still waiting or still weeping for a loved one can enjoy this victory only if it justifies the cause for which the missing and dead suffered. Let us keep them near us and not consign them to the definitive solitude of having suffered in vain. Only then, on this overwhelming day, will we have done something for mankind.

May 12, 1945[474]

We are waiting for a government shakeup,[475] for a change in policy and major new decisions essential if the massive reconstruction effort we need to undertake is to get off the ground. We are waiting, and, in the aftermath of the wild victory

---

[473] This hope for a "final victory" is of course contradicted in the closing lines of La Peste: "He knew, however, this chronicle could not be the chronicle of definitive victory."

[474] Editorial. Text very likely by Camus, who often championed the ideas it contains: hostility toward the politicians of the Third Republic and insistence that they be judged for their actions and not for their past suffering.

[475] The shakeup, which came on June 1, resulted in few changes: Christian Pineau replaced Paul Ramadier (who had been wanting to resign for two months) at the ministry of supply, P.-H. Teitgen became minister of justice, replacing François de Menthon, who was sent to London to serve on the War Crimes Commission, and Jacques Soustelle succeeded Teitgen at the ministry of information.

celebration, we are beginning to hope, we are beginning to say to one another that anything can happen and that tomorrow will witness the birth of the new republic that everyone dreams of. We are still waiting, and the early news is that former premiers Herriot, Daladier, Reynaud, and Blum[476] may join the new government. Thus far we have had to do without their experience, and their wisdom.

If we cared for simplistic formulas, we would sum up our thoughts by saying that the future of France can be decided either by thirty-year-olds or by sixty-year-olds. It appears that the choice has already been made, however, and what is left for us is to state our opinion of a policy that will put the levers of state back in the hands of those who held them for so long with such obstinate blindness.

Given that some of these men have just returned from a harsh captivity, we will temper our remarks. Misfortune has scarred their lives. For that reason alone, they are entitled to respect, and nothing we say is intended as an insult. But it is one thing to give these men the respect they are due and another to decide whether their misfortune is enough to assure us that they possess the political skills the country needs. In that respect they can be judged only on the basis of what they did, not what they suffered. And we are bound to say flatly that what they did does not entitle them to lead this country politically at a time when France needs men who are as determined as they are prudent.

The men being proposed for office took power in a difficult and troubled time. They brought disparate skills and very diverse temperaments to the task. Yet all shared one attitude compounded of weakness mixed with blindness: all retreated in the face of fascist aggression. These are the men who bear responsibility in

---

[476] These names symbolize the period just prior to the war. Edouard Herriot (1872–1957) served as president of the Radical Party from 1919 until his death. He also served as mayor of Lyons and held a number of ministerial portfolios in addition to several terms as premier between 1936 and 1940. When the Chamber of Deputies voted to grant Pétain full powers in July 1940, he abstained, and he did not become an out-and-out opponent of Pétain until August 1942, when the Vichy government abolished the offices of the two parliamentary chambers. After being placed under house arrest, he was deported to Germany but was brought home by Laval in August 1944 in the hope that he would convene the Chamber of Deputies. From 1945 to 1954 he again served as president of the National Assembly.

On Daladier, see the editorial of September 12, n. 63, p. 35.

Paul Reynaud (1878–1966), a republican of the right, deputy, and several-times minister of the Third Republic, most notably as a member of Daladier's cabinet in 1938, he became premier in March 1940. In June he resigned to make way for Pétain. Interned by the government of Vichy and tried at Riom, he was deported to Germany in 1942. On his return he was reelected deputy and served on various parliamentary commissions and the Council of Europe.

Léon Blum (1872–1950) was a state councilor and graduate of the Ecole Normale Supérieure. A writer as well as a politician, he played a very important role in the socialist movement in France. As a collaborator of Jean Jaurès at L'Humanité from 1904, he belonged to the minority of socialists who rejected communism at the Congress of Tours in 1920, at which time he founded Le Populaire, the newspaper of the S.F.I.O. He led the first Popular Front government (June 1936–June 1936) and together with Maurice Viollette worked on a bill to grant French citizenship to certain categories of Algerians (see below, article of May 18, 1945, n. 501, p. 208). As an opponent of Laval and of full powers for Pétain, he was interned, tried at Riom, and handed over to the Germans, who deported him to Buchenwald. After the Liberation, he resumed his editorship at Le Populaire, called for a reform of the Constitution, and briefly led a socialist government in December 1946. Reynaud and Blum were repatriated in May.

whole or in part for the murder of Ethiopia, the destruction of the Spanish Republic, the conquest of Austria, and, finally, thanks to Munich, the occupation of Prague by German troops that no one of our generation will ever forget. No doubt their motives at least partly reflected their desire for peace. Yet it was the joint action of these experienced politicians that ultimately led Daladier to lose the peace as well and to declare war under the worst possible conditions. To put it bluntly, it is hard to imagine a policy more consistent in its failure or more foolish in its conception.

We are therefore obliged to say that these politicians have had their chance, and their success was mediocre, to put it mildly. There is no dishonor in that.

Political life consumes souls in abundance, and not all of them can be first-rate. But the present period is one in which weakness, even if it is paternal, and routine, even if it is unconscious, cannot and should not be regarded as adequate credentials.

We are well aware that such language may seem harsh or out of place. We know that these men endured their misfortune with dignity. Pardon us, however, if we do not single them out more than is fitting in a world in which millions of people have experienced severe hardship and deserve an end to their terrible suffering. In the end this punishment is not so awful. We do not condemn these politicians as human beings. We merely deny them the privileges and power of which they've already had enough. Retirement awaits them: we say this without irony. There they will find the peace and respect appropriate to men who may have made mistakes but did not betray the country's trust. No doubt it is also true that they will not find the marvelous intoxications of power. Today, however, we all need a different kind of power, a power that can come only from intelligence and a steadfast will. When one measures MM. Daladier, Herriot, and Reynaud[477] against the enormous effort required, how can one fail to perceive that the harder they bite their tongues, the louder this country will speak.

May 13–14, 1945
Crisis in Algeria[478]

When one looks at the recent disturbances in North Africa, it is wise to avoid two extremes.[479] One is to describe as tragic a situation that is merely serious. The other is to ignore the grave difficulties with which Algeria is grappling today.

---

[477] Note that Léon Blum is not impugned with the others.

[478] This text inaugurates a series of six articles devoted to Algeria. All were published in a prominent place on page one in large type under bold headlines, and Albert Camus' byline appeared immediately underneath. Five of these articles, including this one, were reprinted in 1958 in *Actuelles III: Chroniques algériennes, 1939–1958*, along with the editorial of June 15, which served as their conclusion.

[479] On May 1, demonstrators demanding the release of Messali Hadj clashed with police in Algiers and Oran. On May 8, the armistice celebration was marred by nationalist demonstrations in eleven Algerian cities. In Sétif and Guelma in the Constantinois, these demonstrations developed into riots that continued

To adopt the first attitude would be to play into the hands of interests out to persuade the government to take repressive measures that would be not only inhumane but also impolitic. To adopt the second would be to continue to widen the gap that for so many years has separated the metropolis from its African territories. In either case, one would be opting for a shortsighted policy as harmful to French interests as to Arab ones.

The survey[480] that follows is the fruit of a three-week visit to Algeria, and its only ambition is to reduce the incredible ignorance of the metropolis in regard to North African affairs.[481] I tried to be as objective as possible as I traveled more than 1,500 miles along the Algerian coast as well as inland to the limits of the southern territories.

I visited not only cities but also the most remote *douars*, and I listened to the opinions and firsthand accounts of bureaucrats and native farmers, of colonists and Arab militants. A good policy is first of all a well-informed policy. Of course this survey is just that: a survey. But if the facts I report are not new, they have been checked. I therefore hope that they can be of some use to those charged with coming up with a policy that can save Algeria from spinning out of control.

Particular Problems[482]

Before going into detail about the North African crisis, however, it may be useful to dispose of a certain number of prejudices. To begin with, I want to remind people in France of the fact that Algeria exists. By that I mean that it exists apart from France and that its problems have their own peculiar texture and scale. Hence one cannot resolve those problems by following the metropolitan example.

One simple fact will suffice to illustrate what I mean. All French schoolchildren learn that Algeria, which falls under the jurisdiction of the ministry of the interior, consists of three *départements*. Administratively, that is true. In fact, however, those three *départements* are the size of forty typical French *départements* and have a population equivalent to twelve. So the metropolitan bureaucracy thinks it has done a great deal when it sends 2,000 tons of grain to Algeria,

---

until May 13, leading to terrible repression that produced many victims, the exact number remaining a matter of controversy to this day. *Combat* did not report these events until May 12 in a brief article entitled "Agitation in Algeria, Where Food Shortages Have Given Rise to Severe Discontent among the Natives." The paper reported that the council of ministers had conducted "lengthy discussions" of the situation in Algeria, "where the administration is encountering severe difficulties stemming in part from shortages in the supply of food to the native population." The council took unspecified steps to remedy the situation and issued instructions to the governor-general concerning the maintenance of order.

480 Camus uses the word *enquête*, which he also used at the end of "Misère en Kabylie," a report he did in 1939 for *Alger-Républicain* (reprinted in *Actuelles III*). This demonstrates the continuity of Camus' thinking and attitudes.

481 Camus arrived in Algeria on April 18 and returned to Paris on May 7 or 8, as is shown by his letters to his wife, in which he describes his travels in various parts of the country.

482 The subtitles were not reprinted in *Actuelles III*.

but that amounts to exactly one day's consumption of the country's 8 million inhabitants. The next day they have to start all over again.

The Political Awakening of the Muslims

As for the political dimension, I want to point out that the Arab people also exist. By that I mean that they aren't the wretched, faceless mob in which Westerners see nothing worth respecting or defending. On the contrary, they are a people of impressive traditions, whose virtues are eminently clear to anyone willing to approach them without prejudice.

These people are not inferior except in regard to the conditions in which they must live, and we have as much to learn from them as they from us. Too many French people in Algeria and elsewhere imagine the Arabs as a shapeless mass without interests. One more fact will set them straight.

In the most remote *douars*, 500 miles from the coast, I was surprised to hear the name of M. Wladimir d'Ormesson mentioned.[483] The reason for this was that, a few weeks ago, our colleague published an article on the Algerian question that Muslims deemed to be ill-informed and insulting. I'm not sure that the journalist for the *Figaro* will be glad to know how quickly he made a reputation for himself in Arab lands, but it does tell us a great deal about the political awakening of the Muslim masses.

Finally, if I point out one more fact of which too many French people are ignorant—namely, that hundreds of thousands of Arabs have spent the past two years fighting for the liberation of France—I will have earned the right to move on to other matters.

Algeria Has to Be Conquered a Second Time

In any case, all this should teach us not to prejudge anything about Algeria and to refrain from repeating clichés. In a sense, the French have to conquer Algeria a second time. To sum up my impressions from my visit, I should say that this second conquest will not be as easy as the first. In North Africa as in France, we need to invent new recipes and come up with new ways of doing things if we want the future to make sense to us.

---

[483] In *Le Figaro* for March 8, 1945, under the title "Imperial Worries," Wladimir d'Ormesson (see editorial of September 8, 1944, n. 52, p. 31) wrote about shortages in Algeria, empty stores, and a state of utter misery. His political analysis deserves to be cited as a good example of current opinion: "Agitators are taking advantage of the widespread misery to kindle the flames of discord. Everyone knows how easy it is to launch demagogic appeals and lead credulous mobs with words. When professional politicians resort to such tricks, it is only to be expected. What is unacceptable is when they are abetted by officials (sometimes high officials), the press, and even the official radio stations. What is not acceptable is for some Frenchmen to dare to speak openly of the 'scandal of French colonization.' Where do they think such tactics will lead?"

The Algeria of 1945 is enduring the same economic and political crisis it has always endured, though never before to this degree. In this lovely country, now glorious with spring blossoms and sunshine, people suffering from hunger are demanding justice. We cannot remain indifferent to their suffering, because we have experienced it ourselves.

Rather than respond with condemnations, let us try to understand the reasons for their demands and invoke on their behalf the same democratic principles that we claim for ourselves. My goal in the remaining articles of this series is to support this effort simply by supplying objective information.

(to be continued)

P.S. This article was complete when an evening paper[484] appeared with an article accusing Ferhat Abbas, president of the "Friends of the Manifesto," of having personally organized the Algerian disturbances. This article was obviously written in Paris on the basis of fragmentary information. Nevertheless, it is unacceptable to make such a serious accusation on the basis of such flimsy evidence. There is much to be said for and against Ferhat Abbas and his party. We will in fact be discussing him. But French journalists must recognize that a problem this serious cannot be resolved by intemperate appeals for blind repression.

ALBERT CAMUS

May 15, 1945
Famine in Algeria[485]

The most obvious crisis afflicting Algeria is an economic one.[486]

Algeria already shows unambiguous signs of this to the attentive visitor. The leading taverns serve drinks in cut-off bottles with the edges filed down. Hotels give you wire coat hangers. Bombed-out stores have fallen beams in their windows rather than glass. In private homes it is not uncommon for the bulb used to light the dining room to be moved to the bedroom after dinner. There is a shortage of manufactured goods, no doubt because Algeria has no industry, but above all there is an import crisis. We will be looking at its effects.

---

[484] The reference is to an article by Yves Grosrichard in *France-Soir* for May 13–14, published under the unambiguous headline "Algerian Disturbances Fomented by the Agitator Ferrat-Abbas [*sic*]." After expressing the hope that "the measures taken by the government to deal with the food supply and the military situation will calm the disturbances," the article concluded: "According to our information, the party of the 'Manifesto' and its leader have considerable funds at their disposal. Opposed by the *caids*, whose loyalty is beyond doubt, as well as by the religious caste of *ulemmas*, and vigorously condemned by all democratic elements in North Africa from the communists to the 'moderates,' though secretly approved, it seems, by a minority of wealthy 'Doriotist' families, Ferrat Abbas and his henchmen appear to be in the pay of foreigners."

[485] Article reprinted in *Actuelles III*, without subtitles. The content and tone of this piece are reminiscent of "Misery in Kabylia." Kabylia was already suffering from famine in 1939.

[486] *Combat* published this note: "See the beginning of this survey in our May 13 issue."

The news that must be shouted from the rooftops is that most Algerians are experiencing a famine. This is the reason for the serious disturbances we have heard about, and this is what needs fixing.[487]

The population of Algeria is nine million in round numbers. Of these nine million, eight million are Arabo-Berbers, compared with a million Europeans. Most of the Arab population is scattered throughout the vast countryside in *douars*, which French colonial administrations have combined into mixed villages.

The basic diet of the Arabs consists of grains (wheat or barley), consumed in the form of couscous or flatbread. For want of grain, millions of Arabs are suffering from hunger.

Famine is still a dreadful scourge in Algeria, where harvests are as capricious as the rainfall. In normal times, however, the reserves maintained by the French administration made up the shortfall caused by drought. There are no longer any reserves in Algeria, because they were transferred to the metropolis for the benefit of the Germans. The Algerian people were therefore at the mercy of a bad harvest.

No Water since January

That misfortune has happened. Let me mention just one fact to give you an idea of how bad it was. Throughout the high plateaus of Algeria, there has been no rain since January. These vast fields are covered with wheat no higher than the poppies that stretch off to the horizon. The land, covered with cracks like a lava flow, is so dry that double teams had to be used for the spring planting. The plow tears at the flaky, powdery soil incapable of holding the sown seed. The harvest expected for this season will be worse than the last, which was already disastrous.

Some Figures

I beg the reader's indulgence if I cite some figures. Normally, Algeria requires some 18 million quintals of grain. As a general rule, its production is roughly equal to its consumption: for instance, the 1935–36 harvest of all grains combined was 17,371,000 quintals. Last season's total was barely 8,715,000 quintals, however, which is just 40 percent of normal needs.

This year's forecasts are even more pessimistic, with a maximum expectation of roughly 6 million quintals.

The drought is not the only reason for this terrifying shortage. The acreage devoted to grain has decreased, because there is less seed and also because fodder is not taxed, so that certain heedless landowners chose to grow it rather than essential grains. Certain temporary technical difficulties also play a part: deteriorating

---

[487] All reports about the riots in Sétif, from the government as well as the press, said the same thing. Unlike most of them, however, Camus did not rely exclusively on this explanation, and his survey would take a much more political turn. Note that on the same day, *Combat*, like other papers, published a communiqué from the ministry of the interior concerning the riots in Sétif and Guelma, which claimed more than a hundred victims and were blamed on the P.P.A. and "certain elements of the 'Friends of the Manifesto' movement." The paper reported that order had been restored and mentioned numerous declarations of loyalty to France. It also published an A.F.P. dispatch concerning the killing of Europeans in Sétif and Périgotville.

equipment (a plow blade that used to cost 20 francs now goes for 500), fuel rationing, and labor shortages due to the military mobilizations. What is more, demand for grain has increased owing to rationing of other foods. Without help from the outside world, it is clear, therefore, that Algeria cannot feed its population from its own soil.

130 to 150 Grams of Grain per Day

To witness the consequences of this famine is enough to break your heart. The administration was obliged to reduce the grain allowance to 7.5 kilograms per person per month (farmworkers receive 18 kilograms from their employers, but they are a minority). That works out to 250 grams per day, which is not much for people whose only staple is grain.

Yet even this famine ration could not be honored in the majority of cases. In Kabylia, in the Ouarsensis, in the South Oranais, and in the Aurès (to take widely separated regions), four to five kilograms per month was the most that could be distributed, which comes to 130 to 150 grams per person per day.

Is it clear what that means? Is it clear that in a country where sky and land are invitations to happiness, this means that millions of people are suffering from hunger?[488] On every road one sees haggard people in rags. Traveling around the country, one sees fields dug up and raked over in bizarre ways, because an entire *douar* has come to scratch the soil for a bitter but edible root called *talrouda*,[489] which can be made into a porridge that is at least filling if not nourishing.

The reader may be wondering what can be done. To be sure, the problem is a difficult one. But there is not a minute to waste, and no one's interests can be spared, if we want to save these wretched people and stop hungry masses egged on by criminal madmen from resuming the savage[490] massacre in Sétif. In my next article I will indicate what injustices must be ended and what emergency measures must be taken in the economic sphere.

(To be continued.)

ALBERT CAMUS

May 16, 1945
Algeria Asks for Ships and Justice[491]

What can we do for the millions of Algerians who are suffering from hunger? It doesn't take exceptional political lucidity to observe that only a policy of massive imports can change the situation.

---

[488] Cf. the first text of "Misery in Kabylia," entitled "Greece in Rags," which was not included in *Actuelles III*: "In one of the most attractive regions of the world, an entire people is suffering from hunger." (*Fragments d'un combat*, p. 279.)

[489] In *Actuelles III*, this word was spelled *tarouda*.

[490] The word "savage" was omitted in *Actuelles III*.

[491] Article reprinted in *Actuelles III* under the title "Boats and Justice," and without subtitles. The original title is reminiscent of an article in "Misery in Kabylia" entitled "To Live, Kabylia Demands!"

The government has just announced that a million quintals of wheat will be distributed in Algeria. That is good. Bear in mind, however, that this amount is enough to meet the needs of only about a month's consumption. There is no way to avoid sending the same quantity of grain to Algeria next month and the month after that. The import problem has thus not been solved, and it will continue to require the utmost energy.

I am by no means unaware of the difficulty of the undertaking. To restore the situation, feed the Arab population properly, and eliminate the black market, Algeria will need to import 12 million quintals. That amounts to 240 shiploads of 5,000 tons each. Given the state in which the war has left us, everyone understands what that means. But given the urgency of the situation, it must also be recognized that we can allow nothing to stand in our way and must, if necessary, demand that the world provide the necessary ships. When millions of people are suffering from hunger, it becomes everybody's business.[492]

When we have done this, however, we still will not have done everything we can, because the gravity of the Algerian affair does not stem solely from the fact that the Arabs are hungry. It also stems from the fact that their hunger is unjust. Hence it is not enough to give Algeria the grain it needs; that grain must also be distributed equitably. I would have preferred not to write this, but it is a fact that the distribution is not equitable.

The Wrongs of the Caïds

For proof of this assertion, consider first the fact that in this country, where grain is almost as scarce as gold, it can still be found on the black market. In most of the villages I visited, it was possible to buy grain not at the official price of 540 francs per quintal but at an underground price ranging from 7,000 to 16,000 francs per quintal.[493] The black market is supplied with wheat siphoned from official supplies by thoughtless colonists and native overlords.

Furthermore, the grain that is delivered to distribution points is not distributed equally. The caïdship, that most harmful institution, continues to wreak havoc.[494] The caïds, who act in a sense as stewards representing the French administration, have all too often been entrusted with the task of overseeing distributions of grain, and the methods used are often highly idiosyncratic.

The distributions carried out by the French administration itself are inadequate but generally honest. Those carried out by the caïds are generally unfair, governed by self-interest and favoritism.

---

[492] The same expression can be found at several places in *La Peste* (e.g., pp. 67 and 125).

[493] *Combat* note: "To make clear what this means, wheat at 10,000 fr. per quintal puts the price of a kilogram of bread at around 120 fr. The average daily wage of an Arab worker is 60 fr."

[494] In "Misery in Kabylia," Camus had spoken out against the imposition of the caïdship, a typically Arab institution, on Kabyle regions. The caïd acted as judge, administrator, and chief of police rolled into one. It is easy to imagine how such a position could be used, and the very term "caïd" came to have a pejorative connotation.

Finally, to save the most painful point for last, the ration distributed to natives throughout Algeria is inferior to that distributed to Europeans. This is the case officially, since a European is entitled to 300 grams per day, compared with 250 for an Arab. Unofficially, the situation is even worse, since the typical Arab receives only 100 to 150 grams, as I mentioned earlier.

The people of Algeria, animated by a sure and instinctive sense of justice, might perhaps accept the need for such severe rationing in principle. But they do not accept (as they made clear to me) the idea that because it was necessary to limit rations, only Arab rations should have been reduced. People who have not been stingy with their blood in this war are justified in thinking that others should not be stingy with their bread.

This unequal treatment, together with various other abuses, has created a political malaise, which I will deal with in forthcoming articles. But within the context of the economic problem that concerns me now, it is further poisoning an already grave situation, and it is adding to the suffering of the natives a bitterness that could have been avoided.

To quell the cruelest of hungers and heal inflamed hearts: that is the task we face today. Hundreds of freighters filled with grain and two or three measures of strict equality: this is what millions of people are asking of us, and perhaps this will help to make it clear why we must try to understand them before we judge them.[495]

Albert Camus

May 17, 1945[496]

"Our food consists of one liter of soup for lunch and coffee with three hundred grams of bread for supper. . . . We are covered with lice and bugs. . . . Jews are dying every day. After they die, they are piled up in a corner of the camp to wait until there are enough of them to bury. . . . For hours or days on end, whenever the sun shines, a foul odor spreads through the Jewish camp and through ours."

The camp pervaded by death's dreadful odor is Dachau.[497] We have known about it for quite some time, and people are beginning to tire of the sheer number of atrocities. Delicate souls find these accounts monotonous and reproach us for continuing to speak of them. But France may change its tune when it learns that this latest cry was uttered by one of Dachau's thousands of political deportees just a week after their liberation by American troops. These men have been kept in their camp awaiting a repatriation that is not yet in view. In the very place where they thought they had attained the ultimate depth of suffering, they are

---

[495] This remark set Camus apart from most other commentators.

[496] Editorial. Reprinted in *Actuelles*.

[497] In 1933 a concentration camp was set up at Dachau in Bavaria to detain opponents of the Nazi regime. The "Jewish camp" held 25,000 Jews sent from Auschwitz in July 1944 in even worse physical condition than other deportees. The mortality rate was terrifying.

today experiencing even worse distress, because now their confidence has been shaken.

The excerpts we quote are taken from a four-page letter sent by an internee to his family. References are available in our offices for anyone to see. We had previously received a good deal of information indicating that this was the way things stood with our deported comrades. We refrained from speaking of it, however, while awaiting more reliable reports. We can wait no longer. The first message to have reached us from the camp is decisive, and we cannot help but proclaim our outrage and anger. This shameful situation must end.

When the German countryside abounds with food, and Hitler's generals fill their stomachs as usual, it is indeed shameful for political detainees to go hungry. When "honored deportees"[498] are repatriated immediately by airplane, it is shameful that our comrades are still scanning the same forlorn skies they have been contemplating for years. These men aren't asking for much. They don't want any special treatment. They aren't asking for medals or speeches. They want only to return home. They have had enough. They were willing to suffer for the Liberation, but they cannot understand why they should suffer from the Liberation. Yes, they have had enough, because everything has been spoiled for them, even this victory, which to a degree unknown to a world uninterested in matters of the spirit, is also their victory.

People need to know that a single hair from one of these prisoners' heads is of greater importance to France and the whole world than twenty of the politicians whose smiles are recorded in countless photographs. They, and they alone, were guardians of honor and witnesses to courage. That is why people need to know that while it is already unbearable for us to know that they are suffering from hunger and disease, we will not allow them to despair of our assistance.

Our comrade's letter, each line of which is grounds for outrage and revulsion, recounts the way in which the news of victory was received in Dachau: "Not one hurrah," he writes, "not one demonstration: this day brought us nothing." Can anyone comprehend what these words mean, given that these are men who, rather than wait for victory to arrive from across the sea, sacrificed everything in order to hasten the day for which they hoped with every fiber of their being? Yet when that day came, it found them amid stinking cadavers, their spirit confined by barbed wire and struck dumb by a world stupider and more unconscious than they could have imagined in their darkest hours.

We will not stop with speaking out on the matter. But if this man's cry is not heard, if immediate measures are not announced by Allied organizations, we will repeat our demand, and we will use every means at our disposal to spread the news and let the whole world know what fate the victorious democracies have reserved for witnesses who allowed their throats to be cut so that the principles for which they stand would have at least the appearance of truth.

---

498 The allusion is to ministers and officials of the Third Republic, including Daladier, Blum, and Reynaud, who were reported to camps in Germany but held under conditions markedly different from those of other deportees.

May 18, 1945

Natives of North Africa Estranged from a Democracy from Which
They Saw Themselves as Excluded Indefinitely[499]

As grave and urgent as the economic privation from which North Africa is suffering is, it cannot by itself account for the Algerian political crisis. If we discussed the famine first, it was because hunger is the first priority. But when we
have done everything that needs to be done to feed the Algerian population, we
still will only have scratched the surface. Or, to put it another way, we will still,
at long last, need to come up with a policy for North Africa.[500]

Far be it from me to try to formulate a definitive policy for North Africa in
the space of two or three articles. This would please no one, and truth would not
be served. But our Algerian policy is so distorted by prejudice and ignorance that
to offer an objective account based on accurate information is already to render
an important service. That is what I propose to do.

An Abandoned Hope

I read in a morning newspaper that 80 percent of the Arabs wished to become
French citizens. In contrast, I would sum up the current state of Algerian policy
by saying that, indeed, Arabs used to want to become citizens but no longer do.
When you've hoped for something for a long time and your hopes are dashed,
you avert your eyes and your erstwhile desire disappears. That is what has happened to the indigenous peoples of Algeria, and the primary responsibility for
this is ours.

French colonial doctrine in Algeria since the conquest has not been notable
for its coherence. I shall spare the reader the history of its fluctuations, from   ▸
the notion of an Arab kingdom favored by the Second Empire to that of assimilation. In theory, it was the idea of assimilation that triumphed in the end.
For the past fifty years or so, France's avowed goal in North Africa was gradually
to open the way to French citizenship for all Arabs. Let it be said at once
that this idea remained theoretical. In Algeria itself, the policy of assimilation
met with unremitting hostility, primarily on the part of the most influential
colonizers.

---

[499] Fourth article on Algeria, reprinted in *Actuelles III* under the title "Le malaise politique." The subtitles
were omitted.

[500] The originality of these statements at this point in time cannot be overstated. Official communiqués
and most newspapers continued to blame the riots on the famine and the actions of "agitators." See, for
example, *Le Figaro* for May 22, in which Philippe Roland published an article entitled "Positions and
Dimensions of the Algerian crisis," which objectively described the economic situation (using the same
figures that Camus cited) and explained that "the Muslims [are] manipulated by propaganda from contradictory extremes" leading to "a crushing of the spirit . . . that ultimately disorients and disconcerts even
the least receptive Muslim."

Explaining the Attitude of North African Natives

There exists a whole arsenal of arguments—some of them apparently convincing at first sight—which have until now sufficed to keep Algeria immobilized in the political situation we have described.

I won't discuss these arguments. But it is clear that on this issue as on others, some day a choice will have to be made. France had to state clearly whether, on the one hand, it considered Algeria to be a conquered land whose subjects, stripped of all rights and burdened with additional duties, would be forced to live in absolute dependence on us, or, on the other hand, it attributed to its democratic principles a value universal enough to be able to extend them to populations for which it had accepted responsibility.

France, to its credit, chose, and having chosen, it was obliged, if words were to mean anything, to follow the logic of its decision to the end. Special interests opposed this venture and tried to turn back the clock. But time inexorably marches on, and people evolve. No historical situation is ever permanent. If you are unwilling to change quickly enough, you lose control of the situation.

The Blum-Viollette Plan[501]

Because French policy in Algeria ignored these elementary truths, it was always twenty years behind the actual situation. An example will help to make this clear.

In 1936, the Blum-Viollette plan marked a first step toward a policy of assimilation after seventeen years of stagnation. It was by no means revolutionary. It would have granted civil rights and voting status to roughly 60,000 Muslims. This relatively modest plan aroused immense hopes among the Arabs. Virtually the entire Arab population, represented by the Algerian Congress,[502] indicated its approval. But leading colonists, banded together in the Financial Delegations[503] and the Association of Mayors of Algeria,[504] mounted a

[501] In 1936, at the behest of Algeria's governor Maurice Viollette, the government of Léon Blum sought to establish a formula for citizenship that would have treated political rights separately from private status, thus allowing a certain number of Muslim natives—veterans, recipients of military decorations, and holders of elementary education certificates and university degrees, among others—to become French citizens without giving up their personal status. Under the auspices of the Maison de la Culture of Algiers, Camus had worked actively on behalf of this plan (see the complete text in *Fragments d'un combat*, I, pp. 143–144, and "Manifeste des Intellectuels d'Algérie en faveur du projet Viollette" in *Essais*, p. 1328).

[502] The Algerian (or Muslim) Congress was an umbrella organization of Algerian political movements, except for Messali Hadj's Etoile Nord-Africaine. It originated with the Council of Ulemmas, founded by Sheikh Ben Badis in 1931, and supported the Popular Front.

[503] Les Financial Assemblies were local assemblies responsible for dealing with budgetary matters, in which Europeans held two-thirds of the seats.

[504] The Association of Mayors of Algeria consistently opposed all reform and, with support from right-wing parties in France, played a decisive role in seeing to it that the Blum-Viollette plan was never put to a vote in parliament. On their activities, see *Fragments d'un combat*, I, pp. 122–139.

counteroffensive powerful enough to ensure that the plan was never even presented to the Chambers.

Ordinance of March 7 [505]

The dashing of this great hope naturally led to a very radical disaffection. Now the French government is proposing that Algeria accept the ordinance of March 7, 1944, whose electoral provisions more or less emulate those of the Blum-Viollette plan.

If this ordinance were really enforced, it would give the vote to roughly 80,000 Muslims. It would also eliminate the exceptional legal status of Arabs, a goal for which North African democrats have fought for years. In effect, Arabs were not subject to the same penal code or even the same courts as Frenchmen. Special tribunals, more severe in their punishments and more summary in their procedures, kept Arabs in a permanent state of subjection. The new ordinance has eliminated that abuse, and that is a very good thing.

Time Marches On

Arab opinion, much dampened by all that has taken place, remains reserved and wary, however, despite all the good things in the new plan. The problem is quite simply that time marches on. The fall of France was followed by a loss of French prestige. The 1942 landing[506] brought Arabs into contact with other nations and spurred them to make comparisons. Finally, one cannot ignore the fact that the Pan-Arab Federation[507] is a constant temptation for the people of North Africa, whose misery only adds to all their other grievances. As a result of all this, a plan that would have been welcomed enthusiastically in 1936 and would have solved a great many problems is today met only with wariness. Once again we are late.

Peoples generally aspire to political rights only in order to set themselves on the road to social progress. The Arab people wanted the right to vote because they knew that, with it, and through the free exercise of democracy, they could eliminate the injustices that are poisoning the political climate of Algeria today.

---

[505] The ordinance of March 7, 1944, adopted by the Provisional Government in Algiers, granted Muslims all the rights and duties of Frenchmen and opened all civilian and military posts to them without loss of personal status. It expanded the representation of Algerians from one-third to two-fifths in all local assemblies, broadened the Muslim electoral college to include all Algerians above the age of twenty-one, and abolished all measures of exception (*statut de l'indigénat*, Régnier decree). On this ordinance, see the editorial of October 13, 1944, n. 138, p. 70, and the texts of Belloul (December 1, 1944, and January 9, 1945).

[506] See editorial of September 4, 1944, and n. 44, p. 27.

[507] The Pan-Arab Federation, which would later become the Arab League, included Saudi Arabia, Egypt, Iraq, Jordan, Lebanon, Syria, and Yemen.

They knew that they could eliminate inequalities in wages[508] and pensions, as well as more scandalous inequalities in military allowances and, in a more general sense, everything that helped to perpetuate their inferior status. But the Arabs seem to have lost their faith in democracy, of which they were offered only a caricature. They hope to achieve by other means a goal that has never changed: an improvement in their condition.

That is why, to believe my sample, Arab opinion is in its majority indifferent or hostile to the policy of assimilation. This is most unfortunate. But before deciding what ought to be done to improve the situation, we must have a clear sense of what the political climate in Algeria is today.

Arabs today face any number of possibilities, and since, historically, every aspiration of a people finds political expression, Muslims have lately found themselves drawn to a remarkable figure, Ferhat Abbas, and his "Friends of the Manifesto" party. In my next article, I will discuss this important movement, the most important and novel to have appeared in Algeria since the early days of the conquest.[509]

ALBERT CAMUS

May 19, 1945 [510]

The day before yesterday we protested the fate reserved for deportees who remain in German camps.[511] Yesterday our comrades at *France-Soir*[512] tried to give our protest a political interpretation that we reject categorically. To attempt such a thing is not only puerile, it is in bad taste in dealing with so grave an issue. We here are not defending anybody. We have only one goal: to save the most precious of French lives. Neither politics nor the nation's sensitivities have any place in this distressing situation.

In any case, this is not the moment to begin leveling accusations, because there is no shortage of blame. This is the moment to act quickly, to hit hard at those with lazy imaginations and carefree hearts who are costing us so dearly. We must act, and act quickly, and if our voices can stir up what needs to be stirred up, we will use them and spare no one.

The Americans are now promising us that they will use their aircraft to bring home five thousand deportees per day. This promise was made after we launched

---

[508] One of the articles of "Misère de la Kabylie" was entitled "Insulting Wages."

[509] See article of May 20–21, p. 212.

[510] Editorial. Reprinted in *Actuelles*, chapter "La chair."

[511] See editorial of May 17.

[512] In *France-Soir* on May 19, under the title "Don't Accuse to Let Yourself Off the Hook," Philippe Viannay (who was, as the paper noted, the founder of *Défense de la France*, as *France-Soir* was originally known, and who had "personally gone to Germany to investigate the conditions surrounding the repatriation of our deportees") expressed the view that while the Americans bore some responsibility for the situation, there was above all a "dreadful failure on the part of the French, who have failed to defend their own," who weren't working hard enough, and who were devoting too many transportation resources to officials and not enough to deportees.

our appeal, and we greet it with joy and satisfaction. The matter of the camps under quarantine remains to be dealt with, however. The camps at Dachau and Allach[513] have been decimated by typhus. On May 6, detainees were dying at the rate of 120 per day. Deported doctors in the camp have asked that the quarantine perimeter be expanded beyond the camp itself, which is overcrowded and where every inch of ground is infected, to include the S.S. camp a few miles away, which is clean and comfortable. This request has yet to be granted, as it should be.

When all the problems have been resolved, blame must be assessed, and it will be. But for now we must wake up everyone who is asleep, without exception. We must tell them, for example, that it is unacceptable for our deported comrades not to have regular correspondence with their families and for their homeland to seem as far away today as in the days of their greatest despair. We must also tell them, to give another example, that what these broken-down operations need is not jars of jam but medical supplies along with all the equipment necessary to save a few of these irreplaceable lives.

In any case, we will continue to protest until we are fully satisfied. If our previous article stirred emotions, so much the better. It would have been better still, of course, if no article had been needed to stir up emotions. There are things that can be seen at Dachau that should have sufficed. But this is the time for action, not regrets.

To be perfectly clear, our grievance is not specifically directed at the Americans. As everyone knows, we here are doing all we can to promote friendship with the Americans. The charge we bring is a general one, however, and the guilty should acknowledge their mistakes, make amends, and put things right by rectifying their oversights and errors. Men and nations do not always see where their true interests and true riches lie.

In all the democracies, governments of every stripe are in the process of proving in this instance that they do not know where their true elites are. They are in pestilential camps, where the few survivors of a heroic troop are still fighting against the indifference and carelessness of their own governments.

France in particular has lost its finest sons in the voluntary combat of the Resistance.[514] The country is gauging the extent of this loss every day. Each of the men who is dying today in Dachau weakens it further and adds to its woe. Because we here are only too well aware of this, we are terribly jealous of these men and feel that we must defend them with every ounce of our strength, without regard for anyone or anything, until they are liberated a second time.[515]

---

[513] Allach was attached to Dachau.

[514] Camus returns to this idea again and again; see the editorial of October 27, 1944, p. 90.

[515] The editorial of May 23, which was not written by Camus, follows up on this one and states: "Our protests, together with those that have been raised throughout France against the situation of the political deportees, have had their effect." Repatriation did in fact accelerate, and the Dachau deportees were transferred to German villages. The newspaper pointed out, however, that there were camps other than Dachau and demanded that everything possible be done to ensure a rapid repatriation.

May 20–21, 1945
Arabs Demand a Constitution and a Parliament for Algeria[516]

I said in my last article that a substantial number of North African natives, having given up on the policy of assimilation but not yet won over by pure nationalism, had turned to a new party, the "Friends of the Manifesto." I therefore think it would be useful to make French people familiar with this party, which, like it or not, has to be reckoned with.[517]

The leader of this movement is Ferhat Abbas,[518] a native of Sétif, a university graduate with a degree in pharmacy, and, before the war, one of the staunchest proponents of the assimilation policy. At that time he edited a newspaper, *L'Entente*, which defended the Blum-Viollette plan and called for the establishment in Algeria of a democratic political system in which Arabs would enjoy rights corresponding to their duties.

Today, Abbas, like many of his coreligionists, has turned his back on assimilation. His newspaper, *Egalité*, whose editor Aziz Kessous[519] is a socialist as well as a former proponent of assimilation, is calling for Algeria to be recognized as a nation[520] linked to France by ties of federalism.

The Man

Ferhat Abbas is fifty years old. He is undeniably a product of French culture. The epigraph of his first book was a quotation from Pascal. This was no accident. He is in fact a man in the Pascalian spirit, combining logic with passion with some considerable success. The following thought is very much in the French style: "France will be free and strong by dint of our freedoms and our strengths."

---

[516] Fifth article on Algeria, reprinted in *Actuelles III* (with addition of a note on Ferhat Abbas) under the title "The Party of the Manifesto."

[517] Camus knew the political situation in Algeria well, not only from his own political activities but also because he had covered the trial of Sheikh El Okbi for *Alger-Républicain* in June 1939 (see *Fragments d'un combat*, pp. 412–510).

[518] Camus gives an excellent account of the career of Ferhat Abbas (1899–1985). Having served as general councilor, municipal councilor for Sétif, and financial delegate before the war, Abbas saw the failure of the Blum-Viollette plan as proof of the impossibility of assimilation. In 1938 he founded the Algerian Popular Union for Conquest of the Rights of Man and the Citizen. Although he was careful to say that "attachment does not mean assimilation," he did not yet envisage an Algeria separate from France. The program of the Manifesto, and the creation of the "Friends of the Manifesto" party, marked a clear shift in his demands. From May 1945 until independence, Ferhat Abbas would play an important role in the history of Algeria. After serving in Tunisia as president of the Provisional Government of the Algerian Republic and later as president of the Algerian Assembly, he was completely sidelined.

[519] Aziz Kessous exercised official responsibilities in Ferhat Abbas's party. A member of the S.F.I.O., he tried, even after November 1954, to bring French and Algerian liberals together by founding a newspaper, *Communauté algérienne*. In *Actuelles III* Camus reprinted a letter he had written to Kessous under the title "Letter to an Algerian Militant," which had appeared in the first issue of the newspaper.

[520] In *Actuelles III* a note was attached to this statement indicating that "to be precise, Ferhat Abbas spoke of an Algerian republic."

Ferhat Abbas owes his style to our culture, as he is well aware. Even his humor bears the French stamp, as is evident from the following classified ad, which appeared in uppercase characters in *Egalité*: "Exchange one hundred feudal lords of all races for 100,000 French teachers and technicians."

This cultivated and independent man has evolved along with his people, and he has set forth their aspirations in a manifesto that was published on February 10, 1943, and accepted by General Catroux[521] as a basis for discussion.

The Program

What does the manifesto say? In truth, taken on its own terms, the text limits itself to a detailed critique of French policy in North Africa and to the assertion of a principle. That principle, which takes note of the failure of the assimilation policy, is that there is a need to recognize an Algerian nation linked to France but distinctive in character. According to the manifesto, "it is now clear to everyone that this assimilation policy is an *inaccessible reality* [my italics] and a dangerous instrument designed to serve the interests of the colonization."

Building on this principle, the manifesto asks that Algeria be given its own constitution in order to ensure that Algerians will enjoy full democratic rights and parliamentary representation. An appendix added to the manifesto on May 26, 1943, and two more recent texts from April and May 1945, further flesh out this position. The amended manifesto calls for recognition, an end to hostilities, and an Algerian state with its own constitution, to be drafted by a constituent assembly elected by universal suffrage of all people residing in Algeria.

The general government would then cease to be a bureaucratic agency and become a true government, with top positions equally divided between French and Arab ministers.

As for the assembly, the "Friends of the Manifesto" were aware that any proposal for strictly proportional representation would have met with hostility in France, since with eight Arabs to every Frenchman in the population, the assembly would then become a de facto Arab parliament. As a result, they agreed that their constitution should allow for 50 percent Muslim representatives and 50 percent Europeans.

The "Friends of the Manifesto" and Their Demands

Not wishing to wound French sensibilities, the "Friends" conceded that the assembly's powers would include only administrative, social, financial, and economic matters, with all issues of external security, military organization, and diplomacy being entrusted to the central government in Paris. To be sure, this

---

[521] General Catroux (1877–1969) served as governor of Indochina in 1939–1940 before joining General de Gaulle in London. In 1943, when de Gaulle and the Provisional Government arrived in Algiers, he became governor-general of Algeria and state commissioner on the National Liberal Committee. Later he served as ambassador to the Soviet Union. Though appointed minister for Algeria in 1956, he was unable to take up his duties.

basic principle went hand in hand with certain social demands, all of which are aimed at bringing as much democracy as possible to Arab politics. Nevertheless, I believe that I have gotten the gist of the document right and have not misrepresented the thinking of the "Friends of the Manifesto."

The Manifesto and the Algerian Nationalists

In any case, these ideas, and the man who represents them, have attracted the support of a substantial part of the Muslim community. Ferhat Abbas has drawn together a very diverse group of men and movements, such as the sect of the Ulemmas, Muslim intellectuals who preach in favor of a rationalist reform of Islam and who were until recently proponents of assimilation, as well as socialists, to name just two examples. It is also quite clear that elements of the Algerian Popular Party,[522] an Arab nationalist party that was dissolved in 1936 but continued to propagandize illegally in favor of Algerian separatism, have joined the "Friends of the Manifesto," which they see as a good platform for action.

They may be the ones who compromised the "Friends of the Manifesto" in the recent disturbances. But I know from a direct source that Ferhat Abbas is too shrewd a politician to have recommended or wished for such excesses, which he knew were likely to strengthen the hand of Algerian reactionaries. The man who wrote that "not one African will die for Hitler" has given sufficient guarantees on this subject.

The reader will form his own conclusions as to the program I've just laid out. Whatever your opinion may be, however, you need to know that this program exists and that it has had a deep impact on Arab political aspirations.

If the French administration had decided not to follow General Catroux in his provisional approval of the manifesto, it might have noticed that the whole political construct of the manifesto derives its strength from the fact that it considers assimilation to be an "inaccessible reality." It might then have concluded that it would be enough to make the reality accessible to cut the ground out from under the "Friends of the Manifesto." But it chose instead to respond with imprisonment and repression. This was stupidity, pure and simple.

ALBERT CAMUS

May 23, 1945
It Is Justice That Will Save Algeria from Hatred[523]

A political portrait of Algeria today would not be complete without taking note of French democrats who live in daily contact with the grave problems we have

---

[522] The Algerian Popular Party, created by Messali Hadj in March 1937, replaced the North African Star, an offshoot of the Communist Party, of which it had taken control in 1927 and which had just been dissolved. Hadj was imprisoned and later deported to Brazzaville. When the A.P.P. was dissolved, he founded the Movement for the Triumph of Democratic Liberties.

[523] This sixth article in the series on Algeria was not reprinted in *Actuelles III*. Camus most likely thought it outdated in 1958.

described in previous articles. Make no mistake, however: democratic elements are in the minority.

Bear in mind that the Vichy regime found its warmest supporters in Algeria, where traces of it remain. With the exception of *Alger-Républicain* (and, to a lesser extent, *Oran-Républicain*), all the Algerian dailies collaborated. They have retained something of that period, as a glance at any of them reveals. Yet they are still allowed to publish, no doubt without M. Teitgen's knowledge.

If these newspapers have large readerships, it is because democracy has not had a good press in North Africa. Many of these readers are high officials of the General Government. This is what is sometimes called a "clarified political situation."

Our Last Chance

There are democrats, however. The Radical Party, the Socialist Party, and the Communist Party are unanimous in this regard. I've read in several places that the Communist Party is engaged in agitation in Algeria. I am obliged to say that this is the exact opposite of the truth.[524]

The Communist Party, which is opposed to the "Friends of the Manifesto," was behind the creation of a movement open to Arabs called the "Friends of Democracy." The position championed by this movement enjoys the practical support of the Radicals and Socialists. All backed the ordinance of March 7, 1944, which they considered to be a step toward equality of political rights. All call for this ordinance to be extended and denounce the social abuses that are the cause of so much suffering in Algeria.

I believe that their program can be summed up in three points: 1) extension of the ordinance of March 7 to all Arabs in possession of a school-leaving certificate and all who fought for France; 2) elimination of the regime of mixed communes and expansion of indigenous municipal rights; 3) egalitarian social policy.

This program, which is reasonable and humane, is widely believed to be France's last chance to safeguard its future in North Africa.

New Men

But a new politics calls for new methods and new men. For example, there would be no point in extending political rights to everyone with a school-leaving certificate while doing nothing to increase the number of such people.

At the present time, according to the administration's own figures, one million Muslim children are without schools. This incredible failure can be remedied only by building new schools and accelerating the training of teachers. By the same token, the government cannot allow officials to take it upon themselves to modify its ordinances and sabotage their application, as is happening in Kabylia today, to judge by prefectoral instructions I saw with my own eyes.

---

[524] The Communist Party would support the Algerian insurrection from 1954 to 1962. That may be one of the reasons why this article was not published in *Actuelles III.*

New men are therefore needed. And at a time when so many young French people are searching for a way and a reason to live, it may be possible to find a few thousand capable of grasping the fact that a land awaits them in which they can their fellow man and their country at the same time serve.[525]

I have now traced the economic and political outline of the Algerian problem as clearly as I know how. This is only an outline, of whose insufficiencies I am well aware. But as I said at the outset, my only ambition was to clarify a situation obscured by blindness and prejudice. Thus far I have done so objectively. In concluding, however, it seems to me that I must add a personal note.

As anxious conquerors, we have something to learn from the wisdom of Arab civilization. In order to learn from that civilization, we first have to understand it and serve it. Granted that we have nothing to teach, it is obvious that we have something for which we need to ask forgiveness.

Our feverish and unbridled desire for power and expansion will never be excused unless we make up for them by unwavering attention to the pursuit of justice and the spirit of self-sacrifice. Despite the repressive actions we have just taken in North Africa, I am convinced that the era of Western imperialism is over.

The material civilization that we bring with us can save itself only if it someday brings more complete liberation to everyone it subjugates. Then we will win the friendship of the people who depend on us. Otherwise, we will reap hatred, like all vanquishers who prove themselves incapable of moving beyond victory. Unfortunate and innocent French victims have lost their lives, and this crime in itself is inexcusable. But I hope that we will respond to murder with nothing other than justice, so as to avoid doing irreparable harm.[526]

"I Accuse Europe"

This problem also transcends our borders. "I Accuse Europe" is the title of one of Ferhat Abbas's pamphlets. On this point, at least, Europe can side with the prisoner. More than that, Europe should accuse itself, since with all its constant upheavals and contradictions, it has managed to produce the longest, most terrible reign of barbarism the world has ever known.

Today, the free men of Europe are victorious; they have for the time being halted the terrible course of this decadence. Now they want to turn history on its head, and in this they can surely succeed if they are willing to make the

---

[525] This call would no longer have made sense in 1958.

[526] This protest was quite isolated. In a report published in *Le Figaro* on July 13, 1945, under the title "What I Saw and Learned in Algeria," Pierre Dubard (who had previously reported that "the repression is over") quoted the prefect of Constantine, who claimed to be "boiling" with "rage against the savagery of the natives": "The rapidity of the repression saved Algeria." The work of Kateb Yacine contains an account of "acts of repression" in Sétif. A note in *L'Homme révolté* alludes to these events after discussing the systematic massacre of the population of Lidice by the Nazis: "It is striking to note that atrocities that remind us of these crimes were committed in the colonies (India, 1857; Algeria, 1945; etc.) by European nations in obedience to the same irrational prejudice of racial superiority" (*Essais*, p. 590).

necessary sacrifices. But the only way to make this revolution is to make it totally. They will save Europe from its demons and low gods only if they liberate all people who depend on Europe.

At the conclusion of this survey, I have only one question for the French, who today know what hatred is: "Do you truly want to be hated by millions of people, as you have hated thousands of others? If so, let things continue on their present course in North Africa. If not, welcome these people among you and treat them as equals, using all appropriate means."

I have no doubt about the response of the French people, or of any reasonable man. But what about those in government? Maybe it's time to envisage a period in which governments will govern in accordance with reason, which under today's conditions means boldly and generously.[527]

---

[527] To complement this series of articles on Algeria (which would conclude with the editorial of June 15), *Combat* on May 25 published a response to accusations made against Camus by Quilici in *La Bataille*. Although it is quite clear that Camus did not write this response, it is likely that he approved its language. Here is the text, entitled "Contempt has never turned anyone into a French citizen":

"In the weekly *La Bataille*, M. Quilici vehemently attacks our friend Albert Camus for his inquiry into conditions in Algeria. Ever since he arrived in Paris, M. Quilici has distinguished himself in the eyes of respectable people. Indeed, he seems to have set himself the task of insulting men associated with the interior resistance. Nevertheless, we have never answered his attacks, because it seemed to us that their quality did not warrant a response. The case in point is no better in that respect, but we are obliged to respond because the issue raised by these attacks is too serious to leave the job to just anyone.

"To discredit Camus's information on Algeria, M. Quilici attacks the intellectual arrogance of anyone who would claim to know the situation in North Africa after three weeks of research. Hence we must point out that Camus is North African by birth and upbringing. He has spent most of his life in Algeria, and until the armistice of June 1940 the only political problem that interested him was the Algerian problem. The Kabyles have not forgotten the investigations of poverty in Algeria that Camus published in *Alger-Républicain* a few months before the war.

"M. Quilici suspects Camus of not caring enough about French victims in Algeria. But how could he not, since his whole family lives there both in cities and in colonial villages vulnerable to the rebels? Therefore, if he asks that we respond to hatred not with hatred but with justice, there is a good chance that he does so not on a whim but only after careful consideration.

"For the rest, we will not mince words. M. Quilici previously published an article on Algeria that was a veritable provocation on account of the disgraceful contempt it showed toward Arabs. He has not stopped. On the one hand, he approves of the democratic solution that Camus advocated and that implies a need for greater assimilation, while on the other hand he seems to regret the fact that Arabs are not required to ride in special cars on Algerian railroads. Contempt has never turned anyone into a French citizen, and for all its show of loyalism, we know of no more vile text than M. Quilici's, which does a disservice to the country to which he seems to think he has exclusive rights.

"Furthermore, M. Quilici sees proof that the disorder in Sétif was orchestrated in the fact that it broke out at the end of the war, as in 1871. Indeed, it is likely that the disorder was orchestrated, but the proof doesn't seem convincing to us, and we find it hard to imagine a rebel leader waiting to send his troops into battle until the forces of repression can easily be mobilized against them.

"As for the tactic of blaming our American friends for the troubles in Algeria, the silliness of the charge speaks for itself. We here believe that France is an adult country capable of acknowledging its mistakes as well as defending its rights. That is what M. Quilici calls the taste for universality. But this comes from an inadequate vocabulary, and from his confused idea of the meaning of honesty.

"Make no mistake: M. Quilici's attitude is significant. If he represented himself alone, it wouldn't mater much. But too many men like him offer Algerians a misleading image of France. The reason for our anger

May 25, 1945[528]

Yesterday, General de Gaulle delivered a speech that brought us a great deal of satisfaction.[529] That the production of coal and electricity and the entire credit system be placed in the service of the nation before the year is out—these are reforms for which we fought hard. We fought the government itself, and that gives us all the more leave today to voice our total approval.

General de Gaulle, moreover, has set these reforms in their real perspective and shown that, in addition to the domestic reasons for implementing them, there would be international consequences as well. This is ground on which we are quite pleased to follow him. Indeed, there is not a single domestic issue that does not also have global repercussions and that is not influenced in turn by international politics.

We will be what we are worth. Others will judge us by what we produce. And we won't be able to produce anything if we don't put the chief instruments of production into the hands of the nation and don't set the entire country to work on a single project: reconstruction. If the nation is to work, it must feel that it is working for itself and not in order to cement the privileges of a few.

The solidarity in misfortune and destruction that France has just experienced must not be forgotten in the hour of her rebirth. After the defeat, the French people learned that the nation was theirs and not the exclusive property of a few specialists. That is why they ask that their sacrifices serve the common interest and only the common interest.

Therefore the announcement of these reforms, even if it does not solve any of the great problems of the moment, may well contribute to their solution. Workers cannot accept the harsh constraints of wage and price controls unless they have proof that those constraints have a purpose and they are not the only ones to bear their burden. Solutions to our problems will be even further advanced if, as General de Gaulle has promised, everything possible is done to improve the food supply. If rationed products truly find their way into the hands of workers, their condition will be improved. The government must bend all its effort to this task.

---

will be clear when we say that there are Frenchmen in Algeria whose first feelings of shame came when they saw how men like M. Quilici conceived of their role in a conquered land. M. Quilici wants people in Algeria to speak the language of hatred, but the problem is serious enough, and we feel enough scruples about the French future in North Africa, to urge the government to turn a deaf ear to such appeals and to state publicly that France will never acknowledge such language as its own."

Combat

[528] Editorial. Text very likely by Camus: it approves of a severe style, exempt from all demagogy and proposing specific reforms, and it calls for constructive effort—all notes that Camus struck repeatedly in his editorials.

[529] *Combat* printed the text of de Gaulle's speech announcing a number of reforms in response to demands voiced by resisters in the spirit of the N.C.R. program. These reforms were implemented in 1945–1946: they included a reform of the bureaucracy, nationalization of credit (December 2, 1945), nationalization of gas and electricity (April 8, 1946), insurance (April 25, 1946), and creation of the Charbonnages de France (May 17, 1946).

To be sure, yesterday's speech offered no prospect of comfort and no hope of a tranquil existence. We have never had any doubt that what France expects is years of toil and effort. But that toil is freely embraced, and when the government has done what must be done in order to ensure that it is also just, then all decent people will unite in the common effort.

We are not among those who believe that effort is a substitute for happiness. Of course each individual has the right to judge for himself. But nations have the duty to regard the happiness of each citizen as sacred. The years of labor that await us are therefore not an end in themselves. But they await us, and we must do what is necessary. If the government sees to it that justice accompanies our efforts, our toil will seem less harsh.

May 26, 1945[530]

While awaiting the ministerial shakeup that has, to be sure, been a long time coming, some recently repatriated legislators are calling for a return to "Republican legality" and the "Constitution of 1875." This demand has, as one might expect, met with a highly favorable response in the Radical Party press.[531]

May we say that we find this ambition somewhat surprising? Because ultimately, if it were a matter of strictly observing the laws in force in 1939, the man in power right now ought to be not de Gaulle but Pétain. Called upon by M. Albert Lebrun to constitute a ministry in 1940 and endorsed by an overwhelming majority of both chambers, which voted to grant him full powers, he and he alone came to power in conformity with the law. And as for the Constitution of 1875, it was once again all those respectable parliamentarians who authorized Pétain to modify it to suit himself. They exhibit a curious logic when they invoke a legality and a constitution that they helped to destroy.

The regime in France today is an extralegal one; more precisely, it is obliged to strike a compromise between legislation passed by Vichy and the laws of the Third Republic without being able to found its power on either one and without the mandate to overhaul the legal system completely.

The latter remains a possibility, however. Although the role of the present government is to make a transition (always a thankless task), and although it is not required to establish new institutions until universal suffrage has spoken, the public has demonstrated its desire for certain specific reforms clearly enough to allow the government to start charting a new course. In this regard, the recent municipal elections may be seen as having removed any remaining doubt.[532]

---

530 Editorial. Text possibly by Camus.
531 Camus was in the habit of attacking the Radical Party.
532 The municipal elections of April 29 and May 13 marked beyond question a victory of the left: the Communist Party, the Socialist Party, and the M.R.P.

In fact, what matters is not the discussion of legality, which is doomed to go nowhere. The provisional government is being asked only to act in a democratic way, that is, in the interest of freedom and justice.

National elections are impossible before all prisoners have returned home. But the government should not seize on this as a pretext to ensconce itself in a fortress surrounded by police and special secret agents. Now that the war in Europe is over, the government should state all its intentions in regard to both domestic and foreign policy so that the choice to be laid before the voters will be clear. It should strive to expose all its work to the light of day.

If the election of the Constituent Assembly is to have a meaning, the issues of the day must be debated publicly, and the government must stop shrouding its policies in vague explanations. Offering relief to one group and then another cannot continue forever. The necessities of History cannot always be finessed.

Some legislators in the past and some members of the government today remind us of the Spanish cardinal of the Renaissance who went into battle with his armor on backward in order to make people think that he was always advancing, when in fact, according to one of his colleagues, he was constantly retreating.

May 27, 1945[533]

The foreign affairs committee of the Consultative Assembly has just called for France to break off diplomatic relations with Franco. In addition, France and England are proposing to reconsider the status of Tangier, which the Spanish dictator altered unilaterally in the middle of the war in accordance with his usual notion of democratic procedure.[534] Thus the issue of Spain is once again on the agenda.

In fact, it would have been surprising if it had not come up. At a time when free men everywhere are celebrating the defeat of fascism, one has to ponder the paradox that the entire Iberian Peninsula remains under fascist rule, while the rest of the world appears to regard this as natural.

The issue is clear, however. As everyone must know, if Franco remains in power, it is because the Allies want him there. If the victorious nations purely and simply ended their relations with Franco's Spain, the Phalangist regime would not survive for more than a few days. It is no secret that the Spanish economy is propped up by the Allies. If it endures, it is because no one is doing what it would take to kill it.

This is a serious matter. The Allied governments, including the French government, run the risk of being misunderstood by millions of people who fought for the very principle of liberty. They risk lending credence to the idea that they prefer a dictatorship they control to a republic that might not be to their liking. This will bring them into conflict with people who have always believed that

---

[533] Editorial. Text probably by Camus, following up the editorial of November 21, 1944, p. 116.

[534] In June 1940, after the armistice, Franco seized Tangiers. See editorial of November 21, 1944, n. 269, p. 117.

fascism had to be destroyed wherever it was found, down to its very last citadel, even if that means Spain.

There is no danger, however, that they will find their actions self-contradictory, because they already are. There is not a single line in any speech delivered by any Allied leader during the war that is not contradicted by the very existence of the Franco regime. For there is still one place in the world where the spirit of mediocrity and cruelty reigns, where prisoners are shot despite the interventions of French officials, and where hundreds of thousands of fighters have been held in prison for years for the crime of hope. We need not remind our readers what those fighters mean to us.[535]

It seems clear that, in spite of all the destruction of the past few years, diplomats have not changed their ways. Apparently there are words to which they will always be deaf.

Yet if governments are always ready to contradict themselves, individuals and nations can no longer do so in today's world. They have paid too dearly for their principles to allow them to be twisted for the sake of a political compromise. All people of all nationalities who rejected Munich and Hitler reject Franco. If it is true to say that total war must inevitably lead to total victory, then we are bound to say that our victory will not be complete as long as Spain remains enslaved.[536] Patience is a word that may still have meaning in the bureaucracies of various capitals. It has no meaning for the prisoners of Madrid or for anyone who has just experienced the endless impatience of defeat and subjugation. People of all countries are tired of secret diplomacy. They want the last Hitlerian government in Europe to disappear, or else they demand that the Allies state clearly and bluntly the reasons for their indulgence and forgetfulness.

May 31, 1945[537]

The Syrian affair, which we have been analyzing daily on the basis of information gleaned from a variety of sources, needs to be approached cautiously.[538] It would be good if we were in a position both to acknowledge our wrongs and

---

[535] We have previously encountered Camus's attachment to republican Spain (see the editorials of September 5, October 5 and 24, November 21, and December 10, 1944, and January 7–8, 1945).

[536] The last sentence is reminiscent of one in an article published in the underground *Combat* that was certainly written by Camus: see p. 1 above.

[537] Editorial. Text probably by Camus.

[538] The Franco-British crisis in Syria and Lebanon (placed under French mandate in 1919) was set against a background of French equivocation as to independence for the states of the Levant. Though promised by the Viénot accords in 1936, independence never became a reality. It was proclaimed in 1941 by General Catroux, the high commissioner for the region, after Free French Forces entered Syria, and guaranteed by British troops. Nationalist demonstrations took place in Beirut on May 8, 1945, and clashes erupted afterward. The situation took a turn for the worse on May 29, when French outposts in Damascus came under attack; the city was bombarded the following night. French and British troops were not evacuated until 1945. *Combat* followed these events quite closely thanks to reporting by its special envoy Pierre Kaufmann. The newspaper also stressed the importance of Middle East oil.

defend our rights, because that would be a position of true strength. But the complexity of all issues touching on the Arab countries is compounded in this case by international influences that have been making themselves felt in the Middle East. In the face of so much confusion, we seem incapable of speaking in a clear voice that would strengthen our position.

The influence that has made itself felt on the Algerian issue stems from England. Because we here are particularly attached to the Franco-British entente, and because we hope that in the future it will become a political reality in which the two countries will find compensation for their reciprocal weaknesses, we regret that England's views were expressed primarily in the official communiqué that we published two days ago, a communiqué that pointed a finger of accusation at us.

This is not to say that we ought to reject every accusation and stubbornly deny that we have made mistakes. We ought to acknowledge our errors and admit that the scuttling of the independence treaty of 1936 was not the right thing to do. But England should also own up to its mistakes and try to find common ground with us so as to safeguard the just rights of the Syrian and Lebanese people for their sake alone and not for the benefit of rival imperialisms. Fortunately, a segment of the British public grasps this. In the *Manchester Guardian,* for instance, we read that "anyone who has studied our treaty with Iraq cannot regard the French proposals as extravagant, for they bear a striking resemblance to the terms of our agreement. But the way in which these demands have been presented and the negotiations carried on is singularly lacking in wisdom." The liberal newspaper adds, moreover, that British officials have made France's situation more difficult, because "they have not always negotiated honestly or tactfully enough."

This is the kind of thing that needs to be said. But if we are to speak in this voice, the Western nations must stop looking upon the Middle East as a closed preserve over which ownership is to be asserted. Europe must seek to play an emancipatory role in its overseas territories rather than engage in a battle over conflicting interests. Given the way things are going and minds are evolving, we have a long way to go. But that is no reason why principles cannot be laid down, and in this respect French policy should set an example to the greatest possible extent. In our present historical situation, to take such a position would serve both the interests of justice and our own interests. For, around the world, twenty nations that have suffered and fought for freedom are waiting for some country to demonstrate at last in word and deed that it intends truly to consecrate freedom's triumph.

In return, we could ask that, in the absence of any kind of international society, which the democratic nations seem incapable of creating, France be granted rights not incompatible with the states of the Middle East.

It's probably already too late, however. In Syria rebellion is already under way, Damascus has been shelled, and hostilities have begun. The hope of a just and peaceful settlement has vanished. Whatever comes of these operations, which will cost still more French lives, they signify a bitter failure.

June 1, 1945[539]

Mr. Churchill's ultimatum—for it is an ultimatum—and President Truman's statement have placed France in a very grave situation, which is quite likely to evolve to its detriment.[540] Yesterday we said what we thought about the Syro-Lebanese affair. Our views have not changed. But today the conflict has moved beyond the states of the Levant: it has brought the American and British governments into conflict with the French government. General de Gaulle's entire foreign policy is under attack.

We have never been tender with that policy. We have steadfastly pointed out its dangers. Even today, it strikes us as odd to propose a policy based on strength and power when the means for such a policy are lacking. This choice makes us vulnerable to being called to order twice in the same day, reminded first in the House of Common that we are acting as though we'd won the war, when we were beaten, and then in Washington that if we have an army at all, it's thanks to equipment and arms from other countries. The facts puncture inflated notions of our power: they confirm our criticisms, and such confirmation is a bitter pill to swallow.

Since the conflict now is among allies, however, it is essential to add that our policy was not alone in being faulty. Everybody knows that international diplomacy is hardly as disinterested and generous as official communiqués might suggest. Clearly the conflicts in the Middle East would not have turned this bitter if not for the presence of rich oil fields. Although it is legitimate for an impoverished France to defend its economic interests, this is not the ground that France has chosen. Indeed, it has been weakened by its errors in other areas, errors that are made worse by its unwillingness to acknowledge them. The unkept promise of independence to Beirut and Damascus is today the best weapon in the hands of those who would like to see France disappear from the Levant.

To be sure, from the reoccupation of the Rhineland by German troops right on to the Liberation, we have known governments that always gave in to force, not always without bluster but always without firing a shot. That is the extreme opposite of the policy of Charles de Gaulle, but only in the sense that extremes meet, as they say: the results are identical.

We briefly hoped that France would draw strength from its weakness by adopting a new tone in its dealings with the world, the tone of truth and, up to a point, of impartiality. We did not think that it would take upon itself the injustices and errors of its past policies on the vain pretext of preserving the nation in all its power. What has been defeated can't be preserved.

---

[539] Editorial. Text probably by Camus, like the previous one, which it follows up directly.

[540] On May 31, Churchill sent de Gaulle a message announcing that he had ordered the commander in chief of British forces in the Middle East to take action, adding: "With a view to avoiding a clash between British and French forces, we call upon you immediately to issue to French troops an order to cease fire and withdraw to their barracks. Once fire has ended and order has been restored, we shall be ready to begin tripartite discussions in London." Washington approved of London's action.

We are forced to repudiate forever methods and individuals condemned by events. We are obliged to take risks and to innovate if we want France to survive with some dignity. We cannot walk in Foch's boots,[541] nor in M. Lebrun's shoes.[542]

That is why we should not allow ourselves to be blinded by this crisis, which in other times would have brought down the government—and which may still be exploited, particularly abroad, to that end. As deep as our disagreement with General de Gaulle is on these issues, he must remain in office if France is to establish the Fourth Republic, whose first elected officials should, we now know, take office before the end of the year.

And then—if we may use a rather shopworn word—France will either be revolutionary or it will cease to be.

June 5, 1945[543]

Henri Frenay is one of our comrades-in-arms.[544] To say that he was the man who created the underground "Combat" movement in 1940 is enough to give you some idea of the moral weight he carries among us. Because of that camaraderie, we have always shied away from praising him and even hesitated to defend him in a few cases when we should have. For the same reason he has always shied away from calling upon us for support. All this goes without saying, and we're not about to change our basic attitude in this regard.

Nevertheless, carrying scruples too far would risk putting us in a false position, compromising both friendship and truth. Today we find ourselves in that situation. Still, we are not going to say that the work of the minister for prisoners has been a model of its kind, nor are we going to adduce commonsense arguments that would cut the ground out from under various demagogic attacks. Instead, we want to make a different point: that there is a principle that must be respected if political and social life are to be possible, namely, the principle of liberty.

Suppose, then, that all the criticisms of the minister for prisoners were accurate. Suppose that it was right to convene a group of prisoners just barely returned home and invite them to voice their legitimate demands. Suppose, finally, that the meeting at La Mutualité this past Saturday had been organized by people who had only the public interest in mind.[545] Having come under attack, the minister for prisoners asks to be heard. He asks his accusers to hear him out.

---

[541] Marshal Foch (1851–1929), supreme commander of Allied troops in the final months of World War I, signed the armistice of 1918.

[542] Albert Lebrun (1871–1950) served as president of the Republic from 1932 to 1940. He resigned when the armistice was concluded in June 1940.

[543] Editorial. Text very likely by Camus.

[544] Commissioner for Prisoners of the C.F.N.L. in Algiers in 1943, Henri Frenay became minister for prisoners and deportees at the Liberation.

[545] On June 2, a meeting called by the Association of Prisoners of War of the Seine drew 25,000 repatriated prisoners, who protested the insufficiency of government assistance and called for the resignation of Henri Frenay. In December 1945, when Frenay was attacked by *L'Humanité*, he sued for libel, but the case

However one views the substance of the case, it is worth noting that our past and present ministers have not accustomed us to quite so much independence or to the kind of courage that it takes to leave the sanctuary of one's office behind and face a resolutely hostile crowd. This willing acceptance of responsibility and sense of obligation are nevertheless what we would like to see in our government officials.

And they refused to listen to Frenay. Newspapers of a certain ilk shout every day in unison that the minister is wrong about everything and invite an embittered and disappointed mob to shout along with them. The minister had said he was going to prove that he's right about certain issues. Undoubtedly that's precisely what the organizers were afraid of, since they refused to hear him out. What new moral code holds sway that allows the simplest request for fairness to be dismissed without a second thought? And what do the repatriated prisoners (a million strong) think about a France that has regained its freedom only to witness the birth of new forms of servitude?

The prisoners' cause is a great cause. The very idea of using them for partisan ends should turn the stomach of anyone with a shred of decency. But it is up to the prisoners themselves to defend their cause and make sure that it is not tainted by acts of injustice, like the anti-Semitic demonstrations of the other day, or by blind partisan passions. Frenay may be wrong, and we have reported on the prisoners' disappointments when we thought it necessary to do so.[546] But the basic right of every man to be heard when he is accused cannot be denied, even to a minister. This principle needs to be stated and defended. These methods are intolerable, not only because they are the methods we fought against for four years but also because they harm interests that should be sacred to us all.

June 15, 1945[547]

After being briefly traumatized, the French public is turning its attention away from Algeria. As attention fades, various papers have taken advantage of the situation to publish articles that attempt to show that it wasn't as bad as it seemed, that the political crisis in the country was of limited scope, and that it could all

---

was dismissed. *Combat* published a note in support of his case: "*L'Humanité* has in particular accused M. Frenay of having deliberately slowed the repatriation of prisoners and deportees, of having barred a thousand foreign children interned at Buchenwald from entering France, of having sought to imprison Spanish resisters upon their return from Germany, etc. Argument in court proved that those assertions were false, but Judge Albert, who issued the writ, held that they were not defamatory, thereby demonstrating, perhaps, to anyone who might still have been unaware of it, that the way in which certain magistrates define honor explains why they still sit on the bench despite having sworn an oath to Pétain when times were different."

546 See the editorials of May 17 and 19, pp. 205 and 210.

547 Editorial. Text reprinted in *Actuelles III* in conclusion to the series on the "Crisis in Algeria."

be blamed on a few professional agitators.[548] To be sure, these articles are not distinguished for their documentation or objectivity. One characterizes the recently arrested president of "Friends of the Manifesto" as the father of the Algerian Popular Party, whose leader has long been Messali Hadj, now also under arrest. The other refers to the Ulemmas as a nationalist political organization when it is actually a reformist religious confraternity, which in any case supported the assimilation policy until 1938.

No one has anything to gain from these hasty, ill-informed surveys, nor for that matter from the inspired studies that have appeared in *Le Monde* and *L'Aube*.[549] It is true that the presence of professional agitators is an essential element for understanding the Algerian massacre, but it is also true that those agitators wouldn't have been able to accomplish much had they not been able to take advantage of the political crisis, to which it would be pointless and dangerous to close one's eyes.

That political crisis, which had been going on for many years, has not miraculously disappeared. On the contrary, it has deepened, and all the news from Algeria suggests that it has now gathered around itself an atmosphere of hatred and suspicion that can hardly improve matters. The atrocious massacres of Guelma and Sétif have provoked deep resentment and outrage among the French in Algeria. The subsequent repression has made the Arab masses fearful and hostile. In this climate, political action that is both resolute and democratic seems unlikely to succeed.

That is no reason to give up hope, however. The minister of national economy has laid out plans for a resupply effort that, if maintained, should suffice to alleviate the disastrous economic situation. But the government needs to extend the ordinance of March 7, 1944, in order to prove to the Arab masses that no amount of bad feeling will ever interfere with its desire to export the democratic regime that the French enjoy to Algeria. What needs to be exported, though, is not fine speeches but concrete actions. If we want to save North Africa, we need

---

[548] On May 15, *Le Figaro* published a communiqué from the ministry of the interior together with the comment that "although the situation is not extremely grave, it nevertheless remains serious." On May 17, *L'Aube* commented that "order has not been restored in Algeria." *L'Humanité* did not deny the gravity of the events but explained them as the result of plots by prominent colonists, Vichyite officials, and a fifth column that contrived the famine in order to provoke riots.

[549] In *Le Monde* of May 18 and 24, Jacques Driand published two articled in a series entitled "The North African Crisis." The first, entitled "The French Malaise," saw France's weakened condition, the rise of Algerian nationalism, and the economic crisis as reasons for the riots, pointed out that North Africans were excluded from politics but not from war, and concluded that "the situation is not tragic" but could become so if the French administrative structure were abandoned or discredited. The second, entitled "Europeans and Native," asked that repressive measures be kept to "the just and reasonable."

In *L'Aube* for June 1 and 2, two article appeared by Paul-Emile Viard, dean of the law faculty in Algiers, under the title "Where Is Algeria Headed?" Paternalistic in tone, these articles stood out for clearly posing the political problem of providing representation for Algerians and calling for enforcement of the ordinance of March 7, 1944. Viard, no doubt responding to Camus' article of May 20–21, which pointed out that Ferhat Abbas had quoted Pascal in the epigraph of his first book, wrote that "you can't turn a person into a French citizen simply by attaching the label 'citizen' to him, even if he uses a sentence from Pascal as the epigraph to his book."

to tell the world of our determination that France be represented there by its noblest laws and by the most just of its people. We must remember this determination, and no matter what the circumstances or how heated the attacks in the press, we must stick to it. Let us be clear that we will save nothing of what is French in Algeria or anywhere else if we do not save justice.

As we have seen, talking this way won't please everyone. It isn't that easy to overcome prejudice and blindness. But we still think that our position is reasonable and moderate. The world today is seething with hatred. Everywhere, violence and force, massacres and riots fill the air from which we thought the worst poisons had been drained. Whatever we can do for truth—French truth and human truth—we must also do to oppose hatred. Whatever it takes must be done to bring peace to people lacerated and tormented by suffering that has gone on too long. For our part, at any rate, let us try not to add anything to Algerian bitterness. Only the infinite power of justice can help us reconquer Algeria and its people.[550]

June 27, 1945[551]

M. Herriot has just made an unfortunate statement.[552] An unfortunate statement is one that comes at an inopportune moment. M. Herriot has spoken at a moment that is no longer his and about a subject that may be deemed untimely.

[550] In connection with the articles on Algeria, it may be of some interest to mention a communiqué that *Combat* published on August 8, 1945, entitled "North African Intellectual Sentenced to Twenty Years at Hard Labor." The case in point was the trial in Algiers before a military court of several men accused of crimes dating back to October 1944. Among the accused was Ben Ali Bouckort, who, "after being convicted of reconstituting the Algerian Popular Party and accused of inciting his countrymen to riot against French sovereignty, was sentenced to twenty years at hard labor, loss of civic rights, and confiscation of all his property." A note from the editors added: "As the press agencies were publishing the bulletin you have just read, a friend of Ben Ali Bouckort's passed on to us a letter from him dated May 28: 'I have been in prison since October 1944. I was arrested following a search in which the manuscript of a book I had written was found. It was a 340-page monograph about Algerian problems inspired by the doctrine of February 10, 1943.'"

The editors' note continued: "We are entitled to ask whether the memory of the riots in Constantine led the military judges to impose a penalty whose severity looks a great deal like injustice. Clearly, Bouckort, who has been in prison since October 1944, cannot have had anything to do with the bloody events of the following spring. And we are entitled to ask whether sending intellectuals to jail is the best way to succeed with a policy of assimilation."

It is plausible to think that Bouckort's friend was none other than Albert Camus and that the comments on the communiqué were written by him. In July 1936, Bouckort was, along with Omar Ouzegane, secretary general of the Algerian Communist Party, the erstwhile local section of the French Communist Party, which later became a regional section. Camus was at that time a member of the party (see introduction, pp. xxxi–xxxii). Furthermore, Ouzegane, with whom Camus had ties, and Bouckort both wrote for *Alger-Républicain*. It is more than likely that he remained in contact with them, even though they followed very different political trajectories.

[551] Editorial. Reprinted in *Actuelles*, chapter on "Morality and Politics."

[552] Camus had been quite critical of the Radical Party, and of Herriot in particular, since 1937. On Herriot, see the editorial of May 12, 1945, n. 476, p. 197. In a speech delivered to the Radical Federation of the Rhône, Herriot said: "I wonder if the present generation is fully qualified to give previous generations lessons in morality."

Even if he were right, he is not the ideal person to charge the nation with immorality or state that the present generation was in no position to give lessons to the prewar generation.

This judgment is unfair in the first place because it is too general. It is true that the French have a penchant for betting against themselves. Although this fault is forgivable in people who have fought hard and suffered long for their country, it is difficult to be equally indulgent toward a man whose political experience should have warned him and whose past positions should have made him more modest.

Nothing should ever be condemned in general, and a nation less than anything else. M. Herriot should know that this generation does not claim to give lessons in morality to the preceding one. But it has the right, won in a time of terrible calamity, to dismiss out of hand the morality that led to that catastrophe.

To be sure, it wasn't the political views of M. Herriot and his Radical colleagues that doomed us. But their morality—a morality without obligations or sanctions, in a France tailor-made for shopkeepers, tobacconists, and legislative banqueters—did more to sap the soul and drain the energy of the French than more glaring perversions would have done. In any case, it is not M. Herriot's morality that gives him the right to condemn the French of 1945.

This nation is searching for a new moral code: that much is true. Things are still in a state of flux. But it has given enough proof of its honor and spirit of sacrifice to insist that the politicians who represented it in the past not offer scornful comments in rebuke. We understand quite well why M. Herriot might feel vexed at seeing a certain prewar political morality rejected. The French are tired of middle-of-the-road virtues; they now know what a moral conflict extended to an entire nation can cost in the way of dislocation and pain. Hence it is not surprising that they are turning away from false elites, elites that were from the beginning elites of mediocrity.

Whatever wisdom and experience M. Herriot may possess, many of us believe that he no longer has anything to teach us. He may still be of use, however, since by contemplating what he and his party once represented and weighing that against the prodigious effort that France still must make if it is to be reborn, we come to see that no comparison is possible and that the reconstruction of France calls for other men, less faint of heart.

It may be that in M. Herriot's entourage, two hours on the black market is preferable to a week of work. We can assure him, however, that there are millions of French people who are working and keeping their mouths shut. They are the people by whom the nation should be judged. That is why we believe that it is as foolish to say that France needs moral reform more than it needs political reform as it would be to say the reverse. It needs both, precisely so that the entire nation isn't judged by the scandalous profits being reaped by a few wretched individuals. We here have always emphasized the requirements of morality, but it would be foolish to allow sermons on morality to hide the need for political and institutional reform. We need to pass good laws if we want to have good citizens.

Our only hope is that, for a decent interval at least, those good laws will keep the professors of virtue from returning to power, the professors of virtue responsible for making the words "deputy" and "government" symbols of derision in France for many long years.

Combat Magazine, June 30–July 1, 1945[553]
Images of Occupied Germany

For a man who has lived under Hitlerian occupation, even one who knew Germany before the war, this country retains unexpected signs of bloodshed that are hard to forget. Imagining it from afar, blanketed by foreign armies, squeezed between now hostile borders, its cities transformed into shapeless rubble and its people bent beneath the weight of the most awful hatred, one conjures up an apocalyptic image appropriate to its violent past and trying present.

That, at any rate, was my vague sense of things, and en route to the German border, bouncing over roads torn up by the war, what I saw reinforced my premonition. Nothing that one encounters in eastern France is likely to gladden the heart. In peacetime I would already have felt uncomfortable here, given my preference for sun-drenched lands. In a word, I would have found it hard to breathe. But amid the rubble and the barren fields ravaged by war and dotted with military cemeteries overshadowed by ungenerous skies, a powerful sense of dismay comes over the traveler as well. This is indeed the land of the dead. And how many there are! Three times in a century millions of men have fertilized this arid land with their mutilated bodies. All died in this small space, and for conquests so fragile that they cannot bear comparison with the numbers of the dead.

Everything here speaks of human suffering. True, being here makes it easier to understand Barrès.[554] What a pity it is, though, that one can no longer share his hope. We now know what our prospects are, and for a long time to come. His was a confidence that can no longer be ours. Is it any wonder, then, that one approaches Germany with a heart wrung by bitterness? Can we imagine that country without thinking of it as bearing some resemblance to what was, in part,

---

[553] Article published in *Combat Magazine*. *Combat* more than once attempted to launch a magazine that came out on Saturdays. This never became a regular publication, in part because of difficulties connected with the shortage of paper (leading at times to government bans on the publication of such supplements) and in part because of the financial problems that plagued the paper in general. On August 18, *Combat* published a noteworthy communiqué: "The difficulties that the Parisian press is facing in regard to the supply of paper have forced us to suspend publication of our Saturday supplement, *Combat Magazine*. We will resume publication as soon as a more intelligent paper policy is instituted by the competent authorities. In the meantime, we beg our readers' indulgence."

[554] Maurice Barrès (1862–1923), a novelist and political essayist who was born in the Vosges and became a spokesman for French nationalism.

its own handiwork? How can we expect it not to greet us with the hideous, drooling snout of war?

Idyllic Germany

So let me say at once that this expectation was quickly disappointed. On the contrary, what strikes you immediately upon entering French-occupied Germany is the surprising air of happiness and tranquillity that you find everywhere, except for the few cities that were destroyed. I hasten to say that I am speaking of the Rhineland, of the duchy of Baden-Württemberg, that is, of rural and Catholic Germany, which suffered less from the war than the rest of the country.

Still, the contrast is surprising. For upon leaving a part of France that lies in ruins and is inhabited by suffering humanity, you enter a fertile and prosperous region filled with splendid children and robust, smiling maidens. There is dancing in the meadows. Variegated bouquets are everywhere, and small children dangle cherries from their ears. To be sure, there are no men. Yet peaceful old couples take evening strolls, women in light dresses gather in the hay, and villages resembling children's toys look elegant and clean—all signs of a happy and comfortable life. In sum, the traveler finds himself in an idyllic Germany and thinks at times that he must be dreaming.

The beauty of the children, in particular, is striking. On the eve of my departure, I happened to find myself in old Montmartre and studied the children in our streets, with their prematurely old faces, their knees bigger than their calves, and their concave stomachs. Here, by contrast, one sees small bodies almost naked, tanned and firm and well-nourished, their heads held high and their laughter bright. In this respect, one quickly becomes convinced of the truth of an American report according to which the only country in Europe to win the war biologically was Germany. In any case, that was my first impression, and I did not stay in Germany long enough to be obliged to change it. I offer my impression for what it's worth, leaving the reader free to draw whatever conclusions he might wish.

Vacation Impressions

Still, this land is occupied, and occupied by the French army. The word "occupation" has a special meaning for us, and I was curious about German reactions now that the wheel has turned.

The French occupation is no doubt harsh. Nevertheless, it has remained within the limits set by the justice a victor is entitled to impose, or so it seemed to me. At first there were excesses, but since then, I learned, looting and rape have been harshly and at times mercilessly punished. On the other hand, violations of the law of occupation are met with sanctions without a moment's hesitation, and the military government in Germany has maintained an iron discipline. For instance, all men are required to salute French officers, manufactured goods have been systematically reappropriated, and space has been requisitioned as needed. Add to that the uncertainty that Germany must endure as to its future (whereas we were never without hope under Nazi occupation), and you might expect the reaction to be one of despair or at any rate dejection.

In fact—and I hasten to add once again that this is only a first impression—the most noticeable thing about the Germans under occupation is how natural they seem. After five years in which many things happened that were anything but natural, there is something surprising about this.

The South Germans are living among French soldiers as if they had always lived that way. Not wearing a uniform, I found lodging with one of the locals. I was welcomed cordially; my host came to bid me good night; and I was told that the war was not a good thing and that peace was better, especially eternal peace. Not one of our young soldiers is without a female companion. That only adds to the startling impression one has on the shores of Lake Constance of watching people on vacation, as an army of tanned and healthy young men, having made their way from North Africa via Tunisia, Italy, and Alsace, swim, canoe, and banter with one another in spacious dormitories decorated with flowers, while others paddle their conquests around the calm waters of the lake, with the Alps looming in the background.

These are the first images to come to my eyes, and I offer them for what they are worth. I doubt that I will surprise anyone, though, if I say that they made a deep impression on me, in the first place because they were unexpected and then, too, because I came from a country that reacted and suffered rather differently.

There is no doubt a lot to say on this topic, and someday, perhaps, I must try to say it. All I can do here is record the state of uncertainty in which I found myself throughout my travels in Germany, incapable as I was of reconciling what I knew with what I saw. To give a proper idea of my confusion, I must mention a distracting thought that came to me as I listened to my host, a man who resembled the kindly grandfather you find in some fairy tales. He was speaking to me quite sensibly about the eternal peace that Christ brings to each individual, and I was thinking of a woman I know who was deported to Germany and used as a prostitute by the S.S., who tattooed the following inscription on her stomach: "Served for two years in the S.S. camp at———."

I could not connect these two worlds, which are the very image of our unhappy, war-torn Europe, divided between victims and executioners[555] and seeking a justice that can never be reconciled with its pain. For me, at least, that is the meaning of the few images of Germany that I sketched above. The reader will understand, I trust, if I leave it at that, without attempting to draw any further conclusions.

ALBERT CAMUS

[555] The pairing of these two terms is striking. It recurs in the series of articles that Camus wrote in 1946. In this feature piece, quite different in tone from his editorials, Camus was aiming not for picturesque description but for the moral symbolism of what he saw during his brief visit to the German Rhineland.

August 2, 1945[556]

Since the Court of Justice has acknowledged that it has been wasting its time up to now, and since the Pétain trial is promising to take a new turn,[557] let us try to speak without excessive passion about a case that has stirred up so much bitterness and distressed so many people in France.

Thus far the trial has been notable chiefly for its humor. When we say humor, everyone should understand that we mean black humor. There is savage irony in the fact that in a trial on which the honor and to some extent the future of France depend, witnesses have been called for the prosecution who in fact have no right to make accusations. We understand full well why M. Daladier has said nothing about his trip to Munich, while M. Reynaud can't stop explaining why he made the peculiar choice of Pétain as his collaborator. After much effort, we can even understand M. Mornet when he tries to explain why he agreed to appear before the Court of Riom.[558] Yet M. Daladier did in fact go to Munich, M. Reynaud really did bring Pétain into the government, and M. Mornet definitely did go to Riom. All this prevents them from making a proper judgment of the armistice and even from judging it at all. The first two bear a part of the responsibility that the trial has brought to light, and as for the third, it would be astonishing to see him in his present position if we didn't already know that men like him come out on top in every regime.

Nevertheless, this irony is unbearable, as is this case, which consists in looking for plots that cannot be proven and in diverting what should be a trial for treason into a consideration of the armistice, which can be called an error but cannot be proven to be a crime. The point is not to prove that Pétain was wrong to believe in the armistice. That has already been proven by another man, whose stature looms larger than ever in comparison with these wretched disputes in which each witness pleads his own case from beginning to end. Only one witness had the right to speak, and it is a great misfortune for the country that decency compels him to remain silent.

The whole truth remains to be established, however. It is the truth that the trial ought to serve and not the passions of the parties or the compromised reputations of a few political men. We need to establish whether or not Pétain served Germany, whether or not his policy made a Hitlerian victory more likely, whether or not he is responsible for the deportations, tortures, and executions

---

[556] Editorial. Text probably by Camus. The criticism of Daladier and Reynaud, the rejection of the death penalty, the irony, and certain images may reasonably be attributed to Camus.

[557] The Pétain trial began on July 23. It would end on August 15 with a death sentence, which was commuted two days later by General de Gaulle to life imprisonment, in accordance with the express wishes of the court. All the papers followed the trial. *Combat*'s correspondent was Georges Altschuler, who submitted daily reports, but a widely reproduced photograph shows that Camus also attended the trial.

[558] The Court of Riom was the tribunal instituted by Vichy to try those responsible for the defeat, including Blum and Daladier. The trials went badly for Vichy, but the accused remained in detention, and most were deported to Germany. Mornet, the prosecutor in the Pétain trial, had sworn an oath to Pétain, like virtually all other magistrates.

that have been visited upon us, and, finally, whether or not he was, willingly or unwillingly, the servant of the enemy and the agent of his infamies. Once these questions have been answered, a judgment must be rendered. We count ourselves among those who await that judgment with anguish, for it will decide whether we were right or wrong in everything that we, along with the majority of the French who kept faith with hope, believed. But if such an expectation is to be realized, we need judges and witnesses capable of transcending themselves and rising above their futile passions.

To us, setting all bitterness aside, Pétain's responsibility still seems immense. We hope, however, that this trial will be conducted in such a way that, if that responsibility exists, it will become clear to the entire world. We will not allow ourselves to be carried away by the clamor of hatred. For instance, we do not believe that the death penalty is desirable in this case. First, because we must resolutely tell the truth, namely, that every death sentence is an affront to morality, and second, because in this particular case the death penalty would make a martyr of this vain old man and thereby enhance his image even in the minds of his enemies. Nevertheless, we are waiting for an explicit judgment based on grounds that everyone can understand.

These years of filth, this night of shame, cry out to be illuminated by the light of justice. We do not appear to be headed toward that light. It may not be too late, however, to call upon the Court of Justice to recognize that it, too, bears a terrible responsibility, that it is charged with seeing to it that the appalling sacrifices of our elites are given their meaning or deprived of it. And it is also charged with proving to those who followed General de Gaulle either that they were dupes or that they fought for the truth.

August 4, 1945[559]

Many things have a claim on the attention of the people of metropolitan France these days: the Palais de Justice,[560] Potsdam,[561] and the supply problem. Still, we must not avert our eyes from Algeria, on which the future of the nation in part depends. Municipal elections have just been held there. They are the first indication we have of the current political temperature in North Africa.

These elections came only after a long delay, and it is a good thing that that political error has now been repaired. But a similar consultation with the voters,

---

[559] Editorial. Text probably by Camus, following directly on the "Crisis in Algeria" articles and the editorial of June 15.

[560] Where Pétain's trial was being held.

[561] From July 17 to August 2, a conference in Potsdam brought together Stalin, Truman, and Churchill (who was replaced on July 28 by Clement Attlee after Churchill suffered a defeat at the polls). In this follow-up to the Yalta Conference, the three leaders set the conditions for the occupation of Germany, instituted a policy of population transfers to replace the policy of protection for minorities, approved the new Polish border, and issued an ultimatum to Japan.

which followed the grave disturbances of recent memory, left room for a good deal of anxiety. There was reason to fear, first of all, that the French of Algeria would show their hostility to the Arab people by rejecting the policy of assimilation in any form, and, furthermore, that the Arabs would refuse en masse to vote in order to demonstrate the bitterness that remained in the wake of indiscriminate repression.

Though we do not necessarily share the optimism of the unofficial communiqués, we can say that the situation, as reflected in the vote, is not as desperate as it may have seemed. The French of Algeria have demonstrated great wisdom by voting en masse for the lists of fighting France, whose candidates defended, in particular, the assimilation policy and the ordinance of March 7, 1944.[562] In doing so, they showed that they did not hold the Muslim masses responsible for the senseless acts of a few criminals. It is reasonable to think that this should help to restore a climate of confidence in Algeria.

The dramatic change in the situation can be measured by the fact that cities such as Sidi Bel Abbes, which have always been bastions of reaction and even fascism and on whose walls it was possible to read "Vive Hitler!" and "Vive Franco!" signs in letters the height of a grown man, have voted to install socialist-communist city governments.[563]

As for the Arab voters, the unofficial communiqué is right to say that more Arabs voted than were expected to vote. But some 40 percent withheld their votes, and that is a sign that should not be underestimated. Furthermore, last Sunday's vote has to be interpreted with caution, since according to the ordinance of March 7, a maximum of 80,000 Arabs had the possibility of expressing themselves through the ballot box. For a nation of 8 million people, that is a small number, too small to draw any general conclusions. One can say, however, that a certain number of Arabs did go to the polls, and therefore the damage is not yet irreparable.

These very modest successes may serve as encouragement to the government. But they should be taken as encouragement to move ahead, not to sink back into slumber. The Algerian crisis is a very long way from being resolved. The elections show only that the policy of assimilation is not necessarily defunct and that a small chance remains that it can be made to bear fruit. But if this is to happen, we must show we really want it and want nothing else. As a first gesture, to be made as soon as possible, we should extend the benefit of the ordinance of March 7 to everyone with a school-leaving certificate and to all Arabs who fought for us in the war. This would be nothing more than justice, and that should be enough to get it passed, since it is only natural that those who agreed to shed their blood for us should be allowed to express themselves. What is more, such a step would give proof of our good faith and regain some of the hearts and minds of loyal friends whose trust we have lost as a result of long years of dilatory and unjust policy.

[562] On this important ordinance, see "Crisis in Algeria."
[563] The municipal elections gave the left a clear victory.

August 7, 1945[564]

General Franco has officially announced that Spain will not ask to be seated at the upcoming international conferences. True, the Potsdam communiqué had already made it clear that Spain would not be invited. The general's fine independence of spirit loses some of its luster as a result.

To be completely fair, we hasten to point out that General Franco is not alone in contradicting himself. For even as the discussions were taking place in Potsdam,[565] Sir Victor Mallet, the new British ambassador, was presenting his credentials to the Spanish dictator. And we have it on good authority that the Americans are continuing to invest capital in the peninsula. The U.S.S.R. has at least been consistent. It has just broadcast an appeal calling upon the Spanish people to disown their government.

In any case, affairs in Spain are coming to a head. Franco appears to be in quite a difficult position. He would be in an even more difficult position if he weren't being propped up with one hand while being pushed off his perch with the other. It is nevertheless hard to see how this support can continue without shocking the moral sensibility of the world, although it is true that it wouldn't be the first time. That is why Franco's Spain is seeking compromise. There is talk of Don Juan,[566] but that surely comes of a penchant for legends. News reports speak of installing a military government to lay the groundwork for free elections, while in the meantime Spanish republicans are being sentenced to death.

All that is well and good, but it is time to get back to the logic of the situation and the constitutional aspect of the issue. The legitimate government of Spain, elected by the people, is the one that was overthrown by General Franco's coup. It is now being reconstituted in Mexico. Its legitimacy comes from the Cortes, which represents the popular will. The meeting of the Cortes, which would put an end to divisions in the republican camp, would result in a new government, in which Mr. Negrín might be the prime minister.[567] This government is the only one that a democracy may recognize, for it is the only one that can proceed to a fair popular vote. If that vote indicates that the Spanish want a monarchy, then and only then might the monarchy be accepted. Such an outcome is highly doubtful, moreover. But as a first step the democracies should recognize the constitutional government, honor the principle of legitimacy that it embodies, and give it a mandate in order to return freedom of expression at long last to the unhappy people of Spain.

When that has been done, it should be borne in mind that it is Franco who has been banned from the international conferences, not Spain. Having long

---

[564] Editorial. Text probably by Camus, continuing the themes of previous editorials on Spain, in particular those of November 21 and December 10, 1944, pp. 116 and 137.

[565] See the previous editorial.

[566] Don Juan, count of Barcelona, was the son of Alphonse XIII, who was exiled from Spain when the Republic was established in 1931 and abdicated in its favor.

[567] On these points, see the editorial of November 21, 1944, p. 116.

fought for the common cause, suffered in silence, and set an example of pride, the people of that poor but great country have won a place among the world's democracies. They would bring to the conferences the voice of honor and of the justice for which they shed so much blood. It is a voice that the French will understand better than others, since they can share with Spain memories of misfortune and the anguish of lost liberty.

August 8, 1945[568]

The world is what it is, which isn't much. This is what everyone has known since yesterday, thanks to the formidable concert that the radio, newspapers, and news agencies have unleashed on the subject of the atomic bomb. Along with much other enthusiastic commentary, we have been given to understand that any average-sized city can be totally leveled by a bomb the size of a soccer ball. American, British, and French newspapers have poured forth a steady stream of elegant dissertations concerning the future, the past, the inventors, the cost, the peaceful uses and military implications, the political consequences, and even the independent character of the atomic bomb.[569] We can sum it all up in a sentence: the civilization of the machine has just achieved its ultimate degree of savagery.[570] A choice is going to have to be made in the fairly near future between collective suicide and the intelligent utilization of scientific discoveries.

In the meantime, one has the right to think that there is something indecent about celebrating in this way a discovery that has been put to its first use by the most formidable destructive rage that man has exhibited for centuries. In a world that has torn itself apart with every conceivable instrument of violence and shown itself incapable of exerting any control while remaining indifferent to justice or even mere human happiness, the fact that science has dedicated itself to organized murder will surprise no one, except perhaps an unrepentant idealist.

These discoveries must be reported and commented on for what they are and announced to the world so that man has a proper idea of his destiny. It is intolerable for these terrible revelations to be wrapped in picturesque or humorous essays.

Even before now it was not easy to breathe in this tormented world. Now we find ourselves confronted with a new source of anguish, which has every likelihood of proving fatal. Mankind has probably been given its last chance, and the papers have seized on this as a pretext for a special edition: "Extra! Extra! Read

---

[568] Editorial. Reprinted in *Actuelles*, chapter on "Morality and Politics."

[569] Study of the newspaper accounts is indeed edifying: they consist essentially of scientific articles about the making of the bomb and about the atom.

[570] This unequivocal judgment stands virtually alone among press commentaries on the use of the atomic bomb. In *Le Figaro* of August 10, under the title "The Bomb," François Mauriac did speak of "universal anguish," "destructive genius," and "love of death pushed to a climax." But his article, which included references to Renan, Anatole France, Edmond Rostand, and Francis Jammes, has none of the vigor of Camus'.

all about it!" But surely the subject deserves a moment's reflection and far more than a moment's silence.

There are also other reasons for withholding our applause for the futuristic romance that the newspapers have been laying before us. When we see Reuters' diplomatic editor proclaiming that this new invention nullifies or renders obsolete the decisions made at Potsdam[571] and makes it pointless to worry about whether the Russians are in Königsberg or in Turkey at the Dardanelles, we cannot avoid drawing the conclusion that in this fine chorus there lurk certain intentions having nothing to do with the objectivity of pure science.

Let there be no mistake about our meaning. If the Japanese surrender now that Hiroshima has been destroyed and they face the intimidation of the atomic bomb, we will rejoice.[572] Nevertheless, we shrink from using news as grave as this as a basis for any decision other than to argue still more energetically in favor of a genuine international organization in which the rights of the great powers will not outweigh the rights of small and medium-sized nations, and in which war, a scourge now made definitive by the fruits of the human mind alone, will no longer be decided by the appetites or doctrines of any one state.

Given the terrifying prospects that mankind now faces, we see even more clearly than before that the battle for peace is the only battle worth fighting. This is no longer a prayer but an order that must make its way up from peoples to their governments: it is the order to choose once and for all between hell and reason.

August 14, 1945[573]

We previously indicated our slight anxiety on the subject of the strategic bases that President Truman has asked for.[574] This was more in the nature of a question than a protest, for which, given the current state of our information, we have no basis. President Truman announced that the United States would seek to negotiate treaties granting it the military bases it needs around the world. Since it is likely that some of those bases will be on French territory, we feel that the issue at least deserves our attention and that in any case it cannot be resolved unilaterally, as Mr. Truman thinks. As is often the case these days, the interests of France and those of international democracy converge on this point, or so it seems to us.

---

[571] On the Potsdam conference, see the editorial of August 4, n. 561, p. 233.

[572] Hiroshima was bombed on the night of August 6, Nagasaki on August 9. On the same day, the Soviet Union declared war on Japan, which offered to surrender on August 10. The surrender was accepted by the Allies on August 11 and went into effect on August 14.

[573] Editorial. Text probably by Camus.

[574] In the editorial of August 11, devoted to Japan's surrender offer (and which appears not to have been written by Camus), we read the following: "This is not the time or place to express the hope that America will not give in to the heady intoxication of this power or to question the wisdom of the strategic bases that President Truman asked for yesterday. Today's events compel us to set our anxieties and worries aside, at least for a while."

On this point, M. Emile Buré characterizes us as doctrinaire pacifists in
L'Ordre and, even though the minor anxiety we expressed was contained in an
article praising our transatlantic allies, accuses us of denouncing American imperialism.[575] M. Buré does not share our opinion, and he minces no words in saying so. Indeed, he states his position so bluntly that we have to pinch ourselves
to make sure we're not dreaming. Indeed, M. Buré reveals that, while spending
the war in New York, he wrote in a Gaullist newspaper[576] that our country could
offer, in exchange for American aid for our colonies, to grant the Americans
sovereign authority over naval bases in those same colonies. And that is not all:
"An American industrialist of French ancestry objected at the time that I was
making this offer before being asked, and I argued that in this case it was good
to make the offer in order to make sure that what was asked would not be too
great to give."

After that, however, he continues to cast the editors of *Combat* in the role of
doctrinaire pacifists and unrepentant internationalists. M. Buré, who is neither
doctrinaire nor pacifist and who has a clear idea of French policy, begins by offering up strategic bases for which no one has asked and which he is unauthorized
to give. We are most definitely living in a strange world, in which the people who
mock pacifists are the same people who gladly give away pieces of their country,
in which Gaullist newspapers publish things that would make General de Gaulle
jump out of his skin, and in which French journalists receive lessons in propri-
ety from American industrialists, who at least have the virtue of remembering
their roots.

Nevertheless, we will not spurn the title "pacifists" that M. Buré so scornfully
ascribes to us. In daily struggle throughout the Occupation, the pacifists at *Combat* formed an idea of war and peace that is not necessarily one that could have
been formed in New York. It is on the basis of that idea that they feel entitled to
be pacifists. They grew familiar with and accepted the responsibilities and duties
of war. We are naïve enough to think that peace will be achieved when democracy is established not only within nations but among them. We are not now
moving toward such an international society, because the era is in fact one of
imperialism. M. Buré notwithstanding, there is an American imperialism, just as
there are Russian and British imperialisms. We are not so naïve as to think that
those imperialisms can be ignored or even to deny that they are in some ways
justified. Nevertheless, we hold that we are under no compulsion to choose
among those imperialisms and to hand our bases over to the power of our choice,

---

[575] In *L'Ordre*, a political and business daily that resumed publication in February 1945, Emile Buré, the
paper's editor, quoted a passage from President Truman's speech on the need for present and future
American bases in his August 12–13 editorial and then added: "Whereupon our doctrinaire pacifists from
Combat began sharpening their knives for an attack on nascent or, rather, growing American imperialism.
We will not follow their lead." Buré stated that America needed colonial expansion in order to complete
the revolution that went hand in hand with the war now ending and that its request for bases was legitimate. He thought that it would be quite acceptable for France to offer the United States bases in its
colonies in exchange for American aid for the colonies.
[576] Buré pointed out that he edited the paper, which was called *France-Amérique*.

even if such a choice were to gain us certain economic advantages. The best course open to us is to plead unremittingly in favor of an international democracy that will harm the interests of no one while fostering solidarity among nations. That is how we think we can best serve the cause of world peace, the precariousness of which we sense even more acutely than before, if such a thing is possible, now that the war is over. The contrast with the example of M. Buré shows that our way of serving the cause of peace is also the best way of serving France and preserving her honor.

August 15, 1945[577]

Yesterday the *Washington Times Herald*[578] declared that "the United States did not defeat Japan in order to return lost European colonies to their former masters." It was not the first American paper to make such a statement, nor, assuredly, will it be the last. The paper made it clear that it was referring to Hong Kong, the Dutch Indies, and Indochina. Now we know where we stand. We do not know the British or Dutch views on the matter, but in regard to Indochina we surely have something to say.

On this subject it is not easy to give shape to the contradictory emotions we feel. Nevertheless, we have stated our position regarding the rights of colonized peoples and our duties toward them with sufficient clarity that we can try to organize our reactions without opening ourselves up to the suspicion that we are giving in to imperialist prejudice. What is at issue for us in this case is not at all the right of the peoples of the East to independence. The issue is solely to decide the degree to which that independence is to become a reality and whether idealism cannot be used here as the businessman's best ambassador.

In the world we live in, one can lay it down as a principle that a nation without economic potential cannot be a free nation. In the world of San Francisco,[579] the European colonies in the East have no choice other than to accept the political stewardship of Europe or the economic stewardship of the United States. It may be that ill will toward Europe and the grave errors of the European system of colonization are driving the peoples of the East to prefer the second of these forms of servitude to the first, at least for the time being. But they will soon come to see that the one leads to the other. In any case, given the world that has been

---

[577] Editorial. Text probably by Camus.

[578] The editorial of August 16 (which cannot be attributed to Camus on the basis of style) gives further details about the *Washington Times Herald*. "This paper is the mouthpiece of an isolationist and reactionary newspaper trust, the Mac Cormick Press [*sic:* The group's name was actually McCormick Press, named for its owner, press baron Robert McCormick] . . . which opposed American rearmament before Pearl Harbor, only reluctantly assented to America's entry into the present conflict, and launched multiple attacks on all its country's allies."

[579] The San Francisco Conference, which took place from April 25 to June 26, 1945, drafted the United Nations Charter in the wake of the Dumbarton Oaks and Yalta Conferences. It thus established a new world order, which was not the order advocated by Camus and *Combat*.

offered to us, it is impossible to settle for the satisfactions of idealism as our share while others reserve for themselves the more concrete benefits of realism.

The real solution is one that will serve the cause of the colonized peoples without redounding to the benefit of any other nation. The goal is not to replace one system of colonization with another. It is to get to the heart of the problem, that is, the political and economic conditions that today make any just solution impossible. In other words, what needs to be reformed is not Hong Kong or Indochina but the world created by the San Francisco Conference itself. Whether dealing with Germany or the Far East, one is regularly forced to the same conclusion. As long as there is no international order based on equality and cooperation among peoples, no order in which economic wealth is distributed among all nations, the world's great problems will be susceptible only of solutions that are imperfect or dangerous when they are not downright scandalous.

August 17, 1945[580]

Now that the war is over, we have time to think about the peace. This is perhaps the only thing today for which it is worth mobilizing ourselves once again. To be sure, there is also the fate of France, but the fate of France is inseparable from the peace, because it is inseparable from the world, because solitude is a word that no longer makes sense, and because the world no longer consists of this nation and that nation but is more like a great suffering body in need of healing.

Neither France nor Europe will survive another war: this is a truth of which we must persuade ourselves. In the case of a new conflagration, neither will even have a chance to act. As things currently stand, Europe can no longer be anything but a battlefield. This calls for deep reflection.

Since it proved impossible to establish the basis of a true international democracy in San Francisco,[581] we can say that tomorrow's conflicts will inevitably be conflicts of empires. And we can predict that the causes of these imperial conflicts are likely to reside in Europe. Since we are facing struggles for influence, let us acknowledge that Europe has unfortunately been fertile ground for such struggles, because of its divisions as well as its riches. Flanked on one side by the Slavic world and on the other by the Anglo-Saxon world, it is equally tempting to both empires; it is divided between them; and, with historical inevitability, it is tempted to model itself after one or the other.

Therein lies the immediate danger. The point is not whether it is desirable for Europe to be Soviet or American. It is to understand that to the extent it gives itself over totally to either one of these influences, it will be inviting a counterattack by the other. If the Anglo-Saxon influence obliges Europe to slow the movement of the deep social reforms its people want and allow reactionary

---

[580] Editorial. Text probably by Camus.
[581] On the San Francisco Conference, see the editorial of August 15 and n. 579, p. 239.

cliques to have their way, the Soviet Union will intervene. If the influence of the Soviet Union compels Europe to transform its reconstruction effort in a way that crushes all freedom, the United States will intervene. Nothing can change that situation one iota, and the fate of our continent depends on doing whatever it takes to achieve a synthesis in which the civilizations of the East and the Atlantic can find common ground, and which they will respect.

The peace of the world depends in large part on how quickly the European spirit succeeds in reconciling justice with liberty. As each of us reflects on these difficult issues, we must be ever mindful of the immense consequences that the resolution of this problem would entail. We must approach our internal debates in this deeply tragic perspective. Elections are one thing, and no doubt an important one.[582] But how ridiculous it is to believe that we would be able to confine our action to these futile debates, when the fate of the world depends on a formula that has yet to be found. If Europe is to turn its mind to the search for this formula, France has its place in this quest. We would like that place to be in the vanguard. And we would like to be able to say of this admirable and disconcerting country that after a long history in which it has seen everything, from victories without posterity to defeat overcome, it has again found the strength to give the world its final word and win the peace.

August 22, 1945[583]

The first National Assembly of the Press held its opening session in Paris yesterday. The press has a leading role to play in public life, yet problems that go to the heart of its activities arouse little interest on the part of the general public. It is a good thing that the assembly immediately turned its attention to the issues of paper and distribution. Even if the public evinces little interest in these matters, the investigations undertaken by the assembly will nevertheless teach the French that what is commonly called freedom of the press depends on many factors, not all of which are under the control of journalists themselves. In particular, people may finally learn that the absurd paper policy[584] that the ministry of information has had in place for more than a year now has undermined the theoretical freedom that journalists acquired during the insurrection.

We will not comment further on this aspect of things, however. We would like to express just one wish, namely, that after looking into the technical problems that are so important for our work, the Assembly of the Press not disband without taking up the fundamental problem of resistance journalism: the method of

---

[582] The election ordinances had just been published. Cantonal elections were set for September 23 and 30. General elections, along with a referendum to choose between a return to the constitution of 1875 and the election of a Constituent Assembly with or without full powers, were set for October 21, 1945.
[583] Editorial. Text very likely by Camus.
[584] See the communiqué included in the note to the article "Images of Occupied Germany" (June 30–July 1), p. 229.

information. A free press is a press that polices itself. If we are to be superior to the prewar press, we must be able to criticize ourselves.[585]

Have we completed the anticipated revolution in this regard? Certainly not. A look at the Paris evening papers is enough to show that most of them take the old *Paris-Soir* as their model![586] One has only to glance at their huge headlines, out of all proportion to their actual news content, or read their articles, written in the indicative even though the dispatch they are reporting on is in the subjunctive, or notice the emphasis on the pungent detail at the expense of the real news. The morning papers are on the whole more modest. But the newspapers least threatened by the temptation of the sensational are the newspapers of opinion. On the other hand, they are more vulnerable to political passions, and that is true of us as much as of our sister publications. They can and sometimes do lose their balance when they become more concerned with their own particular truth rather that the truth in general and more keen to denounce the flaws of their adversaries than to point out their strengths or acknowledge their good faith.

Only through careful reflection on these problems and stumbling blocks can journalism regain the dignity it lost through years of disingenuous and spineless compromise. The public still needs newspapers, but the more people need them, the warier they become. The Assembly of the Press would do well to deal frankly with this problem, and it could demonstrate the good intentions of the new journalists by elaborating a professional code of conduct and establishing a board of review to look into serious violations of that code.

There can be no doubt that the French press will not be free without paper. Nor can there be any doubt that even with paper it will not be free unless it sets the conditions of its own freedom. In particular, it is difficult to imagine an independent press if journalists hesitate to write what they think on occasions when they are sure of being mercilessly insulted by thirty newspapers obedient to the orders of a political party.

August 23, 1945[587]

The Radical Party congress has taken it upon itself to save the Republic.[588] Everyone knows, of course, what superhuman efforts the party has already made to that end, what laudable enthusiasm it displayed in passing the Daladier

---

[585] In the interview Camus gave to *Caliban* in August 1951, "One of the Finest Professions I Know," he said, "This profession forces you to judge yourself" (*Essais*, p. 1565).

[586] Camus was of course contemptuous of this paper, of which he obtained firsthand knowledge in 1940 and which remained for him the symbol of bad journalism: see the editorial of September 1, 1944, and n. 36, p. 24.

[587] Editorial. Text quite likely intended as a follow-up to that of June 27, p. 227. Reprinted in *Actuelles*.

[588] The Radical Party congress took place on August 20. *Combat* published only brief and highly critical reports on August 22 and 23. On August 22, a report on the speeches of Daladier and Herriot was introduced with the following sentence: "Their task seems to have been to justify their personal politics and that of the Radical Party."

edicts,[589] and what a rare spirit of self-sacrifice its deputies showed in bowing before Philippe Pétain[590] as they had previously bowed before Gaston Doumergue.[591] So much sacrifice and devotion entitle the Radicals to treat the resistance in a cavalier manner today and to extol instead the virtues of M. Daladier and M. Herriot.[592]

They are indeed back, and they return quite pleased with themselves. M. Daladier did not shrink from mentioning Munich.[593] Minds given to objectivity and not averse to forgetting might well grant that he proved that he had no choice but to go to Munich as one goes to Canossa.[594] It then follows that M. Daladier was explaining how the superior political minds of the Third Republic managed to lead a country that had only just emerged victorious from one war to the brink of another through a series of capitulations. But when M. Daladier summed up his personal political history by saying that France could be proud of what it had tried to accomplish back then, he must forgive us for thinking that he carried his argument one step too far.

For France is not in fact proud of what it tried to do back then. And if so many men joined a struggle they often felt to be hopeless in the years between 1940 and 1944, it was precisely because they were not proud of what M. Daladier's France had done and felt that something needed to be fixed.

If M. Daladier had any imagination whatsoever, he surely would not have written the word "proud." Whatever his intentions may have been, he must have realized that that adjective would wound many men for whom pride was a matter of deep concern and who for a long time suffered in silence because they could not think of the Czechs or the workers of Vienna[595] without an unbearable sense of shame. And if M. Daladier, even lacking imagination, had exhibited the

[589] In *Alger-Républicain*, Camus had denounced the policies adopted by the Daladier government in April 1938. For his severe criticism, see the articles in *Fragments d'un combat*, I, pp. 229–238. On Daladier, see the editorial of September 12, 1944, n. 63, p. 35.

[590] On July 10, 1940, two-thirds of Radical deputies, 171 in all, voted in favor of granting Pétain full powers. Twenty-seven voted against. Herriot himself abstained along with nine others, and thirty-six were absent. The day before, Edouard Herriot, who was then president of the Chamber of Deputies, called upon all the deputies to rally around Marshal Pétain: "In its distress our nation has rallied around Marshal Pétain, whose name we all venerate. Let us be careful not to disrupt the harmony that has developed under his authority." Quoted by Olivier Wieviorka, *Les Orphelins de la République*, p. 56. See also ibid., pp. 147–148. On Herriot, see the editorial of May 12, 1945, n. 476, p. 197.

[591] Gaston Doumergue (1863–1937) represented the Cartel des Gauches and served as president of the Republic from 1924 to 1931. He then retired from public life but was called back, with support from the Radical Party, to serve as prime minister in 1934 after the February 6 riot. His proposal for a constitutional reform that would have strengthened the executive aroused worry and led to his resignation a few months later.

[592] Daladier and Herriot were frequent Camus targets: see, among others, the editorial of May 12, 1945, p. 197.

[593] The Munich accord that Daladier signed abandoned Czechoslovakia to Hitler yet failed to preserve peace. See the editorial of September 12, 1944, p. 35.

[594] A castle in Tuscany where King Henry IV of Germany begged forgiveness of Pope Gregory VII in 1077.

[595] Allusion to the crushing of the workers' militias that demonstrated in Vienna in February 1934 under the government of Chancellor Dollfuss.

appropriate modesty, he would have recognized that the right thing to ask of France was not that it should rejoice in what was in fact a surrender but that it should feel incapable of taking pride in such a thing.

Obviously, though, that is not the issue for these somber ghosts. For them the issue is the upcoming elections, and M. Daladier cannot run in his district without portraying black as white and Munich as a glorious victory. That is what accounts for his rage to justify himself in opposition to France, as well as his condescending readiness to judge the new state of affairs in the country. M. Herriot took a haughty attitude toward the Fourth Republic. The speakers exhibited disdain for the young men who showed so little respect for so many glorious parliamentary triumphs. Those young men were after all mere irregulars, whereas the Radical Party in M. Herriot's henceforth immortal phrase is the "heavy infantry" of the Republic.

What could be done, however, when the heavy infantry failed to deliver and its generals surrendered? There was no choice but the difficult one of building another army and saving the nation from the disaster precipitated by the infantry's retreat. Those irregulars turned out not to be such awful fellows after all. And they aren't accusing M. Daladier of the crime of having slowly strangled the Republic in 1938 while at the same time besmirching its honor. Nor are they asking M. Herriot to explain the homage to Pétain that he personally penned. All these things were only to be expected, of course, and we're not about to be persnickety about them. We aren't asking these men for any explanations, excuses, or briefs in their own defense. All we ask of them is a little modesty and a lot of silence.

Of course the Radical Party has also taken the liberty of defending democratic freedoms. So there we are, on a footing of equality with them. Yet when we contemplate what preceded this declaration and note that the congress stated its desire to free the French from Marxist enslavement even as M. Herriot was joining the Communist-leaning M.U.R.F.,[596] it is easy to see that we are not talking about the same freedom: the Radical Party's freedom has to do only with the election campaign. As to the other freedom, the real freedom, the one that cannot do without either pride or honor, we feel that we have the wherewithal to defend it without the Radicals and, if need be, in opposition to M. Daladier and M. Herriot.

August 24, 1945[597]

At the Radical Party congress, M. Herriot complained that he was attacked in *Combat* for having dared to say that France stood in need of moral reform.[598] The word "dared" is a bit excessive. For the courage in question is one that we

---

[596] The M.U.R.F., or Unified Movement of the French Resistance, was organized at the behest of the Communists. Herriot, who had been a colonel in the Red Army since 1933 and who was liberated from his German prison by the Red Army, served on the movement's governing council. He was also honorary chairman of the Union de la Jeunesse Républicaine de France, an umbrella organization of Communist youth groups.
[597] Editorial. Text very likely by Camus, following up the previous day's editorial.
[598] In one of his interventions at the congress, at which he was elected president of the Radical Party, Herriot declared: "I will respond first to the attack of a newspaper that previously criticized me for having

demonstrated before he did, and we therefore have every right to tell him that it doesn't carry much weight. What is more, M. Herriot is not correct in what he says. He was attacked in *Combat* not for having said that France stood in need of moral reform but for having proposed the Third Republic as a model of morality. It was possible at that time to believe that if the French needed lessons in morality, it was certainly not the great parliamentarians of the Third Republic who were qualified to give it to them.

When M. Herriot pretends to deplore the anonymous authorship of our articles, he is resorting to rhetorical sleight of hand, and of the worst sort. For our editorials, whose authors are known to everyone in the world of journalism and which are the daily voice of our newspaper, are the collective responsibility of the *Combat* team.[599] In regard to M. Herriot in particular, that team is only too glad to accept responsibility for them.

M. Herriot is also wrong to mock the new press, for it is thanks to the new press that he does not need to address his complaint to a managing editor who had nothing to do with offending him and can deal instead with an editor who knows what he's talking about. In the "purification" press that so delights the president of the Radical Party, the people who write the articles are also responsible for what they write. That is one reform that the Radical ministers invariably forgot to include in their platform, so attached were they to all sorts of moralities, including some dubious ones. In any case, this reform will enable M. Herriot to demand satisfaction from us. We urge him most strenuously to do so.

Of course it is perfectly clear that he wouldn't dare. He talked about it, to be sure, but you have to speak in a stentorian voice when you're addressing a Radical congress, and it doesn't get you very far. M. Herriot demonstrated similar consistency when he both expressed his admiration for Pétain and nevertheless contributed to his condemnation.[600] Who would care about that today? The great moral rule of our former parliamentarians is in effect that no commitment is ever binding.

In any event, we shall add to our crimes. The men who fought so that the Radical Party could once again meet in congress and offer its apologia for Munich think that they, too, have the right to profit from our newly won freedoms to speak their minds. Criticism of individuals is of little importance right now. But it is quite true that it would be the ultimate misfortune of France if the

dared to say that France stood in need of moral reform. In the old days, you could ask some poor devil of a managing editor to justify an attack. I thought that nowadays authors would have the courage to sign their articles." For the original criticism, see the editorial of June 27, p. 227, reprinted in *Actuelles*.

599 The editorial signed by Camus on February 9, p. 170, had already proclaimed the solidarity of the editorial writers.

600 On July 31, *Combat* reported on Herriot's testimony for the prosecution at the trial of Pétain. In fact, Herriot did not oppose the Vichy regime for the first two years. It was Laval's decision in August 1942 to eliminate the two Chambers (whose bureaus were still functioning) that led him to change his mind. On this point see Olivier Wieviorka, op. cit., pp. 277–280.

nation of shopkeepers that generations of professional politicians created for us were to make a comeback. Never again do we want to see the likes of these men, petty in their virtues as in their vices, grave in their speeches but frivolous in their actions, satisfied with themselves but dissatisfied with others. The years that lie ahead of us will not be a time for banquets and speeches. If France does not come up with better men and better ideas than in the past, it will sink into a mediocrity worse than death. The surprising thing is that M. Herriot can still wax indignant over the fact that we feel this so strongly. The astonishing thing, to put it bluntly, is that along with so many others he feels no compunctions about returning to public life.

To tell the truth, though, astonishment of this sort requires a certain naïveté. When a class has so lost its ability to discern human qualities that it can speak of M. Herriot as a possible successor to General de Gaulle, one can only tip one's hat and wait. The judgment of the people will come. It will prove to these men that France has had it with them and that the time has come for this country, on pain of death, to elect leaders who inspire something more than a contemptuous smile.

August 26–27, 1945[601]

We have proved to be excellent prophets: M. Herriot's words turned out to be as empty as we said they were. He complained to the Radical Party congress about not being able to sue the people responsible for slandering him at *Combat*, and despite the fact that we provided him with full details, he has decided not to do anything other than write an article for *La Dépêche de Paris*.[602] Anyone who reads it can see that it doesn't amount to much. Indeed, M. Herriot is still complaining that he can't find the name of our paper's managing editor. This is because he is so feckless in everything he does, including reading. Otherwise he would

---

[601] Editorial. Text very likely by Camus, following up the editorials of August 23 and 24.

[602] *La Dépêche de Paris*, which began publishing in February 1945, was the successor to the underground paper *Patrie et liberté*. Billing itself "a republican daily paper," it was an instrument of the Radical Party. In its August 26–27 issue, Herriot published a "Response to *Combat*" with the subtitle "For the Team Player." Herriot said that he was not shocked to be attacked but rejected the "prohibitions on returning to public life" issued by *Combat*. He added: "Though intended to be insulting, all of this is simply ridiculous. And what pedantic poverty! The young thinker who seeks to beat me down strikes me as having more clichés [i.e., slides] in his collection than an old photographer. . . . 'We are a team,' the courageous pamphleteer adds. . . . Don't exaggerate your notoriety. . . . Despite your revolutionary pretensions, my Radical friends and I are well aware that you are serving the cause of the right with your hostility to those who defended the Republic in desperate times and who did so without wearing masks. You will never be anything but speculative revolutionaries, amateurs without influence over the people. The moment a rapprochement among democrats seems possible, you denounce it. . . . You are only serving the enemies of the Republic." Herriot even went so far as to accuse *Combat* of "feebly imitating" the *Action française*. Claiming to be defending deportees and prisoners from attacks by "the team player," he wrote: "Ah, what a resonant name: the team! So that is the new formula that you want to substitute for the old parties. Some difference!"

have found the name he was looking for in the place appointed by law, where it appears every day.[603]

That said, and to spare M. Herriot the difficulty he creates for himself by avoiding the real issue, we are going to give him the names of the members of the editorial committee of *Combat*: Pascal Pia, Albert Camus, Marcel Gimont, and Albert Ollivier. These are names with which M. Herriot is unfamiliar, because these men are not involved in politics and never will be. As surprising as it may seem to M. Herriot, they do not deem themselves indispensable to their country and will not be running in the next election. But that is why they feel as they do. And there will be at least a few free journalists to say publicly to M. Herriot and his ilk that they are useless and indeed, in the present situation, harmful.

Now that everything is clear, perhaps M. Herriot will stop treating this controversy in a way that allows him to evade the real issues. For the president of the Radicals, who as he says has a thick skin and who thickened it still more in all sorts of situations that we take pride in having avoided, is well versed in the art of avoiding embarrassing questions. We therefore need to confront him with facts he would rather not see.

What facts are those? We share with many others the view that politics as it was practiced by M. Herriot and his friends is a thing of the past. We want no more of them. Why? Because these men had plenty of time to show what they could do and even more what they could not do. And because, to put it bluntly, they never did and never will own up to their responsibilities. The frivolous way in which M. Herriot has returned to launch his election campaign after having congratulated Marshal Pétain on having made us a gift of his person is one indication of that.[604] Another is the fact that M. Herriot did not dare touch on that subject in his article.

We have still other reasons for our opinion. M. Herriot and his party have taken a rather haughty attitude toward the resistance. Their disdain is matched only by their bad conscience. We have always done what we had to do to make sure that resistance credentials not be mistaken for a badge of entitlement. Because of these we can be as firm as we are calm in saying to M. Herriot that no member of the resistance would have agreed to be rescued from the Germans by Pierre Laval.[605] This is because they had a clear idea of who they were and what their duty was.

In any case, these are the arguments that M. Herriot must refute if he wants to prove that our position is incorrect. Once again, however, we are certain that he won't. He will continue to shadowbox. He will again resort to his petty parliamentary ruses. He will speak emotionally about General de Gaulle while

[603] The name of Pascal Pia was indeed noted each day as "managing editor." There is also some contradiction in Herriot's allusion to the editorial writers as a "young thinker," which suggests that his identity is known, while at the same time reproaching him for writing anonymously.

[604] In June 1940 Pétain said, "I am making a gift of my person to France to assuage her misfortune."

[605] In August 1944 Laval had obtained Herriot's release in order to enlist his help in calling the Chamber of Deputies back into session. Herriot refused.

allowing fellow delegates to attack him for three days running and encouraging his friends to designate him, Edouard Herriot, the man who wrote admiring letters to Marshal Pétain, as the inevitable successor to the man of June 18. He will accuse us of furthering the right-wing agenda without fear of provoking our readers to laughter and without scruples about writing such a thing at the conclusion of a congress dedicated entirely to the repudiation of essential structural reforms.[606] To be frank, he will do as he has always done.

But we will also do as we have always done, and with all the requisite energy. M. Herriot insisted on maintaining a humorous tone throughout his article. We beg his pardon if we don't follow his lead. We have nothing against humor, except for the kind that comes at the end of campaign dinners, which some people say is contagious. For us, there are some subjects that can never again serve as a pretext for humor. There was a time when the spectacle of mediocrity in power served only to amuse crowds and edify sages. Since then, we have shed too many tears. No, we can no longer separate M. Herriot's France from the memory of our abjection. And surely he will be the only person in France who continues to find that amusing.

August 28, 1945[607]

Many readers have asked us to take a position on the upcoming election and indicate how they ought to vote. Although we do not feel very well qualified to guide voters through the labyrinth of electoral subtleties, we have no compunction about offering our advice in this particular case, because this is a vote for principles, not individuals. *Combat*'s position on these issues can be translated into practical advice quite readily.

Two questions have been put to the voters. First, they are asked whether they want a Constituent Assembly to be charged with the task of drafting a new constitution. They should know that if they say "no," they will be indicating a preference for a return to the Constitution of 1875. We think that the answer to this first question should be "yes." Why? First, because the Constitution of 1875 has outlived its usefulness: we know its defects and its qualities, and the former seem to us to outweigh the latter. Second, because, like it or not, approval of the Constitution of 1875 will be taken as a blank check by former members of parliament whom we no longer wish to see in government. (Voters would do well to ponder the fact that the Radical Party is calling for a "no" vote.)

The second question concerns the government's plans to modify the powers of the Constituent Assembly if the voters choose to have one. This plan actually incorporates the counterproposal submitted to the Consultative Assembly by

---

[606] The Radical Party congress called for a return to the Constitution of 1875 and prewar political institutions.

[607] Editorial. Text very likely by Camus.

M. Vincent Auriol[608] and M. Claude Bourdet.[609] To understand what is at issue here, you have to remember that the now-defunct Consultative Assembly clashed with the government over the principle of governmental responsibility. The Assembly wanted the government to be responsible to the future Constituent Assembly, while the government, seeking what it saw as desirable stability for its policies, rejected this demand. The Auriol-Bourdet counterproposal, which forms the essential basis of the text that will be laid before the voters, reconciles these two conflicting points of view. It establishes the principle of governmental responsibility, a crucial point for any republican, but it also sets forth provisions necessary to ensure ministerial stability. The Assembly can withdraw its confidence from the government, but it can do so only after a certain number of days of reflection. The government is still entirely responsible to the Assembly, but the Assembly must be fully aware of what it is doing when it exercises its sovereignty, and the government will not be at the mercy of a momentary whim. In any case, we believe that the answer to this second question ought to be "yes." (Bear in mind that the Radicals are recommending a "no" vote.)

The truth is that you have to wonder why unity was not achieved. Or, rather, you would have to wonder if you didn't know all too well how sausage gets made in politics. Because ultimately there are three things about which anyone who has given any thought to this country's woes would have to agree: 1. We need a new democracy. 2. It must be full democracy, which means that the government must be responsible to the people. 3. It must be an effective democracy, and in order for that to happen there must be no return to the ministerial instability that plagued the Third Republic.

A "yes" vote on both questions in the referendum preserves all three principles. No consideration of any individual or party outweighs this basic fact. In the days to come, some will try to hide this fact by offering their own interpretations along with the usual deceptions, campaign rhetoric, and partisan speeches. But every French citizen can hold fast to the basic principles that ought to guide his vote. The rest is of no importance.

August 30, 1945[610]

We beg the reader's indulgence if we begin today with a basic fact: there can no longer be any doubt that the postwar purge has not only failed in France but is now completely discredited.[611] The word "purge" itself was already rather distressing.

---

[608] Vincent Auriol (1884–1966) was an active member of the S.F.I.O. He served as a minister in the Popular Front government and was one of eighty deputies who refused to vote in favor of granting full powers to Pétain. He joined de Gaulle in London. Later he served as president of two Constituent Assemblies and then as president of the Republic from 1947 to 1954.

[609] Claude Bourdet, an important resistance leader, exercised his moral right to purchase the title "Combat" and continue publication of the newspaper.

[610] Editorial. Reprinted in *Actuelles*, chapter on "Morality and Politics."

[611] As early as January 5 Camus expressed his fear that the purge would fail and that reconstruction would therefore fail as well. See p. 163.

The actual thing became odious. It had only one chance of not ending that way, and that would have required that it be carried out in a way that was neither vengeful nor thoughtless. It seems that the straight path of justice is not easy to find amid the cries of hatred coming from one side and the special pleading of guilty consciences coming from the other. In any case, the failure is complete.

The reason for this is that politics got mixed up in it, with all its varieties of blindness. Too many people clamored for the death penalty, as if imprisonment at hard labor were an inconsequential punishment. By contrast, too many others screamed "terror" when sentences of a few years were meted out to those guilty of denunciations and other dishonorable acts. And we found ourselves powerless to do anything about either. Maybe the best thing for now is to do what we can to see to it that the more flagrant injustices do not further poison the atmosphere, which is already difficult for many people in France to breathe.

Today we want to talk about one of those injustices. The same court that condemned Albertini,[612] the L.V.F.[613] recruiter, to five years at hard labor, has sentenced the pacifist René Gérin, who wrote the literary column for *L'Œuvre* during the war, to eight years of the same. Neither logic nor justice can account for this. We here do not approve of René Gérin's politics. Total pacifism seems to us a poorly worked out position, and we now know that there inevitably comes a time when it can no longer be sustained. Nor do we approve of the fact that Gérin wrote for *L'Œuvre*, even on literary subjects.

Nevertheless, the punishment should be proportionate to the crime, and men should be judged for what they are. Hard labor is not an appropriate punishment for a few literary articles, even in an Occupation newspaper. In other respects, Gérin's position has never wavered. One need not share his views, but at least his pacifism was the logical consequence of a perfectly respectable concept of man. A society judges itself when, owing to a lack of clear definitions and ideas, it proves incapable of punishing genuine criminals and instead imprisons a man who only by accident found himself keeping company with phony pacifists who loved Hitlerism and not peace. Can a society that wants to make itself over and claims to be in the process of doing so afford to overlook the basic need for clear distinctions?

Gérin did not denounce anyone, nor did he participate in any of the enemy's undertakings. If his literary collaboration with *L'Œuvre* was deemed worthy of punishment, then the punishment should have been proportioned to the crime. An exaggerated sentence of the sort just handed down fixes nothing. It merely fosters the suspicion that the verdict was the judgment not of the nation but of a class. It humiliates an individual without doing anyone any good. It discredits a policy, to everyone's detriment.

---

[612] Georges Albertini, an associate of Marcel Déat, under whom he served as chief of staff at the ministry of labor and as secretary general of the Rassemblement National Populaire, the collaborationist, pro-fascist party created by Déat. He wrote for *L'Atelier*, a collaborationist paper.

[613] The L.V.F., or Legion of French Volunteers against Bolshevism, was established shortly after Germany attacked the Soviet Union in July 1941 and recruited French volunteers to fight on the eastern front.

In any case, this sentence cries out to be reduced, not only so as to spare a man suffering disproportionate to his mistakes but also to preserve justice itself and to make it, in this one case at least, respectable. Although René Gérin was not in our camp, it seems to us that on this matter resistance opinion ought to be with us, in order to save whatever still can be saved in this realm.

September 1, 1945[614]

The postwar has begun. A year has passed since the liberation of France. First Germany, then Japan, fell to their knees. Justice has not yet arrived, but we have at least emerged from an abject condition in which injustice reigned. No sooner had France emerged from the insurrection than it began its yearlong effort to breathe normally again. We aren't quite there yet, but we're well on our way. On the eve of the elections, we can say that we have turned a corner, and it is time to offer an assessment of the past difficult year.

It might not be a bad idea for each of us to contribute the results of his own experience to this collective assessment. For instance, a newspaper like this one, which deliberately set out to become one of the voices of the new France, needs to ask itself what it accomplished in the past year. For reasons of space, we will confine our comments to just one aspect of the question.

We cannot emphasize too strongly that our experience has been limited. Our ambitions were restrained. We believed that each French citizen should try to innovate in his or her own way. Our job was to report the news. We had to break with past practice in a domain where the past had done a great deal of harm. We had to create the conditions necessary for honest reporting and objective discussion. As to the latter, we believed that it would be possible to create a climate in which the various tendencies of French political life could confront one another without clashing. Our idea was not, as some believed and others still fear, to rival Marx and Christ. It was not our intention to make fools of ourselves. Being neither Communists nor Christians, we simply wanted to make dialogue possible by pointing out differences and highlighting similarities. In this respect, our year of work has ended in abject failure.

We tried, for instance, to engage in dialogue with the Communists. We still remember the long editorial in which we tried to set forth our hesitations and our sympathies as honestly as we could.[615] We received no response. But a few weeks later, on a subject of no importance at all, they turned on us, even though we had tried to strike a certain tone, one that we know touches us personally when it comes from an adversary (and we are not really adversaries at all!). But they would have none of it.

---

[614] Editorial. Text very likely by Camus. This rather somber assessment no doubt reflects the general sentiment of the *Combat* staff, but the references to the editorial of October 7 and to the polemic with Mauriac argue in favor of attributing it to Camus.

[615] The reference is probably to the editorial of October 7, 1944, p. 62, which was later reprinted in *Actuelles*.

We then tried to engage in dialogue with the Catholics, or at any rate with one Catholic, M. François Mauriac. Admittedly, some foolish things were said on both sides, but the exchange got off to a good start; dialogue seemed possible. It ended when M. Mauriac wrote an article in a tone that reduced us to silence.[616]

We did not conclude from these experiences that others were making dialogue impossible. We concluded, rather, that we had yet to find the words needed to bring us together, words that would have united us without requiring us to renounce our differences. Despite our provisional failure, we remain convinced that this country and this world cannot be saved until they find the right words, the right vocabulary. We are all still shading our meaning, or at any rate hurling back and forth words that each of us interprets differently. People sometimes tell us that the world needs to be made over. That may be true, but we cannot make the world new until we have given it a new lexicon. Let the realists stop shouting: the new dictionary we need is being written little by little in the blood of warfare and the clamor of revolution. Our one hope is this, that a little thought might go a long way toward preventing a lot of bloodshed.

The conditions under which journalists operate do not always lend themselves to deep thought. Journalists do what they can, and if they inevitably fail, at least they can toss a few ideas into the air for others to develop into more efficient instruments. The ideal might be for the country's political journalists to return for a time to voluntary silence, but that is impossible. History forbids it. In this respect, French public life will no doubt continue to be what it is, namely, an arena in which powerful orthodoxies confront one another while a few solitary voices try to make themselves heard.

In other respects, the signs are more comforting. The letters a newspaper receives tell it not about the state of public opinion but about the opinions of its readers. Still, a certain tone and a certain set of basic requirements about which everyone agrees provide useful information. Thus we know that thousands of men and women join us in our fundamental demand. We are increasingly persuaded that the cruel games of traditional politics go over the heads of the people and do not correspond to their desires. And it is the people who are right. It is the people who, by exerting their will, will slowly but surely save France. Yes, we have boundless confidence in the people of this country. That is the one great certainty that we take from this first year of work.

The rest will come when it comes. Men toil, suffer, insult and maim one another in pursuit of a goal they do not always clearly perceive. But that goal always resides in man himself: in fact, it is man himself, and his liberation. The entire history of the world is the history of freedom. We knew this a year ago in the great exultation of the insurrection. Since then, we have come to know it a little better, and we also know that the long quest for freedom is an infernal struggle in which even good intentions can inflict wounds. This new knowledge is nothing to be sneezed at: we have learned we must think hard, be wary of our own impulses, and not give up hope in others. Hence we conclude that, as

---

[616] See the article of January 11, p. 168.

disappointing as this past year has been, it was nevertheless fruitful. Tomorrow will be better.

November 15, 1945

France is in a state of siege.[617] It is in a state of economic siege, and as long as each of us fails to notice this, defeat is certain. What we must decide first is not whether we should adopt a policy of power or prestige, whether we should serve one bloc and oppose another or assert our independence as a nation. Regardless of whether we think in terms of power or alliance, of whether we wish to be solitary or in solidarity, we need the means to make good on our intentions. Either we will rebuild this nation, or we will cease to exist as a fact to be reckoned with.

That is why no Frenchman would underestimate the importance of the composition of the new government or the astonishing partisan disputes that preceded it. Indeed, what we must do now is utter a cry of alarm, and we must do it long enough and loud enough to make the country and its representatives aware of what lies ahead and of the responsibilities they now face.

What does this mean? It means that there is as little point in shouting "Program first!" as there is in shouting "de Gaulle first!" The government's program must contribute to reconstruction if it is to amount to anything. And even if it is very good, it will be of no avail unless it is clearly explained. What we need as much as a good program is a good ministry. It is on this score that General de Gaulle and the parties will be challenged.

Because this ministry will not be good, and therefore the program will not be useful and reconstruction will fail and the country will come apart, if the government is not united by acceptance of a common set of responsibilities. This ministry will not be good if a liberal minister of finance refuses to give a Socialist minister of national economy the means to put the country back on its feet, or if the department of war siphons off for itself what a Communist might have tried to funnel into public health. The parties must fully commit themselves, because the country will not allow them to shirk their responsibilities, nor will the times.

Now that General de Gaulle has agreed to form a new government, the next time is to determine the conditions that will ensure that the government's work will be as effective as possible. We know in advance that it will not be completely effective, and that steps perilous to democracy will need to be taken. How can the dangers be avoided? France must above all be saved from disaster.

---

[617] Editorial very likely by Camus. This is the only text to which Camus can possibly be referring in his November 19 letter to Pascal Pia. Unlike other *Combat* editorials of this period, which were very negative, this one proposes concrete measures, and one cannot help but notice the formula "solitaires ou solidaires," which is repeated in the singular in "Jonas ou l'Artiste au travail." Recall, however, that Camus, in this same letter, protested the "softening and confusing corrections" to which his text had been subjected. It is impossible to say exactly what he was referring to, however.

Our opinion—which we call upon others to ponder in an appropriately serious way—is that General de Gaulle should combine the key ministries in a sort of war cabinet, to which the other ministries will be subordinate. Foreign affairs, finance, national economy, and interior will coordinate their efforts with reconstruction as their objective. And they will be jointly responsible for the results. Since the country has designated three large parties to represent it,[618] these three parties will have to divide the key ministries and their associated responsibilities. Since the Communist Party has often called for increased production and expressed its legitimate concern that the economy not be dominated by trusts, it seems well suited to take charge of the ministry of national economy. However the ministries are divided, it is essential that all decisions be unanimously approved by the "war cabinet," and the ministers along with their parties should be jointly responsible for carrying them out.

In seven months[619] we should know whether France is dead or alive. Life is like walking: the proof is in the progress. Progress will come only with resolution, responsibility, and determination. Anything else will meet with sanctions seven months from now in the form of the people's wrath and the foundering of the ship of state.

---

[618] The elections marked victories for the Communists, Socialists, and Christian Democrats.
[619] The referendum on the Constitution would take place in May 1946. The first proposal was rejected. New legislative elections were held in June.

C H A P T E R 3

November 19–30, 1946
"Neither Victims nor Executioners"

Camus' contribution to *Combat* in 1946 consisted of just eight articles in the series entitled "Neither Victims nor Executioners," but this group of articles enjoyed a very special status, as the typesetting emphasized. The first article was preceded by the headline "Today, Albert Camus. The Century of Fear."

The presentation highlighted the importance of these pieces. They appeared on page one, enclosed in a frame. Their subtitles, in large type, served as headings, and the overall title, "'Neither Victims nor Executioners,' by Albert Camus," was repeated in the center of each text. Publication began on November 19, 1946, and continued on November 20, 21, 23, 26, 27, 29, and 30.

Alone among Camus' journalistic writings, these texts were copyrighted.[1] They were also reprinted exactly a year later, in November 1947, in the journal *Caliban* (no. 11), before being included in *Actuelles* with the same overall title and subtitles in a special chapter oddly dated "November 1948." These articles were clearly conceived as a group that could stand on their own, a short essay inspired by events but relatively detached from the news of the day. They were written with serial publication in mind: even in manuscript, each article begins with an initial title, and the pieces are numbered sequentially and almost equal in length. Each brief chapter contributes to a consistent overall purpose. One passage that would appear in "The Century of Fear" was originally written for the conclusion. The typescript,[2] with its deletions, emendations, and additions, makes it possible to consider variant formulations.[3] It reveals the care taken in writing and editing these pieces. All the corrections contribute to the clarity and vigor of the writing. But the manuscript also reveals that Camus experienced a certain difficulty in saying what he wanted to say, as can be seen, in particular, in the major changes he made to the article "A New Social Contract." Further evidence of the difficulty he faced can be seen in a note he made in October: "Distress I feel about the idea of writing these articles for *Combat*."[4]

---

[1] "Copyright by Albert Camus and *Combat*."

[2] Preserved in the Fonds Camus, CMS2, Ae1-01-07; the article of November 19 was written out entirely by hand; the others were partially typed and corrected by hand. The article of November 26, "International Democracy and Dictatorship," is missing.

[3] Only the most important or significant changes are reproduced here.

[4] *Carnets* II, p. 183. This note was explicitly intended as a "follow-up to the preceding" paragraph, in which he spoke of his profound disarray: "There are times when I don't think I can bear the contradiction any longer. When the sky is cold and nothing in nature sustains us. . . . Better to die, perhaps." These notes were clearly written between the beginning of October ("October 1946. 33 years old in one month," p. 180) and October 29, the date mentioned explicitly on p. 185.

Clearly Camus had come a long way from the articles he had written in the grip of enthusiasm some two years earlier. Indeed, his return to the pages of *Combat* after a lengthy absence was dictated by two necessities. First, he hoped to help the newspaper, whose financial position had become quite critical, so much so that Pia envisioned stopping publication. Second, he was determined to sound a cry of alarm and to raise a voice of protest against the reign of terror that was under way around the world and against the legitimation of murder that lay behind it. "Neither Victims nor Executioners" does not stand apart in Camus' thinking; the anxieties it expresses were a constant with him. The themes of these articles are to one degree or another similar to those of "Remarque sur la révolte,"[5] which appeared in 1946, or the lecture entitled "The Human Crisis,"[6] which was delivered at Columbia University in New York in March 1946, and the brief article "Nous autres meurtriers."[7] He developed these themes in "Le temps des meurtriers," a lecture given in São Paulo,[8] and they are the source from which *The Rebel* sprang. They resonate deeply with *The Plague*. And they echo discussions that Camus had in October with Arthur Koestler,[9] Manès Sperber,[10] Sartre, and Malraux on the place of Marxism in the new world order. Koestler and Sperber denounced the crimes of the Soviet regime and the "conspiracy of silence" that surrounded them; no doubt they were among the first to do so. Sartre did not want to take sides against the Soviet Union. Malraux worried about the political value of the proletariat. And Camus wanted to place his hope in a modest, relative form of utopia, rejecting both nihilism and "political realism."[11] Like *The Rebel*, "Neither Victims nor Executioners" forcefully made the case that nothing can justify murder.

Camus had previously paired the terms "victims" and "executioners."[12] In his article of June 30, 1945, "Images of Occupied Germany," published in *Combat*

---

[5] Nothing less than an outline of *The Rebel* (*L'Homme révolté*), this piece appeared in "L'Existence" and was reprinted in *Essais*, pp. 1982–1997. Many notes in the *Carnets* show the degree to which Camus' concerns revolved around the themes of rebellion and murder.

[6] "The Human Crisis," the French text of which seems to have been lost, was published in *La Revue des Lettres modernes*, Série Albert Camus 5, 1972, pp. 157–176, by Peter Hoy. A French translation appeared in *La Nouvelle Revue française*. In *Albert Camus, voyageur et conférencier, le voyage en Amérique du Sud*, Archives Albert Camus no. 7, 1995, Fernande Bartfeld was able to reconstitute fragments of this text from the lecture on "Le temps des meurtriers" (see the next note).

[7] Published in *Franchise*, no. 3, November–December 1946, and reprinted in Bartfeld, *Albert Camus, voyageur*, pp. 47–49.

[8] Published in Bartfeld, *Albert Camus, voyageur*, pp. 50–72.

[9] Koestler, Arthur (1905–1983). An English-speaking Hungarian, whose book *Darkness at Noon*, published in France in 1946 under the title *Le Zéro et l'Infini*, forcefully denounced the rigged Moscow trials, Koestler had been a Communist and participated in the Spanish civil war.

[10] Sperber, Manès (1905–1984), was an Austrian-born essayist and novelist who published *Analyse de la tyrannie* in 1938. In his work he considered the commitment of intellectuals in the face of totalitarian regimes.

[11] See *Carnets* II, pp. 185–186.

[12] This association calls to mind Baudelaire's poem "L'Heautontimorouménos": "Je suis la plaie et le couteau / . . . Et la victime et le bourreau" [I am the wound and the knife / . . . the victim and the executioner." But Baudelaire has in mind the torments of the individual conscience.

Magazine, he evoked "unhappy, war-torn Europe, divided between victims and executioners."[13] In September 1945 he made this note: "We are in a world in which we must choose to be either victim or executioner—there is no other choice. And the choice is not easy."[14] The November 1946 articles offered a response to this dilemma in the form of a refusal to choose. Camus here seeks a political and moral way out of what seems to him a historical dead end. In France, the "spirit of the resistance" is a thing of the past, relations with the Communists are beset with conflict, and partisan differences have turned virulent. Churchill had just used the expression "iron curtain" to describe the barrier between the Soviet Union and the West.

Hence these articles were entirely in tune with the news of the day, yet they were written with such lucidity and foresight that they reflect today's concerns and sensibility to an astonishing degree.

November 19, 1946
Neither Victims nor Executioners
The Century of Fear[15]

The seventeenth century was the century of mathematics.[16] The eighteenth century was the century of physical science, and the nineteenth the century of biology. Our twentieth century is the century of fear. Fear isn't a science, you may be thinking. Well, to begin with, science is no stranger to fear, since the latest theoretical advances have led science to repudiate itself, and since its practical applications threaten the entire earth with destruction. Furthermore, even if fear can't be considered a science in itself, there is no question that it is a method.

Indeed, what is most striking about the world we live in is first of all the fact that most people, broadly speaking, are deprived of any future (other than believers of one sort or another).[17] No worthwhile life is possible without projection onto the future, without promise of development and progress. To live with one's back to a wall is a dog's life. But people of my generation and of the generation just now taking its place in factories and classrooms have lived and are living more and more like dogs.

---

[13] See p. 229.

[14] *Carnets* II, p. 141.

[15] The original text, entirely handwritten, includes a number of phrases that have been scratched out. No typescript has survived. Several passages from this introductory article appeared in the typescript of "A New Social Contract," which Camus clearly intended originally to be the conclusion. This shows that the whole series was conceived as a single essay.

[16] This observation previously appeared in a footnote to Camus' preface to Chamfort's *Maximes et anecdotes* (Monaco: Incidences, 1944), reprinted under the title "Introduction to Chamfort" in *Essais*, pp. 1099–1109.

[17] *Actuelles*: the parenthetical phrase is omitted.

Of course this is not the first time that people have faced a materially obstructed future. In the past, however, they used to overcome obstacles by speaking out or shouting out their discontent. They appealed to a different set of values, on which they pinned their hopes. Today, no one is talking (apart from those who repeat themselves), because the world seems to us to be led by forces blind and deaf to warnings, advice, and supplications. Something in us succumbed to recent experience. That something is man's eternal confidence, which always fostered the belief that we could elicit human reactions from other human beings by speaking to them in the language of humanity.[18] We have witnessed lying, humiliation, killing, deportation, and torture, and in each instance it was impossible to persuade the people who were doing these things not to do them, because they were sure of themselves and because there is no way of persuading an abstraction,[19] or, to put it another way, the representative of an ideology.[20]

The long dialogue among human beings has now come to an end. And of course a man who cannot be persuaded is a man who makes others afraid. So that alongside people who stopped speaking because they deemed it pointless to try, a vast conspiracy of silence has arisen and continues to spread, a conspiracy accepted by those who quake in fear and who find every reason in the world to hide their quaking from themselves, and encouraged by those who find it in their interest to do so. "You must not talk about the purge of artists in Russia, because that would play into the hands of the reactionaries." "You must keep silent about the British and American decision to keep Franco in power because to talk about it would play into the hands of communism." As I said earlier, fear is a method.

Between the very general fear of a war for which everyone is preparing and the very specific fear of lethal ideologies,[21] it is therefore quite true that we live in terror. We live in terror[22] because persuasion is no longer possible, because man has

---

[18] An earlier formulation of this, which appears in the typescript of "A New Social Contract," combined a passage indicated below (see note 22) with the end of this sentence: "Yes, we live in terror because persuasion is no longer possible, became man shrinks from living in a world in which it is no longer possible to hope that we can *elicit human reactions from other human beings by speaking to them in the language of humanity.*" This whole passage was crossed out.

[19] In *The Plague* the scourge is several times compared to an abstraction that has to be combated.

[20] In the manuscript, after "ideology" begins a new sentence, with no paragraph break: "And of course . . ." The intervening sentence is omitted.

[21] Manuscript: the word "lethal" is omitted.

[22] Typescript of "A New Social Contract": "*Yes*, we are in terror because man has been delivered entirely into the hands of history . . . of messianism without subtleties of any kind." The passage then continued: "But we cannot escape from abstraction, and kill the fear somewhat, by means of rational argument modest in its conclusions and the efforts of passion. As restrained as our hopes may be, they justify trying. 'I think that we ought to be fanatical,' a now-fashionable revolutionary once said, 'but that doesn't exclude either wisdom or common sense.' Use common sense, then, in pondering these facts. In the long struggle ahead, we can never have enough of such quiet fanaticism." This entire passage was deleted. The revolutionary alluded to is Saint-Just. Camus quotes this passage in *Carnets* II, p. 162.

been delivered entirely into the hands of history and can no longer turn toward that part of himself which is as true as the historic part, and which he discovers when he confronts the beauty of the world and of people's faces.[23] And because we live in a world of abstraction, a world of bureaucracy and machinery, of absolute ideas and of messianism without subtlety. We gasp for air among people who believe they are absolutely right, whether it be in their machines or their ideas.[24] And for all who cannot live without dialogue and the friendship of other human beings, this silence is the end of the world.

In order to escape from this terror, we need to be able to think and to act on the basis of our thoughts. But the problem is that terror does not create a climate conducive to thinking. My view, however, is that rather than blame our fear, we should regard it as a basic element of the situation and try to remedy it. Nothing is more important, for this affects the fate of a large number of people in Europe, people who, having had enough of violence and lies, having seen their fondest hopes dashed, and being loath to kill their fellow human beings even in order to persuade them, are equally loath to see themselves persuaded in the same manner. Yet this is the dilemma that the vast masses of Europeans face, those who belong to no party[25] or who are uncomfortable in the party they have chosen, who doubt that socialism has been achieved in Russia or liberalism in America, and yet acknowledge the right of people on both sides to assert their version of the truth while denying those same people the right to impose that truth by murder, either individual or collective. Among those who wield power today, these people are without a kingdom. They will be able to gain recognition for their point of view (without necessarily securing its triumph) and reclaim their homeland only when they can consciously formulate what they want and express this in terms simple enough and strong enough to bind a range of energies. And if fear is not the right climate for proper reflection, then they must first come to terms with fear.

In order to come to terms with fear, we need to understand what it signifies and what it rejects. It signifies and rejects the same fact: a world in which murder is legitimate and human life is considered futile. Therein lies today's primary political problem. Before dealing with the rest, we have to take a position on this. Before we can build anything, we need to ask two questions: "Yes or no, directly or indirectly, do you want to be killed or assaulted? Yes or no, directly or indirectly, do you want to kill or assault?"[26] Anyone who answers yes to these questions is automatically caught up in a web of consequences that is bound[27] to

---

[23] Cf. *Carnets* I, p. 152: "Women's faces, joys of sunshine and water, that is what they are killing."

[24] In the manuscript, the next three sentences do not appear.

[25] Manuscript: who belong to no party, who *do not believe* that socialism . . .

[26] Manuscript: killed or *tortured.*

[27] Manuscript: a web of consequences that is bound (and I was thinking of the socialists) to change the way in which . . .

change the way in which the problem is posed. My aim is to detail just two or three of those consequences. In the meantime, honest readers may wish to ask themselves these questions and answer them.[28]

ALBERT CAMUS

November 20, 1946
Neither Victims nor Executioners
Saving[29] *Bodies*[30]

After saying one day that, given the experience of the last two years, I could no longer accept any truth that might place me under an obligation, direct or indirect, to condemn a man to death, various people whose intelligence I respect told me that I was living in utopia, that there was no political truth that might not someday lead to such an extremity, and that one was obliged either to run that risk or to accept the world as it is.

This argument was forcefully presented. But the people who presented it expressed themselves with such force, I believe, because they lack imagination when it comes to other people's deaths. This is one of the faults of our century. Just as we now love one another by telephone and work not on matter but on machines, we kill and are killed nowadays by proxy. What is gained in cleanliness is lost in understanding.

Still, the argument has another strong point, albeit indirect: it raises the issue of utopia. In short, the world that people like me are after is not a world in which people don't kill one another (we're not that crazy!) but a world in which murder is not legitimized. We are therefore living in utopia and contradiction, to be sure, since the world we live in is one in which murder is legitimized, and we ought to change it if we don't like it. But it seems that it can't be changed without running the risk of committing murder. Murder thus leads to murder, and we will continue to live in terror either because we resign ourselves to it or because we seek to eliminate it by means that replace one form of terror with another.

Everyone, in my view, should think about this. For what strikes me amid all the polemics, threats, and eruptions of violence, is everyone's good intentions. Everyone, on the right and on the left, apart from a few rogues, believes that his truth is likely to make men happy. And yet the conjunction of all these good intentions leads to this infernal world, in which men are still being killed, threatened, and deported, preparations are being made for war, and it is impossible to say a word without instantly being insulted or betrayed. One cannot help

---

[28] Manuscript: . . . and answer it. For my part, I have learned over the past two years in particular that there is no truth I would place above the life of a human being.
This sentence was deleted and then inserted at the beginning of the manuscript of the next article, which proves that they were conceived as a whole.
[29] Manuscript: in French, *sauvez* instead of *sauver*.
[30] Text partially handwritten, partially typewritten.

concluding that if people like us live in contradiction, they are not alone, and those who accuse them of utopian thinking may be living in a utopia of their own, different no doubt but in the end more costly.

We must therefore admit that the refusal to legitimize murder forces us to reconsider our notion of utopia.[31] In that regard, it seems possible to say the following: utopia is that which is in contradiction with reality. From this point of view, it would be completely utopian to want people to stop killing people. This would be absolute utopia. It is a much lesser degree of utopia, however, to ask that murder no longer be legitimized. What is more, the Marxist and capitalist ideologies, both of which are based on the idea of progress and both of which are convinced that application of their principles must inevitably lead to social equilibrium, are utopias of a much greater degree. Beyond that, they are even now exacting a very heavy price from us.[32]

In practical terms, it follows that the battle that will be waged in years to come will not pit the forces of utopia against the forces of reality. Rather, it will pit different utopias against each other as they try to gain a purchase on the real, and the only choice remaining will be to decide which form of utopia is least costly.[33] My conviction is that it is no longer reasonable to hope that we can save everything, but we can at least hope to save the bodies[34] in order to keep open the possibility of a future.

We see, therefore, that the refusal to legitimize murder is no more utopian than today's realistic attitudes.[35] The only question is to decide whether the latter are more or less costly. This is a question that we need to resolve as well, and that is my excuse for believing that it may be useful, with utopian principles in mind, to set forth the conditions necessary for pacifying minds and nations. If we ponder this matter free of fear as well as pretension, we may be able to help create the conditions for a just philosophy and for a provisional accord among those of us unwilling to be either victims or executioners. Of course the remaining articles[36] will not seek to state a definitive position but only to correct some misleading notions that are abroad in the world today and to attempt to state the problem of utopia as accurately as possible. The goal, in short, will be to define the conditions for a modest political philosophy, that is, a philosophy free of all messianic elements and devoid of any nostalgia[37] for an earthly paradise.

ALBERT CAMUS[38]

---

[31] Manuscript: After "notion of utopia," a new sentence: "To stay with generalities before moving on to the concrete, we will say simply that . . ."

[32] Manuscript continues: "In practical terms, the battle that is now beginning . . ."

[33] Manuscript continues: "We can no longer hope . . ."

[34] Manuscript: " . . . save the bodies. We see, therefore . . ."

[35] Manuscript: "today's so-called realistic attitudes. It remains to be seen if they are more or less costly."

[36] Typescript: "Of course the [three] (crossed out) [four] (crossed out) remaining . . ."

[37] Manuscript: "devoid *of any notion* of an earthly paradise."

[38] As with all the articles in this series, the following notice appeared at the end: "Copyright by Albert Camus and *Combat*. Rights of reproduction reserved for all countries." This distinctive feature deserves special mention, as noted earlier.

November 21, 1946
Neither Victims nor Executioners
Socialism Mystified[39]

If we admit that the state of terror in which we have lived for the past ten years, whether acknowledged or not, is not yet over, and that this is today the single greatest factor in the malaise of individuals and nations around the world, then we need to look at how terror can be combated. This raises the problem of western socialism. For terror can be legitimized only if one adopts the principle that the end justifies the means.[40] And this principle can be embraced only if the efficacy of an action is taken to be an absolute end, as in nihilist ideologies (everything is permitted, success is what counts) or philosophies that take history as an absolute (first Hegel, then Marx: since the goal is a classless society, anything that leads to it is good).

Therein, for example, lies the problem faced by French Socialists. They have discovered that they have scruples. They have seen violence and oppression at work, after having had only a fairly abstract idea of what those things were. And they asked themselves if they would be willing, as their philosophy demanded, to practice violence themselves, even if only temporarily and for a quite different purpose. In a recent preface to Saint-Just, a writer[41] spoke of men who had felt similar scruples in terms dripping with contempt: "They shrank from the horror." Truer words could not be spoken. And for that they earned the disdain[42] of souls strong enough and superior enough to embrace horror without flinching. But at the same time they gave a voice to the anguished appeal stemming from the millions of mediocre men and women among whom we count ourselves, the people who are the very stuff of history and who must some day be reckoned with, all the disdain notwithstanding.[43]

A more serious approach, we think, is to try, rather, to understand the contradictory and confusing situation in which our socialists find themselves. It then becomes obvious that not enough thought has been given to the crisis of conscience in French socialism as revealed by the party's recent congress.[44] It is quite clear that our Socialists, under the influence of Léon Blum and even more under

---

[39] Text partly handwritten and partly typed.

[40] Camus returns to this point at length in *The Rebel.*

[41] The allusion is to Jean Gratien's preface to the *Œuvres of Saint-Just* (Paris: Editions de la Cité Universelle, 1946).

[42] Manuscript: "earned the contempt."

[43] Manuscript: "even if one is contemptuous of it."

[44] The 38th Congress of the SFIO (and not the 18th, as indicated in a note in the *Essais*, p. 1513), which took place from August 29 to September 1, 1946, witnessed a clash between Léon Blum's "humanism" and Guy Mollet's "Marxism." In a still-famous speech, Blum attacked the "totalitarian vestiges" in the "slogans rather than convictions" championed by Mollet, and in very Camusian terms called for "democracy and justice," but he was not backed by the majority. Mollet succeeded Daniel Mayer as the party's secretary general.

the threat of events, gave unprecedented priority to moral issues (the end does not always justify the means).[45] Their legitimate desire was to invoke a small number of principles more important than murder. It is no less obvious that the same Socialists want to maintain Marxist doctrine, some because they believe that it is impossible to be a revolutionary without being a Marxist, others because they are understandably loyal to the history of the party, which persuades them that one cannot be a Socialist, either, without being a Marxist. The last party congress had highlighted these two tendencies, and the principal task of this congress was to reconcile them. But there is no reconciling the irreconcilable.

For it is clear that if Marxism is true, and if there is a logic to history, then political realism is legitimate. It is equally clear that if the moral values favored by the Socialist Party are fundamentally right, then[46] Marxism is absolutely false because it claims to be absolutely true. From this point of view, the well-known idea that Marxism will ultimately be transcended in favor of a more idealist and humanitarian philosophy is merely a joke, an inconsequential dream. Marx cannot be transcended, because he pursued the logic of his system to the ultimate end. Communists are rationally justified in using the lies and violence of which the Socialists want no part, and they are justified by the very principles, the very irrefutable dialectic, that the Socialists nevertheless wish to maintain. One can't help being astonished by the sight of the Socialist congress ending with a straightforward juxtaposition of two contradictory positions,[47] the sterility of which was repudiated in the last elections.[48]

In this respect, the confusion persists. A choice was necessary, and the Socialists would not or could not choose.

I chose this example not to condemn the Socialists but to illuminate the paradoxes of our time. To condemn the Socialists, one would have to be superior to them. This is not yet the case. On the contrary, this contradiction seems to me to be shared by all the people I've mentioned, who want a society that is both happy and worthy, who want men to be free in a condition that can at last be described as just, but who still hesitate between a freedom in which they know full well that justice is finally duped and a justice in which they see clearly that freedom is eliminated at the outset.[49] This unbearable anguish is generally derided by those who know what has to be believed and what needs to be done. But I am of the opinion that rather than mock this unbearable anguish, we should use our reason and insight to understand what it means, to interpret the

---

[45] Typescript: "If we grant that the avowed or unavowed state of terror in which we have been living for the past ten years is not yet over, we can understand the legitimate desire of the socialists to refer . . ."

[46] Typescript: "then the Marxist theory of mystified consciousness is false and with it the whole critique of idealism and Marxism itself [deleted]. From this point of view . . ."

[47] Typescript: "contradictory positions. In this respect, . . ."

[48] The reference is obviously to the elections of November 10, 1946 (and not November 1948, as indicated in a note on p. 1513 of the *Essais*), in which the SFIO finished third, behind the Communists and the M.R.P.

[49] The balance between justice and freedom would become one of the themes of *The Rebel*.

virtually total condemnation of the world that provokes it, and to identify the feeble hope that underlies it.[50]

Indeed, hope resides in this contradiction itself, because it is forcing or will force the Socialists to choose. Either they will admit that the end covers the means, hence that murder can be legitimized, or else they will renounce Marxism as an absolute philosophy and limit their attention to the critical aspects, which is often still valuable. If they choose the first alternative, their crisis of conscience will be over, and situations will be clarified. If they choose the second, they will demonstrate that the end of ideologies is upon us, that is, the end of absolute utopias that destroy themselves owing to the heavy price they eventually exact when they seek to become part of historical reality. It will then be necessary to choose another utopia, one that is more modest and less ruinous. In any case, the refusal to legitimize murder makes the question unavoidable.[51]

Yes, this is the question that must be asked, and no one, I believe, would dare answer it lightly.

ALBERT CAMUS

November 23, 1946
Neither Victims nor Executioners
The Revolution Travestied[52]

Since August[53] 1944, everybody in France has been talking about revolution— and always sincerely, no doubt about that. But sincerity is not in itself a virtue. There are kinds of sincerity so confused that they are worse than lies. What we need today is not to speak the language of the heart but simply to think clearly. Ideally, a revolution is a change of political and economic institutions intended to increase freedom and justice in the world. Practically, it is a series of often unfortunate historical events that brings about this change for the better.

Can we say that this word is used today in its traditional sense? When people in France hear talk of revolution, what they envision, assuming they keep their wits about them, is a change in the mode of ownership (generally taken to be a move to collective ownership of the means of production) achieved either through legislation by the majority or through seizure of power by a minority.

It is easy to see that this set of ideas makes no sense in the current historical situation. For one thing, the seizure of power by violent means is a romantic idea

---

[50] Typescript adds: "I have pondered—to put it simply, after a year of journalism—my own inability to have anyone shot in the name of some truth or illusion of truth. Like many other people today, I have concluded that I cannot accept any truth" [the rest of the sentence is missing in the manuscript]. Perhaps Camus noticed that he was repeating a sentence from "Saving Bodies."
[51] Manuscript skips next phrase and continues at "No one, I believe . . ."
[52] Typescript with some handwritten additions.
[53] Typescript: *April* 1944.

consigned to fantasy by advances in the technology of weaponry. The repressive apparatus can avail itself of the force of tanks and planes. Hence it would take tanks and planes merely to equal its power. 1789 and 1917 remain dates, but they are no longer examples.

Yet even if we assume that such a seizure of power is possible, and regardless of whether it is achieved by force of arms or by legislation, it would be effective only if France (or Italy or Czechoslovakia) could put itself in a box and cut itself off from the world. Indeed, in our current historical situation, in 1946, a change in property relations would have such an impact on, for example, American loans that our economy would find itself under threat of death. A right-wing revolution would be no more likely to succeed because of the comparable imped-iment that Russia creates for us with[54] millions of Communist voters and with its position as the greatest continental power. The truth —and I apologize for stating plainly what everybody knows but nobody says—is that we, as French-men, are not free to be revolutionaries. Or at any rate we can no longer be soli-tary revolutionaries, because there is no place in the world today for either conservative or socialist politics within the borders of a single nation.

Hence the only revolution we can talk about is an international one. To be precise, the revolution will either be international or it will not happen. But what can this phrase mean today? There was a time when it was possible to believe that international reform would come about through successive or simultaneous national revolutions—a series of miracles, as it were. If the foregoing analysis is correct, however, the only revolution that is conceivable today is one that would extend an already[55] successful revolution. This is something that Stalin saw quite clearly, and it is the most benevolent explanation that one can give of his policy (the other alternative being to deny Russia the right to speak on behalf of revolution).

What this comes down to is to look at Europe and the West as one nation, in which a large and well-armed minority might come to power after lengthy strug-gle. But since the conservative force (namely, the United States) is equally well armed, it is easy to see that the notion of revolution has now been replaced by that of ideological warfare. To put it more plainly, there is no possibility of an international revolution today without an extremely high risk of war. Any future revolution will be a foreign revolution. It will begin with a military occupation, or, what amounts to the same thing, a threat of occupation. It will make sense only when the occupying power has won a final victory over the rest of the world.

Within nations revolutions are already quite costly, but in view of the progress they are supposed to bring, people generally accept the need for the damage they do. Today, the cost to humanity of any war must be objectively weighed against the progress one might hope to see from the seizure of world power by Russia or America. It is of the utmost importance, I believe, that in weighing the pros and

---

[54] Typescript: "with *five* million."
[55] Typescript: "already" is omitted.

cons we use a little imagination for once and try to envision what a planet that holds some 30 million still-warm bodies would be like after a cataclysm that would claim ten times as many lives.

Let me point out that this manner of reasoning is perfectly objective. It takes only reality into account, taking no position for the time being on ideological or sentimental judgments. In any case, it should give pause to those who speak lightly[56] of revolution. What this word portends *today* must either be accepted or rejected in toto. If you accept it, you must consciously acknowledge responsibility for the war to come. If you reject it, you must either admit that you prefer the *status quo*, which is a completely utopian position insofar as it assumes that history is immobile, or else you must redefine the word "revolution," which means accepting what I shall call a relative utopia. Having thought about the question for a while, I have come to the conclusion that those who want to change the world effectively today have to choose among carnage, the impossible dream of bringing history to an abrupt halt, or the acceptance of a relative utopia that leaves some chance of human action.[57] It is not difficult to see, however, that the relative utopia of which I speak is the only real possibility, the only one inspired by the spirit of reality. What fragile possibility is there of saving ourselves from carnage? This is the question to which we shall turn in our next article.

ALBERT CAMUS

November 26, 1946
Neither Victims nor Executioners
International Democracy and Dictatorship [58]

Today we know that there are no more islands and that borders are meaningless. We know that in an ever-accelerating world, in which the Atlantic can be crossed in less than a day and Moscow communicates with Washington in a few hours, we are forced to embrace solidarity or cooperation depending on the situation.[59] What the 1940s taught us was that harm done to a student in Prague also injured the worker in Clichy, that blood shed on a riverbank in Central Europe could bring a Texas farmer to spill his blood in the Ardennes, a place he had never seen. There is no longer any such thing as isolated suffering, and no instance of torture anywhere in the world is without effects on our daily lives.

---

[56] Typescript: adds the word "today" after "lightly."
[57] The notion of "relative utopia" is central to *The Rebel.*
[58] There is neither a typescript nor a manuscript of this text in the archives.
[59] Here and throughout the article it is possible to see a worried anticipation of globalization. Camus also joined the movement in support of Gary Davis, the self-proclaimed "citizen of the world." See the reports on his activities in *Combat* during November 1948, and Camus' two articles, "What Is the UN Accomplishing?" December 9, p. 301, and "Responses to the Incredulous," December 25–26, 1948, p. 304.

Many Americans would like to go on living within the confines of their society, which they judge to be good. Many Russians, perhaps, would like to carry on with their statist experiment separate from the capitalist world. They cannot now and never will. By the same token, no economic problem, no matter how minor it seems, can be resolved today without international cooperation. Europe's bread is in Buenos Aires, and Siberian machine tools are manufactured in Detroit. Today, tragedy is collective.

Hence we all know, beyond the shadow of a doubt, that the new order we are seeking cannot be merely national or even continental, much less Western or Eastern. It has to be universal. It is no longer possible to hope for incomplete solutions or concessions. Compromise is what we have now, and that means anguish today and murder tomorrow. Meanwhile, history and social change are accelerating. The twenty-one deaf men—future war criminals—who are discussing peace at this very moment are engaged in monotonous dialogues, quietly sitting in the middle of a torrent that is sweeping them toward an abyss at a thousand miles an hour.[60] Yes, the new world order is the only issue of the day, overshadowing all the disputes about the constitution and the election law. It is the issue that cries out for us to use our intelligence and our resolve to do something about it.

What can we do today to achieve world unity and to bring about an international revolution that will improve the distribution of human resources, raw materials, commercial markets, and spiritual wealth? I see only two possibilities, two ultimate alternatives. The world can be unified from above, as I said the other day, by one state more powerful than the rest. Either Russia or America can play this role. Neither I nor anyone I know has anything to counter the contention of some that both Russia and America have the means to rule the world and to unite it around an image of their own societies. I am loath to accept this as a Frenchman and still more as a Mediterranean. But I will not deal with this emotional argument.

Here is my only objection, one that I discussed in a recent article: such unification cannot take place without war or, at the very least, an extreme risk of war. I will even grant, though I do not believe, that this might not be atomic war. Even so, the war of tomorrow would leave mankind so impaired and so impoverished that the very idea of a world order would surely be anachronistic. Marx could justify the war of 1870[61] as he did because it was the war of the Chassepot rifle and was localized. From the standpoint of Marxism, a hundred thousand deaths are nothing compared with the happiness of hundreds of millions. But the certain death of hundreds of millions of people is too high a price to pay for the supposed happiness of those who remain.[62] The dizzying progress

---

[60] Since July 29, the peace conference that was to define the borders of the countries that had allied themselves with Germany had been meeting in Paris at the Luxembourg Palace.

[61] According to Roger Quilliot, Camus was probably referring to letters from Marx to Engels, Paul Lafargue, and Kugelmann in which he explained that the war had taught the proletariat how to use arms and that the Prussian victory would lead to a "centralization of state power . . . useful to the centralization of the working class." See *Essais*, pp. 1513–1514.

[62] This would become one of the themes of *The Rebel*.

of armaments—a historical phenomenon unknown to Marx—forces us to look at the means-ends problem in a new light.

In this case, moreover, the means would shatter the ends. Whatever the desired end may be, as noble and necessary as it conceivably is, and regardless of whether or not it seeks to bring happiness to humankind or to establish justice and freedom, the means to that end represent a risk so conclusive, so disproportionate to the likelihood of success, that we objectively refuse to run it. That brings us back to the second means of achieving universal order, which is by mutual agreement of all parties. We will not ask if this possible, because here we take the point of view that nothing else is possible. So first we must ask ourselves what is involved.

This agreement of all parties has a name: international democracy. Everybody at the U.N. talks about this, of course. But what is international democracy? It is a democracy which is international. Forgive me for this truism: the most obvious truths are also the most distorted.

What is national democracy, and what is international democracy? Democracy is a form of society in which the law is above those who govern, the law being the expression of the will of all, represented by a legislative body. Is that what people are attempting to establish today? They are indeed elaborating for us an international law. But that law is made and unmade by governments, that is, by the executive. We are therefore in a regime of international dictatorship. The only way out is to place international law above governments, which means that that law must be made, that there must be a parliament for making it, and that parliament must be constituted by means of worldwide elections in which all nations will take part. And since we do not have such a parliament, the only option open to us is to resist this international dictatorship on an international level using means not in contradiction with the ends we seek.

ALBERT CAMUS

November 27, 1946
Neither Victims nor Executioners
The World Moves Quickly[63]

It is obvious to everyone that political thought increasingly finds itself overtaken by events. France, for example, began the war of 1914 with the resources of 1870 and the war of 1939 with the resources of 1918. But anachronistic thinking is not peculiar to the French. For now it will suffice to note that, to all intents and purposes, today's political systems seek to settle the world's future by employing principles shaped in the eighteenth century in the case of capitalist liberalism and in the nineteenth century in the case of so-called scientific socialism. In the former case a philosophy born in the early years of modern industrialism, and in the latter a doctrine contemporaneous with Darwinian evolutionism and Renanian optimism, seek to reduce to equations the era of the atomic bomb, sudden

[63] Typescript with handwritten corrections and additions.

upheaval, and widespread nihilism. There can be no better illustration of the increasingly disastrous gap that exists between political thought and historical reality.

Of course the mind is always a step behind reality. History races ahead while the mind meditates. But this unavoidable gap is widening today as the pace of history accelerates. The world has changed far more in the past fifty years than in the previous two hundred. And today we see everyone focused on the issue of establishing borders, when people everywhere know that borders are now abstractions. Yet it was the principle of nationalities that apparently held sway at the Conference of the Twenty-One.

We[64] must take this into account in our analysis of historical reality. Today we shall focus on the German question, which is a secondary issue compared with the clash of empires that hangs over us. Yet if we were to come up with international solutions to the Russian-American problem, we would still be in danger of being ignored. The clash of empires is already close to taking a back seat to the clash of civilizations. Indeed, colonized civilizations from the four corners of the earth are making their voices heard. Ten or fifty years from now, the challenge will be to the preeminence of western civilization.[65] It would therefore be better to anticipate this by opening the World Parliament to these civilizations, so that its law will truly become universal law and the order that it consecrates will truly become the world order.

The questions that have arisen lately in connection with the right of veto are misleading, because the opposing sides in the U.N. debate are misleading. The Soviet Union will always have the right to reject the will of the majority as long as it consists of a majority of ministers and not a majority of peoples represented by their delegates and until all nations are represented. If a meaningful majority should ever be assembled, everyone will either have to obey it or reject its law, which is to say, openly declare its will to dominate.[66]

By the same token, if we never lose sight of the acceleration of history, we stand a chance of finding the right way to approach the economic issues of the day. The question of socialism did not look the same in 1930 as it did in 1848. The abolition of private property gave way to techniques for collectivization of the means of production. Those techniques involved not only the fate of private property but also the increased scale of economic issues. And just as there will be no political solution that is not international, so, too, will any economic solution have to deal with international means of production such as oil, coal, and uranium *as a first priority*. If there is to be collectivization, it must deal with the resources that are indispensable to everyone and should in fact belong exclusively to no one. Everything else is just political speechifying.[67]

---

[64] Typescript: "Well, we must . . ."
[65] On this point, too, Camus' premonitory clarity of mind is worth noting.
[66] Manuscript: "will to power."
[67] This entire paragraph was added by hand.

This approach to the question looks utopian to some, but for those who refuse to accept the risk of war, there is no choice but to embrace these principles and defend them wholeheartedly. How do we get there from here? The only way imaginable is for former socialists to come together with individuals who today find themselves politically isolated around the world.

There is in any case one further and final response to the accusation that these principles are "utopian." For us, the choice is simple: either utopia or war, which is where outmoded ways of thinking are taking us. The choice today is between anachronistic political thinking and utopian thinking. Anachronistic thinking is killing us. Wary as we are (and as I am), realism therefore forces us to embrace the relative utopia I am proposing. When this utopia has been absorbed into history[68] like so many others before it, people will no longer be able to imagine any other reality. For history is nothing other than man's desperate effort to turn his most perspicacious dreams into reality.

Albert Camus

November 29, 1946
Neither Victims nor Executioners
A New Social Contract[69]

Let me summarize what I have said so far. The fate of people of all nations will not be settled until the problems of peace and world organization have been settled. There can be no effective revolution anywhere in the world until this revolution has taken place. Anyone in France who says anything different today is either wasting his breath or has a personal stake in the outcome. I will go even farther. Not only will there be no lasting change in the mode of property ownership anywhere in the world, there will not even be any solution to the simplest problems—supplying people with their daily bread, ending the hunger that is wracking bellies across Europe, ensuring an adequate supply of coal—until peace has been created.[70]

---

[68] In *Actuelles*, the word "history" is capitalized here and in the next sentence.

[69] Partially typewritten text with handwritten additions and numerous corrections. The text was intensively revised. It was first conceived as a conclusion to the series, and in fact one section was moved to the final article "Toward Dialogue," for which no separate manuscript or typescript of a final draft exists. Another section, which was at the end of this article, was moved to "The Century of Fear." See notes 15, p. 257, and 18 and 22, p. 258. Long passages were deleted from the final version. Others are not found in the manuscript (everything from "Any thought that recognizes" to "of a doomed society"). *The Rebel* includes an analysis of Rousseau's *Social Contract* under the title "A New Gospel" (*Essais*, pp. 523–526).

[70] In the typescript, this is followed by the following two paragraphs (with a few handwritten corrections): "For people pondering these questions, I therefore see no more urgent need than to commit all their energy, resistance, and time, their ballots (for as little as they are worth), their talent, and their resources to demand a worldwide solution to alleviate the burden of misery and fear. And this movement must

Any thinker who honestly acknowledges his inability to justify lies and murder will be led inescapably to this conclusion if he cares at all about truth. He will have no choice but to assent to the argument as set forth thus far.

In so doing he will acknowledge that: 1. domestic politics taken in isolation is essentially of secondary importance and in any case intellectually incoherent; 2. the only real issue is the creation of an international order, which will finally bring about lasting structural reforms tantamount to a revolution; 3. the only strictly national issues that remain are administrative problems that must be dealt with for now as effectively as possible, until a more general and therefore more effective solution can be achieved.

It must be granted, for instance, that the French Constitution can be judged only in terms of what it does or does not contribute to the creation of an international order based on justice and dialogue. Seen in this light, the indifference of our Constitution to the most basic of human liberties deserves to be condemned. It must be granted that the provisional organization of a more efficient logistical system is ten times more important than the issue of nationalizations or the votes tallied by this or that party. Nationalizations will not endure if they are limited to one country. And while it is true that the logistical problem cannot be resolved within a purely national framework either, it is nevertheless a more pressing issue that calls for expedient solutions, even if they are temporary.

Taken together, these observations may yield the criterion for judging domestic politics that has thus far been lacking. *L'Aube* may well publish thirty editorials a month opposing the thirty editorials of *L'Humanité*, but none of those pieces can make us forget that both newspapers, along with the parties they represent and the men who lead them, agreed to the annexation of Brigue and Tende without a referendum,[71] which means that they were allies for the purpose of destroying international democracy. Whatever their reasons, good or bad, M. Bidault and M. Thorez both opted for the principle of international dictatorship. Hence

---

develop not only within each country but above all in the international arena, initially by way of preaching. That is the primary task, the most urgent necessity we face, and the only one that can be effective or truly realistic.

"Otherwise, there is little that we can expect from governments, which will find themselves overwhelmed by their burdens until this issue is resolved. And governments themselves are well aware of this. Their primary task seems to be to survive, and then, depending on which parties join in coalition, to give assurances to the foreign power of their choice. On all other matters any possible solutions are therefore provisional. The only two issues that count are that of creating an international order that will at last bring about durable structural reforms tantamount to revolution, and that of devising some temporary system for meeting daily needs and managing the flow of resources. And since those who are in charge of international organization today have managed to get themselves stuck in a dead end, *individuals, working both within their own countries and across borders, must one by one enter into a new social contract that will unite them* again *in accordance with a more reasonable set of principles.*" The italicized portion of the last sentence was moved to a point later in the text. See n. 73, p. 272.

[71] The Treaties of Paris, signed in February 1947 between the victorious powers and the former allies of Germany, provided among other things for the surrender by Italy to France of the villages of Brigue and Tende. The annexation took place after a referendum at the end of the year.

regardless of how we may judge their decision, they represent not political reality but rather utopian thinking of the most unfortunate kind.

Yes, domestic politics does not deserve to be accorded so much importance. You cannot cure the plague with remedies for a head cold.[72] A crisis that is tearing apart the entire world cannot be resolved without a universal solution. There must be order for all so that the burden of misery and fear that each must bear can be reduced: that, for now, is our logical objective. This demands action and sacrifice, and that means people. And while there are many people nowadays who condemn violence and murder in their heart of hearts, there aren't many willing to recognize that this obliges them to reconsider the way they think and act. Yet those who are willing to make the effort can expect to find reasonable hope along with rules for action.

Admittedly, not much can be expected from the governments now in power, since these live and act by lethal principles. Hope therefore requires us to take the more arduous path, to start over and build anew a living society within the doomed society we are living in now.[73] Hence individuals, working both within their own countries and across borders, must one by one enter into a new social contract that will unite them again in accordance with a more reasonable set of principles.

The peace movement I mentioned should be able to link up with communities of labor inside nations and with international study groups. These working communities, organized in a cooperative way and on the basis of free contract, would bring relief to as many people as possible, whereas the study groups would attempt to define the values on which the new international order[74] should be based while at the same time advocating for that order at every available opportunity.

More precisely, the task of these groups should be to meet the confusions of terror with clear language and at the same time to set forth the values that a

---

[72] Tarrou makes the same point in *The Plague*: "They are never a match for epidemics. And the remedies they imagine are hardly up to treating a head cold." (*La Peste*, p. 118.)

[73] The passage excised from the manuscript earlier was moved here.

[74] In the typescript, another sentence was inserted here: "Again, this relative utopia is the only chance." This was followed by a lengthy passage, of which only the last words would make it into the final text. "This, by the way, is so un-utopian that elements of such groups can be seen in the real world today. The example given here is only an example, intended to serve as a general idea of what I have in mind. A good model for the kind of contractual organization that is rethinking our society's mode of production is the working group that Marcel Barbu has established in Valence. In France we have many highly intelligent and distinguished minds, but few, so far as I know, have noticed the importance of Barbu's experiment and its true significance for the present age. He has created a community of 150 men of various beliefs (including Marxists, Christians, and unaffiliated members) who say that they are happy to be there. It has been in existence for eight years. Other, similar communities have been established. People say that they will fail, but for the moment they are surviving, and in any case they will have rescued a few of misery's hostages for at least eight years. This community has not promised all these workers dignity and inner peace within four generations; it has given them these things in the space of a few years. Once again, ultimate liberation depends on international reform. But experiments like Barbu's, which is creating a new type of human relationship based on the free choices of human beings with respect for differences and liberty for all, shows that in the meantime it is possible to make some progress toward overcoming universal disorder and hatred. This progress can be made permanent only when a worldwide organization has been achieved. Until then it is threatened. But it makes hope possible.

world at peace will find indispensable: their first objectives could be to formulate an international code of justice whose first article would abolish the death penalty everywhere[75] and to give a clear statement of the principles necessary for any civilization based on dialogue. This work would meet the needs of an era that can find no philosophy which offers the grounding necessary to satisfy the craving for friendship that Western minds are experiencing today. Clearly, however, the point of this exercise should not be to elaborate a new ideology. It should be simply to search for a new way of life.

In any case, these are themes for reflection, and I cannot explore them in any depth in the space available. But to put things more concretely, let us imagine a group of people determined, in all circumstances, to set example against power, preaching against domination, dialogue against insult, and plain honor against wily cunning; a group of people who would refuse all the advantages of society as they find it today and accept only the duties and responsibilities that tie them to others; and who would attempt to redirect teaching, above all, and, in addition, the press and public opinion in keeping with the principles of conduct I have just set forth. These people would be acting not in a utopian way but rather in accordance with the most genuine realism. They would be laying the groundwork for the future, and in so doing they would immediately begin to break down some of the walls that we find so oppressive today. If realism is the art of taking both the present and the future into account at the same time, of obtaining the most while sacrificing the least, then who can fail to see that the most unmistakable reality belongs to these men and women.

Whether these people will come forward or not,[76] I do not know. It is likely that most of them are pondering the situation right now, and that is good. Yet there can be no doubt that the effectiveness of their action depends on their finding the courage to give up some of their dreams for now in order to hold fast to what is essential, which is to save lives. At this point, moreover, before it is all over, it will perhaps[77] be necessary to raise our voices.

ALBERT CAMUS

"These are the relations that must be extended whenever possible, because what is at stake is the building of a living society within the doomed society in which we are living now. Men who would assert in everyday political debate that the only real issue is to build an international society; who would prove that all other disputes, both constitutional and electoral, are pointless, and who would insist on international solidarity and organization; who would simply define the common and provisional values they find indispensable for rejecting murder and pursuing their goals; who would demand *general abolition of the death penalty* in the West; *who would reject all the advantages of society as they find it today and accept only the duties and responsibilities that tie them to others;* who would in all circumstances prefer *preaching to domination and dialogue to insult;* and who would bring to the press and above all to the schools *the principles of conduct set forth here; those men . . .*"

[75] Although Camus had often previously expressed his revulsion at the death penalty, this was perhaps the first time he phrased it this way.

[76] In the manuscript, the phrase "I do not know" was omitted, and the sentence continued with the next sentence as its second clause.

[77] Manuscript: "it might perhaps be necessary."

November 30, 1946
Neither Victims nor Executioners
Toward Dialogue[78]

Yes, it might be necessary to raise our voices.[79] I have thus far refrained[80] from calling upon the power of the emotions. What is crushing us today is a histori-cal logic that we created out of whole cloth, on the knots in which we are about to choke. Emotion is not what is needed to slice through the knots of a logic gone awry. Only reason can do that—reason that knows its limits. Yet I do not want to end with the suggestion that the future of the world can dispense with the powers of indignation and love. I am well aware that it takes a lot to get peo-ple mobilized and that it is hard to gird oneself for a battle in which the objec-tives are so limited and there is barely a glimmer of hope. But the point is not to dragoon people into acting. On the contrary, the key is that they must not be dragged and that they must have a clear idea of what they are doing.

To save what can still be saved just to make the future possible: that is the great motivating force, the reason for passion and sacrifice. What is required is simply that we reflect and clearly decide whether we must add to the sum of human suffering for still indiscernible ends, whether we must acquiesce while the world blankets itself with arms and brother again kills[81] brother, or whether, to the contrary, we must economize as much as possible on bloodshed and pain simply to give other generations, better armed than we are, their chance.[82]

I, for one, am practically certain that I have made my choice. And having cho-sen, it seemed to me that I ought to speak, to say that I would never count myself among people of whatever stripe who are willing to countenance murder, and I would draw whatever consequence followed from this.[83] Now I have said my piece, and I shall end. But before that, I would like readers to know something of the spirit in which I have been writing thus far.

We are being asked to love or to hate one or another country or people. But a few of us are only too well aware of our similarity to our fellow human beings to accept this choice. The right way to love the Russian people, in recognition of

---

[78] No separate manuscript exists for this text, but it incorporates a passage originally intended for "A New Social Contract."

[79] Repetition (with slight alteration) of the final clause of the previous article.

[80] The whole passage from "I have thus far refrained" to "indignation and love" appears in the typescript of "A New Social Contract," where it is followed by a passage that would ultimately appear in "The Cen-tury of Fear," which is crossed out and replaced by the heavily corrected handwritten text that is repro-duced here, beginning with "I am well aware."

[81] Manuscript: "brother *oppresses* brother."

[82] Manuscript: "bloodshed and pain [and] *reject terror* simply to *ensure the existence* of other generations that will be better armed than we are." The manuscript ends here.

[83] Here again, the affinity with *The Rebel* deserves mention.

what they have never ceased to be—what Tolstoy and Gorky called the world's leavening—is not to wish upon them the vagaries of power but to spare them a new and terrible bloodletting after all they have suffered in the past. The same is true of the American people and of the unfortunate people of Europe. This is a fundamental truth, but of a kind all too often forgotten in the tumult of the day.

Indeed, what we need to resist today is fear and silence and the division of minds and souls that these entail. What we must defend is dialogue and communication worldwide. Servitude, injustice, and falsehood are scourges that interfere with such communication and prevent such dialogue. That is why we must reject them. But those scourges are today the very stuff of history, and many people therefore look upon them as necessary evils. It is also true that we cannot escape from history, since we are in it up to our necks. But we can aspire to do battle within the historical arena in order to save from history that part of man which does not belong to it. That is all I wanted to say. Before closing, in any case, I would like to try to define my attitude, and the spirit in which I wrote these articles, a little more clearly, and I ask my readers to reflect on what I am about to say with open minds.

A vast experiment has now set all the nations of the world on a course governed by the laws of power and domination. I do not say that this experiment should be prevented from continuing. It needs no help from us, and for the moment it cares nothing for those who oppose it. Hence the experiment will go on. I simply raise one question: what will happen if this experiment fails, if the logic of history on which so many people are now relying proves wrong? What will happen if, despite two or three wars, despite the sacrifice of several generations and not a few values, our grandchildren, supposing they exist, find themselves no closer to achieving the universal society? The survivors to the experiment will not even have the strength to bear witness to their own agony. Since the experiment is continuing and it is inevitable that it will continue for some time to come, it is not a bad thing that some people set themselves the goal of preserving, in the apocalyptic period that awaits us, the modest way of thinking that does not claim to solve all problems but is always ready at a moment's notice to ascribe a meaning to everyday life. What is essential is that these people weigh carefully, once and for all, the price that they will be obliged to pay.

Now I can end. What I think needs to be done at the present time is simply this: in the midst of a murderous world, we must decide to reflect on murder and choose. If we can do this, then we will divide ourselves into two groups: those who if need be would be willing to commit murder or become accomplices to murder, and those who would refuse to do so with every fiber of their being. Since this awful division exists, we would be making some progress, at least, if we were clear about it. Across five continents, an endless struggle between violence and preaching will rage in the years to come. And it is true that the former is a thousand times more likely to succeed than the latter. But I have always believed that if people who placed their hopes in the human condition were mad, those who despaired of events were cowards. Henceforth there will be only one honorable choice: to wager everything on the belief that in the end words will prove stronger than bullets.[84]

ALBERT CAMUS

---

[84] These last words inevitably recall the interview that Camus gave to *Demain* in 1957, which appeared under the title "Our Generation's Wager."

CHAPTER 4

March 17–June 3, 1947

After the departure of Pascal Pia, Camus served for two and a half months as editor in chief of *Combat*. He published six editorials and two articles, all titled and signed. There is a certain unity to these texts. They reflect their author's disillusionment and fears in regard to France's domestic, colonial, and international policies. Like the previous articles, moreover, they attest to Camus' exalted conception of journalism.

By January his name was appearing in the columns of the newspaper, but it was as a writer that he responded to Joan Desternes's survey of American literature. Although this text obviously does not have the same status as the others, it seems legitimate to include it in its chronological place, in that it serves as a reminder that the journalist was *also* a novelist: he was finishing *The Plague*, which would appear in June. The publication of the book was greeted warmly, including an article by Maurice Nadeau. On June 14, the paper announced that "Albert Camus has received the Prix des Critiques," and the announcement was accompanied by a picture and a comment by Dominique Arban: "At *Combat*, each of us feels that something good has happened to us personally."

January 17, 1947
"What do you think of American literature?
— 'Literature of the basic,' answers Albert Camus." [1]

Of course it's a fashion. But every fashion has its reasons. Americans are astonished by the success their writers have been enjoying in Europe. ([Erskine] Caldwell sells ten times as many books in Paris as in New York.) I'm not. The American technique in novel writing is one of easy fluency—hence it will always do well. [2] But if you compare a Steinbeck to a Melville, [3] you'll see that the

---

[1] Jean Desternes's survey of American literature, which began on January 3, was published in the literary section of the paper.

[2] In an interview published in *Les Nouvelles littéraires* on November 15, 1945, Camus had said that "the American technique in novel writing seems to me to lead to a dead end. True, I used it in *The Stranger*. But that was because it suited my purpose, which was to describe a man who was apparently without conscience. If the method is generalized, it leads to a world of automata and creatures of instinct. That would be a considerable loss. So even while giving the American novel its due, I would give a hundred Hemingways for one Stendhal or one Benjamin Constant. And I regret the influence of American literature on so many young writers."

[3] Camus' admiration of Melville is well-known. See the preface he wrote to *Les Ecrivains célèbres* (Paris: Editions Mazenod, 1952), vol. 3, reprinted in *Théâtre, Récits, Nouvelles* (Paris: Gallimard [Pléiade], 1991), pp. 1899–1903.

American literature of the nineteenth century, whose greatness was universal, has been replaced by a magazine literature.

But how do you explain the influence of what Americans are producing on our literature?

I see two explanations, one of which is obvious, while the other is more personal, and I offer it for what it is worth. The first is the taste for efficiency and speed, a predilection that is very widespread nowadays and which I do not disdain, but which has lately been introduced into narrative techniques. The narrative is silent about everything that until recently constituted the proper subject of literature, namely, to put it crudely, the inner life. Man is described but never explained or interpreted. The result is that you can write a novel today using only your memory and your eyes. All the rest—inward experience, meditation, knowledge of man and of the world—is not necessary. The novel is thus placed within reach of everyone. If you can see, you can write, and since everyone can see, everyone can write, etc.

And the second explanation?

This is more in the nature of an impression, which I offer in the most tentative way. Here it is: we get a misleading impression of American novels when we read them in French, because we have a tradition of (and taste for) compression, insinuation, and understatement, so we take a technique that never says anything important and impute to it the intention to say a range of things that may never have been intended. We read *Of Mice and Men*[4] in the same spirit in which we read *La Princesse de Clèves*.[5] But the characters in American novels, unlike the prince de Clèves, are really basic beings. If the prince de Clèves says nothing, it is because his pain is so acute that in the end he will die of it. If Steinbeck's George says nothing, it is because he has nothing to say, other than an overwhelmingly powerful but confused feeling, which is never truthfully articulated.

In other words, the art of the American novel strikes you as more elementary than universal?

Exactly, it is universal only at the level of the elementary.[6] The technique is peerless when it comes to describing a man with no apparent inner life (and I used it in this way). But to use it generally, as we are seeing today, would be tantamount to eliminating nine-tenths of what we treasure in art and life. This would be a tremendous loss. The [American] literature that we read (with the

---

[4] By John Steinbeck.

[5] In July 1943, in a special issue of the journal *Confluences* (nos. 21–24) devoted to "Problems of the Novel," Camus published a very fine articled entitled "L'intelligence et l'échafaud" on the classical French novel, in which he gives a great deal of space to Madame de Lafayette and expresses his admiration for *La Princesse de Clèves*. See *Théâtre, Récits, Nouvelles*, pp. 1887–1894. See also *Carnets II*, pp. 60–62. When Mauriac responded to the same survey (*Combat*, January 26–27), he said: "Albert Camus told me recently that there was nothing better than *La Princesse de Clèves*."

[6] See, in *Carnets II*, p. 114, this note from 1943: "On the American novel: it aims for the universal. Like classicism. But whereas classicism aims for an eternal universal, contemporary literature, owing to circumstances (interpenetration of borders), aims at a historical universal. This is not man for all times but man for all places."

exception of Faulkner[7] and two or three others who, like him, have had no success over there) is eminently useful as a source for cultural study, but it bears only the most distant relationship to art.

Is there a social explanation for this phenomenon?

There is always a social explanation for what we see in art. Only it doesn't explain anything important. Nevertheless, it seems clear to me that the commercialization of literature, the influence of advertising, the prospect of making millions of dollars on one book if it is basic enough and self-indulgent enough to become a best seller are partial explanations. Writers are not saints, and even if they were, they would not be writers. How many European writers would hesitate if given the choice between becoming a millionaire manufacturer of books and remaining a great but unknown talent? If there are great writers in America today, there is a good chance that we don't know who they are. Think of the bitter detachment and independence of the great Melville, who died in squalor, unknown to his contemporaries, surrounded by his neglected masterpieces. Think of Poe, who first won praise in Europe, or Faulkner, whose novels appear in editions of a few thousand while the unspeakable *Forever Amber*[8] sells millions.

There has been a debate around For Whom the Bell Tolls, *has there not?*

Yes, and quite a pointless one. Hemingway should be given his due. *The Sun Also Rises* is a very good book. But his book about Spain is a children's book compared with Malraux's *Espoir* (*Man's Hope*).[9] I was very disappointed that he chose to stick an MGM-style love story into the middle of the prodigious events that took place in Spain. You can't mix Hollywood with Guernica.

Are you completely hostile to American literature?

No, because I've found in America both the reasons for this literature and the promise that it will someday be surpassed, if it hasn't been already. And I am in sympathy with some of those reasons (in my country, in North Africa, people also live in this brief and violent way), as I am with the promise. America is bursting with still unused vitality, and it is not done surprising the world. But it may surprise the world in quite facile and violent ways (as one says that a color is "violent"), or it may do so by resurrecting the tranquil and boundless genius that has already produced Melville and Hawthorne.[10] America will choose. But the best thing we can do for it is not to imitate its most vulgar works but to stick to the rigorous realm of art where its greatest minds have already staked out a place.

To set an example?

No, we can no longer serve as an example for America. It has its own course to follow, as we have ours, which is no longer easy. But we can sometimes tell

---

[7] In 1957 Camus adapted *Requiem for a Nun* for the stage.

[8] By Kathleen Winsor. The book was a great success in France.

[9] Camus greatly admired Malraux.

[10] Camus probably felt some affinity with Nathaniel Hawthorne. In *Carnets II*, p. 296, he reproduced a comment Melville had made about him: "He did not believe, and he could not be satisfied with unbelief."

America that it is wrong, to help it out, and in the end we may be right. Art is the only realm in which honesty and toughness are sometimes rewarded. When *The Grapes of Wrath* and *Tobacco Road* have been forgotten, people will still be talking about *Moby Dick* and *The Scarlet Letter*.[11] Our role is to say so, if that is what we think.

Perhaps one ought to modify this slightly. The best works are not always the most influential works, but the worst works in a country's literature sometimes serve as vehicles for what is good in the greatest works. And to complete the circle, bad influences may thus stimulate great works. There is in art a kind of justice or miracle, you might say.

Conclusion?

Stay calm.

March 17, 1947
The Deaf and Dumb Republic[12]

The therapeutic silence is over for now.[13]

After a hiatus of more than four weeks, our newspaper is back on the newsstands. To be sure, various benevolent observers had predicted its demise. Clearly these reports were premature. Other reports, from sources no less friendly, hinted that *Combat* had suffered the ultimate misfortune of virtue by selling itself to wealthy libertines.

Alas, it seems that the only virtue that *Combat* can claim for itself is the kind that lacks intelligence, by which we mean the kind that is stupid enough to risk dying of hunger. Poor but free before the strike, *Combat* is back, poorer than ever but still free and determined to stay that way. Just as it lived on the income from its sales and advertising a month ago, it continues today to rely solely on its readers.

But we will save that subject for later. For now we owe it to our readers only to provide certain information and to the government to relate certain truths. This interminable strike has been a veritable financial hemorrhage for all newspapers. It has threatened their very survival, and this has been especially true of independent papers. A series of governments now bears the immense responsibility of never having adopted a statute regulating the press despite our incessant appeals, and the extended duration of this latest strike has only increased the likelihood that newspapers backed by money will replace those dailies that have

---

[11] *The Grapes of Wrath* is by John Steinbeck, *Tobacco Road* by Erskine Caldwell, *Moby Dick* by Herman Melville, and *The Scarlet Letter* by Nathaniel Hawthorne.

[12] Editorial.

[13] Because of a printers' strike, *Combat* did not appear from February 15 to March 17. This long hiatus undermined its precarious financial position and ultimately led to its demise.

managed to remain free. The present government has no excuse to offer in this regard.

It has no excuse because, despite the obligations of an austerity policy approved by both the newspapers and the unions, it refused from the outset to assume its responsibilities. In the early days of the strike, Prime Minister Ramadier[14] refused to intervene in the conflict, which he described as "not being of a political character." The two parties in contention, both working within the framework of the austerity policy, tried to reach an agreement in which wage increases would be granted only in return for worker agreement to improvements in the production process. In agreement with the government, newspapers were scheduled to appear seven days a week. On March 10 and 12, two agreements were signed, only to be rejected by the government. On March 14, the government even reversed its decision to authorize a seventh day of publication. Afterward, the ministers involved accompanied M. Vincent Auriol[15] on a trip to Toulouse, the urgent character of which is well-known.

In keeping with an old tradition, the government therefore took the position that a policy of nonintervention in fact meant intervention, but only in a negative sense. Neither liberal nor *dirigiste*, it chose to let the market have its way while blocking all progress toward a workable solution. To put it rhetorically, this might be considered an attitude but not a doctrine. And since plain talk is essential, we will say that the government, which does not exist so far as doctrine is concerned, seems to us suspect in its attitude.

At a time when striking butchers no longer honor any meat ration and legislators who presume to lead the nation without being able to control themselves try to pacify Indochina by participating in infamous duels,[16] while a few of us persist in worrying anxiously about the fate of the freedom that was for years the primary concern that kept us going, the general silence of the press, the suppression of press forums on the radio along with broadcasts featuring journalists who cover parliament, and surreptitious censorship of broadcast editorials do not suggest that the policy adopted is one that can be openly avowed. It is merely a policy of silence of the sort that totalitarian regimes execute more skillfully and, to be honest, with greater candor.

M. Ramadier reportedly stated that the silence of the press saved the Republic from a dark conspiracy, which, to hear him tell it, made use of this newspaper. This is news to us, but it sheds a new light on the singular notions of a republican prime minister so taken with the eloquence of his ministers as to believe that no one else serves the cause of democratic truth, and indeed that anyone else in the country who speaks out can only be strengthening the hand of what are commonly referred to as reactionary conspiracies. The Republic of

---

[14] Paul Ramadier had been prime minister since January 22, 1947.

[15] Vincent Auriol was elected president of the Republic on January 16, 1947.

[16] Allusion to a duel with pistols in which Gaston Defferre was involved.

which M. Ramadier dreams, in short, is a deaf and dumb one that can be subjected with impunity to the therapeutic methods of Sganarelle.[17]

We, for our part, believe that there is no democracy without dialogue[18] and that every policy needs to be balanced and constrained by the judgments it warrants. Since we have regained our freedom of speech, it should be used today to forcefully denounce an attitude that deliberately runs the risk of destroying the only values that seem to us worth fighting for along with the only privilege that we defend with all our might, namely, the privilege of saying here, every day, in total freedom, what we think is just and what we believe deserves to be condemned.

ALBERT CAMUS

March 21, 1947
Radio 47[19]

I do not have the privilege of knowing M. Max Régnier.[20] For want of time and perhaps also of taste, I rarely listen to the Radio Nationale. I did, however, listen to its news during the newspaper strike, out of an innocent desire to be informed. But innocence is never well treated in this world, and I learned fairly quickly that what distinguishes our radio network is its mysterious faculty of announcing events that never took place and its unusual readiness to present systematically biased reports. In that department it has to be granted that our radio beats our daily press by several lengths, which I would have thought humanly impossible.

In short, I never listened to M. Max Régnier. Like everyone else, I know that his program was highly successful, and I was happy for him, since I have a disinterested taste for satirical songwriters. I also know that M. Régnier is accused of having undermined the credit of the state by inconsiderately relating certain declarations made by our minister of finance. If true, M. Régnier was surely in the wrong. Being ignorant of the facts, however, I hesitate to judge the substance of the case. Still, the method of banning what one was incapable of preventing may be worthy of a word or two of comment.

The most remarkable effect of this tactic has certainly been to give increased importance to a program that would otherwise have been less effective. In this respect, the government has not acted politically enough. In another respect,

---

[17] Allusion to Molière's play *Le Médecin malgré lui*.

[18] It is hardly necessary to point out how much Camus insists on the need for dialogue in politics as elsewhere.

[19] Editorial.

[20] The daily radio broadcast of the very famous satirical songwriter Max Régnier had just been canceled. He had made a number of jokes about the fall of the franc and the scant resources of the Banque de France and was in effect accused of "undermining the credit of the state."

however, it may have acted far too politically. Such touchy intolerance of a few jokes may be justified by a desire to protect the public credit, but it seems less legitimate when it is also directed against the last glimmers of freedom left in broadcasting. The case of M. Régnier is of no importance in itself, but the whole range of measures of which this decision is one is far more shocking.

Of course it is always possible to prohibit the open forum of journalists covering parliament. (In a related note, I call M. Ramadier's attention to the fact that the Paris Forum remains a credit to broadcasting and that it should therefore be canceled.) One can always truncate the editorials cited in the press reviews, cancel after the first infraction any program that does not use the sound of marching feet as its background, and generally impose sanctions on any emission that to any degree makes up for the partisan character of a clearly subservient broadcast medium. But in doing so one deprives oneself of the right to denounce conspiracies against the Republic, and one runs the risk of imitating M. Daladier, who in 1939 imagined that he was sending Frenchmen off to fight for democracy while at the same time he did away with that democracy by means of edicts and emergency decrees.[21]

One of our great statesmen is supposed to have asked the following question, which has a particular resonance in this age of propaganda: "So you believe in the news, do you?" We count ourselves among those who nurse certain reasonable illusions in this regard. Yes, we believe in the news. Standing with the imbeciles, by which I mean those who are not prepared to commit murder in order to win an argument, free speech is the only thing we have left to defend what we believe to be true. That is why we cannot allow that freedom to be tampered with, whether out of inadvertence, stupidity, or calculation, for it is a freedom that is defended as much by song and public debate as by philosophical treatises and political speeches.

ALBERT CAMUS

March 22, 1947
No Excuse for This[22]

Yesterday's issue of this newspaper contained a courageous later to M. Ramadier from Father Riquet,[23] a resister and deportee. I have no idea what Christians may think about this letter, but my conscience will not allow me to let it pass

---

[21] Camus' contempt for Daladier has been evident throughout these editorials. See the article of September 12, 1944, n. 63, p. 35, and of May 12, 1945, p. 196.

[22] Article, set off in a framed box in publication. Reprinted in *Actuelles*, chapter "Deux ans après."

[23] Father Michel Riquet, a resister deported to Mauthausen and later Dachau, was then pastor of Notre-Dame of Paris, a position in which he remained until 1955. His widely noticed sermons dealt with the major issues of the day from a Christian point of view. In the Joanovici case, convents and religious homes were searched by the police, and monks and nuns accused of harboring former members of the Milice

without comment. Indeed, it seems to me that unbelievers should feel even more obliged than others to express outrage at the unspeakable attitude that a part of the press has adopted in this case.

I have no desire to justify anything whatsoever. If it is true that certain religious conspired against the state, they should indeed be subject to the laws that this country has adopted. To date, however, France has not, to my knowledge, countenanced the idea that responsibility might become collective. Before so many journalists and party hacks denounced convents as dens of murderers and traitors and the entire Church as the center of a vast and obscure conspiracy, one wishes that they had simply taken the trouble to remember.

Had they done that, they might have recalled a time when certain convents camouflaged a very different sort of conspiracy with their silence. They might have held up as an example to the tepid and faltering the actions of a few heroic souls, who without lengthy discussion quit their pacific communities for the tortured ones of the camps of destruction. Since we were among the first to denounce the failings of certain religious dignitaries,[24] we have the right to point this out at a time when other journalists neglect the duties and dignity of their profession and transform themselves into slander-mongers.

Whatever responsibility must be borne by a government that has clearly revealed only what suited itself and that chose the most propitious moment for doing so, the responsibility of journalists is greater still, for they denied what they knew and averted their eyes from what remains our sole justification, namely, the suffering we shared for four years. For newspapers that enjoyed the honor of publishing underground, this is an unforgivable failing, an affront to the noblest of memories, and a challenge flung in the face of justice. When *Franc-Tireur*,[25] responding to Father Riquet without printing his letter, screams, "Who is still faithful to the spirit of the Resistance? Those who are trying to save the torturers of deported priests from justice or those who want to punish them?" it forgets that if there is one justice that should be applied to the enemy, there is another, superior in spirit, that ought to be applied to brothers in arms. In strictest justice, an effort should have been made not to lump a vast number of innocents together with a handful of the accused while gleefully ignoring all whose throats had been slit. There is definitely no excuse for this.

---

were arrested. The minister of the interior, Edouard Depreux, accused them of "protecting militiamen and other collaborators." On March 21, *Combat* published Father Riquet's letter of protest to Prime Minister Ramadier. In this letter, which also appeared in *L'Aube*, Riquet recalled his own enlistment in the Resistance and deportation and spoke out against the climate of slander, hatred, and inquisition he saw as a leftover from the German occupation.

[24] See the editorials of September 16 and December 26, 1944, pp. 38 and 152.

[25] On March 18, 1945, *Franc-Tireur* ran the following headline: "La Santé [Prison] Will Not Be Short of Chaplains." On the front page, under the title "And Now for the Cassock Conspiracy," the paper published a long article by Madeleine Jacob, which spoke of "networks" going all the way to the Vatican and noted: "It was already public knowledge that the convents steadfastly offered the widest and most solicitous asylum to all who had belonged to the Milice, the L.V.F., the Gestapo, and, to put it in a nutshell, Vichy. The beneficiaries of this asylum merely had to know which door to knock on with which secret knock."

But what good does it do to protest, really? The calculating spirit is deaf; we are preaching to the wilderness. Who cares anymore about the Resistance and its honor? After two years in which so many hopes were wrecked, it is with a heavy heart that we repeat what we have said in the past.[26] Still, we must. We speak only about what we know, and we feel ashamed for those we love, and for them alone. I can hear the mockery already. "Guess what! *Combat* now stands with the Church." That, of course, is without importance. As unbelievers, the only hatred we feel is for hatred itself, and so long as there is a breath of freedom in this country, we will go on refusing to join those who scream insults and stand only with those who bear witness, whoever they may be.[27]

ALBERT CAMUS

April 22, 1947
The Choice [28]

It seems that one must choose.[29] Nothing is more urgent, to believe those who press us to make a choice. With them this is an idée fixe. "What are you waiting for? Are you for the R.P.F.[30] or against it? There is something a little comical about such insistence. After all, the house is not yet on fire. Fragrant flower carts wend their way through springtime Paris,[31] and the air is mild. The leisure of liberty is almost palpable. In political heads, however, an obsessional fever rages, and so we are forced to set down some basic truths. Here they are.

Combat, if memory serves, was not created to be the newspaper of a party. It was created so that a few men could come together to exercise free criticism while respecting the nuances of their respective opinions. Nothing more and nothing less. Just because General de Gaulle has organized a movement does not mean that we have to clamber up on stage alongside him. Until further notice, the R.P.F. is nothing other than a new element in the political life of this country. It is therefore appropriate that it be treated exactly the same as the other parties. In

---

[26] It was no doubt this sentence that justified the title given to this chapter in *Actuelles*. This was not an error, contrary to Roger Quilliot's contention in a note (*Essais*, p. 1511).

[27] See *La Peste*, p. 278: "This chronicle . . . could only stand as witness to what had to be done." See also, among other texts, "Le Témoin de la liberté," a lecture given in December 1948 and reprinted in *Actuelles. Essais*, pp. 399–406.

[28] Editorial.

[29] This editorial led to a break between Camus and Albert Ollivier, who, as a backer of de Gaulle and supporter of the R.P.F., had wanted to respond to it. See his letter, quoted in the introduction, p. xxxi.

[30] General de Gaulle had just founded the Rassemblement du Peuple français. Spurred on by René Capitant and André Malraux, among others, this "movement," which refused to consider itself a party, saw itself as united "in the effort to renovate and reform the state." It drew people hostile to communism, including many former resisters. It lasted ten years.

[31] Cf. *La Peste*, p. 11: "Spring was evident only in the quality of the air and the baskets of flowers that modest vendors brought in from the suburbs."

that light, excommunication and worship strike us as equally puerile attitudes. After all, a certain number of Frenchmen share our view that the national dilemma is not entirely summed up by the choice between de Gaulle and Thorez and that it is still permissible to maintain one's sangfroid.

As one might expect, our columns will not be used to insult General de Gaulle. We, at least, have not lost our memories. But the justice we accord him is compatible, we believe, with independent judgment. Just as we were able to criticize him in the most uncompromising way (and frequently alone) when he presided over the government, so, too, will we judge the R.P.F. by its actions and not by its principles, several of which remain vague. These are simple ideas, but simplicity nowadays seems rather unusual. One has to be more specific.

It is no secret that the party to which we feel closest is the Socialist Party (with all the disappointments that entails). Despite this, the Socialist position in practice has not always thrilled us, and we have never hesitated to say so in an appropriately objective form. Similarly, while General de Gaulle is for us the man who restored the French Republic (which gives him certain rights), he is also the man who agreed to the election law from which today's parties derive their strength. This, in our view, makes it difficult for him to offer a truly telling critique of the system organized by those same parties.

I can hear the objection that will be raised to this line of argument: we treat ourselves too handsomely. I'm not certain of this, and we here can attest that our role is not the easiest. In the end, though, it may be good for this country that a forum continues to exist far from the deafening tumult of partisan voices, a forum where independent minds can still bear witness without pretentiousness or fear. It is good that freedom can still be exercised, at least for a little while, and even if it must swim against the tide. In the age of lies, even the clumsiest frankness is preferable to the best-orchestrated ruse. Here, at least, it is still possible to breathe, as lonely as the effort may sometimes seem. Those are our reasons. Now as in the past, the purpose of *Combat* is to avoid the blindness born of enthusiasm as well as hatred and preserve what few grounds continue to sustain our fragile hope.

ALBERT CAMUS

April 30, 1947
Democracy and Modesty[32]

The new parliamentary year has begun.[33] Wheeling, dealing, and chicanery are about to resume. The same problems that have eluded us for the past two years will face the same dead ends. And every time a free individual tries to say in

---

[32] Editorial. Reprinted in *Actuelles*, chapter "Deux ans après," with the erroneous date "February 1947."
[33] The beginning of the parliamentary year coincided with the end of the Easter recess.

simple language what he thinks of all this, an army of watchdogs of every ilk and stripe barks furiously to drown out any response.

None of this gladdens the heart, of course. Fortunately, those who nurse only reasonable hopes continue to have healthy hearts. Those people in France who have experienced the full brunt of the past ten years have at least learned not to fear for themselves but only for others. They have come to terms with the worst. They remain calm and steady. Let us therefore repeat calmly and steadily, with the unalterable naïveté that others so kindly see in us, the basic principles without which, in our view, no acceptable political life is possible.[34]

There may be no good political regime, but democracy is surely the least bad of the alternatives. Democracy is inseparable from the notion of party, but the notion of party can easily do without democracy. That happens when one party or group imagines itself to be in possession of the absolute truth. That is why the Assembly and deputies today need to ingest a dose of modesty.

Today's world offers any number of grounds for modesty. Is it possible to forget that neither the National Assembly nor any government possesses the means to solve the problems that beset us? The proof of this assertion can be seen in the fact that in dealing with those problems, our legislators have invariably run up against international disagreements. Are we short of coal? The reason is that the English refuse to let us have coal from the Ruhr and the Russians refuse to let us have coal from the Saar. Are we short of bread? M. Blum and M. Thorez hurl back and forth statistics about the tons and quintals of wheat that either Moscow or the United States should have shipped to us. There is no better proof that the role of the Assembly and government can for now only be an administrative one and that France, in short, is dependent on others for what she needs.

The only thing to do is to acknowledge this, draw the necessary consequences, and try, for instance, to work together to define the international order without which no domestic problem can ever be resolved anywhere. In other words, we need to forget about ourselves for a while. If we did, deputies and parties would acquire some of that modesty that good and genuine democracies require. After all, a democrat is a person who admits that his adversary may be right, who therefore allows him to speak, and who agrees to consider his arguments. When parties and people are so convinced by their own arguments that they are willing to resort to violence to silence those who disagree with them, democracy no longer exists. Modesty is therefore salutary in republics at all times. France no longer possesses the means of power. Leave it to others to say whether that is good or bad. It is in any case an opportunity. Until we either regain our power or renounce it, the possibility remains for us to set an example. But France can set an example for the world only if it proclaims the truths it is able to discover within its borders. In other words, it must demonstrate by the actions of its government that domestic democracy cannot be complete until an international

---

[34] Here Camus returns to the theme of many of the editorials of 1944 and 1945. In November 1948 he published an article in *Caliban* entitled "La démocratie, exercice de la modestie," which continues this text. See *Essais*, pp. 1580–1583.

order has been established and that such an international order cannot be democratic unless it renounces violence and its attendant distress.

As the reader will already have divined, these meditations are intentionally untimely.[35]

ALBERT CAMUS

May 7, 1947
Anniversary

On May 8, 1945, Germany signed the most important surrender agreement in all history. General Jodl[36] stated at the time that he believed "the surrender document places Germany and the German people in the hands of the conquerors." Eighteen months later, Jodl was hanged at Nüremberg. It was not possible to hang 70 million Germans, however; Germany is still in the hands of the conquerors; and this anniversary of the surrender is not a day of rejoicing. Victory also has its inescapable obligations.

The problem is that Germany is still on trial, and that makes it difficult, especially for a Frenchman, to say or do reasonable things when it comes to the German question. Two years ago, on Dönitz's orders, the Flensburg radio[37] broadcast an appeal in which the provisional leaders of the defeated Reich expressed their hope that "the atmosphere of hatred that envelops Germany everywhere will gradually give way to a spirit of reconciliation among nations, without which there can be no recovery." This lucidity came five years too late, and Dönitz's hope was only half realized. The hatred of Germany has given way to a bizarre sentiment in which wariness and a vague rancor are mixed with an old indifference. As for the spirit of reconciliation—

The three minutes of silence that followed the announcement of Germany's surrender has thus been extended to an endless state of dumbness, in which occupied Germany continues to live in stunned disbelief, somewhat scornfully neglected by the rest of the world. No doubt this is due to the fact that Nazism, like all predatory regimes, could expect anything from the world but to be forgotten. It began our apprenticeship in hatred. Perhaps that hatred could have been set aside, since human memory evaporates as rapidly as history moves on. But the calculation and cold, meticulous precision of the Hitlerian regime

---

[35] The phrase "untimely meditations" is taken from Nietzsche, and Camus had used it before as the title of an article published in *Soir-Républicain* on November 6, 1939, and signed "Nero." See *Fragments d'un combat*, p. 637. Here it ironically contradicts the volume title.

[36] Alfred Jodl was a general who was very close to Hitler and who played an important role in devising German strategy in World War II. As Dönitz's chief of staff, he signed the surrender agreement for Germany in Rheims on May 7, 1945. Tried at Nüremberg for war crimes, he was sentenced to death and hanged.

[37] Dönitz announced the German surrender from the city of Flensburg in Schleswig-Holstein.

continue to weigh on countless hearts. The functionaries of hatred are not as quickly forgotten as the possessed. This is a valuable warning to all of us.

So there are some things that people of my generation can never forget, but I don't think that any of us would want, on this anniversary, to trample a defeated enemy underfoot. Absolute justice is impossible, just as eternal hatred and eternal love are impossible. That is why a return to reason is essential. The Age of the Apocalypse is over.[38] That of mediocre organization and compromise without grandeur has begun. Wisdom and a predilection for happiness counsel that the latter is to be preferred to the former, even though we know that mediocrity leads to apocalypse. But this respite allows time for reflection, and today that reflection should dissuade us from reviving dormant hatreds and lead us instead to establish a proper order in Germany.

Regardless of our inward passions and of the memories of our rebellions, we know full well that there can be no peace in the world without a pacified Germany, and there can be no pacification of Germany if it is forever banished from the international order. If dialogue with Germany is still possible, it is reason that insists upon its resumption. We must add just as forcefully, moreover, that the German problem is in fact a secondary one, though some seek to transform it into the most important issue of the day in order to divert our attention from what is glaringly obvious, namely, that Germany today is not so much a threat as a prize in the contest between Russia and America. The only urgent problems of our time are those that bear on the relations—agreement or hostility—between these two powers.[39] If agreement can be reached, Germany and several other countries will face a reasonable future. Otherwise, Germany will be submerged in a broad general defeat. What this means is that France should prefer the application of reason to the politics of power in all circumstances. The choice today is between actions that will probably be ineffective and those that will certainly be criminal. This, in my view, is not a difficult choice to make.

In any case, the effort to employ reason is proof of self-confidence. It is proof that we feel strong enough, come what may, to go on fighting and pleading for justice and freedom. Today's world is not a hopeful place. We may soon find ourselves once again facing the Apocalypse. But the surrender of Germany—a victory against all reason and against all hope—will stand for many years to come as a symbol of the impotence of force that Napoleon once described in such melancholy terms: "In the long run, Fontanes, the spirit is always mightier than the sword."[40] In the long run, yes—but of course it is a good rule of conduct to believe that the free spirit is always right and will always triumph in the end, for

---

[38] Camus may have in mind not only the Apocalypse of the New Testament but also the section of Malraux's *Man's Fate* that follows "The Lyric Illusion" and is entitled "Experiencing the Apocalypse."

[39] Once again it is worth pointing out the clarity of Camus' political vision.

[40] Camus was quoting from memory a sentence he had recorded in his notebooks, with which he began an article entitled "Pour preparer le fruit," which appeared in *La Tunisie française* in January 1941. This text was reprinted in 1954 under the title "Les Amandiers" in *L'Eté*. "'Do you know,' said Napoleon to Fontanes, 'what I admire most in the world? It is the impotence of force when it comes to founding

when the spirit ceases to be right, all mankind will be wrong and human history
will have lost all meaning.

ALBERT CAMUS

May 10, 1947
Contagion

There can be no doubt that France is a far less racist country than others I have
had a chance to visit. That is why it is impossible not to denounce the signs of
this stupid and criminal malady that have lately reared their heads in one place
or another.

A morning newspaper ran this banner headline on page one: "Raseta the murderer." That is one sign, because quite obviously the Raseta case is currently
under investigation, and it is impossible to publicize such a serious charge in
such a manner before the investigation is complete.[41]

I should say at once that the only nonsuspect news I have about events in
Madagascar consists of accounts of atrocities committed by the rebels and reports
on certain aspects of the repression. I therefore feel nothing but equal repugnance
for the methods of both sides. The question, however, is whether or not M. Raseta
is a murderer. There can be no doubt that no honest man would presume to make
up his mind about this until the investigation is complete. In any case, no journalist would have dared to use such a headline if the alleged murderer had been
named Dupont or Durand. But M. Raseta is Malagasy, so he must somehow or
other be a murderer. Such a headline is therefore of no consequence.

Nor is this the only sign of racism in France. No one is surprised to learn that
the unfortunate student who killed his fiancée used the presence of "sidis,"[42] as
they say, in the forest of Sénart to divert suspicion from himself. If Arabs go for
a walk in the woods, it cannot be simply because spring has arrived. It can only
be to murder their contemporaries.

By the same token, you can always be sure, sooner or later, of finding a
Frenchman, often an intelligent Frenchman, eager to tell you that Jews are prone

---

something. There are only two powers in the world: the saber and the spirit. In the long run, the saber is
always defeated by the spirit." *Carnets I*, p. 186; *Essais*, p. 835. In the *Carnets*, Camus wrote *garder* (to
keep) instead of *fonder* (to found). In the article and the essay, Camus commented: "Clearly conquerors
are sometimes melancholic." Here he retains the idea of "melancholy."

[41] Riots had erupted in Madagascar on March 29. *Combat* reported on these disturbances throughout the
month of April. The government tended to minimize the events somewhat, and most of the press followed
suit, with the notable exception of *Franc-Tireur*, which accorded ample space in its pages to Dr. Raseta,
one of the leaders of the Democratic Movement of the Malagasy Revolution, which would ultimately be
dissolved. On April 9, *Combat's* "special correspondent," Marie-Louise David, stressed the seriousness of
the events in her in-depth analysis. Raseta, a deputy from Madagascar, was assaulted in the corridors of
the Palais-Bourbon. A warrant was issued for his arrest even before his parliamentary immunity was lifted.
This measure led to a break with the Communist ministers, who voted no confidence in the government.

[42] [The word is an insulting slang term for North African immigrant—Trans.]

to exaggerate. Of course this Frenchman has a Jewish friend who's not of that sort, but still—As for the millions of Jews who were tortured and burned, our Frenchman naturally disapproves of such methods, to put it mildly. It's just that Jews exaggerate, and they have no business supporting one another, even if they learned their solidarity in a concentration camp.[43]

Yes, these are signs. But they are not the worst. One year ago in Algeria, methods of collective repression were used.[44] And *Combat* recently revealed the existence of the "spontaneous confession chamber" in Fianarantsoa.[45] This is not the place to get into the root of the problem, which is of a different order entirely. The nature of the solution is worth reflecting on, however.

Three years after being subjected to a policy of terror themselves, Frenchmen are reacting to this latest news with the indifference of people who have seen too much. Yet the facts are there, the clear and hideous truth: we are doing what we reproached the Germans for doing.[46] I am well aware that we have been offered an explanation, namely, that the Malagasy rebels have tortured Frenchmen. But the cowardly crimes of our adversaries do not excuse our becoming cowardly and criminal in turn. I haven't heard that we were building crematory ovens to avenge ourselves on the Nazis. We put them on trial, as far as I know. Clear, firm justice is the proof that a society is ruled by law, and it is justice that should represent France.

In fact, the true explanation lies elsewhere. If the Hitlerians applied their shameful laws to Europe, the reason was that they believed their race to be superior, hence the law for Germans could not be the same as the law for enslaved peoples. If we French revolted against their terror, it was because we believed that all Europeans were equal in rights and dignity. But if Frenchmen can now hear of the methods used in some instances by other Frenchmen against Algerians and Malagasies and not react, it is because they are unconsciously certain that we are in some way superior to those people and that it makes little difference what means we choose to demonstrate that superiority.

I do not propose to resolve the colonial problem here, nor do I mean to offer any excuses. My purpose is simply to call attention to signs of a racism that dishonors so many countries already and from which we need to protect our own. Therein lay, and should lie, our true superiority, and some of us are terribly afraid that we are losing it. If it is accurate to say that the colonial problem is the most complex of all the problems we face, and if it is going to shape the history of the next fifty years, it is no less true to say that we will never be able to solve it if we allow the most pernicious of prejudices to influence our judgment.[47]

---

[43] Certain passages in this article anticipate the tone of *La Chute*.

[44] Allusion to the events of Sétif. See "Crisis in Algeria" in May 1945, pp. 198 ff.

[45] On May 2, Marie-Louise David wrote: "The repression was and still is terrifying. I will mention only the 'Gestapo-style' torture chamber in Fianarantsoa, to use the description offered by a torturer assigned to make the rebels talk."

[46] No other newspaper published a similar condemnation.

[47] Camus's tone here is reminiscent of his position on Algeria.

It is no part of my purpose, however, to plead for a foolishly sentimental approach that would embrace all races in one undifferentiated effusion of affection. People are not all alike. I am well aware of the deep differences of tradition that separate me from an African or a Muslim. But I also know what unites me to them, and that is something in each of us that I cannot despise without debasing myself. That is why it is necessary to say clearly that these signs of racism, whether glaring or covert, point up what is most abject and senseless in the human heart. Only when we have vanquished that flaw will we win the difficult right to denounce the spirit of tyranny and violence wherever it arises.

ALBERT CAMUS

June 3, 1947
To Our Readers[48]

The political and managing editors and staff of the daily *Combat* are resigning today, although the newspaper will continue to appear. This calls for a certain amount of explanation, and I shall try to be clear.

The number of *Combat*'s readers today should be sufficient to ensure the existence of a newspaper without ambitions. But to be frank, the conditions under which daily newspapers operate have evolved to the point where only large circulation papers can break even. I leave it to readers to ponder what this law of economics portends for freedom of thought. Despite the fact that *Combat* is currently losing money, it made enough in previous years that it should have been able to continue for another year in the hope of increasing its circulation by reorganizing and redoubling our effort to attract new readers. This was well within the realm of possibility. But the printers' strike evaporated the few million francs that represented the fruit of the assiduous labor of our collective. Of course we could have sought money from outside and could even have obtained money without seeking it. There was no shortage of offers, as you may imagine (and many of them were both honorable and generous). Nevertheless, we did not think we were entitled to accept them, in view of the situation in which we

---

[48] This editorial marked the end of Camus' *Combat*. It was followed immediately by a text by Claude Bourdet entitled "*Combat* Continues." Bourdet wrote: "*Combat* is more than a newspaper. It is the most sacred heritage of a sinister and glorious period." After saying a brief word about the underground *Combat*, Bourdet hailed the "great daily newspaper" it had become, "whose courage and independence are now proverbial . . . having succeeded in winning the esteem of journalists the world over." He pointed out that he was among those responsible for putting together the paper's original staff and that he shared their "concern for independence" and "absence of prejudice." He pledged that "neither the political line nor the tone" of the newspaper would change. He listed the collaborators who would continue to work with him and concluded with the following: "It is clearly understood that if Camus and those comrades who are about to take a well-deserved rest wish to return to daily journalism, the pages of *Combat* will remain open to them as before."

found ourselves. For some weeks now, the *Combat* staff has tried with diminished means to fight on in an attempt to save the paper and protect our employees' jobs. In the end, however, we had to acknowledge that we, the present editorial staff, had reached the end of our tether.

We are not the exclusive owners of the name *Combat*, however. The newspaper belongs, morally and legally, to all who wrote, printed, and distributed it during the Occupation. Once we decided to give up our own claim to the name, we were therefore obliged to turn it over to the militants of the "Combat" movement. With the approval of the Fédération des Amicales "Combat," our comrade Claude Bourdet, one of the founders of the underground newspaper, who was arrested and deported on account of his activities and whose political leanings have always been close to those of this paper, has decided to take charge himself of the job of running it. As we leave our posts, therefore, it is to Claude Bourdet that we entrust an enterprise whose meaning for us I do not need to describe. There was also another reason for our decision, of considerable importance: our concern to save the jobs of our employees and protect the livelihood of our staff. I will not insist on this point, but it will serve to give readers a precise idea of the responsibilities we bore.

The political and managing editors of the paper are thus withdrawing and turning the operation over to new leadership. We want this to be perfectly clear. We offer our sincerest wishes for the success of a venture we have cherished. But just as the comrades who will put out the paper in the future should bear no responsibility for positions we have taken, so, too, should our departure relieve us of responsibility for any positions they may take in the future. It should nevertheless be clearly understood that Claude Bourdet intends to pursue the line of objectivity and independence that he has always followed. Otherwise, the staff of the paper remains as it was.

It remains for me to thank our readers for the confidence and devotion they have shown us throughout. There are several ways to thrive in journalism. I hardly need mention that we who joined this daily poor are leaving it just as poor. Our only wealth has always been concentrated in our respect for our readers. If we in turn have on occasion earned their respect, this was and will remain our only luxury. It is of course possible that we made mistakes over the past three years (who does not make mistakes when obliged to speak daily?). But we never abdicated any of the responsibilities that constitute the honor of our profession. The fact that this newspaper is not like other newspapers was for all these years a source of pride for us. There is no other decent way to express our feelings as we leave *Combat* today.

ALBERT CAMUS

CHAPTER 5

1948–1949

In 1948, two things led to the reappearance of Camus' name in the pages of *Combat* as both subject and author: the creation of *L'Etat de siège* (*State of Siege*) and the action of Garry Davis, the "citizen of the world," whom Bourdet and Camus supported.

The newspaper gave considerable publicity to the performance of *State of Siege* at the Théâtre Marigny.[1] On October 27 it reported on the play's dress rehearsal, and the next day it published a photograph of Camus together with Jean Louis Barrault and Maria Casarès. On October 29 there was an article by Jacques Lemarchand,[2] accompanied by a Maurice Henry drawing. On November 19, *Combat* published an excerpt from the play.[3] On November 23 there was a report on a lecture by Barrault,[4] who championed the idea of a work created in conditions of "total freedom." It was therefore logical for Camus to choose *Combat* to respond, two days later, to an article that Gabriel Marcel published on *State of Siege* in *Les Nouvelles Littéraires*. This was a particularly logical choice in light of the fact that Camus' response was more political and moral than literary and continued the argument he had begun developing in his editorials about Spain and his series "Neither Victims nor Executioners."

Camus' departure from *Combat* did not mean that he had given up on making his political views known, particularly his dream of an international organization of socialists and pacifists. Although he did not join the "Rassemblement démocratique révolutionnaire," or R.D.R., a political movement in which various socialists were joined by Jean-Paul Sartre, David Rousset, and Georges Altman, he did take a keen interest in it and supported it with articles in *La Gauche*[5] and *Franc-Tireur*. It will come as no surprise that his position in this regard was close to that of *Combat*, as it was to *Combat*'s position with respect to Garry Davis, who attempted to create an international movement to promote world peace. In May, Garry Davis renounced his American citizenship and proclaimed himself a "citizen of the world." In September, he camped out in front of the Palais de Chaillot, where the U.N. held meetings from September until December of 1948. He claimed the status of "citizen of the world" and hoped to gain a hearing at the U.N. Around him he formed a "Council of Solidarity," which included intellectuals, writers, artists, and journalists, among them

---

[1] The director was Jean-Louis Barrault, who also played the role of Diego. The music was by Arthur Honegger, and the sets were designed by Balthus. Maria Casarès played Victoria.

[2] Lemarchand "wondered if Jean-Louis Barrault hasn't obliged Camus to present a different play from the one he wrote" and deplored the fact that the words of the text took a back seat to the direction.

[3] The excerpt was from the first scene between Diego and Victoria.

[4] By Emile Scotto-Lavina, who noted that the audience did not respond strongly to the play, which closed after only twenty-three performances.

[5] A bimonthly publication of the R.D.R.

Georges Altman, Claude Bourdet, André Breton, Albert Camus, Jean Hélion, Emmanuel Mounier, Jean Paulhan, Abbé Pierre, Raymond Queneau, Vercors, and Richard Wright. In November and December *Combat* devoted considerable space to rallies in support of Davis in which members of this council participated, and the newspaper frequently summarized or published in full Camus' remarks on these occasions. On November 19, Davis attempted to interrupt a U.N. session with a demand for world government. He was arrested. In the November 20–21 issue, Maurice Henry reported on Camus' remarks at an impromptu press conference given after the arrest by writers belonging to the council who had been present in the hall:

> Camus stressed the importance of Garry Davis's arrest, which leaves the U.N. in an untenable position. The man was arrested in effect for advocating the cause that the U.N. claims to champion. The author of *The Plague* added that the Council of Solidarity had decided to do everything it could to support the movement that the arrest of Garry Davis cannot fail to ignite.

Emile Scotto-Lavina's report on December 14 of the international writers' meeting at the Salle Pleyel, which was attended by Sartre, Rousset, Breton, Wright, and Carlo Levi as well as Camus, took a sentence of Camus' as its title: "This century is searching in vain for reasons to love, which it has lost." It included excerpts from his speech, the text of which was later published in *La Gauche* and reprinted in *Actuelles* under the title "Witness for Freedom." For *Combat* there was no doubt a symbolic value attached to the name "Camus." On December 7, *Combat* published the text of an appeal to the U. N., "For Peace," signed by five hundred intellectuals. It noted that "among the personalities most familiar to readers of this newspaper, A. Camus, H. Calet, J. Lemarchand, Roland-Manuel, Maurice Nadeau, and Bernard Voyenne signed this petition."

A year and a half after his departure, readers clearly had not forgotten Camus. And Camus himself remained an attentive reader of the paper: he noticed that it mentioned him among the members of the jury for the Prix de la Villa d'Este.[6] The next day, the paper printed a correction, quoting from a note Camus had sent:

> *Combat*, which is always well informed, is for once a little too well informed. It has me down as a member of a literary jury, for the Prix de la Villa Este, which I had never heard of until now. This is very flattering, but the fact is that I am not now a member of any jury and do not expect to become one any time soon. Tell your readers this when the opportunity arises, for the sake of the foundation giving the prize as well as for the principle of the thing.

---

[6] See the November 29, 1947, issue. The Prix de la Villa d'Este was a literary prize. The jury included George Duhamel, André Maurois, and the Tharaud brothers. After quoting from Camus' note, the writer of this piece concluded that "since Camus added that he would buy us a drink soon, we won't wait a day longer to print this correction." This shows that Camus maintained friendly relations with some members of the paper's staff.

Camus' signature appeared along with André Breton's on a petition published in the February 26–27 and March 10 issues, which pleaded for a commutation of the death sentences of ten Greek intellectuals (former resisters sentenced to death by the Germans) who again faced the death penalty after being convicted of trying to leave Greece secretly. *Combat* supported the petition and reported that it had resulted in a commutation of the sentences. Finally, in March 1949, *Combat* published a letter from Camus and René Char protesting the sentencing of Algerian war veterans. Unless I am mistaken, this was the last text that Camus published in *Combat*. After the exclusion of Claude Bourdet, the paper quickly became the exclusive property of Henri Smadja, and it thereafter had nothing in common with the paper of Pia and Camus.[7]

November 25, 1948
Why Spain?[8]

RESPONSE TO GABRIEL MARCEL

I will respond here to just two passages in the article you wrote about *State of Siege* in *Les Nouvelles littéraires*.[9] I do not wish to respond to the criticisms that you and others have made of the play as a theatrical work. When one presents a play or publishes a book, one submits to criticism and agrees to accept the censure of one's contemporaries. Whatever one might wish to say in response, it is better to remain silent.

Nevertheless, you abused the critic's privilege when you went so far as to express your surprise that a play about totalitarian tyranny should be set in Spain, whereas you would have preferred that it be set in Eastern Europe. You further authorize me to reply when you write that this choice reflects a lack of courage and honesty. True, you are kind enough to suggest that I was not responsible for

---

[7] In February 1950 Camus wrote: "It would be better for the name to disappear than for it to be exploited by the current management. . . . The name without M. Smadja, or M. Smadja without the name." Letter quoted in Y. M. Ajchenbaum, *A la vie, à la mort*, p. 326.

[8] Text reprinted in *Actuelles*, standing alone, with the erroneous date "December 1948."

[9] Marcel's criticism was on the whole quite harsh. On November 4, *Les Nouvelles littéraires* published a caricature by Ben, and on November 11 it published Marcel's article, entitled "Theater: Albert Camus's 'State of Siege.'" The Christian existentialist philosopher, who was also a playwright, ripped both the play and its author to shreds, speaking of "a veritable academicism in the maniac," asserting that "the whole thing is entirely artificial, entirely cerebral," and concluding that "after this I can no longer think of this writer as a dramatic author." The passage that provoked Camus' response is worth quoting: "I don't think it was very courageous or even honest to have set the action in Spain, in Cadiz, rather than in some Dalmatian or Albanian port, for example, or some sub-Carpathian town. I cannot help thinking that this circumstance is probably not the fault of M. Camus himself, whose bravura is obvious. Any impartial and well-informed person will agree that for some time now the news most apt to plunge those who retain a concern for human dignity and freedom into despair has not been coming from the Iberian peninsula. It appears that an effort was made to find a substitute in order to calm the wrath of those who, like it or not, are the work's primary targets in 1948—I repeat, in 1948."

the choice in question (to speak plainly, you are thus blaming wicked Barrault, whose name you have already blackened with countless crimes). But the sad truth is that the play is set in Spain because I, and I alone, chose to set it there after giving the matter due consideration. I must therefore take your accusations of opportunism and dishonesty as being directed at me. This being the case, it should not surprise you that I feel compelled to respond.

Very likely I would not bother to defend myself against these charges (for to whom can one justify oneself nowadays?) if you hadn't touched on a subject as grave as the situation in Spain, for I really don't need to tell the world that I wasn't trying to please anyone in particular when I wrote *State of Siege*. I wanted to attack head-on a type of political society that has been or is being organized on both the right and the left along totalitarian lines. No impartial observer can doubt that this play takes the side of the individual, of flesh in the noblest sense, and ultimately of mortal love against the abstractions and terrors of the totalitarian state,[10] whether it be Russian, German, or Spanish. Men of somber learning reflect daily on the decadence of our society and look for its deeper causes, which no doubt exist. But for simpler souls, the evil of the present age is characterized by its effects, not by its causes. It is called the state, whether police or bureaucratic. Its proliferation everywhere on a variety of ideological pretexts make it a mortal danger for all that is best in each of us, as does the insulting security it derives from mechanical and psychological methods of repression. In this sense, contemporary political society is contemptible, regardless of its content. That is all I said, and that is why *State of Siege* is a declaration of independence that aims to spare no one.

Having said all this as clearly as I can, your question remains: Why Spain? I confess that if I were you, I would be rather ashamed to ask it. Why Guernica,[11] Gabriel Marcel? Why this place, where for the first time Hitler, Mussolini, and Franco demonstrated to a world still asleep amid its comforts and its miserable morality what totalitarian methods were like? Why this place, which affected us as well? For the first time, people of my generation saw injustice historically triumphant.[12] Innocent blood flowed while Pharisees chattered on, as, frankly, they are still doing today. Why Spain? Because a few of us refuse to wash that blood from our hands. Whatever reasons there may be for anticommunism, and I know some good ones, we will never accept it if it goes so far as to forget the injustice done to Spain, an injustice which, with the complicity of our governments, has been allowed to continue to this day. I have stated as forthrightly as

---

[10] This echoes one of the themes of "Neither Victims nor Executioners," as well as the premises of the chapters of *The Rebel* concerned with "state terrorism."

[11] Guernica, a city in northern Spain, was bombed by German planes on April 27, 1937, killing some 2,000 people. This massacre, which took place on a market day, foreshadowed the bombings of World War II and inspired a famous painting by Picasso.

[12] We have already seen what Spain meant to Camus. He often said that the Spanish civil war was the beginning of World War II.

I could what I thought of the Russian concentration camps.[13] Yet those camps are not about to make me forget Dachau, Buchenwald, or the nameless agony of millions of people and the dreadful repression that has decimated the Spanish Republic. Yes, despite all the commiseration our illustrious political leaders have offered, all these things must be denounced together. I am not about to make excuses for the hideous plague in Western Europe just because the same plague is also wreaking havoc in the East. You write that for people who are well-informed, the news most likely to dash the hopes of those who believe in human dignity is not now coming from Spain. You, Gabriel Marcel, are not well-informed. Just yesterday, five political opponents of the regime were sentenced to death. But you make yourself ready to be ill-informed by cultivating forget-fulness. You forget that the first armies of the totalitarian war were steeped in Spanish blood. You forget that in 1936 a rebel general, acting in the name of Christ, assembled an army of Moors to set against the lawful government of the Spanish Republic; you forget that he led an unjust cause to victory in the wake of unforgivable massacres and thereupon launched an atrocious repression that has gone on for ten years now and is not over yet. Yes, indeed, why Spain? Because you and so many others have lost your memory.

And also because I, together with a small number of other people in France, still find it impossible at times to be proud of my country. To my knowledge, France has never handed Soviet dissidents over to the Russian government. That will come, no doubt; our elites are prepared to do anything. When it comes to Spain, on the other hand, we have already done such things. Owing to the most scurrilous clause in the armistice, we surrendered Spanish Republicans, includ-ing the great Luis Companys,[14] to Franco on Hitler's orders. And Companys was shot while this terrible traffic went on. That, of course, was Vichy; it wasn't us. We merely put the poet Antonio Machado[15] in a concentration camp in 1938, a camp he left only to die. Yet on the day the French state set itself up as recruit-ing sergeant for the totalitarian executioners, who spoke out? Nobody. No doubt because, like you, Gabriel Marcel, those who might have protested found that none of this amounted to much compared with what they most detested in the Russian system. So their attitude was, "What difference can one more death by firing squad make?" But it's a vile wound that a firing squad leaves in a man's face, and gangrene ultimately set in. Gangrene has won out.

---

[13] *Combat* added the following note: "See *La Gauche*, October 1948." This note was omitted when the piece was reprinted in *Actuelles*. Camus published several articles in that organ of the R.D.R. The one in question was entitled "We Will Never Be for the Socialism of Concentration Camps," which appeared in *Actuelles* under the title "Second Response," in the chapter entitled "Two Responses to Emmanuel d'Astier de la Vigerie."

[14] On Companys, see the editorial of January 7–8, 1945, n. 404, p. 167.

[15] Antonio Machado (1875–1939) was a Spanish poet who supported republican Spain. He died in Collioure shortly after leaving the refugee camp at Argelès.

So where are the murderers of Companys? In Moscow or in this country? The answer is, Here. So we must admit that we shot Companys, that we are responsible for what followed. We must admit that we are humiliated by this and that the only way to repair the damage is to preserve the memory of a free Spain that we betrayed, as we did in our own petty place and way. To be sure, there is not a single major power that did not betray Spain, except Germany and Italy, who shot Spaniards in the face rather than the back. But that cannot be a consolation, and free Spain continues, by its silence, to ask us for reparations. I have done what little I can, and that is what you find scandalous. If I had more talent, the reparation would have been greater: that is all I can say. Cowardice and deceit in this case would have been to condone the status quo. But I shall say no more on this subject and suppress my feelings, out of respect for you. There is just one thing I would add: no man of sensibility should have been surprised, given that I wanted to give voice to the flesh and to pride as against the shame and shadows of dictatorship, that I chose the Spanish people. I couldn't, after all, choose the international subscribers to the *Reader's Digest* or the readers of *Samedi-Soir* and *France-Dimanche*.

No doubt you are waiting eagerly for me to bring this piece to a conclusion by explaining why I gave the role I did to the Church. On that point I will be brief. You judge that role to be odious, whereas in my novel it was not. But in my novel I was obliged to do justice to the Christian friends whom I met during the Occupation and with whom I joined in a just fight. In my play, by contrast, I had to say what role the Church played in Spain. If I portrayed that role as odious, it was because in the eyes of the world it was odious. As harsh as that truth may be for you, you may take consolation from the fact that the scene that bothers you lasts no more than a minute, whereas the one that continues to offend the conscience of Europe has been going on for ten years. And the entire Church would have been mixed up in the unbelievable scandal that saw Spanish bishops bestowing their benedictions on the rifles of firing squads if two great Christians had not spoken out immediately: one of them, Bernanos, is now dead,[16] while the other, José Bergamin,[17] lives in exile. Bernanos would not have written what you have written on this subject. He knew that the declaration with which my scene ends—"Christians of Spain, you have been forsaken"—was not an insult to your faith. He knew that to have said anything else, or to have remained silent, would have been to insult the truth.

If I were to rewrite *State of Siege*, I would still set it in Spain. For me, that is the bottom line. It should be clear to everyone that the play condemns not just Spain as it has been and as it is today but also, through Spain, all totalitarian societies.

---

16 Camus was of course an admirer of Georges Bernanos, as we have seen.

17 José Bergamin (1895–1983) was a Spanish writer and critic, a Catholic who backed the Spanish Republic. He was obliged to flee first to Mexico and later to South America. He tried to return to Madrid in 1958 but was forced to flee again and died in France.

I would not do so, moreover, at the cost of shameful complicity. We can keep the right to protest against terror only if we speak out in this way. That is why I cannot share your view when you say that we are in absolute agreement on the subject of political order, because you are willing to keep silent about one terror the better to combat another. Some of us are unwilling to keep silent about anything. What makes us sick to our stomachs is our political society in its entirety. There will be no salvation, moreover, until everyone who is still worth anything has totally repudiated it in order to begin looking for a path to renewal somewhere other than in its insuperable contradictions. Until then we must fight. And we must fight with the knowledge that totalitarian tyranny is built not on the virtues of totalitarians but on the vices of liberals. Talleyrand's gibe is contemptible: a blunder is not worse than a crime. In the end, however, the blunder ends up justifying the crime and providing the criminal with his alibi. This plunges the victims into despair and is on that account culpable. Indeed, it is precisely this that I cannot forgive in contemporary political society: it is a machine that makes people desperate.

You will no doubt find a great deal of passion in this letter for a small pretext. So let me speak for once in my own name. The world I live in disgusts me, but I feel myself in solidarity with the suffering people in it. There are many ambitions that I do not share, and I would not be comfortable if I were obliged to avail myself of the paltry privileges reserved for those who compromise with the world in order to make their way. To my way of thinking, though, there is one ambition that all writers ought to possess: the ambition to bear witness and to cry out whenever possible, to the extent that our talent permits, on behalf of those who share our servitude. That is the ambition that you attack in your article, and I will go on denying you the right to do so as long as the murder of a human being elicits your outrage, apparently, only to the extent that the victim shares your ideas.

ALBERT CAMUS

December 9, 1948
What Is the UN Accomplishing?[18]

Q. What are you doing here?
A. What we can.

---

[18] This text was published with the following brief introduction: "Below is the text of remarks delivered at the Salle Pleyel on December 3 by the author of *The Plague*." It was reprinted under the title "I Respond" in *La Patrie mondiale*, a newspaper created, according to an announcement published in *Combat*, on December 22 by "a group of young people" and "aided" by certain writers, who were none other than the members of the Council of Solidarity with Garry Davis, Camus among them. Its goal was to "combat all war psychosis and replace it with a peace psychosis."

Q. What are you accomplishing?

A. What is the UN accomplishing?

Q. Why isn't Davis going to speak in Soviet Russia?

A. Because they won't let him in. In the meantime, he is speaking to the Soviet delegate along with the rest.

Q. Why don't you give up your French nationality?

A. That is a valid if somewhat perfidious objection, which is to be expected since it comes from friends. Here is my answer: Davis gave up a good many privileges when he relinquished his American citizenship. To be French today carries with it more burdens than privileges. If your standards for yourself are high, it is very difficult to renounce your country when it is in trouble.

Q. Doesn't Davis's gesture seem to you rather theatrical and therefore suspect?[19]

A. It is not his fault if plain facts are today considered theatrical. Not to say that the two cases are the same, but Socrates, too, put on a constant show in the marketplace of his time. No one managed to prove him wrong other than by condemning him to death. And that indeed is precisely the form of refutation that is most widely used in contemporary political society. But it is also the way in which that society customarily admits its degradation and impotence.

Q. Don't you see that Davis is serving American imperialism?

A. By giving up his American citizenship, Davis took his distance from that imperialism and all the rest. This gives him the right to condemn imperialism, a right that it seems to me difficult to grant to those who want to impose limits on all sovereignty except that of the Soviet Union.

Q. Don't you see that Davis is serving Soviet imperialism?

A. The answer is the same as to the previous question but the other way around. I would add this: the two forms of imperialism are like twins. They grow together and cannot do without each other.

Q. Sovereignty is a reality. Don't you see that realities must be taken into account?

A. Cancer is also a reality. We nevertheless try to cure it, and nobody has yet had the effrontery to say that to cure a cancer that has attacked an overly sanguine temperament, the patient should eat more steak. Of course doctors have never taken themselves for popes in possession of the whole truth. That is their advantage over politicians.

---

[19] After turning in his American passport and proclaiming himself a "citizen of the world," Garry Davis camped out in front of the Palais de Chaillot, where the UN was in session. He hoped to be allowed to speak.

Q. Still, is it anything other than utopian to think that sovereignty can be limited in the historical circumstances that exist today? (Objection presented by *Le Rassemblement* in an unsigned article.[20])

A. I'll let General de Gaulle answer *Le Rassemblement*. In speaking of the Ruhr, he said that no one was obliged to have a good solution to the problem ready in order to be able to recognize and reject a bad one. In any case, Davis is proposing a solution, and you are declaring it to be utopian. You remind us of the father who invokes "realities" to warn his children against being too adventurous. Sometimes, though, the child honors the family by disobeying the father and quitting the family grocery. In other words, history is never anything other than utopia made flesh.

Q. Don't you see that the USA is the only obstacle to the establishment of socialism in the world? (Sometimes this question is put differently: Don't you see that the Soviet Union is the only obstacle to freedom in the world?)

A. If you have the war you foresee with an obstinacy worthy of being put to better use, the destruction and suffering it will cause, which will greatly overshadow the destruction and suffering due to World War II, will make it impossible to predict what the future will bring. I would not bet much on either liberty or socialism in a Europe reduced to rubble and filled with people not without the strength even to cry in pain.

Q. Does that mean you would choose surrender before war?

A. I know that some of you are only too glad to offer a choice between hanging and the firing squad. That is your idea of freedom. We are doing what we can to see to it that such a choice does not become inevitable. You are doing what you can to make it inevitable.

Q. But if it is inevitable, what will you do?

A. If you succeed, as I do not think you will, in making it inevitable, we will have no choice but to suffer the world's agony. The rest is mere journalism, and of the worst kind.

I am done, but before I go, I would like to put one question to those who disagree with me. It's my turn now. Are they so sure in the depths of their hearts that the political belief or doctrine that inspires them is infallible enough for them to heedlessly reject the warnings of those who remind them of the woes of millions of people, the cries of the innocent, and the simplest forms of happiness, and who ask them to weigh those poor truths in the balance against their hopes, no matter how legitimate? Are they sure enough of being right to risk

---

[20] *Le Rassemblement* was the weekly newspaper of the R.P.F. In January 1948 it took over from *L'Etincelle* (created in April 1947). As successor to Jacques Baumel, Albert Ollivier served as managing editor after June 1948. He had been working for the paper since February 1948, attacking both social democrats and Christian democrats. Other writers who had quit *Combat* also wrote for this paper, including Jean Chauveau and Pascal Pia.

even one chance in a thousand of making atomic war more likely? Indeed, are they so sure of themselves, and so prodigiously infallible, that we must concede everything to them? That is the question we put to them, a question they have heard before, to which we are still awaiting an answer.

ALBERT CAMUS

December 25–26, 1948
Responses to an Unbeliever[21]

ALBERT CAMUS TO FRANÇOIS MAURIAC[22]

To answer you is to astonish myself. You, however, won't react as *Le Populaire* did, when it took as an attack a mere expression of my surprise on learning that the Socialists not only were not the first to support one man's solitary peace initiative but were instead quick to heap ironies on it.[23] One is very alone in the Church, you wrote. Imagine the feelings of those who lack faith as consolation for the shortcomings of their churches!

A number of writers, myself among them, were sounded out about offering our support and protection to a man who had single-handedly taken courageous

[21] This text was published in a two-page special edition produced by the Centre de Recherche et d' Expression Mondialiste, which was close to the R.D.R. and to the Council of Solidarity supporting Davis. It described itself as "a first attempt at an international newspaper" and an "effort to create a free forum of world conscience, which will deal with the new issues common to all people." Under the title "People of the World," this two-page paper appeared every two weeks for a few months in 1949. The December 25–26 edition included, in addition to Camus, articles by Richard Wright, Henry Usborne, and Emmanuel Mounier. The title of this piece did not lack for humor, given that it was addressed to the very Catholic François Mauriac, whose "unbelief" concerned the possibility of a worldwide movement of the sort envisioned by the "Davis committee." Camus was also responding to reactions to his article of December 7 in *Franc-Tireur*, entitled "L'embarras du choix" (see *Essais*, pp. 1583–1586) and to his *Combat* article of December 9, "What Is the UN Accomplishing?" reproduced above.

[22] In *Le Figaro* of December 11–12, under the title "Nous nous éloignons infiniment de ce que nous aimons," Mauriac answered Camus' article "What Is the UN Accomplishing?" He began by saying that, although he had been tempted to follow Garry Davis, he was held back by a "reflex of common sense," and went on to analyze Camus' remarks: "Albert Camus, in *Combat*, easily dismisses all the objections to Davis but one: 'Don't you see that Davis is serving Soviet imperialism?'" Mauriac quotes the comment about the two forms of imperialism being twins and says that he doesn't understand its "scope." He then says: "The only reason for the U.N. to exist is precisely to create the conditions under which the Soviet Union and America cannot do without each other and agree to work together to save the world." He adds that he has signed a petition on this subject, which he says "is something different from launching an unstoppable movement, setting in motion uncontrollable forces indifferent to any contingencies that may arise, including Soviet imperialism." He compares Davis to Chamberlain, who was also a peace-loving man.

[23] It was the December 4–5 issue of *Le Populaire* that "heaped ironies" on the December 3 meeting in a brief report on "Salle Pleyel, aviary of peace," in which it remarked, "Peace is a bird, but which one? Was it Camus-the-blackbird, ironic and passionate? '*Le Populaire*,' he says, 'asks why Garry Davis is not going to speak in Soviet Russia. The answer is that they won't let him in, by Jove!' No, handsome blackbird, *Le Populaire* is glad that the Garry Davis affair could become an issue in Paris and doubts that it ever could in Karkhov." The paper then went on to deal with "Mounier-the-osprey" and "Vercors-the-stork."

and significant action only to be rewarded with sneers from newspapers that as you know never miss an opportunity to do honor to this country. What we were asked to do was in effect to defend Davis against the bureaucracy and call attention to his act of bearing witness. This we felt we could not refuse. Thereupon we were immediately denounced as Chamberlains, Daladiers, even Marcel Déats.[24] Leave aside the fact that one of my former collaborators at *Combat* wrote with no obvious signs of shame in *Le Rassemblement* that I repented of having been a resister.[25] Of course I know that he has no idea what he's talking about. And leave aside the fact that I find myself once again under indictment, as it were, by the likes of M. Pierre Hervé.[26] Some callings are irresistible, and as we should have learned by now, the police mentality has its apostles. But you astonish me.

Although I see no reason for the disdainful way in which you speak of the Davis Committee intellectuals, I readily grant that the profession of writer is no guarantee of infallibility. This truth applies to all writers, however. It is also the case that one can be a writer without suffering from a total lack of intellectual courage. I am not authorized to speak on behalf of my friends, but I never heard any of them describe Soviet imperialism as a contingency. At least some of them recognize it as a fact, and they will never acquiesce in the socialism of

---

On December 8, Henri Noguères responded to the *Franc-Tireur* article "L'embarras du choix" with a piece entitled "Pacifisme et publicité." He protested what he called Camus' "underhanded attack on *Le Populaire* on the pretext of pacifism": Camus, he said, had argued that "the Communists interpret every wish for peace expressed in this form [that is, as a refusal to choose between taking the American or the Russian side] as objective aid to the Americans. *Le Rassemblement* (and *Le Populaire* for that matter) respond immediately that, objectively speaking, to use your word, naïve prudence of this sort serves Russian imperialism." Treating Camus as a "notable propagandist for pacifism," Noguères criticized him for "tossing *Le Populaire* in the common grave along with all the other warmongers," for "counting the Socialists among the enemies of peace," and for pretending to believe that those who did not want to fight either the Russians or the Americans were few in number. He then asserted that such people "do not by any means regard [Camus] as their spokesman."

[24] Chamberlain and Daladier of course signed the Munich treaty in 1938 in the hope of preserving peace by sacrificing Czechoslovakia, while Déat was an advocate of collaboration with the Germans.

[25] In *Le Rassesmblement* of December 11 a note entitled "M. Albert Camus Repents" quoted a passage from Camus's December 7 article in *Franc-Tireur* ("L'embarras du choix"): "Despite the terrible bitterness and shame we may feel at the thought of vast prison camps in which countless human beings cling to life, we must not lose sight of the fact that peace gives us a chance to see these injustices repaired, while war does not." This was followed by a comment: "Here you have the illusion that M. Albert Camus is nursing in *Franc-Tireur*: he no longer believes that totalitarian ventures should be resisted by force." This note was not signed. Was the "former collaborator at *Combat*" Albert Ollivier or Jean Chauveau?

In the same issue of *Le Rassemblement*, Pascal Pia, commenting on the December 3 meeting and the reactions of the Communists, offered a pointed comment on "the last word in 'third-force' philosophy due to M. Albert Camus." On December 18, in an article entitled, "March with the People or Force the People to March?" Pia attacked the pacifism of Camus and Sartre (whose article had appeared in *Franc-Tireur* on December 10): "There is no point to an antiwar campaign unless it is to discourage in advance all resistance to a totalitarian state that aims to control our country. The recent 'Peace and Freedom' sessions sponsored by the Communist Party were inspired by no other concern than this."

[26] Pierre Hervé was a Communist journalist.

concentration camps (which in fact has more to do with concentration camps than with socialism). To put it plainly, they will not shade the facts. Their honesty therefore leaves them defenseless against your question. If Garry Davis succeeds in making his ideas known, which is likely to happen only in the West, won't that just hasten the victory of Russian imperialism?

Let me first approach the problem from the other side. Suppose you're completely right. What should you do? What you aren't doing. For if the Russian threat takes precedence over all others in both time and space, and if reluctance to go to war risks making war more likely, then we should drop everything else and take whatever steps are necessary in the full knowledge that they may lead to war. We should immediately enlist the support of the only force that can stop or even slow the Russians, namely, the United States, and that means that we must accept their foreign policy (whether we do so cheerfully or not changes nothing in the end). Since the Russians have put [foreign] Communist Parties in the vanguard, we must combat Communism by throwing our support to the only movement in France capable of opposing Communism by force, namely, Gaullism. As far as I know, you are not doing either of these things, and I do not say this for the pointless pleasure of catching you out but rather to urge you to show a little more indulgence toward our own inconsistency, assuming it exists. In any case, you have to admit that once we begin to think in terms of imperialism, aggression, and tactics—in terms of the Cold War, in other words—the position I have just set forth is the only logical one. If I'm not mistaken, it is the position of some of de Gaulle's sincere supporters.

Personally, I regard this logic as inevitable the moment one begins to think as you do. But I have something against the consequences of that logic, and I am going to draw out some further implications of the position that ought to be yours. In Cold War terms, everything in France should be subordinated to the struggle against the Communist Party, and this implies imposing certain limits on the way we think, rightly or wrongly, about democracy. Everything else should take a back seat to the need to enhance our military power, which will have its drawbacks for our economy. When I say that the brunt of the economic consequences will be borne, in the first instance, by workers of all classes, I don't think I'm exceeding the limits of the plausible. In foreign policy, if we, as realists, are to take part in the Cold War, you'll need to overcome some of your scruples. If Tsaldaris[27] better serves the cause of anti-Bolshevism, you'll need to close your eyes to the executions in Athens, to the island prison colonies, and to the politics of repression. And that is not all. You were among the first to speak out

---

[27] Tsaldaris, the Greek prime minister, pursued a repressive policy against the Communists. After the troubles of 1944 (see the editorials of November 29 and December 5 and 9, 1944, pp. 126, 133, and 135), Greece endured civil war from the end of 1946. Camus intervened on several occasions to defend condemned Greek intellectuals (see "L'enfant grec" of 1955 in *Camus editorialiste à l'Express*, pp. 118–121).

against Franco's rebellion. For that you deserve credit. But since Franco has given military assurances to the United States and stands as an obstacle to Russian ambitions, you'll need to support him, hope that he thrives, and on occasion shake his hand. If you don't, you'll be serving Russian imperialism. In short, if you don't agree from the beginning to an aggravation of social injustice, limitation of our liberties, executions in Greece, and Franco's prisons, you will be serving Russian imperialism just as we do.

There are additional consequences, moreover, that seem to me just as hard to swallow. In my view, those who believe that the Cold War is the only way of avoiding the other kind of war without serving Russian imperialism face a dilemma as embarrassing as the one we face. If Russian imperialism is what they say it is, there can be no doubt that time is on its side, that the Russians will one day have atomic weapons along with a restored economy, and on that day they will be ready to rule the world. The proponents of the Cold War are therefore obliged to accept the idea of preventive war or else find themselves speechless when challenged by others more realistic than themselves: "By not declaring war right away, you are serving Russian imperialism." If you follow the logic of the argument whose premises you accept, there is no escaping the conclusion: "Anything is preferable to Soviet domination, even immediate atomic war."

Given such a consequence, I am sure that you can understand our hesitations. How can we applaud such mad confidence when we know the depths of our ignorance, when we are forced to compare a menace we know well with another that we can only imagine. There has been no dearth of warnings, however. When Niels Bohr,[28] who is of necessity well-informed, writes that "a million people could be blown up and lose their lives in a single day; these figures are frightening, yet they may still fall short of the reality," it seems to me that one needs to weigh the pros and cons a little longer than you and others have done. I am aware that Paulhan[29] finds it foolish to say that wars are dreadful because they destroy human beings. I personally subscribe to this foolishness, but even if we discount the dead, our conception of liberty may find it hard to adapt to a gutted Europe or a France that will never recover from a Third World War, as you know and everyone else knows.

In any case, an argument that leads to a choice between cemeteries and concentration camps may be rigorous, but, rigor aside, I cannot get past the idea that something must have been left out. Maybe it is true that rigor will someday lead to this unenviable choice. On that day each man will do what he must. After all,

---

[28] Niels Bohr (1885–1962) was a Danish physicist, the founder of atomic theory, for which he won the Nobel Prize in 1922.

[29] Jean Paulhan (1884–1968) was a writer and critic regarded as the "gray eminence of letters." From 1925 to 1940 he directed the *Nouvelle Revue Française*. In 1943 he joined the Resistance. As an editor at Gallimard he played a key role in the publication of *L'Etranger* and *Le Mythe de Sisyphe* in 1942.

the men of my generation are prepared for the worst, and in any event it is quite true that I am not inclined to accept just any peace. But what we do or don't do then will of course be important only to us. Gulls, too, screech when it storms, but I imagine that they do so for their own pleasure.

Given the situation we are in, do you still find it useful to pour scorn on people who are searching for what little hope there may still be of preserving both peace and freedom and who are still trying to think clearly? For that is all we are about. You can poke fun at Davis's effort to put salt on the dove's tail. Obviously there is a way of capturing the dove of peace without making a fool of oneself with grains of salt; you can blast it at point-blank range. While rigorously effective, such a method is clearly not one of which Davis wishes to avail himself. He has refused to accept the fine rigor of the killing machines and for the time being has been content to expose the falsehoods and absurdities of our international society. The dreams that you and others ascribe to him surely do not come from what he has said or done. You have been ill-informed, something that happens to every journalist.

You seem, in fact, to look upon Davis as a conscientious objector. Where did you get that idea? I have never heard Davis say that war must always be avoided. He said that he would be the first to enlist as a pilot in an international police force. He simply believes that there is a still a possibility that there will be no war and that there is still a chance that tyrannies can be ended without taking Europe along with them. He has said what everyone thinks, that the only organization charged with preserving world peace is paralyzed by unbending sovereignties. His gesture has brought this essential contradiction to light. He has also shown every international organization of the present or future what the true goals of a League of Nations should be. That is all, but it is a great deal, and that is what we believed merited our support. Just tell me what will give the U.N. delegates more to think about, assuming that they are still capable of thought: the petition that you and five hundred other intellectuals signed, or Davis's act.

I think the answer is Davis's act, and I'll tell you why. I believe that it is still imperative to try to save Europe and France from an unparalleled catastrophe. We have to save as many lives as we can in order to preserve the energies that may change the face of war and peace. Since war and surrender are not yet our options, since France cannot fight without weapons supplied by others, I see usefulness and decency in any enterprise that does not bet on the inevitability of war and does not lead to a choice between two shameful alternatives, surrender on the one hand or silence on the killings in Greece and the repression in Spain on the other. At a time when everyone is forced to wager, it seems preferable to me to wager on a reasonable hope. Neither Davis nor his supporters claim to be bringing the truth to the world. They know full well that their ultimate path lies elsewhere, as does their true calling. They have merely uttered a cry of alarm, as befits their station, and it is perfectly possible that they are crying in the wilderness. But before smiling at what they have done, at least consider the filthy air of shame and calculation that surrounds the truths and faiths that have been imposed on today's world. May you at least—you least of all—not cast the first stone.

March 14, 1949

Only Privates Are Traitors

A LETTER FROM ALBERT CAMUS AND RENÉ CHAR[30]

We read in *Combat* that two Algerian soldiers have been sentenced to death by a court-martial in Algiers for desertion under fire. Their entire platoon surrendered to the enemy nine years ago in the Meuse in the midst of a general rout of French forces. We ask you to compare this merciless sentence (recalling the climate of 1940) with the far more moderate punishments meted out to generals accused of having offered their services to the enemy after being made prisoners of the German army. We further ask you to inform your readers that it is extremely rare for Algerian subjects to enjoy the rights of French citizenship, even though they are subject, as we have just seen, to the same duties. It is our hope, at least, that these comparisons will enable readers to appreciate the singular lesson in morality that our courts have just administered to the people of France and Algeria.

---

[30] This brief protest, cosigned by René Char, was, I believe, Camus' last publication in *Combat.*

1944–1948

Although it would be impossible to provide a complete summary of events in this tumultuous period of history, I thought it essential to present a succinct chronology as a complement to Camus' articles. Even when his pieces are not directly related to the events mentioned, it is important to know the context in which they were written. This chronology borrows freely from those published by Jacques Julliard in *La IVe République: Naissance et Mort* (Paris: Calmann-Lévy, 1968), and Jean-Pierre Rioux in *La France de la IVe République: I: L'ardeur et la nécessité, 1944–1952* (Paris: Editions du Seuil, 1980).

1944	
The Consultative Assembly, created in Algeria, and the Provisional Government of the French Republic return to Paris.	
Articles by Camus	Events
August 1944	
21: "Combat Continues . . ." 21: "From Resistance to Revolution"	20–30: Liberation of French territory as far as the foothills of the Vosges, with persistent pockets of resistance.
	20–25: Liberation of Paris.
	21: Start of Dumbarton Oaks conference, which will lay the foundations for the U.N. A place on the Security Council is reserved for France, which is not represented at the meeting.
22: "Time for Justice"	
23: "They Shall Not Pass"	
24: "The Blood of Freedom"	
25: "The Night of Truth"	
29: "Intelligence and Character"	
30: "The Age of Contempt"	
31: "Critique of the New Press"	

Continued

September 1944

1: "The Reform of the Press"

2: "The Democracy to Come"

2: Provisional Government in Paris holds first meeting of Council of Ministers.

4: "Morality and Politics"

6: "The End of a World"

6: First use of V2 rockets in the bombing of London.

7: "Our Brothers in Spain"

8: "Justice and Freedom"
8: "Critical Journalism"

9: General de Gaulle shakes up his government, forms a government of national unity. Yves Chataigneau is named governor-general of Algeria.

10: "The new government is constituted."

12: "Comrade, you write us . . ."

12: De Gaulle, in a speech at Chaillot, says that major sources of wealth must revert to collective ownership.

14: Allied forces enter Germany.

15: "In 1933, an eager, frenetic personage . . ."

15: Special courts of justice replace courts-martial and military tribunals, marking the beginning of the official purge.

16: "A wire service report . . ."

17: "What are the people of Germany doing?"

19: "The National Liberation Movement . . ."

20: "We spoke the other day about the German people . . ."

22: "As everyone knows, newspapers are today subject to military censorship . . ."

23: "Four years ago . . . Germany lost the war . . ."

23: Decree incorporating the FFI (internal resistance forces) into the regular army.

26: "With the arrest of Louis Renault . . ."

27: "Please forgive us, but we are not yet done with the case of Renault."

28: "One can read the communiqué of the Council of Ministers elsewhere."

29: "We are emerging from euphoria."

29: Jefferson Caffery arrives to represent the U.S. to de facto French authorities (the Provisional Government had been recognized de facto since July 11).

30: "Mr. Churchill has just delivered a speech . . ."

October 1944

1: "People say, 'Tell us in a few words, what is it you want?'"

3: "The *Daily Mail* has just published an interesting article on the French press by Allan Forbes."

4: "It is no secret that the Underground Press Federation . . ."

5: "We have said before in this space . . ."

5: Law on the right to vote for women.

6: "There was plenty of noise . . ."

7: "In Algiers on March 26, 1944 . . ."

7: End of Dumbarton Oaks conference.

8: "Yesterday, the National Council of the Resistance . . ."

11: "The situation of the press poses problems."

12: "There is much talk of order right now."

12: Edict concerning the composition of the Consultative Assembly, expanded to include delegates from the internal resistance and former deputies.

13: "It is impossible to exaggerate the importance of the statements . . ."

Continued

14: "Mr. Churchill said in his most recent speech . . ."

15: "We beg our readers' indulgence . . ."

17: "We must return once again to the recognition of the French government."

18: "Let us say a few words about the purge."

18: Law concerning the confiscation of unlawful profits.

19: "France's participation in the allied military government . . ."

20: "We are not in agreement with M. François Mauriac."

21: "Yes, the drama that France faces . . ."

21: "Money versus Justice."

22: "The *Daily Express* has just published . . ."

23: De jure recognition of the Provisional Government by the Allies.

23–25: Congress of NLM cadres. Attempt to unify the various resistance movements around the program of the NCR.

24: "We wish to protest here . . ."

25: "We hesitated to respond to the invitation . . ."

27: "It was difficult for us to speak, as we did yesterday, about René Leynaud."

28: Banning of the patriotic militias over the objections of the NCR.

29: "The day before yesterday, the minister of information delivered a speech . . ."

31: "We can discuss the case of M. Stéphane Lauzanne . . ."

November 1944

2: "The Council of Ministers has just established . . ."

3: "Governing is good."

3: "Pessimism and Courage"

4: "Two days ago, Jean Guéhenno published . . ."

5: "The *Officiel* has published the text of an executive order . . ."

7: "For several weeks, some in France have been waiting . . ."

7: First meeting of the expanded Consultative Assembly. Félix Gouin is elected president. Franklin Roosevelt is reelected in the United States.

8: "The Consultative Assembly met yesterday for the first time."

7–8: Extraordinary congress of the S.F.I.O. Discussion of merger with the Communists.

9: "Mr. Roosevelt's election is good news."

10: "Yesterday, the Congress of the Socialist Party held its first meeting."

11: "Our friends from *Défense de la France* are troubled . . ."

14: "It is worth noting that the first issue to be debated . . ."

15: "There is something irritating about the many news reports . . ."

16: "The Government has decided to confiscate the property of Renault . . ."

19: "We need to look closely at what has happened in Belgium."

21: "It is once again time to update the situation in Spain . . ."

22: "It is time for some self-criticism."

Continued

23: "To judge by what one reads in the Paris press, everyone in France is socialist . . ."

23: French troops enter Strasbourg.

24: "The more one thinks about it . . ."

25: "Yes, our armies are on the Rhine . . ."

26: "This is what we have come to: Belgian blood has been shed in Brussels . . ."

26: M.R.P. holds its organizing convention.

27: Communist leader Maurice Thorez returns to Paris.

28: "We get word from many quarters . . ."

28: Creation of "civic chambers" as courts of the purge.

29: "Only just liberated, Europe is in turmoil."

30: "The ministry of information is preparing a decree . . ."

December 1944

1: "The problem of the press . . ."

3: "General de Gaulle has had talks with Marshal Stalin."

3: Beginning of civil war in Greece.

5: "There is a sort of tacit agreement between M. Mauriac and us . . ."

9: "Yesterday, before the House of Commons, Mr. Churchill . . ."

10: "Yesterday, many newspapers rather too hastily announced the resignation of General Franco."

10: Signature of Franco-Soviet pact.

13: "One reads almost everywhere that we are at war."

13: Law nationalizing the coal mines of northern France.

14: "Two days ago, the Consultative Assembly . . ."

15: "The Consultative Assembly yesterday took up the problem . . ."

15–17: Meeting of the Départemental Liberation Committees, on which all the underground resistance movements were represented.

16: "There is a belief in some
quarters that the new press . . ."

17: "When a revolution has broken
out, what must be done to
destroy it?"

18: "The text of the Franco-Soviet
pact has now been made public."

18: First issue of *Le Monde*.

19: German offensive in the Ardennes.

20: "As von Rundstedt was
launching his offensive . . ."

20: The Communist and Socialist
Parties establish a liaison committee.

22: "France has endured many
tragedies . . ."

23: "French Renaissance (Suetonius)"

24: "The Poet and General de Gaulle
(Suetonius)"

26: "The Pope has just delivered a
message . . ."

26: Law on punishment of
collaborators (*indignité nationale*).

29: "Broad questions of policy . . ."

30: "Judge Not"

31: "The Thirteenth Caesar
(Suetonius)"

31: The Communist-dominated
Lublin Committee proclaims itself the
provisional government of Poland.

1945

General de Gaulle forms a government of National Unity
Félix Gouin presides over expanded Consultative
Assembly (Gouin president)
De Gaulle Government (November 21, 1945–January 20, 1946)

January 1945

1: "1945"

1–5: Germans threaten Strasbourg.

2: "*Panem et circenses* (Suetonius)"

2: "We have read with the requisite
respect and approval . . ."

3: "The Agence Française de
Presse has just published a
communiqué . . ."

Continued

5: "The press has lately been preoccupied with injustice."

6: "MinisterTiberius (Suetonius)"

6: Increase in salaries of government officials after massive protests.

7–8: "Spain is growing fainter."

11: "Justice and Charity"

16: Nationalization of Renault factories that did work for the Germans; constitution of a nationalized enterprise.

21–23: Central Committee of the Communist Party meets in Ivry: "Unite, Fight, Work" (Thorez).

23: Germans retreat in the Ardennes.

23–28: First NLM congress. Refusal to merge with the Communists.

27: Charles Maurras is sentenced to life in prison. Soviet forces liberate Auschwitz.

February 1945

3: Minority of the NLM merges with National Front to form the United French Resistance Movement, with ties to the Communists.

9: "To judge by what is being said about us, it would seem that *Combat* . . ."

4–12: Yalta Conference (Churchill, Roosevelt, Stalin). Status of United Nations, Germany, and liberated territories is decided. De Gaulle refuses to meet with Roosevelt on his return trip

6: Execution of Robert Brasillach.

13–14: Bombing of Dresden.

16: "Along with other difficult issues, the Crimea Conference . . ."

17: "'Here, at least, we aren't living amidst lies' . . ."

22: Law on the creation of *comités d'entreprise*.

Tunisian political parties declare themselves in favor of internal autonomy.

28: Pré-Bail Accord.

March 1945

4: Allies reach the Rhine. Creation of the Arab League in Cairo.

9: "For two days, M. Teitgen . . ."

9: Japan attacks in Indochina.

11–12: "Yesterday we published . . ."

11: North Vietnam and Cambodia proclaim independence.

13–18: First trials before the High Court of Justice.

16: "In *Témoignage chrétien* . . ."

18: "Breaking our general rule, we trust that we may just this once speak out . . ."

27: "It is rather vexing and a bit ridiculous . . ."

29: "Truth is a harsh master, allowing no time for rest."

April 1945

3: "What was being celebrated yesterday in the city's streets?"

4: "As the end of hostilities draws near . . ."

5: "'I am a teacher, and I'm hungry.'"

5: Mendès France resigns from government over disagreement on financial policy.

6: "Those who look upon the resignation of M. Mendès France . . ."

9: Nationalization of factories of Gnome et Rhône, manufacturers of aircraft engines who have been supplying the Germans.

10: "The victories on the western front . . ."

Continued

12: Roosevelt dies; Truman succeeds him as president.

14: "His face was the very image of happiness."

15–16: "Mr. Truman has made no secret . . ."

17: "With every step closer to victory . . ."

19 April–13 May: Municipal elections, victory of the left
25: American and Soviet forces converge.
26: Pétain returns to France and places himself in custody.
25 April–25 May: San Francisco conference establishes UN Charter; France refuses to act as inviting power.
30: Hitler commits suicide.

May 1945

1: Dönitz succeeds Hitler.

8: Germany surrenders.

9: "Who would think himself capable of describing this delirious day . . ."

8–12: Riots in Sétif and Guelma, insurrection in Kabylia, followed by very harsh repression. Foreshadowing of Algerian War.

10–30: Prisoners of war and deportees return home.

12: "We are waiting for a government shakeup . . ."

13–14: "Crisis in Algeria"

15: "Famine in Algeria"

16: "Algeria Asks for Ships and Justice"

16: France obtains a seat as permanent member of the Security Council.

17: "'Our food consists of one liter of soup . . .'"

18: "Natives of North Africa Estranged from a Democracy . . ."

19: "The day before yesterday we protested the fate reserved for deportees . . ."

20–21: "Arabs Demand a Constitution and a Parliament for Algeria"

23: "It Is Justice That Will Save Algeria from Hatred"

25: "Yesterday, General de Gaulle delivered a speech . . ."

26: "While awaiting the ministerial shakeup . . ."

27: "The foreign affairs committee of the Consultative Assembly . . ."

28: Blum-Byrnes accord on the liquidation of war debts.

30: In Syria, France bombs Damascus to quell independence movements. The intervention of British forces obliges French troops to return to their barracks, and a cease-fire is signed on May 30.

31: "The Syrian affair . . ."

June 1945

1: "Mr. Churchill's ultimatum . . ."

4–15: Exchange of banknotes.

5: "Henri Frenay is one of our comrades-in-arms."

5: France is awarded a zone of occupation in Germany.

7–25: The NLM breaks up and the Democratic and Social Union of the Resistance is formed out of non-Communist resistance elements.

12: End of press censorship L'Humanité publishes an article by Jacques Duclos on organic unity.

15: "After being briefly traumatized, the French public . . ."

Continued

26: Signing of U.N. Charter Nationalization of airlines by purchase of stock
(which would be united in 1948 under
the aegis of Air France).

27: "M. Herriot has just made an
unfortunate statement."

28: Rent control law.

30 June— 1 July: "Images of
Occupied Germany"

30: Price control and anti-black-
market law.

July 1945

1–22: Bretton Woods conference;
adoption of gold standard and dollar as
international unit of currency.

10–14: Estates General of the
French Renaissance (tied to the
Communists).

18 July–2 August: Potsdam Conference
(Stalin and Molotov, Truman and
Byrnes, Churchill and Eden, then
Atlee and Bevin). Agreement on a peace
treaty for Europe, German reparations,
de-Nazification, Polish frontier on
the Nesse River. France does not
participate.

23: Beginning of Pétain's trial.

August 1945

2: "Since the Court of Justice has
acknowledged . . ."

3: Last session of the Consultative
Assembly.

4: "Many things have a claim on
the attention of the people of
metropolitan France . . ."

6: Atomic bomb dropped on Hiroshima.

7: "General Franco has officially
announced . . ."

8: "The world is what it is, which
isn't much."

8: Soviet Union declares war on
Japan.

9: Nagasaki bombed.

12–15: Congress of S.F.I.O., where organic unity of socialists and communists is rejected.

12: Japan asks to surrender.

14: "We previously indicated our slight anxiety . . ."

15: "Yesterday the *Washington Times Herald* . . ."

15: The High Court sentences Pétain to death while expressing the hope that he will be pardoned, and General de Gaulle does pardon him.

16: In Indochina, Ho Chi Minh calls for a nationwide insurrection.

17: "Now that the war is over . . ."

17: Law on the October elections.

20: Proclamation of the Republic of Vietnam.

22: "The first National Assembly of the Press . . ."

23: "The Radical Party congress . . ."

24: "At the Radical Party congress, M. Herriot complained . . ."

25: Abdication of Bao Dai. Formation of government by Ho Chi Minh

26–27: "We have proved to be excellent prophets."

28: "Many readers have asked us to take a position . . ."

30: "We beg the reader's indulgence . . ."

September 1945

1: "The postwar has begun."

2: Japan surrenders.

5: Benoît Frachon is elected secretary of the C.G.T.

18: Opening of Nüremberg trials.

Continued

23: French reestablish themselves in Saigon.

23–30: Cantonal elections.

October 1945

4: Beginning of Pierre Laval's trial.

4–19: Law on social security.

11: Law on housing crisis.

15: Execution of Pierre Laval.

19: Landing in Indochina of French Expeditionary Force commanded by Leclerc.

21: Referendum and elections to the first Constituent Assembly. Yes to two questions: rejection of institutions of the Third Republic. Elections bring success to Communists, M.R.P., and Socialists; failure for the right and the Radicals.

November 1945

8: Félix Gouin elected president of the National Assembly.

13: De Gaulle unanimously elected head of government.

15: "France is in a state of siege."

December 1945

2: Nationalization of banks and credit.

13: Crisis in Syria and Lebanon; evacuation of French and English troops.

22: Creation of Republican Party of Freedom.

26: Ratification of Bretton Woods accords; currency to be defined in terms of gold and dollars; creation of the International Monetary Fund and the

International Bank for Reconstruction
and Development.

28: Reinstitution of the bread ration
card.

1946

Second Constituent Assembly (National Assembly) (president: Vincent Auriol)
Resignation of General de Gaulle (January 20)
Gouin Government (January 29)
Bidault Government (June 23)
Blum Government (December 16)

January 1946

10: General Assembly of the UN.

20: General de Gaulle resigns in disagreement over shape of government
and rule by parties.

24: Accord between M.R.P., Socialists,
and Communists lays foundations of
tripartite rule.

29: Election of Félix Gouin as head of
government.

31: Vincent Auriol elected president of
the Constituent Assembly.

February 1946

1: Newspaper strike in Paris.

March 1946

6: Sainteny–Ho Chi Minh accord
on recognition of Vietnam as a free
state.

April 1946

3: Resignation of F. de Menthon as
general secretary for the constitution;
replaced by Pierre Cot.

8: Nationalization of gas and electricity.

16: Law on personnel delegates.

Continued

19: Socialist-Communist majority votes in favor of the constitution.

29: C.G.T. leads strike at Renault. Bread ration set at 250 grams.

May 1946

5: Victory of "no" in referendum; the proposed constitution is rejected by 52 percent of voters.

16: Law on works councils.

17: Law on coal mines.

28: Blum-Byrnes financial accords; $650 million in debt is deferred C.G.T. demands higher wages.

June 1946

2: Elections to the Second Constituent Assembly; success of M.R.P.; Communist gains; Socialist losses. In Algeria, success of Union of Friends of the Manifesto, led by Ferhat Abbas.

12: Creation of the C.N.P.F.

16: In Bayeux, General de Gaulle proposes a constitution similar to the one that would be adopted in 1958.

18: Proclamation of the Italian Republic.

19: Bidault becomes head of government.

23: Bidault government based on tripartite rule (Socialists, Communists, M.R.P.).

July 1946

4: Employers and unions meet at Palais-Royal to discuss price stability and wage increases.

6: Opening of Franco-Vietnamese conference at Fontainebleau, with Ho Chi Minh attending.

29: Opening of Peace Conference in Paris.

30 July–3 August: Postal strike.

August 1946

3: Civil service salaries increased by 25 percent.

6: Law on family contributions.

29: 38th Congress of S.F.I.O.

September 1946

4: Guy Mollet elected secretary general of the S.F.I.O.

12: Law on old-age insurance.

14: End of Fontainebleau conference. Provisional accord between Moutet and Ho Chi Minh avoids breakdown of talks.

30: New draft constitution is adopted by the Assembly.

October 1946

13: Constitutional referendum: the proposed constitution is adopted.

15: End of Paris conference.

19: Law on civil service status.

Late October: Scandal in wine and textile industries.

November 1946

10: Legislative elections: Communists advance, Socialists lose ground.

18: Thierry d'Argenlieu meets with Ho Chi Minh.

Neither Victims nor Executioners

19: "The Century of Fear"

20: "Saving Bodies"

21: "Socialism Mystified"

Continued

23: "The Revolution Travestied"

26: "International Democracy and Dictatorship"

27: "The World Moves Quickly"

29: "A New Social Contract"

30: "Toward Dialogue"

23: Shelling of Haiphong by French navy kills several thousand people.

24 November–8 December: Elections to the Council of the Republic.

December 1946

3: Vincent Auriol elected president of the National Assembly.

12: The UN decides on a diplomatic boycott but not an economic boycott of Spain.

16: After failed attempts by Thorez and Bidault, Blum becomes head of government.

19: Insurrection in Hanoi. Economic annexation of the Saar by France.

23: Law on collective bargaining agreements.

1947

Vincent Auriol, President of the Republic
Ramadier Government (January 28)
Schuman Government (November 22)

January 1947

1: Social security plan goes into effect.

2: Prices decreased by 5 percent.

8–15: Newspaper strike in Paris.

8–9: Moutet and General Leclerc leave Indochina.

16: Vincent Auriol is elected president of the Republic.
Blum government resigns.

17: [Response to a questionnaire
on American literature]

21: Edouard Herriot is elected president of the National Assembly.

24: French plan on status of Germany.

28: Ramadier becomes head of government.

February 1947

10: Peace treaty with Finland, Bulgaria, Hungary, Romania, and Italy signed at Trianon.

11 February–17 March: Newspaper strike in Paris.

March 1947

4: Treaty seals Franco-British alliance.

5: Bollaert named high commissioner in Indochina.

10: Moscow conference on Germany.

12: Truman speech on American aid.

17: "The Deaf and Dumb Republic"

18: Monnerville elected president of the Council of the Republic (Senate).

21: "Radio 47"

22: "No Excuse for This"

22: Vote to allocate funds for the military in Indochina. The Communist Party rejects Ramadier's policy.

30: De Gaulle speaks in Bruneval Malagasy insurrection begins.

31: De Gaulle and Ramadier meet Creation of minimum wage (S.M.I.G.).

April 1947

2–12: Repression in Madagascar.

7: In Strasbourg, de Gaulle announces the creation of the Rassemblement du

Continued

Peuple Français (R.P.F.), which is officially born on April 14.

9: Sultan of Morocco denounces the
protectorate.

21: Franco-American agreement on the
Ruhr.

22: "The Choice"

24: Moscow conference on the German
problem fails.
French policy shifts toward that of England and the United States.

29: The C.G.T. assumes leadership of
the Renault strike.

30: "Democracy and Modesty"

May 1947

1: Bread ration reduced to 200
grams per day. Demonstration in
Paris.

4: Dismissal of Communist ministers
who protested the arrest of Malagasy
deputies and voted no confidence in
the government.

7: "Anniversary"

10: "Contagion"

10–21: Incidents in Lyons and
Dijon.

16: Work resumes at Renault.

18: General Juin named resident
general in Morocco.

25: Requisition of personnel in the
electrical and gas utilities.

June 1947

3: "To Our Readers"

1: Numerous strikes.

5: Marshall Plan proposed. France and
England ultimately accept American
aid, while Soviet Union and
Czechoslovakia refuse.

July–December 1947

27 August: Algeria status approved.

September–November: New wave of strikes.

5 October: Constitution of Kominform (news bureau representing communist and workers' parties). This was a response to the Marshall Plan and covered the Communist countries (Soviet Union, Bulgaria, Hungary, Poland, Romania, and Czechoslovakia) as well as the Communist Parties of France and Italy.

19 November: Ramadier resigns.

20 November: Following the failure of Léon Blum to form a government, Robert Schuman is chosen

Accidental death of General Leclerc.

10 December: Inaugural session of the assembly of the French Union.

14–28 December: The S.F.I.O. and M.R.P. declare themselves in favor of a "Third Force."

15 December: Failure of the Big Four meeting in London on the German problem.

1948

January–October 1948

25–30 January: Devaluation of the franc, return to free market in gold, blockage of 5,000-franc notes.

30 January: Assassination of Gandhi.

11 February: Naegelen named governor-general of Algeria.

24 February: Communists seize power in Prague.

Continued

28 February: Creation of Rassemblement Démocratique Révolutionnaire (Altman, Sartre, Rousset).

13 March: American Senate approves the Marshall Plan.

4–11 April: Elections in Algeria.

14 May: Proclamation of state of Israel.

5 June: France recognizes independence of Vietnam.

22 June: Soviets begin Berlin blockade.

19 July: Robert Schuman resigns.

24 July: André Marie forms new government.

25–28 August: Birth of Movement for Peace in Wroclaw.

27 August: Marie government resigns, replaced by Robert Schuman, who presided over a minority coalition.

11 September: Queuille government.

4 October: Two death sentences against Malagasy rebels, including Raseta.

November 1948

November–December: Garry Davis stirs controversy and attracts support after proclaiming himself a citizen of the world.

2: Truman reelected.

25: "Why Spain?"

29: End of numerous strikes that had led to police being called into factories and reservists being recalled to active duty.

December 1948

9: "What Is the UN Accomplishing?"

10: Universal Declaration of the Rights of Man adopted at UN

25–26: "Responses to an Unbeliever"

PARTIAL BIBLIOGRAPHY

I. WORKS BY ALBERT CAMUS

Bartfeld, Fernande. *Albert Camus voyageur et conférencier, le voyage en Amérique du Sud.* Archives des Lettres Modernes, Archives Albert Camus no. 7, Lettres Modernes, 1995.

Grenier, Roger. *Albert Camus, Soleil et Ombre.* Paris: Gallimard, 1987.

Guérin, Jeanyves. *Camus et la politique.* Actes du Colloque de Nanterre, 5–7 June 1985. Paris: L'Harmattan, 1986.

Guérin, Jeanyves. *Portrait de l'artiste en citoyen.* Paris: Bourrin, 1993.

Lebesque, Morvan. *Camus par lui-même,* "Ecrivains de toujours." Paris: Editions du Seuil, 1963.

Parker, Emmett. *The Artist in the Arena.* Madison and Milwaukee: University of Wisconsin Press, 1965.

Todd, Olivier. *Albert Camus: Une vie.* Paris: Gallimard, 1996.

Weyembergh, Maurice. *Albert Camus ou la mémoire des origines.* Brussels: De Boeck University, 1998.

Collective Works

À Albert Camus, ses amis du Livre. Paris: Gallimard, 1962.

Camus, "Génies et réalités." Paris: Hachette, 1964.

II: WORKS ABOUT *COMBAT*

Ajchenbaum, Yves-Marc. *A la vie, à la mort: Histoire du journal "Combat," 1941–1974.* Paris: Le Monde Editions, 1994.

Guérin, Jeanyves, ed. *Camus et le premier "Combat."* Actes du Collque de Paris X-Nanterre. Editions européennes Erasme, 1990.

III. WORKS ON THE HISTORICAL PERIOD

Ageron, Robert. *Histoire de l'Algérie contemporaine.* Paris: Presses Universitaires de France, 1970.

Aron, Raymond. *Mémoires: 50 ans de vie politique.* Paris: Julliard, 1983.

Aron, Robert. *Histoire de la Libération de la France.* Paris: Fayard, 1959.

Aron, Robert. *Histoire de l'épuration.* Paris: Fayard, 1967.

Aron, Robert. *Les Origines de la guerre d'Algérie.* Texts and contemporary documents. Paris: Fayard, 1962.

Azéma, Jean-Pierre, and François Bédarida, eds. *La France des années noires.* Vol. 1, *De la défaite à Vichy.* Vol. 2, *De l'occupation à la Libération.* Paris: Editions du Seuil, 1993.

Azéma, Jean-Pierre, and François Bédarida, eds. *Les Années de tourmente. De Munich à Prague.* Critical Dictionary. Paris: Flammarion, 1995.

Conan, Eric, and Henry Rousso. *Vichy, un passé qui ne passe pas.* Paris: Fayard, 1994. Paris: Gallimard, 1996.

Dahan, Yves-Maxime. *La vie politique à Alger de 1940 à 1944.* Librairie de droit et de jurisprudence, Pichon et Durand-Auzias, 1963.

Dansette, Adrien. *Histoire de la Libération de Paris.* "Les grandes études contemporaies." Paris: Librairie Arthème Fayard, 1946.

Elgey, Georgette. *La République des illusions (1945–1951) ou la vie secrète de la IVᵉ République.* Paris: Fayard, 1965.

Fauvet, Jacques. *La IVᵉ République.* Paris: Librairie Arthème Fayard, 1959.

Frenay, Henri. *La nuit finira: Mémoires de Résistance,1940–1945.* Paris: Robert Laffont, 1973.

Guérin, Alain. *La Résistance: Chronique illustrée, 1930–1950.* 5 vols. Livre Club Diderot, 1972–1976.

Hamon, Léo. *Vivre ses choix.* Paris: Robert Laffont, 1991.

Julien, Charles-André. *L'Afrique du Nord en marche: Algérie, Tunisie, Maroc, 1880–1952.* Omnibus, 2002.

Julliard, Jacques. *La IVᵉ République, Naissance et mort.* Paris: Calmann-Lévy, 1968.

Ollivier, Albert. *Fausses Sorties.* La Jeune Parque, 1946.

Paxton, Robert O. *Vichy France.* New York: Columbia University Press, 1971.

Rey-Goldzeiguer, Annie. *Aux origines de la guerre d'Algérie, 1940–1945, de Mers-el-Kébir aux massacres du Nord-Constantinois.* Paris: La Découverte, 2001.

Rioux, Jean-Pierre. *La France de la IVᵉ République: I: L'ardeur et la nécessité, 1944–1952.* Paris: Editions du Seuil, 1980.

Stora, Benjamin. *Histoire de l'Algérie coloniale, 1830–1954.* Paris: La Découverte, 1991.

Stora, Benjamin. *Histoire de la guerre d'Algérie (1954–1962).* Paris: La Découverte, 1993.

Wieviorka, Olivier. *Les Orphelins de la République.* Paris: Editions du Seuil, 2001.

IV. OTHER SOURCES

Periodicals Consulted

L'Action, Alger-Républicain, L'Aube, Caliban, Le Figaro, France-Soir (ex-Défense de la France), Franc-Tireur, L'Humanité, Le Monde, Le Populaire, Le Parisien libéré, Le Rassemblement (ex-L'Etincelle), Soir-Républicain, Témoignage chrétien, La Table Ronde, Temps présent.

Miscellaneous

L'Année politique 1944–1945. Revue chronologique des principaux faits politiques, économiques et sociaux de la France, de la Libération au 31 décember 1945, ed. M. Seydoux and M. Bonnagous. Editions du Grand Siècle, 1946.

L'Année politique 1946.

L'Année politique 1947.

L'Année politique 1948.

Contat, Michel, and Michel Ribalka. *Les Ecrits de Sartre.* Chronology and annotated bibliography. Paris: Gallimard, 1970.

Archives Consulted

Fonds Albert Camus, Centre de Documentation Albert Camus, Cité du Livre, Aix-en-Provence

Archives Jean Bloch-Michel